MW01089925

THE MACARTHUR NEW TESTAMENT COMMENTARY

MARK 1-8

John MacArthur

MOODY PUBLISHERS/CHICAGO

Cover Design: Smartt Guys design

Library of Congress Cataloging-in-Publication Data

MacArthur, John
  Mark 1-8 / John MacArthur.
    pages cm. – (The MacArthur New Testament commentary)
  Includes bibliographical references and index.
  ISBN 978-0-8024-1030-6
  1. Bible. Mark, I-VIII–Commentaries. I. Title.
  BS2585.53.M225 2015
  226.3'077–dc23
                    2014033026

We hope you enjoy this book from Moody Publishers. Our goal is to provide high-quality, thought-provoking books and products that connect truth to your real needs and challenges. For more information on other books and products written and produced from a biblical perspective, go to www.moodypublishers.com or write to:

Moody Publishers
820 N. LaSalle Boulevard
Chicago, IL 60610

3 5 7 9 10 8 6 4 2

Printed in the United States of America

To Chris Hamilton

a man among men,
a friend among friends,
and a leader among leaders

Contents

Preface

It continues to be a rewarding, divine communion for me to preach expositionally through the New Testament. My goal is always to have deep fellowship with the Lord in the understanding of His Word and out of that experience to explain to His people what a passage means. In the words of Nehemiah 8:8, I strive "to give the sense" of it so they may truly hear God speak and, in so doing, may respond to Him.

Obviously, God's people need to understand Him, which demands knowing His Word of Truth (2 Tim. 2:15) and allowing that Word to dwell in them richly (Col. 3:16). The dominant thrust of my ministry, therefore, is to help make God's living Word alive to His people. It is a refreshing adventure.

This New Testament commentary series reflects this objective of explaining and applying Scripture. Some commentaries are primarily linguistic, others are mostly theological, and some are mainly homiletical. This one is basically explanatory, or expository. It is not linguistically technical but deals with linguistics when that seems helpful to proper interpretation. It is not theologically expansive but focuses on the major doctrines in each text and how they relate to the whole of Scripture. It is not primarily homiletical, although each unit of thought is generally treated as one chapter, with a clear outline and logical flow of thought. Most truths are illustrated and applied with other Scripture. After establishing the context of a passage, I have tried to follow closely the writer's development and reasoning.

My prayer is that each reader will fully understand what the Holy Spirit is saying through this part of His Word, so that His revelation may lodge in the mind of believers and bring greater obedience and faithfulness—to the glory of our great God.

Introduction
to Mark

"The beginning of the gospel of Jesus Christ, the Son of God" (1:1). Those opening words to Mark's gospel not only state the purpose behind its composition but may have served as its original title. However, like the other three gospels, the work has been known throughout church history by the name of its author.

Mark appears several times in the book of Acts, where his name is given as "John who was also called Mark" (Acts 12:12, 25; cf. 15:37, 39). He was a cousin of Barnabas (Col. 4:10), and his mother's home in Jerusalem served as a gathering place for the early church (Acts 12:12). As a presumably young man, John Mark accompanied Paul and Barnabas on their first missionary journey (Acts 12:25; 13:5). But he deserted them at Perga in Pamphylia (Acts 13:13). As a result of Mark's inexcusable failure, Paul refused to take him on a subsequent trip (Acts 15:37–38). The issue sparked a sharp disagreement between Paul and Barnabas, causing them to part ways (Acts 15:39). Barnabas took Mark with him to Cyprus while Paul embarked on a second missionary journey with Silas (Acts 15:39–41).

Though he had betrayed Paul's trust on the first missionary journey, John Mark later became a valued member of the apostle's ministry team. In Colossians 4:10–11, Paul instructed his readers to welcome Mark as one of his "fellow workers for the kingdom" who had proven "to be an encouragement" to him during his first Roman imprisonment (cf. Philem. 24). Some years later, near the end of his life, Paul asked Timothy to "pick up Mark and bring him with you, for he is useful to me for service" (2 Tim. 4:11).

It is likely that John Mark was restored to ministry usefulness, at least in part, through the mentorship of Peter. As a leader in the Jerusalem church, Peter was familiar with the house of Mark's mother (Acts 12:12) and may have met Mark through her. The friendship between Peter and Mark was such that the apostle became a spiritual father figure to Mark, referring to him as "my son" (1 Peter 5:13). If anyone understood the process of restoration after failure, it was Peter, who was graciously restored by Christ after denying Him three times (cf. John 18:15–17, 25–27; 21:15–17). Peter's influence undoubtedly helped Mark overcome the weaknesses and vacillations of his youth so that he could faithfully accomplish what God had called him to do.

AUTHOR

Like the other three, the second gospel does not include the name of its author. However, the universal testimony of the early church confirms it was penned by Mark. The early church father Papias of Hieropolis, writing sometime between A.D. 95–140, explained that Mark's content was derived from the sermons of Peter, an observation consistent with their close relationship. According to Papias,

> Mark having become the interpreter of Peter, wrote down accurately whatsoever he remembered. It was not, however, in exact order that he related the sayings or deeds of Christ. For he neither heard the Lord nor accompanied Him. But afterwards, as I said, he accompanied Peter, who accommodated his instructions to the necessities [of his hearers], but with no intention of giving a regular narrative of the Lord's sayings. Wherefore Mark made no mistake in thus writing some things as he remembered them. For of one thing he took especial care, not to omit

anything he had heard, and not to put anything fictitious into the statements. (*The Exposition of the Sayings of the Lord,* 6; cited in Eusebius, *Church History,* 3.39.15–16)

The second-century apologist Justin Martyr (c. 100–165) similarly described Mark's gospel as the "memoirs of Peter" and suggested it was composed by Mark in Italy. Later Christian leaders, like Irenaeus, Origen, and Clement of Alexandria, echoed similar sentiments. The fourth-century church historian Eusebius of Caesarea (c. 263–339) suggested that Mark wrote his gospel at the request of Peter's hearers:

> A great light of religion shone on the minds of the hearers of Peter, so that they were not satisfied with a single hearing or with the unwritten teaching of the divine proclamation, but with every kind of exhortation [they] entreated Mark, whose gospel is still in existence, seeing that he was Peter's follower, to leave them a written statement of the teaching given them verbally, nor did they cease until they had persuaded him, and so became the cause of the scripture called the Gospel according to Mark. And they say that the Apostle, knowing by the revelation of the Spirit to him what had been done, was pleased at their zeal, and ratified the scripture for study in the churches. (*Church History,* 2.15.1–2)

Whatever the specific catalyst that prompted Mark to write his gospel, the uniform testimony of early tradition affirms that he is its author, likely composing his account while in Rome for the benefit of the believers who were there.

DATE OF WRITING AND INTENDED AUDIENCE

The church fathers disagree on whether Mark wrote his gospel before or after Peter's martyrdom. (Peter was killed under Nero c. 67–68.) Contemporary evangelical scholarship generally places the date of composition before A.D. 70, since Jesus' statement in 13:2 strongly suggests that Mark's gospel was written before the temple was destroyed. Though many modern scholars assert that Mark completed his gospel before Matthew and Luke, enabling them to use his gospel as a source for theirs, that assertion is doubtful. (For more on that point, see the further discussion below.) Thus, the dating of the other gospels is not determinative in establishing the date of Mark. In all likelihood, Mark completed his gospel either while accompanying Peter in Rome (in the late 50s or early 60s) or shortly after the apostle's death (in the late 60s).

Unlike Matthew's gospel, which addressed a Jewish audience, or Luke's gospel, which was composed for a specific individual (Luke 1:3), Mark was written for the Gentile believers of Rome. Mark's audience was clearly non-Jewish, as evidenced by the fact that he translates Aramaic terms (3:17; 5:41; 7:11, 34; 14:36; 15:22, 34); provides explanations for Jewish customs (7:3–4; 14:12; 15:42); omits certain elements of particular interest to Jewish readers, like Jesus' genealogical records; includes fewer Old Testament references than the other Synoptic Gospels; and calculates time according to the Roman system (6:48; 13:35). That the gospel was written for believers in Rome, in particular, is supported by the use of Latin expressions in place of their Greek equivalents (5:9; 6:27; 12:15, 42; 15:16, 39), and the mention of Rufus (15:21), the son of Simon of Cyrene and a prominent member of the Roman church (Rom. 16:13). Those details buttress the claims of the early church fathers that Mark's gospel was written from Rome for the believers there. As a divinely inspired and accurate historical record of the life and ministry of the Lord Jesus, Mark's gospel has remained a profound blessing to countless Christians throughout the ages and a powerful witness to the unbelieving world.

PURPOSE AND THEMES

Mark's purpose for writing is indicated by the opening verse: to articulate "the gospel of Jesus Christ, the Son of God" (1:1). That theme reaches its climax halfway through his sixteen-chapter history. In 8:29, Peter responded to Jesus' question, "Who do you say that I am?" by triumphantly declaring, "You are the Christ." That confession marks the doctrinal highpoint of Mark's gospel. The preceding narrative builds up to it and the subsequent narrative flows from and continues to build on it. The first eight chapters demonstrate that Jesus is the Christ on the basis of His authoritative words and miraculous deeds; the final eight on the basis of His sacrificial death and glorious resurrection. But everything centers on the foundational truth that Peter proclaimed: Jesus is the Christ. He is the Son of God and the Savior of the world.

In surveying that truth, Mark presents Jesus as the Suffering Servant (10:45; cf. Isa. 53:10–12). He emphasizes Jesus' humanity, including His human emotions (1:41; 3:5; 6:34; 8:12; 9:36) and human limitations (4:38; 11:12; 13:32). But he also highlights Jesus' deity as the Son of God (1:11; 3:11; 5:7; 9:7; 12:6; 13:32; 14:61–62; 15:39). Christ's divine authority is evidenced in His power over demons (1:24–27, 32, 34, 39; 3:11, 15; 5:13, 7:29; 9:25), over disease (1:30–31, 40–42; 2:11; 3:5, 10; 5:29, 41–42; 6:5, 56; 7:32–35; 8:23–25; 10:46–52), over sin (2:10), over the Sabbath (2:28; cf. 7:1–13), and over the forces of nature (4:39; 6:41–43, 49–51; 11:14, 20).

Mark moves quickly through much of Christ's ministry, using the word "immediately" (or *euthus* in Greek) more than the other three gospel writers combined. Consequently, he often leaves out the lengthy discourses included in the other gospels and gives only short excerpts. He also omits the account of Jesus' birth, choosing to begin with the Lord's baptism and the start of His public ministry.

Like the other gospel writers, Mark clearly has an evangelistic purpose. The purpose statement of John's gospel applies to Mark's as well: "These things have been written so that you may believe that Jesus is the Christ, the Son of God; and that believing you may have life in His name" (John 20:31; cf. 1 John 5:20). Sinners are commanded to repent and believe in the Lord Jesus Christ (1:15), abandoning the follies of hypocritical religion (cf. 2:23–28; 7:1–13; 12:38–40) in order to follow the Lord in heartfelt obedience (cf. 1:17–20; 2:14; 8:34–38; 10:21; 15:41; 16:19–20).

MARKAN PRIORITY AND THE SYNOPTIC PROBLEM

Because the Synoptic Gospels (Matthew, Mark, and Luke) share striking similarities (e.g., Matt. 9:2–8; Mark 2:3–12; Luke 5:18–26), some modern scholars—who reject the truth of divine inspiration and thus have to explain the similarities in the Gospels—insist that they must have borrowed from one another. Proponents of such literary dependence usually argue that Mark wrote his gospel first, and Matthew and Luke subsequently utilized it as a source to compose their accounts. Additionally, they allege that material appearing in Matthew and Luke but not in Mark was derived from a second source called "Q" (which stands for the German word *Quelle*, meaning "source").

A number of reasons argue against the notion of Markan priority and the "Two Source" hypothesis (i.e., that Mark and Q were the two sources used by Matthew and Luke). First, the overwhelming testimony of the first eighteen centuries of church history affirms that Matthew wrote his gospel first, not Mark. Second, as an apostolic eyewitness to the events he described, Matthew would have had no reason to depend on a non-eyewitness like Mark. Third, though Luke thoroughly investigated the resources available to him (Luke 1:3), he omitted a lengthy section of material from Mark's gospel (6:45–8:26), suggesting he was not aware of it when he wrote his account. Fourth, there are significant places where Matthew and Luke agree against Mark. Those occurrences cannot be satisfactorily explained if Matthew and Luke were both depending on Mark in composing their gospels. Fifth, no historical evidence has ever been found to verify the existence of the supposed Q document. Sixth, the similarities between the Synoptic Gospels can be better explained by the fact that they were recounting the same historical events and thus naturally overlapped. (The gospel of John was written later as a supplement to the Synoptic Gospels, and therefore intentionally focused on material not included in them.) Also, the fact that Matthew, Mark, and Luke orbited in the same circles (among the apostles and early Christians) and undoubtedly had some personal contact with one another (cf. Philem. 24) renders modern theories of literary dependence unnecessary.

When fully considered, the evidence demonstrates that in actuality there is no Synoptic Problem (cf. Eta Linnemann, *Is There a Synoptic Problem?* [Grand Rapids: Baker, 1992] and Robert L. Thomas and F. David Farnell, eds., *The Jesus Crisis* [Grand Rapids: Kregel, 1998], especially Chaps. 1, 3, 6). Sadly, many contemporary evangelicals have rejected the traditional view in favor of an imaginary Q document and the unbelieving speculations of liberal scholarship. Rather than entertaining the skeptical notions of higher critics, believers are much better served when they acknowledge that the same Holy Spirit inspired Matthew, Mark, and Luke to write their gospels (2 Peter 1:21; cf. John 14:26), so that any similarities between their accounts ought to be attributed to His sovereign guidance rather than modern theories of literary dependence.

     F. He Calls the Disciples to an Attitude of Selfless Service (10:35–45)

     G. He Heals a Blind Man in Jericho (10:46–52)

V. The Consummation of Christ's Ministry: Jerusalem (11:1–16:20)

     A. He Enters the City Triumphantly (11:1–11)

     B. He Curses a Fig Tree (11:12–14)

     C. He Cleanses the Temple (11:15–19)

     D. He Teaches Publicly in the Temple (11:20–12:44)

        1. Prelude: The Lesson of the Fig Tree (11:20–26)

        2. Regarding His Authority (11:27–33)

        3. Regarding His Rejection (12:1–12)

        4. Regarding Paying Taxes (12:13–17)

        5. Regarding the Resurrection (12:18–27)

        6. Regarding the Greatest Commandment (12:28–34)

        7. Regarding Christ's True Sonship (12:35–37)

        8. Regarding the Scribes (12:38–40)

        9. Regarding a Widow's Offering (12:41–44)

     E. He Teaches about End Times on the Mount of Olives (13:1–37)

     F. He Is Anointed, Betrayed, and Arrested (14:1–72)

        1. Judas Conspires to Betray Jesus (14:1–2, 10–11)

        2. Christ Is Anointed in Bethany (14:3–9)

        3. He Eats a Final Meal with the Disciples in Jerusalem (14:12–31)

        4. He Prays in Gethsemane (14:32–42)

        5. He Is Betrayed in Gethsemane (14:43–52)

        6. He Is Placed on Trial at the House of the High Priest (14:53–72)

     G. He Is Tried before Pilate and Sentenced to Death (15:1–41)

        1. He Is Placed on Trial in Pilate's Praetorium (15:1–15)

        2. He Is Taken to Golgotha and Crucified (15:16–41)

     H. He Is Buried in the Tomb of Joseph of Arimathea (15:42–47)

     I. He Rises from the Dead (16:1–8)

     J. Postscript to the Gospel of Mark (16:9–20)

The Herald of the New King (Mark 1:1–8)

1

The beginning of the gospel of Jesus Christ, the Son of God. As it is written in Isaiah the prophet: "Behold, I send My messenger ahead of You, Who will prepare Your way; The voice of one crying in the wilderness, 'Make ready the way of the Lord, Make His paths straight.'" John the Baptist appeared in the wilderness preaching a baptism of repentance for the forgiveness of sins. And all the country of Judea was going out to him, and all the people of Jerusalem; and they were being baptized by him in the Jordan River, confessing their sins. John was clothed with camel's hair and wore a leather belt around his waist, and his diet was locusts and wild honey. And he was preaching, and saying, "After me One is coming who is mightier than I, and I am not fit to stoop down and untie the thong of His sandals I baptized you with water; but He will baptize you with the Holy Spirit." (1:1–8)

No narrative is more compelling, and no message more essential, than the gospel of Jesus Christ. It is the greatest story ever told because it centers on the greatest person to ever walk this earth. The history of His earthly ministry is perfectly recorded in four complementary accounts —written under the inspiration of the Holy Spirit by Matthew, Mark, Luke, and John. Their writings, known collectively as the four Gospels, provide a factual record of Jesus' life, death, and resurrection. Matthew and John were apostolic eyewitnesses to the events of which they wrote; Luke thoroughly investigated the details of our Lord's ministry in order to produce his testimony (cf. Luke 1:3–4); and, according to early church tradition, Mark wrote his gospel based on the preaching of the apostle Peter. Though penned by different men, these four accounts harmonize perfectly, providing their readers with a full-orbed understanding of the person and work of the Lord Jesus Christ. (For an integrated harmony of the Gospels, see John MacArthur, *One Perfect Life* [Nashville: Thomas Nelson, 2012].) Of the four gospel writers, only Mark used the word **gospel** (*euangelion*) to introduce his history of the Lord Jesus. In keeping with his quick, staccato style, Mark opens his account with one brief introductory phrase: **"The beginning of the gospel of Jesus Christ, the Son of God."**

The word **gospel** is a familiar one to us—frequently used to designate the first four books of the New Testament. But that is not how the biblical writers employed the term, nor is it how Mark uses it in the opening verse of his historical account. In the New Testament, the **gospel** is never a reference to a book; rather, it always refers to the message of salvation. That is Mark's intended meaning here. His first-century audience would have understood the word "gospel" to mean "good news" or "glad tidings" of salvation. But it had an even more specific meaning that would have been familiar to both Jewish and Gentile people in ancient times.

First-century Jews would have been familiar with the word *euangelion* from its occurrence in the Septuagint—the Greek translation of the Hebrew Old Testament. There it is used to speak of military victory, political triumph, or physical rescue (cf. 1 Sam. 31:9; 2 Sam. 4:10; 18:20–27; 2 Kings 7:9; Ps. 40:9). Significantly, the term is also found in a messianic context, where it points to the ultimate salvation of God's people through the messianic King. Speaking of Israel's future deliverance, the prophet Isaiah proclaimed:

Get yourself up on a high mountain,
O Zion, bearer of good news,
Lift up your voice mightily,
O Jerusalem, bearer of good news;
Lift it up, do not fear.
Say to the cities of Judah,
"Here is your God!"
Behold, the Lord God will come with might,
With His arm ruling for Him.
Behold, His reward is with Him
And His recompense before Him.
(Isa. 40:9–10)

In those verses, the Septuagint translates the Hebrew word for "good news" (*basar*) with forms of the Greek word *euangelion*. In Isaiah 40, this "good news" consisted of more than mere tidings of military victory or physical rescue. It encompassed a message of ultimate victory, triumph, and eternal rescue, making it the best news possible. After thirty-nine chapters of judgment and rebuke, Isaiah concluded his prophetic masterpiece (in chapters 40–66) with promises of hope and deliverance. Those promises proclaimed the reality of God's future reign and the restoration of His people.

In Isaiah 52:7, we find another familiar proclamation of hope:

How lovely on the mountains
Are the feet of him who brings good news,
Who announces peace
And brings good news of happiness,
Who announces salvation,
And says to Zion, "Your God reigns!"

As in Isaiah 40:9, the prophet used the Hebrew term *basar* or "good news" (cf. Isa. 61:1–2), which is again translated by *euangelion* in the Septuagint. Significantly, this passage precedes Isaiah's extended discussion of the Suffering Servant—the Messiah through whom this promised salvation would come (Isa. 52:13–53:12). When Mark stated that this was the **gospel of Jesus Christ,** his use of the word *Christos* (the Greek equivalent of the Hebrew "Messiah") would have made this connection inescapable in the minds of those familiar with the Septuagint. The word **gospel**, which was associated with the Messiah, was a word of enthronement and royal exaltation; the glorious tidings of the

King of kings coming to take His rightful throne.

The term *euangelion* also had special significance to those outside of Judaism. Though largely ignorant of Jewish history, first-century Romans would have similarly understood the term to refer to the good tidings of a coming king. A Roman inscription dating back to 9 B.C. provides insight into how the word **gospel** was understood in an ancient Gentile context. Speaking of the birth of Caesar Augustus, a portion of the inscription reads:

> Whereas the Providence . . . which has ordered the whole of our life, showing concern and zeal, has ordained the most perfect consummation for human life by giving to it Augustus, by filling him with virtue for doing the work of a benefactor among men, and by sending him, as it were, [as] a saviour for us and those who come after us, to make war to cease, to create order everywhere . . . and whereas the birthday of the God [Augustus] was the beginning of the world of the glad tidings that have come to men through him. . . . (*Inscrip. Priene*, cited from Gene L. Gree, *The Letters to the Thessalonians*, Pillar New Testament Commentary [Grand Rapids: Eerdmans, 2002] 94)

The inscription speaks of "glad tidings" (a form of *euangelion*) to describe the birth and reign of Caesar Augustus—a ruler whom the Romans regarded as their divine deliverer. The word **gospel** thus functioned as a technical term, even in secular society, to refer to the arrival, ascendency, and triumph of an emperor.

As these examples from both Jewish and pagan sources illustrate, the first-century readers of Mark's account would have understood the **gospel** to be a royal pronouncement, declaring that a powerful monarch had arrived—one who would usher in a new order of salvation, peace, and blessing. Under the inspiration of the Holy Spirit, Mark chose that word in order to effectively communicate—both to Jews and to Gentiles—that he was presenting the good news of the divine King.

Mark opens his account by noting that this is **the beginning** of his royal declaration. Such naturally stands at the head of his historical account. Yet, it also serves as a reminder that what follows is not the end of the story. The history of Jesus Christ is still being written. The King has not fully taken His throne. One day, He will return to establish His kingdom and He will reign as the eternal Sovereign. Mark's account only begins to tell the story of the arrival, ascendency, establishment, and enthronement of the new King who is far more glorious than all other kings.

In this way, Mark's record of the life of the Lord Jesus opens with language that would signal to his readers that the most glorious King has come—and it is not Caesar. In fact, this divine Monarch sets Himself against all other earthly rivals including Caesar. He is the theme, not only of Mark's history but of all history. And what is His name? Mark wastes no time in declaring who He is: **Jesus Christ, the Son of God.**

The name **Jesus** (Greek, *Iesous*) is His human name. It is a Greek form of the name Joshua (Hebrew, *Yeshua*), which means "Yahweh is salvation." As the angel explained to Joseph, "You shall call His name Jesus, for He will save His people from their sins" (Matt. 1:21). The term **Christ** is not a name but a title. It is the Greek translation of the Hebrew word translated "messiah," which means "anointed one." A royal title, it was used in the Old Testament to refer to the divinely appointed kings of Israel (cf. 1 Sam. 2:10; 2 Sam. 22:51) and ultimately to the great eschatological deliverer and ruler, the Messiah (Dan. 9:25–26; cf. Isa. 9:1–7; 11:1–5; 61:1). Any Jewish reader would have immediately understood the significance of the title—an explicit reference to the promised Savior of Israel.

The name **Son of God** speaks of Jesus' lineage and right to rule. He is one in nature with God—coeternal and coequal with the Father. For those Roman pagans who wrongly regarded Caesar as a god, Mark introduces them to the true divine King: the Lord Jesus Christ. As Nathaniel said to Jesus, "You are the Son of God, You are the King of Israel" (John 1:49). Throughout the course of His earthly ministry, Jesus repeatedly demonstrated Himself to be the divine King, and Mark is careful to present the overwhelming case to his readers (cf. 3:11; 5:7; 9:7; 13:32; 15:39). In the first half of his gospel record (chapters 1–8), Mark highlights the Lord's astonishing words and works. In the second half (chapters 9–16), he focuses on Jesus' death and resurrection. Both sections reach the same inevitable conclusion: through His words, works, death, and resurrection, Jesus proved Himself to be the promised messianic King, the Son of God and Savior of the world. Peter's confession articulates this theme in unmistakable language: "You are the Christ" (Mark 8:29; cf. Matt. 16:16). That this majestic confession stands in the middle of the book is certainly no accident. It represents the very heart of Mark's message: the Lord Jesus is exactly who He claimed to be.

In his account **of the gospel of Jesus Christ,** Mark is consumed with the arrival of the greatest King ever: the messianic Monarch who will introduce His glorious kingdom of salvation and usher in a new era for the world. But Mark's gospel is only the beginning of the good news because the story of Christ's kingdom will continue through all of human history and into eternity. Mark introduces the sovereign Savior by looking at three facets of His royal arrival: the promise of the new King, the prophet of the new King, and the preeminence of the new King.

THE PROMISE OF THE NEW KING

As it is written in Isaiah the prophet: "Behold, I send My messenger ahead of You, Who will prepare Your way; The voice of one crying in the wilderness, 'Make ready the way of the Lord, Make His paths straight.'" (1:2–3)

Having introduced his account as a royal proclamation of the divine King, Mark continues his narrative by introducing the King's forerunner, John the Baptist. Mark's initial focus on John, rather than Jesus, might seem surprising to modern readers. But it is perfectly in keeping with Mark's purpose (to present Jesus Christ as the divine King) and would have been expected by his first-century audience. Earthly monarchs in the ancient world invariably sent official messengers before them to prepare the way, announce their coming, and make the people ready to receive them. So also, the arrival of the divine King was preceded by a royal herald who clearly announced His coming.

In order to introduce John the Baptist, Mark references two Old Testament prophecies—Malachi 3:1 and Isaiah 40:3—each of which foretold the ministry of the Messiah's forerunner. The phrase **it is written** was a normal way for New Testament writers to designate quotations from the Old Testament (cf. 7:6; 9:13; 14:21, 27; Matt. 4:4, 6, 7; Luke 2:23; 3:4; John 6:45; 12:14; Acts 1:20; 7:42; Rom. 3:4; 8:36; 1 Cor. 1:31; 9:9; 2 Cor. 8:15; 9:9; Gal. 3:10; 4:22; Heb. 10:7; 1 Peter 1:16). The fact that Mark does not mention Malachi's name but introduces both with the phrase **"As it is written in Isaiah the prophet"** is not problematic. It was not uncommon at that time, when citing multiple Old Testament prophets, to refer only to the more prominent one and tuck in the others. Because these two prophecies fit together so perfectly and both refer to the same person, they may have been frequently used together by early Christians. The other gospel writers also applied these Old Testament passages to John (cf. Matt. 3:3; 11:10; Luke 3:4–6; 7:27; John 1:23).

Mark's appeal to the ancient Hebrew prophets is an important one, demonstrating that the King's arrival was not a secondary plan or an afterthought. This was the very plan that God had been working out from eternity past. In keeping with that plan, the ancient prophets had predicted the coming of the King's forerunner hundreds of years before he was born.

Mark begins by referencing Malachi 3:1, **"Behold, I send My messenger ahead of You, Who will prepare Your way."** The Lord Jesus Himself declared this passage to refer to John the Baptist (Matt. 11:10; Luke 7:27). John was sent by God **ahead of** the Messiah as a royal herald to **prepare** the **way** for the divine King's arrival. Such preparation came through proclamation. John was called to be a preacher, who made a strong call for people to ready themselves for the new King's arrival. An expanded translation of Malachi 3:1 might read, "Behold, I, Jehovah, send My messenger John the Baptist to be the forerunner for You, the Messiah, and to prepare the people for Your coming."

Mark's use of Old Testament prophecy continues with a reference to Isaiah 40:3, **"The voice of one crying in the wilderness, 'Make ready the way of the Lord, make His paths straight."** This passage expands on the mission of the Messiah's herald. In the ancient world, a royal forerunner was charged with making the road ready for the king's arrival. But how was John to do that for the coming Messiah? Rather than clearing literal roads of physical debris, John sought to remove obstacles of stubborn unbelief from the hearts and minds of sinners. The **way of the Lord** is the way of repentance, of turning from sin to righteousness, and of turning spiritual **paths** that are crooked into ones that are **straight** and holy.

In keeping with his calling, John preached to the multitudes who came to hear him **in the wilderness,** fervently pleading with them to repent. With the fiery **voice** of an impassioned prophet, he was **crying** out with shouts, groans, and pleas for sinners to forsake their sin and seek the Savior. John was both a prophet and the fulfillment of prophecy. He was the last of the Old Testament prophets; yet he was also the forerunner whose ministry the Old Testament prophets had foretold. As the personal herald of the divine King, John was given unparalleled privilege. Because of his elevated role, being so closely associated with the Messiah's coming, he was the greatest prophet to ever live (Matt. 11:11).

As with many passages in the book of Isaiah, the prophecies of Isaiah 40 (including verse 3) anticipated both a short-term, partial fulfillment and a long-term, full fulfillment. In the short-term, the words of Isaiah 40 promised the Jews of the Babylonian captivity that they would one day return to Israel. God would lead them back to their homeland after seven decades of bondage, making a straight path of deliverance for them. When they arrived, the Lord would be with them (cf. Isa. 40:9–11). But Isaiah's prophecy went beyond the Babylonian captivity—since not everything Isaiah prophesied was fulfilled during the Jews' return to Israel in the sixth century B.C. In the long-term sense, Isaiah's prophecy pointed to the coming of the messianic King, and to the one who would precede Him as His forerunner.

All of this was promised in the Old Testament. Mark highlights these promises because he knows they will resonate with his readers, whether Jew or Gentile. The King's arrival—being properly preceded by a royal herald—was promised by God through the Hebrew prophets in centuries past. But there is an additional aspect to those Old Testament prophecies that must not be overlooked. They not only describe the Messiah's forerunner, they also reveal the divine character of the Messiah Himself.

The full text of Malachi 3:1 reads: "'Behold, I am going to send My messenger, and he will clear the way before Me. And the Lord, whom you seek, will suddenly come to His temple; and the messenger of the covenant, in whom you delight, behold, He is coming,' says the Lord of hosts." The implications of that prophecy are profound. In that verse, the Lord explained that the coming King, the one before whom the forerunner would be sent, is "Me"—namely, God Himself. The prophecy continues with a promise that the Lord would suddenly come to His temple. It is no accident that Christ began His public ministry by going to the temple and cleansing it (John 2:13–22). Mark, of course, references only the first part of Malachi 3:1. Under the inspiration of the Holy Spirit, he paraphrases it slightly (changing the "Me" to "You") in order to emphasize that the divine pronoun in Malachi 3:1 refers to the Lord Jesus. His use of this Old Testament passage underscores the divine nature of the Messiah. The new King is none other than God Himself.

The testimony to Christ's deity is also seen in Isaiah 40:3, where Isaiah prophesied that Messiah's forerunner would "clear the way for the Lord in the wilderness" and "make smooth in the desert a highway for our God." The Hebrew word for "Lord" is *Yahweh,* the covenant name for God. The connection is unmistakable: the Messiah is one in nature with Yahweh. The testimony of that reality would be clearly articulated at Jesus' baptism. Just a few verses later, in Mark 1:11, we find the words of the Father, "You are My beloved Son, in You I am well-pleased."

The world had never seen a King like this. The God of the universe broke into history to provide salvation, blessing, and peace. His arrival had been promised from long ago. He was preceded by a royal herald who proclaimed His coming. The King's name is Jesus, and He is the Christ, the Son of God.

THE PROPHET OF THE NEW KING

John the Baptist appeared in the wilderness preaching a baptism of repentance for the forgiveness of sins. And all the country of Judea was going out to him, and all the people of Jerusalem; and they were being baptized by him in the Jordan River, confessing their sins. John was clothed with camel's hair and wore a leather belt around his waist, and his diet was locusts and wild honey. (1:4–6)

After referencing Old Testament prophecy about the Messiah's forerunner, Mark continues by stating his name: **John the Baptist.** The name **John** was common in first-century Israel. It means "the Lord is gracious" and is the Greek equivalent of the Hebrew name "Johanan" (cf.

2 Kings 25:23; 1 Chr. 3:15; Jer. 40:8). The title **the Baptist** is literally "the baptizer," a name that distinguished **John** from others with that same name, and identified him with one of the most recognizable aspects of his ministry. John **appeared in the wilderness,** spending the duration of his ministry along the Jordan River, about twenty to thirty miles south of the Sea of Galilee (cf. John 3:23). He had, in fact, grown up **in the wilderness** (cf. Luke 1:80) and that is where he preached and ministered, away from the hubbub of the cities.

The **wilderness** had great significance in Jewish history; it was a constant reminder of the exodus from Egypt and entrance into the Promised Land. That significance would not have been easily missed by those who traveled to hear John's **preaching** and witness his ministry of **baptism.** As William Lane explains:

> The summons to be baptized in the Jordan meant that Israel must come once more to the wilderness. As Israel long ago had been separated from Egypt by a pilgrimage through the waters of the Red Sea, the nation is exhorted again to experience separation; the people are called to a second exodus in preparation for a new covenant with God. ... As the people heed John's call and go out to him in the desert far more is involved than contrition and confession. They return to a place of judgment, the wilderness, where the status of Israel as God's beloved son must be re-established in the exchange of pride for humility. The willingness to return to the wilderness signifies the acknowledgment of Israel's history as one of disobedience and rebellion, and a desire to begin once more. (*The Gospel according to Mark,* New International Commentary on the New Testament [Grand Rapids: Zondervan, 1974], 50–51)

John's ministry centered on the **preaching** of **a baptism of repentance for the forgiveness of sins.** As noted earlier, in ancient times, the envoy of the arriving king would go before him, removing all the obstacles in the path and making sure the people were ready to receive the king. But how were the people to prepare for the arrival of the messianic King? They needed to forsake their sin and receive God's forgiveness. In order to demonstrate their repentance, John called them to be baptized.

John's **baptism** was a onetime act, distinguishing it from other ritual Jewish washings. In Jewish practice, the closest parallel to John's baptism was the onetime washing of Gentile proselytes, a rite that symbolized both their rejection of paganism and their acceptance of the true faith. The ceremony was the mark of an outsider's becoming a part of God's chosen people. For a Gentile proselyte to be baptized was nothing extraordinary. But John's call for Jews to be baptized was radical. In essence, it required them to see themselves as outsiders who must acknowledge that they were no more fit for the Messiah's kingdom than the Gentiles. John's baptism directly confronted the religious hypocrisy that permeated first-century Judaism. It challenged his listeners to consider the reality that neither being a physical descendant of Abraham nor a fastidious observer of Pharisaical laws were sufficient grounds by which to gain admittance into God's kingdom.

Instead, what was required was an internal change of the person's heart, mind, and will. The word **repentance** (*metanoia*) implies a genuine turning from sin and self to God (cf. 1 Thess. 1:9). True **repentance** involves a transformation of one's nature—making it a gracious work of God (Acts 11:18; 2 Tim. 2:25). The fruit (or subsequent evidence) of that internal transformation is seen in changed behavior. As John the Baptist told the crowds, "Therefore bear fruits in keeping with repentance, and do not begin to say to yourselves, 'We have Abraham for our father,' for I say to you that from these stones God is able to raise up children to Abraham" (Luke 3:8; cf. Matt. 3:8–9).

An initial evidence of that genuine heart transformation was a willingness to be baptized. Those whose self-righteous pride remained would never undergo such a public, humbling act. But those whose minds had truly turned to forsake their sin and pride would eagerly declare themselves to be no better than Gentiles—sinners who recognized their unworthiness and their need to walk rightly before God. Thus, baptism marked the outward profession of inward repentance; it did not generate repentance but was its result (Matt. 3:7–8). Moreover, the act of **baptism** did not produce the **forgiveness of sins** but served as an external symbol of the fact that, through faith and repentance, sinners are graciously forgiven by God (cf. Luke 24:47; Acts 3:19; 5:31; 2 Cor. 7:10). Though John's ministry of baptism preceded Christian baptism (cf. Acts 19:3–4), it served a vital role in preparing the people for the arrival of the Messiah. As the apostle Paul explained many years later, "John baptized with the baptism of repentance, telling the people to believe in Him who was coming after him, that is, in Jesus" (Acts 19:4).

John proclaimed an urgent message of repentance in preparation for the coming of the messianic King. Consequently, his **preaching** focused on divine wrath and judgment. He confronted the Jewish religious leaders with vivid language: "You brood of vipers, who warned you to flee from the wrath to come?" (Matt. 3:7). Speaking of the coming Messiah, he further warned the people, "His winnowing fork is in His hand, and He will thoroughly clear His threshing floor; and He will gather His wheat into the barn, but He will burn up the chaff with unquenchable fire" (Matt. 3:12). John's fiery sermons drove the people to address their sin, as they considered the possibility of being excluded from God's kingdom. Before they could hear the good news of salvation, they needed to be confronted with the bad news regarding their own wickedness. Only through genuine faith and repentance could their sins be forgiven.

No first-century Jew wanted to be left out of the messianic kingdom. And so the people of Israel flocked from the cities into the wilderness in order to hear from this rugged, countercultural prophet. As Mark explains, **all the country of Judea was going out to him, and all the people of Jerusalem; and they were being baptized by him in the Jordan River, confessing their sins.** In the words of one commentator:

> By making the pilgrimage to the Jordan, those who believed John's message showed that they wanted to be visibly separated from those under judgment when the Lord came. They wanted to be members of the future purified Israel. Undergoing John's baptism helped them anticipate that they were not only God's covenant people, but that they would remain in that covenant after God cast others out. In order to be assured that they would be included in the future forgiven Israel whose iniquity would be removed, they needed to repent and ask for personal forgiveness now. (Mark Horne, *The Victory According to Mark* [Moscow, ID: Canon Press, 2003], 27)

Multitudes from **Jerusalem,** Jericho, and **all the country of Judea** came to hear John, to confess their sins, and to be baptized by him. By **confessing their sins,** the people agreed with God that they had broken His law and needed to be forgiven. But in the end, this revival proved to be largely superficial. Sadly, the nation that flocked to John at the peak of his popularity would later reject the Messiah to whom his whole ministry pointed.

The territory of **Judea** was the southernmost division of first-century Israel, with Samaria and Galilee to the north. It included the city of **Jerusalem** and extended from the Mediterranean Sea in the west to the Jordan River in the east, and from Bethel in the north to Beersheba in the south. The **Jordan River** is still Israel's major river, flowing from the Sea of Galilee south to the Dead Sea. Tradition suggests that John began his ministry of baptism at the fords near Jericho.

Having described the nature of John's ministry (in vv. 4–5), Mark continues in verse 6 by describing John himself. The New Testament records many wonderful stories about John the Baptist—from his supernatural conception by aged parents, to his being filled with the Holy Spirit while in his mother's womb, to the fact that Jesus called him the greatest man who had lived up to that time. But Mark leaves out those details. In fact, his description of John is short and to the point: **John was clothed with camel's hair and wore a leather belt around his waist, and his diet was locusts and wild honey** (1:6). John's physical description fits a man who lived in the wilderness, where clothing fashions were ignored for rugged durability, and where **locusts and wild honey** provided viable sustenance.

But there is more here than a superficial statement about John's wardrobe and eating habits. A hairy garment made of **camel's hair,** girded **around** the **waist** by a rough **leather belt,** would have designated John as a prophet. In fact, the prophet Elijah wore similar attire. In 2 Kings 1:8, Elijah is described as "a hairy man with a leather girdle bound about his loins." The reference to Elijah as a "hairy man" describes the hairy garments made of animal skin that he wore. Those garments were held in place by a leather belt around the waist.

The similarities between John and Elijah are hardly coincidental. As the angel Gabriel explained to Zacharias regarding John:

> He will be great in the sight of the Lord; and he will drink no wine or liquor, and he will be filled with the Holy Spirit while yet in his mother's womb. And he will turn many of the sons of Israel back to the Lord their God. It is he who will go as a forerunner before Him *in the spirit and*

> *power of Elijah,* to turn the hearts of the fathers back to the children, and the disobedient to the attitude of the righteous, so as to make ready a people prepared for the Lord. (Luke 1:15–17, emphasis added)

Jesus reiterated the connection between Elijah and John in Matthew 11:12–14. There He told the crowds who followed Him, "From the days of John the Baptist until now the kingdom of heaven suffers violence, and violent men take it by force. For all the prophets and the Law prophesied until John. And if you are willing to accept it, John himself is Elijah who was to come" (cf. Mal. 4:5). The Lord's point was that if the Jews had received John's message as God's message and received the Messiah he proclaimed, he would indeed have been the Elijah-like figure spoken of by Malachi. But because Israel ultimately rejected John's gospel witness, another prophet like Elijah is still yet to come, perhaps as one of the two witnesses of Revelation 11:1–19.

John's diet included **locusts,** which the Mosaic law permitted the Israelites to eat (Lev. 11:22). **Locusts** provided a good source of protein and could be prepared in a variety of ways. Once the wings and legs were removed, the body could be roasted, boiled, dried, and even ground up and baked into bread. **Wild honey** was also available (cf. Judg. 14:8–9; 1 Sam. 14:25–26), and provided a sweet counterpart to locusts. John's simple diet was in keeping with his status as a lifelong Nazirite (cf. Luke 1:15).

Even Mark's short description of John is enough to indicate that he must have been a shocking figure to those who saw him. He claimed to be a messenger from God, but his lifestyle was radically different than the other religious leaders of first-century Judaism. Those leaders (the Sadducees and Pharisees) were refined, well-dressed, and sophisticated. John clearly did not care about worldly comforts and even made a point of refusing them. His austere clothing, diet, and way of life were in themselves a rebuke of Israel's religious elite, who indulged in the pomp and circumstance of their privileged positions. It confronted the common people also—since many of them admired the worldly advantages of their leaders. Significantly, John did not call the people to live or dress like he did. His goal was not to turn them into social recluses or ascetics. Nonetheless, his physical appearance served as a dramatic reminder that the pleasures and pursuits of this world can be stumbling blocks that keep people from rejecting their sin and turning to God.

THE PREEMINENCE OF THE NEW KING

And he was preaching, and saying, "After me One is coming who is mightier than I, and I am not fit to stoop down and untie the thong of His sandals. I baptized you with water; but He will baptize you with the Holy Spirit." (1:7–8)

The sum of John's ministry is articulated in these two verses. The entire purpose behind his **preaching** (literally, proclaiming) was to point his listeners to the **One** who was **coming** after him. That is what it meant to be the forerunner, the herald who directed everyone's attention away from himself and toward the coming King. As John later explained to his disciples, "He must increase, but I must decrease" (John 3:30). He rightly understood and embraced his role as the Messiah's messenger.

Thus he told the crowds, **"After me One is coming who is mightier than I, and I am not fit to stoop down and untie the thong of His sandals."** The Greek includes a definite article, indicating that John was speaking about *the* **One** who was **coming.** John's ministry did not precede just any king or monarch. Rather, he was pointing to *the* divine King whose coming was foretold by the Old Testament prophets. John readily acknowledged that this coming King was **mightier than** he. The Messiah would be greater in every respect, so much so that John did not regard himself as even being **fit to stoop down and untie the thong of His sandals.** Untying the master's sandals and tending his dusty feet was a task performed by the lowest of slaves. John's point, then, was that he did not consider himself worthy to be even the lowest slave of such an infinitely exalted King.

John continued to distance himself from Christ by noting the immeasurable difference between their two ministries: **"I baptized you with water; but He will baptize you with the Holy Spirit."** It is as if John is saying, "All I can do is wash you on the outside with water. But He can transform and cleanse you on the inside." Being baptized **with the Holy Spirit** refers to the regenerative work of salvation (cf. Ezek. 36:24–

27; John 3:5–6). This is not a reference to an ecstatic postconversion experience, as some contemporary charismatics claim. Rather, it is the washing of regeneration and the renewing of the Holy Spirit that occurs at the moment of salvation (Acts 1:5; 8:16–17; 1 Cor. 12:13; Titus 3:5–7). This is the purification of the new covenant, and the transformation of the new birth.

In the upper room, the Lord Jesus promised to send the **Holy Spirit** to His disciples as "another Helper, that He may be with you forever; that is the Spirit of truth, whom the world cannot receive, because it does not behold Him or know Him, but you know Him because He abides with you, and will be in you" (John 14:16–17). That promise was initially fulfilled on the day of Pentecost (Acts 2:1–4). Since that time, every believer experiences the indwelling presence of the Holy Spirit beginning at the moment of salvation (cf. 1 Cor. 6:19).

John's statement regarding the Holy Spirit must have thrilled the hearts of the faithful Jews who heard him preach. In keeping with the promises of the Old Testament, they hoped for the day when God would "pour out [His] Spirit on all mankind" (Joel 2:28), when He would "sprinkle clean water on [them]," and "give [them] a new heart and put a new spirit within [them]" (Ezek. 36:25–26). In that day, their hearts would at last be baptized in the very power and person of God Himself (cf. Jer. 31:33). This supernatural power distinguishes the ministry of the new King from any other. John was not able to give the Holy Spirit. Only God can do that. And the coming King is God in human flesh, and He will baptize sinners with the saving power of the Spirit's regenerative work.

John's message summarizes the heart of the gospel, bringing us back to Mark's use of the term in verse 1. The gospel is good news—the glad tidings of a new King who is bringing a new kingdom. The new King is the long-awaited Messiah. He is God Himself. His kingdom is a kingdom of forgiveness, blessing, and salvation. It comes to those who repent. And those who do will be baptized with the Holy Spirit. This gospel is the culmination of all past redemptive history and the door to all future glory. And John the Baptist, the faithful herald and forerunner, had come to announce His arrival.

The Significance of Jesus' Baptism (Mark 1:9–11)

2

In those days Jesus came from Nazareth in Galilee and was baptized by John in the Jordan. Immediately coming up out of the water, He saw the heavens opening, and the Spirit like a dove descending upon Him; and a voice came out of the heavens: "You are My beloved Son, in You I am well-pleased." (1:9–11)

From the very first verse, the gospel of Mark declares itself to be a joyous proclamation of the divine King: Jesus Christ, the Son of God. The word gospel (*euangelion*), in its first-century context, signified the accession of a king to his throne (1:1). Mark is writing about God's great King, the Sovereign whose coming signaled the beginning of a new era for the world. Because he was writing to a Roman audience, Mark intentionally highlighted details he knew would demonstrate Christ's imperial sovereignty in the minds of his Gentile readers. He began with the King's forerunner, John the Baptist (1:2–8). The messianic King, like any legitimate monarch in the ancient world, was preceded by a royal herald who proclaimed His coming and prepared the way for His arrival. As the prophetic forerunner, John's ministry of preparation was characterized by preaching repentance and pointing his hearers to the coming King.

In this section (1:9–11), Mark continues to emphasize Christ's divine kingship. But the focus shifts from anticipation to arrival, as the King appears on the scene to begin His public ministry. In keeping with his theme, Mark presents Jesus' baptism as a royal coronation ceremony, in which the authority of the messianic King is affirmed by heaven itself.

It was probably a summer day in the year A. D. 26 when, to John's surprise, Jesus was among the crowds who had come to be baptized. As Mark explains, **In those days, Jesus came from Nazareth in Galilee and was baptized by John in the Jordan.** The phrase **in those days** refers to an unspecified point during John's ministry (cf. vv. 4–8). John had likely been preaching before Jesus' baptism for six months or longer.

Reported by all four Gospels (Matt. 3:13–17; Luke 3:21–22; John 1:29–34), this is the only meeting between Jesus and John recorded in the New Testament. Though they were related and later contacted each other through their disciples (cf. Matt. 11:2), there is no indication that they met either before or after this occasion. The meeting was initiated by **Jesus,** who **came** when the time was right for Him to make His first public appearance (cf. Luke 3:21). According to Luke 3:23, He was about thirty years old when He **came from Nazareth in Galilee** to be baptized and begin His ministry.

For the sake of his non-Jewish audience, Mark explains that the small village of **Nazareth** was located in the region of **Galilee**—an area largely populated by Gentiles. (**Nazareth** was so obscure that it is not even mentioned in the ancient Jewish literature of the first century.) **Galilee** had been conquered by the Israelites during the time of Joshua and was part of the northern kingdom of Israel in the days of the divided kingdom. But when the northern kingdom fell to Assyria (in 722 B.C.), the Assyrians deported the Israelites and many Gentiles came to live in the region. Consequently, the Jews of Judea viewed Galilee, and even their fellow Jews who lived there, with a certain level of disdain. According to John 7:41, many found it unthinkable that the Messiah could come out of Galilee. Indignantly they asked, "Surely the Christ is not going to come from Galilee, is He?" Their question betrayed an ignorance of Old Testament prophecy. In Isaiah 9:1–2, the prophet said of the Messiah:

> "But there will be no more gloom for her who was in anguish; in earlier times He treated the land of Zebulun and the land of Naphtali with contempt, but later on He shall make it glorious, by the way of the sea, on the other side of Jordan, Galilee of the Gentiles.

> The people who walk in darkness
> Will see a great light;
> Those who live in a dark land,
> The light will shine on them."

Clearly, it was God's plan all along that the Messiah, though born in Bethlehem of Judea (cf. Mic. 5:2), would grow up in Galilee.

The fact that the Messiah came from an insignificant village in a humble region on the fringes of Jewish society was in itself a rebuke to the corrupt religious system that dominated Judaism at that time. The first-century Jews expected the Messiah to come from Jerusalem—the center of Jewish religious life. Instead, He came from the outskirts, far removed from the apostate religious establishment. Though He grew up in obscurity, the time had arrived for Him to make His first public appearance. Hence, He left Nazareth in order to be **baptized by John in the Jordan.**

The **Jordan** River is the primary river in Israel, flowing south from the Sea of Galilee (680 feet below sea level) toward the Dead Sea (the lowest point on earth at 1300 feet below sea level). The exact spot where John was baptizing at that time is unknown, though it was likely toward the southern end of the Jordan River—near Jericho and the Dead Sea. The gospel of John reports that it was near "Bethany beyond the Jordan" (John 1:28), but the precise location of that town is debated.

Mark has already identified **John** as John the Baptist (v. 4), a name that directly associated him with his unique practice of baptizing Jews. Though the rituals of Judaism included various ceremonial washings, baptism (by full immersion into water) was not a normal part of Jewish religious practice. The closest parallel was Gentile proselyte baptism—in which Gentile converts to Judaism were washed to signify their entrance into Judaism. For John to call the Jews to be baptized, in a way designed for Gentiles, was shocking and unique. To confess they were no better than Gentiles was, for many Jews, undignified and offensive. If baptism was distasteful to the self-righteous sinners in John's audience, how much more objectionable it must have seemed for the Messiah Himself to seek baptism. John's baptism was a sign of repentance, designed for sinners as a declaration that they had forsaken their wicked ways and turned to God. But Jesus was the sinless Son of God. Why would He need to be baptized?

John undoubtedly knew all about Jesus, having learned about the Messiah from his parents, Zacharias and Elizabeth. From birth, John understood that he was to be the Messiah's forerunner. He also knew that Jesus, Mary's son, was the Son of God, the promised Savior of Israel. Yet, it appears that John had never personally met Jesus. John's parents, who were elderly when he was born, likely died when he was relatively young. John himself grew up in the Judean wilderness (Luke 1:80), while Jesus spent His childhood in an obscure Galilean village. And although John, while still a baby in his mother's womb, "leaped for joy" when in the presence of the unborn Christ (Luke 1:44 ESV), there is no indication in Scripture that John and Jesus ever met before Jesus' baptism. This conclusion is strengthened by John the Baptist's remark in John 1:33. Speaking of Jesus, John explained, "I did not recognize Him, but He who sent me to baptize in water said to me, 'He upon whom you see the Spirit descending and remaining upon Him, this is the One who baptizes in the Holy Spirit.'" The word **recognize** (*oida*) means "to know with one's eyes," suggesting that John had never seen Jesus before, or at least not in a very long time. Consequently, John did not recognize Jesus because he did not know what He looked like.

But once that initial moment of unfamiliarity passed—and John suddenly realized who this Man was standing before him—everything he knew about the Messiah flooded into his mind. This was the sinless Lamb of God (John 1:29). His life required no confession or repentance. He needed no conversion or transformation. So why was He coming to be baptized?

Recognizing the obvious incongruity, John responded to Jesus in the way we might expect. According to Matthew 3:14, "John tried to prevent Him, saying, 'I have need to be baptized by You, and do You come to me?'" The phrase "tried to prevent" represents a single Greek verb (*diekōluen*). The imperfect tense indicates that John was continually trying to prevent Jesus, emphasizing how inappropriate it seemed for the Lord to receive a baptism designed for sinners. Rather than baptizing Jesus, John sought to be baptized by Him. To John, that seemed more fitting—since Jesus was the sinless messianic King and John was but His sinful, humble servant (cf. Mark 1:7).

John's attitude toward Jesus was the polar opposite of his response to the Pharisees and the Sadducees. According to Matthew 3:7–8, when John "saw many of the Pharisees and Sadducees coming for baptism, he said to them, 'You brood of vipers, who warned you to flee from the wrath to come? Therefore bear fruit in keeping with repentance.'" When the Jewish religious leaders arrived, John publicly confronted their self-righteous hypocrisy and commanded them to repent. He refused to baptize them on account of their pride, duplicity, and impenitence. When Jesus came, John's reaction was totally different. His reluctance to baptize Jesus stemmed from his realization that Jesus was sinless. If anyone did not need to be baptized, surely it was Him.

From a christological perspective, John's unwillingness to baptize Jesus underscores a foundational theological truth about the character of Christ. It is one of the greatest affirmations of the sinlessness of Christ found in the Gospels. John knew that Jesus was holy, spotless, undefiled, and without sin (cf. Heb. 4:15). That is why he hesitated to baptize Him. John's baptism was a baptism for sinners, and Jesus was not in that category. Thus, even in his reluctance to baptize Jesus, John fulfilled the role of a herald by bearing testimony to the perfection of the divine messianic King.

So for what purpose did Jesus come to be baptized? The answer to that question has been the subject of much speculation and conjecture. But it need not be. A comparison of the four gospel accounts reveals that Jesus came to be baptized for two reasons: first, to fulfill all righteousness and second, to divinely authenticate His ministry.

To Fulfill All Righteousness

According to Matthew 3:15, Jesus responded to John with these words, "Permit it at this time; for in this way it is fitting for us to fulfill all

righteousness." Jesus did not deny John's assessment of His sinless perfection. Rather, He explained that what seemed inappropriate was, in
fact, necessary on this special occasion ("at this time"). The Lord understood that John's reluctance was motivated out of humble reverence and
profound loyalty. Thus, He did not rebuke John for his reticence. Rather,
He asked John to yield to Him, trusting that what He was asking was
according to God's perfect plan.

Jesus answered John's objections by explaining that His baptism
was necessary and proper, so that He might fulfill all the righteous
requirements of God. It was God's will for John to baptize the people (cf.
John 1:33). Because Jesus perfectly submitted to the will of God in everything, it was fitting for Him also to receive the baptism of John. Jesus' obedience was comprehensive and complete—He lived in perfect
alignment to the will of His heavenly Father (cf. John 5:30). He fulfilled
God's requirements perfectly in every respect, yet because God had
authorized John's baptism, Jesus submitted to it.

Moreover, through His baptism, Jesus identified Himself with the
sinners He had come to save. He fulfilled all righteousness, not only
through His life of perfect obedience but also through His substitutionary death on the cross, in which God "made Him who knew no sin to be
sin on our behalf, so that we might become the righteousness of God in
Him" (2 Cor. 5:21). The righteous requirement of God's law was death as a
payment for sin. Christ's death paid that debt in full (Col. 2:14). Centuries
earlier, the prophet Isaiah declared that the Messiah would be "numbered with the transgressors; yet He Himself bore the sin of many, and
interceded for the transgressors" (Isa. 53:12; cf. 1 Peter 3:18). In the first act
of His ministry, the One who had no sin publicly identified Himself with
those who had no righteousness. The sinless Lamb submitted to a baptism designed for sinners—a foreshadowing of the fact that He would
soon submit Himself to a death deserved by sinners.

Symbolically, Jesus' baptism looked forward to the cross, just as
Christian baptism now looks back to it. As the Lord told His disciples in
Luke 12:50, "I have a baptism to undergo, and how distressed I am until it
is accomplished!" On another occasion, He said to James and John, "You
do not know what you are asking for. Are you able to drink the cup that I
drink, or to be baptized with the baptism with which I am baptized?"

(Mark 10:38). Being lowered into the water and then rising again pictured His death and resurrection. He was immersed in the river of death in order to bear the sins of those who would believe in Him.

Thus, it was fitting for Him to be baptized in order that He might fulfill all righteousness—both as an act of obedience to the Father's will and as a way to identify with sinners for whom He would die as a righteous substitute.

To Divinely Authenticate His Ministry

Immediately coming up out of the water, He saw the heavens opening, and the Spirit like a dove descending upon Him; and a voice came out of the heavens: "You are My beloved Son, in You I am well-pleased." (1:10–11)

Mark does not include the dialogue recorded by Matthew that took place between Jesus and John. Instead, Mark focuses on the spectacular event that **immediately** followed Jesus' baptism: the divine coronation of the messianic King. In keeping with the fast-paced style of his gospel, Mark employs the adverb *euthus* (meaning **immediately** or "straightaway") more than the other three gospel writers combined—using it eleven times in the first chapter alone (1:3 [where it is translated as "straight"], 10, 12, 18, 20, 21, 28, 29, 30, 42, 43).

As Jesus was **coming up out of the water,** while He was praying (cf. Luke 3:21), a dramatic scene **immediately** began to unfold. This majestic, Trinitarian scene might best be described as the Messiah's royal commissioning, a glorious event that encompassed both Jesus' official coronation and the divine inauguration of His public ministry. The regal ceremony included two elements—visibly, the Son was anointed by the Holy Spirit; audibly, He was affirmed by His heavenly Father. The renowned nineteenth-century British preacher Charles Spurgeon summarized the significance of this event with these words:

> Try to picture to yourselves the scene that our text describes. . . . As Jesus comes up out of the water, the Spirit of God descends upon Him

in a visible shape—in appearance like a dove—and rests upon Him. John says that "it abode upon Him," as though the Spirit was thenceforth to be His continual Companion and, truly, it was so. At the same time that the dove descended and lighted upon Christ, there was heard a Voice from Heaven, saying, "This is My Beloved Son, in whom I am well-pleased." This was the voice of God the Father—He did not reveal Himself in a bodily shape, but uttered wondrous words such as mortal ears had never before heard! The Father revealed Himself not to the eyes as the Spirit did, but to the ears—and the words He spoke clearly indicated that it was God the Father bearing witness to His beloved Son. So that the entrance of Christ upon His public ministry on earth was the chosen opportunity for the public manifestation of the intimate union between God the Father, God the Son and God the Holy Spirit! (Charles Spurgeon, "Lessons from Christ's Baptism," sermon 3298, March 4, 1866)

The Messiah's coronation was distinctly Trinitarian; yet it was open to public view. When Jesus looked up, **He saw the heavens opening.** But this was not a private vision given only to Him. John the Baptist, presumably among many other bystanders, provided eyewitness testimony to the reality of these glorious events (John 1:32).

Mark's description of the sky splitting open is understandably dramatic. His word for **opened** is a form of *schizō* ("to tear, rip"), the same verb he later used to describe the tearing of the veil in the temple after Jesus' death (Mark 15:38). The imagery is reminiscent of Isaiah 64:1, where the prophet Isaiah cries out to the Lord, "Oh, that You would rend the heavens and come down, that the mountains might quake at Your presence." Isaiah's prophecy anticipated the Messiah's arrival. The day would come when the sky itself would rip open and God would come down.

Given Mark's arresting language, one might expect a violent scene to unfold, but nothing came crashing down through the clouds to the earth. Instead, with beauty and gentleness, **the Spirit like a dove was descending upon Him.** The third member of the Trinity gracefully descended to alight upon the Son, providing a visible symbol of divine blessing, authentication, and empowerment at the outset of Jesus' ministry. Importantly, Mark does not say that **the Spirit** is a **dove**—nor should we allow the imagery to be taken too far (lest we begin to picture the third member of the Trinity as eternally existing in the form of a bird). Mark's point was simply that the **Spirit** in some visible form descended upon Christ with the same delicate gentleness of a dove landing softly on its perch.

In its anticipation of the Messiah, the Old Testament had prom- ised that "the Spirit of the Lord will rest on Him" (Isa. 11:2). That promise was reiterated by God Himself, "Behold, My Servant, whom I uphold; My chosen one in whom My soul delights. I have put My Spirit upon Him" (Isa. 42:1). The name "Messiah" (or "Christ") was a royal title, meaning "Anointed One." At Jesus' baptism, the Holy Spirit visibly anointed Him as a public declaration of His messianic kingship.

Jesus, of course, was fully God. Even in His incarnation, He did not forfeit His divinity. In His deity He needed nothing. But in His humanity, He was being anointed for service and empowered for ministry by the Spirit in a manner reminiscent of the words of Isaiah 61:1,

> "The Spirit of the Lord God is upon me,
> Because the Lord has anointed me
> To bring good news to the afflicted;
> He has sent me to bind up the brokenhearted,
> To proclaim liberty to captives
> And freedom to prisoners."

In His incarnation, the Son of God voluntarily laid aside the inde- pendent use of His divine attributes. As the apostle Paul explains, "Although He existed in the form of God, [He] did not regard equality with God a thing to be grasped, but emptied Himself, taking the form of a bond-servant, and being made in the likeness of men" (Phil. 2:6–7). The Son of God took on human flesh, humbly submitting Himself to the Father's will and the Holy Spirit's power (cf. John 4:34). At every major point of Jesus' ministry, the Spirit was actively at work: His birth (Luke 1:35), His baptism (Mark 1:10), His temptation (Mark 1:12), His ministry (Luke 4:14), His miracles (Matt. 12:28; Acts 10:38), His death (Heb. 9:14), and His resurrection (Rom. 1:4). At every point and in every way, Jesus Christ was perfectly filled with the Holy Spirit. He never resisted, grieved, or quenched the Spirit but always operated under the Spirit's full control, walking in perfect obedience to the will of His Father.

Jesus' anointing with the Holy Spirit was fundamentally unique. The Spirit came upon Him to empower Him for ministry; the Spirit's descent was also a visible sign to John the Baptist and everyone else in the watching crowd that Jesus truly was the Anointed One whose coming had been predicted by the prophets. Here, at last, was the long-awaited King, the Son of God—the One to whom John's ministry pointed.

The visible descent of the Holy Spirit was accompanied by the audible affirmation of the Father: **and a voice came out of the heavens: "You are My beloved Son, in You I am well-pleased"** (1:11). Each member of the Trinity was simultaneously present at Jesus' baptism. The Son in His humanity physically standing in the water, the Spirit visibly descending upon Him, and the Father in heaven audibly voicing His approval. On at least two other occasions, the Father would similarly confirm the person and work of His Son—at the transfiguration (Matt. 17:5) and while Jesus was preaching to a crowd shortly before His death (John 12:28). At Jesus' baptism, the Father's superlative commendation underscored the glorious truth about the Son's absolute perfection.

There were many who bore witness to the ministry of Christ— angels, John the Baptist, His followers. But the Father's witness was the most important of all (cf. John 5:32; 8:18). And what was the Father's testimony? **"You are My beloved Son, in You I am well-pleased."** No prophet had ever been told that. Prophets might be called friends of God (James 2:23), servants of God (Deut. 34:5), or men of God (1 Sam. 2:27). But no prophet was ever called the Son of God. Yet, over fifty times in the gospel accounts, Jesus Christ is called the Son of God. On this occasion, the testimony came from the Father Himself. His words are reminiscent of Psalm 2:7, a passage that the Jews universally regarded as messianic: "I will surely tell of the decree of the Lord: He said to Me, 'You are My Son, Today I have begotten You.'"

The fact that Jesus Christ is the Son of God, as the Father here declares Him to be, is central to the gospel message. It underscores the truth that He is one in essence with God, possessing the same nature as the Father. He is both God and "with God" (John 1:1). "He is the radiance of God's glory and the exact representation of [God's] nature" (Heb. 1:3), "the image of God" (2 Cor. 4:4), and the one in whom the fullness of deity dwells (Col. 2:9). Because of His deity, He is superior to the angels who worship Him (Heb. 1:6–8). Even God's title of Father is a reference to His essential relationship to Jesus Christ, the Son (Matt. 11:27; John 5:17–18; 10:29–33; 14:6–11; 17:1–5; Rom. 15:6; 2 Cor. 1:3; Eph. 1:3, 17; Phil. 2:9–11;

1 Peter 1:3; 2 John 3). When Jesus called God "Father," He emphasized the fact that He shared the same essence and nature as the Father. As John 5:18 explains, even His enemies knew Jesus "was calling God His own Father, making Himself equal with God."

Not only is the Son equal in essence with God, but He is also **beloved** by God. From the Father's perspective, He is **My Son,** the only one who bears that eternal privilege. He is uniquely the object of the Father's highest affection (cf. John 5:20), in a way that is shared with no other like Him. **Beloved** (*agapētos*) expresses the infinitely deep and eternally profound relationship enjoyed by the Father with the Son. Though the same word is used of the Father's love for believers (Rom. 1:7), the Father loves His Son supremely above all others. It is only because believers are in the Son, that they are privileged to receive the Father's love at all (cf. John 17:24–26; Eph. 1:6).

Having "loved [the Son] before the foundation of the world" (John 17:24), the Father is eternally and completely **well-pleased** with Him (cf. Isa. 42:1). Jesus Christ was well-pleasing to His Father in everything that He did. In His incarnation, the Son perfectly submitted to the Father's will, and in His death, He fully satisfied the Father's wrath. The Son would offer Himself as the final sacrifice for sinners, and the Father was delighted to receive that sacrifice (Isa. 53:10). In Old Testament Israel, an acceptable sacrifice to God had to be spotless and unblemished (cf. Ex. 12:5; Lev. 1:3; Deut. 17:1). Only the perfect Lamb of God could ever fully meet those requirements.

In Israel's history, no animal sacrifice had ever ultimately pleased God or fully satisfied His wrath. That is because, as the author of Hebrews explains, "it is impossible for the blood of bulls and goats to take away sins" (Heb. 10:4; cf. 9:12). Those sacrifices only pointed to the cross— where the Messiah Himself would be slain as the perfect substitute for sinners. Hence, the apostle Peter could tell the believers to whom he wrote: "You were not redeemed with perishable things like silver or gold from your futile way of life inherited from your forefathers, but with precious blood, as of a lamb unblemished and spotless, the blood of Christ" (1 Peter 1:18–19). At the cross, God's justice was fully satisfied by the pure sacrifice of the Son. Thus the Father was **well-pleased** with the Son— both in His life and in His death.

No higher testimony to the sinless perfection of Jesus Christ could ever be given. The ultimate authentication of the Son came from the verbal affirmation of the Father accompanied by the visible manifestation of the Spirit. Such constitutes the divine inauguration of the new King—God's sinless, beloved Son who was anointed and empowered by the Holy Spirit to save sinners and establish His kingdom. This is the Messiah's coronation, a ceremony in which the entire Trinity was involved.

Later in Jesus' ministry, when the religious leaders asked Him, "By what authority are You doing these things, or who gave You this authority to do these things?" (Mark 11:28), Jesus answered by pointing them to His baptism:

> And Jesus said to them, "I will ask you one question, and you answer Me, and then I will tell you by what authority I do these things. Was the baptism of John from heaven, or from men? Answer Me." They began reasoning among themselves, saying, "If we say, 'From heaven,' He will say, 'Then why did you not believe him?' But shall we say, 'From men'?"—they were afraid of the people, for everyone considered John to have been a real prophet. Answering Jesus, they said, "We do not know." And Jesus said to them, "Nor will I tell you by what authority I do these things." (vv. 29–33)

Because they were unwilling to acknowledge the legitimacy of John's baptizing ministry—and by extension Jesus' own baptism—the Lord had nothing else to say to them. If they would not recognize His coronation, the discussion was over before it even began. In essence, Jesus was saying, "If you refuse to admit that John was a prophet of God, then you will not acknowledge the reality of what occurred at My baptism, where the Spirit anointed Me and the Father affirmed Me. And if you reject that, then there is nothing else I can add to convince you about the source of My authority." That is how critical Jesus' baptism was. It was His coronation, and the divine inauguration of His public ministry.

The Authority of Jesus Christ
(Mark 1:12–20)

3

Immediately the Spirit impelled Him to go out into the wilderness. And He was in the wilderness forty days being tempted by Satan; and He was with the wild beasts, and the angels were ministering to Him. Now after John had been taken into custody, Jesus came into Galilee, preaching the gospel of God, and saying, "The time is fulfilled, and the kingdom of God is at hand; repent and believe in the gospel." As He was going along by the Sea of Galilee, He saw Simon and Andrew, the brother of Simon, casting a net in the sea; for they were fishermen. And Jesus said to them, "Follow Me, and I will make you become fishers of men." Immediately they left their nets and followed Him. Going on a little farther, He saw James the son of Zebedee, and John his brother, who were also in the boat mending the nets. Immediately He called them; and they left their father Zebedee in the boat with the hired servants, and went away to follow Him. (1:12–20)

The glories of the Lord Jesus Christ are inexhaustible. The fullness of His majesty and the wonder of His person cannot be conceived or contained. Every comprehensible truth about Him enriches His people profoundly, so that they long for more. While His human history is the subject of the four Gospels, the eternal Son is the theme of the entire Bible. Each gospel record is unique, reflecting the perspective and purpose of each inspired author, so the four Gospels present a perfectly harmonious, historically accurate, and Holy Spirit–revealed portrait of Jesus.

In keeping with his condensed, fast-paced style, Mark leaves the account of Jesus' birth to Matthew and Luke, and begins his gospel by focusing attention on the ministry of Jesus' forerunner, John the Baptist (1:2–8). Mark does not linger there. His brief survey of John's ministry quickly shifts to the divine One of whom John preached. When the time came to be revealed to Israel, Jesus left Nazareth and came to the Jordan River. There He was baptized by John (1:9–11)—the event that constituted His divine coronation ceremony and the inauguration of His public ministry.

In the verses that follow (1:12–20), Mark continues His rapid pace. Appropriately, the word **immediately** occurs three times in these nine verses. Whereas Matthew and Luke each provide a detailed account of Jesus' temptation, Mark's brief record is stated in two verses (vv. 12–13). He subsequently skips Jesus' initial ministry in Judea (recorded in John 2:13–4:2), along with His travels through Samaria (John 4:3–42), reentering the story with His arrival in Galilee (vv. 14–15). In verses 16–20, with seemingly no connection to the preceding verses, Mark advances to describe Jesus' calling of Peter, Andrew, James, and John. Once again, the staccato nature of Mark's gospel is evidenced in the brevity of these vignettes. Why does Mark take this condensed approach—moving quickly from one short snippet to the next? Why does he put them together in this way?

The answer goes back to verse 1, where Mark announced that his account was a royal proclamation (or "gospel") of Jesus Christ, the messianic King and the Son of God. It is Mark's tight purpose that keeps his narrative streamlined. In order to move to the main part of the story, Mark proceeds quickly to those details that will clearly establish Jesus Christ's royal credentials. The vignettes Mark selected in these opening verses are not a random assortment of disconnected details but thoughtfully connected events that collectively demonstrate that Jesus is the messianic King. Mark's sequence is designed to show that Jesus was not only preceded by a royal herald (1:2–8), but like any ancient monarch would be, He was crowned and commissioned as a king with one major point of distinction: in His case, He was crowned by God Himself (vv. 9–11)—something no other king could claim. After His baptism, Jesus demonstrated His royal authority over all evil forces by defeating His archenemy in the wilderness (vv. 12–13). Then He exercised His sovereignty by preaching His kingdom message of salvation from sin (vv. 14–15). In the final segment, He commanded His servants to follow Him (vv. 16–20).

This emphasis on Jesus' royal authority provides the common thread through these brief episodes in Mark 1:12–20. The scope of that authority extends to three areas: over Satan and his realm (vv. 12–13), over sin and its dominion (vv. 14–15), and over sinners in their salvation and submission (vv. 16–20). If the new King is to take His rightful throne, He must demonstrate His might and overthrow the usurper. If He is going to conquer the kingdom of sin and free its captives, He must have complete power over evil. If He is to rescue lost people, He must have the prerogative and power to transform them into His righteous servants, so that through them He may advance His kingdom truth and power to the world. Clearly, that kind of authority—over Satan, sin, and sinners—is not only royal, it is divine.

JESUS' KINGDOM MIGHT: HIS AUTHORITY OVER SATAN

Immediately the Spirit impelled Him to go out into the wilderness. And He was in the wilderness forty days being tempted by Satan; and He was with the wild beasts, and the angels were ministering to Him. (1:12–13)

In all three Synoptic Gospels, the account of Jesus' temptation directly follows His baptism. The two events stand in stark contrast. Having received the royal accolades of heaven, Jesus **immediately** faced the fierce assaults of hell. His coronation by the Spirit and confirmation from the Father are followed straightaway by His confrontation with the devil. Given the majesty of His baptism, readers might expect a glorious celebration complete with angelic choirs and resounding doxologies. Instead, they are flung into the desert with hardly a moment to catch their breath. There is no time to relish the joy and glory of the baptism. Mark's description does not even include a transition sentence: **Immediately the Spirit impelled Him to go out into the wilderness.**

One of the paradoxes visible through Jesus' earthly ministry, all the way to the cross, was that He came to earth not only as the messianic King but also as the Suffering Slave. As King, He was exalted and glorified, a point majestically illustrated at His baptism. As the Suffering Slave, He was demeaned and mistreated, a reality vividly demonstrated during His temptation. The most exalted One was also the most humiliated One. The juxtaposition of Jesus' baptism with His temptation manifested those contrasting realities early. The final contrast would come at His death where He was numbered as a criminal while a sign declaring Him to be King hung over His bloody head.

The **Spirit** here is the Holy Spirit. According to Luke 4:1, "Jesus, full of the Holy Spirit, returned from the Jordan and was led around by the Spirit in the wilderness." Being filled with the Holy Spirit, Jesus fully submitted Himself to the Spirit's control. The third member of the Trinity was the power behind all that Jesus did (cf. Luke 4:14, 18). The word **impelled** (*ekballō* in Greek) is a forceful word, meaning "to drive out" or "to compel one to depart." The verb fits Mark's dramatic style and certainly does not imply that Jesus was resistant to the Spirit's leading. Rather, it underscores the reality that the Spirit was in control—perfectly leading Jesus to fulfill each element of the Father's plan.

Mark does not reveal the reason why the Holy Spirit impelled Him to go into the wilderness, but Matthew 4:1 does: "Jesus was led up by the Spirit into the wilderness to be tempted by the devil." Within God's purposes, it was necessary for Jesus to be tempted by Satan himself—to confront the devil in face-to-face combat and defeat him. The Greek word for "tempted" (*peirazō*) is a morally neutral term that simply means "to test." The testing can be either good or evil depending on the intention of the one devising the test. Because Satan is the one doing the testing in this instance, *peirazō* is rightly translated by the English word "tempt."

Although the Spirit led Jesus to the place where He would be tempted, it is important to note that God is never the tempter. James 1:13 is clear that God cannot tempt anyone. God allowed His Son to be tested for the sole purpose that through His victory Jesus might demonstrate His absolute power and authority over the devil's devices. Christ's temptation then did not happen by the will of Satan. In the will of God, it was another way to authenticate the Son.

The stakes could not have been higher, especially following His messianic coronation ceremony. Would He, as the divinely commissioned King, be able to meet and conquer His archenemy? Could He endure the most alluring assaults the devil could devise? He would never be able to establish His kingdom if He were unable to overthrow the usurper. It was His royal duty to crush the serpent's head (Gen. 3:15), "to destroy the works of the devil" (1 John 3:8), and to depose the illegitimate "god of this world" (2 Cor. 4:4). But would He be able to do that decisively when, after fasting for forty days, He was physically weak, emotionally drained, and completely isolated?

The setting for Jesus' temptation was the **wilderness**—a place of desolation where He was removed from people and provision. In a very short period of time, His circumstances had dramatically changed. He had gone from the elevated experience of His coronation, among the massive crowds that surrounded John the Baptist, to utter isolation. At the Jordan River, the Father commended Him, the Spirit descended upon Him, and John the Baptist declared Him to be the Messiah. His public ministry had been supernaturally inaugurated from heaven. After waiting for thirty years, He had been commissioned to commence His earthly mission. At that highest moment, the Holy Spirit drove Him into the desert to face a severe, supernatural assault from hell.

The Judean **wilderness** is an arid, inhospitable desert that stretches west from the Dead Sea toward Jerusalem, encompassing an area roughly thirty-five miles long and fifteen miles wide. The dusty, desolate, and dangerous landscape is broken up by rocky peaks, craggy cliffs, and plunging ravines. The first Adam—tempted by Satan in the garden of Eden, a lush paradise where everything was good—succumbed to sinful temptation despite being innocent and dwelling in a perfect environment. The second Adam, perfectly holy, faced the devil in the middle of a foreboding wasteland—a place utterly unlike Eden. It was there, in the parched heat of a barren desert, that Jesus found Himself all alone and weakened by fasting, accompanied by the fiery serpents and scorpions that lived there (cf. Deut. 8:15). Mark's explanation that **He was with the wild beasts** emphasizes the reality that He was completely isolated from human care. Such untamed animals may have included leopards, foxes, jackals, and wild pigs.

Mark summarized Christ's encounter with the devil in one succinct phrase: **And He was in the wilderness forty days being tempted by Satan.** Both Matthew and Luke indicate that Jesus went the entire forty-day period without food (Matt. 4:2; Luke 4:2). Jesus' fast was not the first forty-day fast recorded in Scripture; both Moses (Ex. 34:28) and Elijah (1 Kings 19:8) went without food for that long. Interestingly, it was those same two Old Testament saints who later met with Jesus at His transfiguration (Matt. 17:3).

Nearly six weeks without eating creates a desperate condition, especially in the location where Jesus was moving. His physical state would have begun to rapidly deteriorate after just two weeks, so that His strength was undoubtedly gone long before the temptation reached its final assault. Yet, as the royal and divine Son, He had to face and conquer His strongest enemy even when He was at His weakest. Mark's description of Jesus' temptation implies that the Lord was being tempted by Satan throughout the entire six-week period—a time of testing that climaxed in the final temptation recorded in Matthew 4 and Luke 4.

The three episodes recounted by Matthew and Luke indicate that Satan primarily attacked Jesus in His role as the Suffering Servant. The devil did not entice Jesus to give up His sovereign prerogative. Rather, he urged Jesus to exercise the power and privilege inherent in His divine status and thus abandon the humiliation of His incarnation. When Jesus was hungry, Satan asked Him to exercise His sovereign power and create bread (Matt. 4:3–4; Luke 4:3–4). After Jesus resisted, the devil took Him to a high mountain and offered Him dominion over all the nations of the world (Matt. 4:8–10; Luke 4:5–8). Again, Jesus rejected Satan's ploy. Finally, the devil brought Him to the pinnacle of the temple, urging Jesus to give a public demonstration of His messiahship by leaping off the edge (Matt. 4:5–7; Luke 4:9–12). Once more, Jesus refused. In the face of each attack, the King responded with Scripture from Deuteronomy.

In each case, Satan attempted to persuade Christ to abandon His humiliation—to exercise His divine right apart from the Spirit's empowerment and outside of the Father's will. To do so would have undermined God's saving purposes. The success of Jesus' earthly mission depended upon His humiliation, ultimately leading to the cross. As Paul told the Philippians, Jesus "humbled Himself by becoming obedient to the point of death, even death on a cross" (Phil. 2:8). If Jesus had abandoned His humiliation and disobeyed the Father's will, He would have demonstrated Himself to be an imposter, another false messiah, who could never have gone to Calvary to die as God's Lamb. The hope of redemption would have ended in failure and defeat. On the other hand, Christ's victory led to the salvation of the elect and His ultimate exaltation (Phil. 2:9–10).

It must be understood that this was not a unique, even singular experience of temptation for Jesus. Hebrews 4:15 explains that He was "tempted in all things [or at all points in His life] as we are, yet without sin." From childhood on, He faced the same enticements to sin that every human being experiences. Nor would this be the last time that He would be tempted. In Luke 22:28, Jesus told His disciples that they were those who "have continued with me in my temptations" (KJV). He was again assaulted in the garden of Gethsemane as He anticipated the cross (Luke 22:53). But He was never tempted so intensely over such an extended period of time as He was in the wilderness. This was Satan's major attempt to cause Him to sin and be discredited as Messiah and Savior.

If the new King was to be triumphant, He had to demonstrate His victory over the devil at his most clever and opportune effort. He could not claim absolute and complete power over sin itself if He did not demonstrate personal power in defeating Satan. His call to deliver sinners would have been meaningless, if He Himself had not been able to quench the fiery darts of the evil one. Hence, His public ministry began by directly confronting the most powerful demon ruler who opposes God and all His purposes.

All the Son of God had known from eternity was infinite honor, power, and divine privilege. Here, as a man at the moment of His greatest weakness, He was urged by Satan to claim what was rightfully His as the Son of God, but in a way that was contrary to the Father's plan. Would Jesus withstand such intense temptations? Would He endure the test, claim victory over the devil's seductive schemes, and thus demonstrate His deity?

Mark's concluding phrase **and the angels were ministering to Him** implies what Matthew and Luke state explicitly—that, indeed, Jesus triumphed over all the temptation Satan brought, emerging victorious from His forty-day isolation in the wilderness. The word **ministering** (*diakoneō*) indicates that these angels provided Jesus with food. But **the angels** also ministered to Him by their very presence, which served as confirmation that the Father who sent them was still well pleased with His Son.

Jesus' subsequent life and ministry prove His divine holiness beyond argument. It was here, during His temptation in the wilderness, that His holiness was assaulted most acutely and relentlessly. It was not until after "the devil had finished every temptation, [that] he left Him" (Luke 4:13) and the angels arrived. Jesus had entered the wilderness as the newly commissioned King. He left as the conquering Monarch. Jesus continued to overpower Satan and demons throughout His ministry.

JESUS' KINGDOM MESSAGE:
HIS AUTHORITY OVER SIN

Now after John had been taken into custody, Jesus came into Galilee, preaching the gospel of God, and saying, "The time is fulfilled, and the kingdom of God is at hand; repent and believe in the gospel." (1:14–15)

Mark followed his brief description of Christ's temptation with an equally terse introduction to Jesus' preaching ministry. At least six months had passed since Jesus' baptism. He had been in Judea, ministering there and even cleansing the temple (cf. John 2:13–4:3). Mark bypassed those events, along with Jesus' journey through Samaria (John 4:4–42), to focus on the beginnings of Jesus' public ministry in Galilee. Mark picks up the history **after John had been taken into custody,** an event he will describe in more detail in 6:17. It was after John the Baptist's arrest that Jesus began His public preaching and miracle working in Galilee. Prior to that, John was still baptizing in the Jordan and Jesus was ministering in Judea, so their two ministries overlapped (cf. John 3:24). After John's arrest, Jesus returned to Galilee for extensive ministry there (cf. Matt. 4:12).

Galilee was the northern region of the land of Israel. From a first-century Jewish perspective, it was regarded as the outskirts, located far from the religious center of Jerusalem. The fact that Jesus launched His ministry in full power in Galilee was in itself a rebuke to the apostasy and corruption that existed in Jerusalem at that time.

When **Jesus came into Galilee,** He was **preaching the gospel of God.** Traveling from town to town, from synagogue to synagogue, and in the countryside, Jesus preached the truth of God's good news about Himself and His kingdom of salvation (cf. Luke 4:14–30). The Father's method of reaching the world in the first century was through the **preaching** (or proclamation) of the **gospel,** first by the Lord Jesus. In the modern age, **preaching** is still the means that God has ordained, as faithful spokesmen herald kingdom truth. Contemporary ministers have the same divine message to proclaim, and faithful ministry always articulates that message clearly and exclusively. **The gospel of God** (a common New Testament term—Rom. 1:1; 15:16; 2 Cor. 11:7; 1 Thess. 2:2, 8–9; 1 Peter 4:17) refers to the truth that comes from **God** Himself to the world concerning the salvation from sin and judgment available only through Jesus Christ.

As in 1:1, the term **gospel** carries with it the idea of royal pronouncement: the arrival of a king and his kingdom. Jesus' **gospel** proclamation was no exception. Thus, He was **saying, "The time is fulfilled, and the kingdom of God is at hand; repent and believe in the gospel."** Christ offered His hearers a place in His eternal kingdom of salvation, the sphere of forgiveness and redemption, if they would repent of their sin and believe in Him as Lord and Savior. The clarity and simplicity of Jesus' message stands as an example for all who would seek to preach and teach faithfully today. Preachers are not called to analyze the culture, give politically charged speeches, or design new gimmicks for persuading the audience. Rather, they are called to proclaim the same message that Jesus Himself preached: the good news of eternal salvation that comes from God.

Christ's announcement that **the time is fulfilled** indicated that His coming marked the turning point of salvation history. The word **time** is *kairos*. It does not refer to clock time or calendar time (like the Greek word *chronos* does) but speaks of the fixed point in history for an event to occur. As Paul explained in Galatians 4:4, "When the fullness of the time came, God sent forth His Son" (cf. Eph. 1:10). Jesus' ministry took place according to God's sovereign timetable. This was the hour for which the world had long been waiting; it was the most significant moment in earth's history. The Savior had arrived to pay in full the penalty for sin and thus provide salvation for all the elect—from the beginning of history to the end.

This was God's great epochal moment. The promises of the Old Testament regarding Messiah and His kingdom of salvation were about to be realized. Christ had come not only to conquer Satan but to destroy sin itself, and its consequences for His people. The new King had come in order to initiate His kingdom. The message was unmistakable: **the kingdom of God is at hand.** In essence Jesus was saying, "Because I am the King, wherever I am My kingdom is present."

The **kingdom** that Jesus proclaimed ought to be understood in three dimensions: as a spiritual kingdom, a millennial kingdom, and an eternal kingdom. Though it is invisible and spiritual in the present, it will one day be manifest as a physical, earthly kingdom. In His first coming, the King preached the good news of salvation. Consequently, He established His spiritual kingdom in the hearts of all who believe (Luke 17:21). Christ's kingdom is being advanced even now, as sinners come to saving faith in Him and are transferred out of the domain of darkness, and into the realm ruled by the Son of God (Col. 1:13). To follow Jesus Christ is to seek the expression and honor of His kingdom and His righteousness. Such is the spiritual and invisible sense of the kingdom.

At His second coming, the King will establish His kingdom in a visible and temporal way here on the earth. According to Revelation 20:1–6, that kingdom will last for a thousand years. During that time, all of the millennial promises of the Old Testament will be literally fulfilled. Jesus Christ will reign as the King in Jerusalem, and the entire world will be under His rule. After the millennial kingdom, God will inaugurate the final eternal kingdom by creating a new heaven and a new earth, where the triune God will reign forever and ever (Rev. 22:1–5).

In the present, the kingdom consists of all who embrace Jesus Christ as their Lord and Savior. The King rules over and is resident in the hearts of those who belong to Him. His kingdom advances one soul at a time. It will continue until He returns to establish His earthly reign followed by His eternal reign.

How does a subject of Satan escape that tyrant and enter Christ's kingdom? Jesus' answer is simple and straightforward: **repent and believe in the gospel.** The word **repent** (*metanoeō*) means to turn to the opposite way. Having turned from their sin and unbelief, sinners must **believe in the gospel**—meaning they turn in faith to the Lord Jesus Christ, trusting in Him and His finished work of redemption from sin and victory over death. As Paul explained in Romans 10:9, "If you confess with your mouth Jesus as Lord, and believe in your heart that God raised Him from the dead, you will be saved." That kind of belief is not a nebulous faith but a wholehearted embrace of the person and work of Jesus Christ.

Having conclusively demonstrated His authority over Satan in the wilderness, and anticipating His final victory over Satan at the cross, Jesus proclaimed the message of deliverance from sin for all who would believe in Him. The whole world has been given an invitation to enter the kingdom of God from the King Himself.

JESUS' KINGDOM MEANS:
HIS AUTHORITY OVER SINNERS

As He was going along by the Sea of Galilee, He saw Simon and Andrew, the brother of Simon, casting a net in the sea; for they were fishermen. And Jesus said to them, "Follow Me, and I will make you become fishers of men." Immediately they left their

nets and followed Him. Going on a little farther, He saw James the son of Zebedee, and John his brother, who were also in the boat mending the nets. Immediately He called them; and they left their father Zebedee in the boat with the hired servants, and went away to follow Him. (1:16–20)

Jesus displayed His authority over Satan in the wilderness and declared His authority over sin in the gospel. Here Mark shows that Christ demonstrated and delegated that authority through the people whom He transformed and empowered for use in His kingdom.

One day, as Jesus was **going along** the shore **by the Sea of Galilee, He saw Simon and Andrew, the brother of Simon.** Jesus already knew these men. According to John 1:35–42, Andrew was with John the Baptist when John pointed to Jesus and declared, "Behold, the Lamb of God!" (John 1:36). After spending the day with Jesus, Andrew went and found his brother Simon Peter, who also came to see the Lord (vv. 40–42). Though several months had passed from that introductory meeting, Jesus pursued these brothers to call them to abandon their mundane work and follow Him to share His eternal work.

The Sea of Galilee is really a large, freshwater lake—sitting approximately 690 feet below sea level and measuring thirteen miles long and seven miles wide at its most expansive points. In the Old Testament, it was known as the Sea of Chinnereth (or *Genneseret* in Greek), a form of the Hebrew word *kinnor* that means "harp" or "lyre" (cf. Num. 34:11; Josh. 13:27). The name was fitting because the lake is roughly shaped like a harp. It also became known as the Sea of Tiberias (John 6:1; 21:1), because the city of Tiberias (founded by Herod Antipas c. A.D. 18) was located on its western shore. That was the name preferred by those influenced by loyalty to the Roman emperor (Tiberius) after whom the city was named.

It was there that Jesus **saw Simon and Andrew, casting a net in the sea; for they were fishermen.** Evidently, after John's imprisonment, they resumed their normal lives as fishermen. The **net** used was likely large and circular, up to twenty feet in diameter, with weights positioned around the perimeter. As experienced fishermen, they would throw the net so that it unfolded in the air, landing flat on the water's surface. As the edges began to sink to the bottom, the net would capture whatever fish were swimming underneath. The **fishermen** would then dive into the water, where they would pull the bottom of the net closed, using a rope that also ran through the perimeter. The loaded net was subsequently affixed to the boat so that the fish could be hauled back to shore (cf. John 21:8).

The lake supported a thriving fishing industry. Ancient sources indicate that it was accessed from at least sixteen harbors, with hundreds of fishing boats. Since fish was the predominant meat in the Mediterranean world, the fishing industry was big business. All indications suggest that **Simon and Andrew** ran a successful catching operation—in partnership with **James the son of Zebedee, and John his brother** (Luke 5:10). They were prominent men, not poor day laborers. **Simon** Peter, for example, owned his own home in the city of Capernaum (Luke 4:38), and **John** was well-known to the high priest (John 18:15).

When He found **Simon and Andrew** along the shore, **Jesus said to them, "Follow Me, and I will make you become fishers of men."** Jesus' statement was a command, not a request. Unlike the rabbis, who instructed the people to follow their legalistic traditions, Jesus commanded these Galilean fishermen to follow Him. And He did so with ultimate authority, a power that no scribe or Pharisee possessed (cf. Mark 1:22). The implications of His command were extreme and unmistakable: Abandon everything, including your careers as fishermen, and **follow Me.** It was a unique, nonnegotiable, all-encompassing mandate from the King to His first chosen subjects. The Lord would later echo that same kind of call in spiritual terms to all who come to Him. He said in Mark 8:34: "If anyone wishes to come after Me, he must deny himself, and take up his cross and follow Me." That first call to the disciples was an illustration of the comprehensive call our Lord gives to all who would enter His kingdom—not the abandonment of an earthly career but of all other masters.

Jesus promised that He would **make** them **become fishers of men,** an analogy they would have immediately understood. Instead of casting nets for fish, they would be trained to preach the gospel for the purpose of gathering in sinners. They would be prepared by Jesus Himself to become heralds of the kingdom through the proclamation of

God's gospel.With this command,Jesus established the means by which His kingdom would advance.He uses transformed sinners whom He sovereignly identifies and summons.Such absolute authority behind such a summons belongs only to the messianic King,who possesses the divine right to demand and gain that kind of allegiance. Remarkably, **immediately they left their nets and followed Him.** Though these rugged fishermen were hardly pushovers, there was no resistance or hesitation on their part. They **immediately** dropped everything to follow Jesus. Their response demonstrates both the Lord's authority and the power that moves in those He calls to respond.

The scene is essentially repeated in verses 19–20, where Jesus called and empowered two more disciples to follow Him: **Going on a little farther, He saw James the son of Zebedee, and John his brother, who were also in the boat mending the nets. Immediately He called them; and they left their father Zebedee in the boat with the hired servants, and went away to follow Him.** The sons of Zebedee were anything but milksops. In fact, they would earn the nickname "Sons of Thunder" (Mark 3:17). On one occasion, they angrily suggested calling down fire from heaven to destroy a village that had refused to welcome them (Luke 9:54). Standing farther down the shore, these fiery siblings were busy **mending the nets,** a critical part of repairing the fishing gear for the next trip out. Their **father Zebedee** and his **hired servants** were there too, all working as part of the larger fishing operation. Yet, in an instant, the "Sons of Thunder" were compelled to leave everything and everyone to follow the Lord Jesus Christ.

That kind of amazing obedience would be repeated with the rest of the disciples too—like Levi, who simply walked away from his tax collection booth to follow Jesus (Mark 2:14). Their response may seem shocking from a human perspective. From the divine standpoint, it is not at all surprising. As Jesus explained to His disciples in John 15:16, "You did not choose Me but I chose you, and appointed you that you would go and bear fruit, and that your fruit would remain, so that whatever you ask of the Father in My name He may give to you." Clearly, the scope of Jesus' authority encompassed the disciples whom He called to follow Him. It was through those regenerated and transformed sinners, and their

proclamation of the gospel, that Jesus would advance His kingdom purposes (cf. Matt. 28:18–20).

The Lord's power over sin and Satan is still demonstrated today
—every time an unredeemed heart is given life and set free from Satan's
dominion and sin's power and penalty (cf. Eph. 2:1–4). Having rescued
believers from sin, the King employs them in His service, empowering
them through His Spirit to be instruments for the advance of His kingdom. All of this takes place under the authority of His sovereign prerogative (Eph. 1:18–23). The One who defeated Satan, both in the wilderness
and at the cross; the One who declared victory over sin, through the
proclamation of the gospel; and the One who continually demonstrates
His power in the lives of those whom He saves and empowers—He alone
is the messianic King. All rule, authority, power, and dominion belong to
Him (Eph. 1:21).

For those who know and love the Lord Jesus Christ, there is no
greater joy than seeing His kingdom advanced through the faithful
proclamation of His gospel. The promise He made to Andrew and Peter
on the shores of the Sea of Galilee still applies to all who are willing to
unwaveringly proclaim His message: **Follow Me, and I will make you
become fishers of men.** In a sermon on that subject, the renowned
nineteenth-century preacher Charles Spurgeon encouraged his hearers
with these words:

> When Christ calls us by His grace we ought not only to remember what
> we are, but we ought also to think of what He can make us. . . . It did not
> seem a likely thing that lowly fishermen would develop into apostles;
> that men so handy with the net would be quite as much at home in
> preaching sermons and in instructing converts. One would have said,
> "How can these things be? You cannot make founders of churches out
> of peasants of Galilee." That is exactly what Christ did; and when we are
> brought low in the sight of God by a sense of our own unworthiness,
> we may feel encouraged to follow Jesus because of what He can make
> us. . . . O you who see in yourselves at present nothing that is desirable,
> come you and follow Christ for the sake of what He can make out of
> you. Do you not hear His sweet voice calling to you, and saying, "Follow
> Me, and I will make you fishers of men?"

Later in that same sermon, Spurgeon balanced his words of encouragement with some apt words of warning.

Jesus says,"Follow Me, I will make you fishers of men;" but if you go in your own way, with your own net, you will make nothing of it, and the Lord promises you no help in it. The Lord's directions make Himself our leader and example. It is, "Follow *Me*, follow *Me*. Preach *My* gospel. Preach what I preached. Teach what I taught, and keep to that." With that blessed servility which becomes one whose ambition it is to be a copyist, and never to be an original, copy Christ even in jots and tittles. Do this, and He will make you fishers of men; but if you do not do this, you shall fish in vain. (Charles Spurgeon, *How to Become Fishers of Men*, sermon 1906)

The Authority of the Divine King (Mark 1:21–28)

4

They went into Capernaum; and immediately on the Sabbath He entered the synagogue and began to teach. They were amazed at His teaching; for He was teaching them as one having authority, and not as the scribes. Just then there was a man in their synagogue with an unclean spirit; and he cried out, saying, "What business do we have with each other, Jesus of Nazareth? Have You come to destroy us? I know who You are—the Holy One of God!" And Jesus rebuked him, saying, "Be quiet, and come out of him!" Throwing him into convulsions, the unclean spirit cried out with a loud voice and came out of him. They were all amazed, so that they debated among themselves, saying, "What is this? A new teaching with authority! He commands even the unclean spirits, and they obey Him." Immediately the news about Him spread everywhere into all the surrounding district of Galilee. (1:21–28)

Life's most critical question is, "Who is Jesus Christ?" How a person answers that question has eternal implications. Nothing is more essential, either for this life or the life to come, than knowing the truth about Jesus. Yet few seem seriously interested in rightly understanding who He is and why He came. Tragically, many people blindly assume that Jesus was merely a good teacher, a moral idealist, or a misunderstood social activist whose life ended in tragedy two millennia ago. That is not how Scripture presents Him, nor is it in keeping with who He declared Himself to be.

The gospel of Mark (like the other three) provides a definitive answer to that question in the very first verse. Mark 1:1 declares Jesus to be the Christ—the messianic King—and the Son of God. He is the divinely appointed ruler to whom all the prerogatives of royalty are due. Moreover, He is God incarnate, worthy of all glory, honor, and praise. He is the Lord of lords, possessing all authority both in heaven and on earth (cf. Matt. 28:18). Consequently, the only right response to His sovereign dominion is to submit and worship Him as the eternal King of kings and the glorious Son of God. Any depiction of Jesus that undermines or belittles His true person and position is not only inadequate, it is blasphemous. Though many demean and disparage Him now, all will one day recognize Him for who He truly is. As the apostle Paul told the Philippians, "At the name of Jesus every knee will bow, of those who are in heaven and on earth and under the earth, and that every tongue will confess that Jesus Christ is Lord, to the glory of God the Father" (Phil. 2:10–11).

Mark 1:21–28 is a passage that dramatically illustrates both the sovereign authority of Jesus Christ and the stubborn unwillingness of unbelieving sinners to recognize and submit to that authority. The passage comes on the heels of Mark's introduction (in vv. 1–20), in which he presented five proofs to demonstrate that Jesus is indeed the divine King: Jesus was preceded by a royal forerunner (1:2–8), experienced a divine coronation ceremony (1:9–11), defeated His archenemy the prince of darkness (1:12–13), proclaimed the kingdom message of salvation (1:14–15), and commanded His kingdom citizens to follow Him (1:16–20). Heralded by John, commissioned by the Father, filled with the Spirit, victorious over sin and Satan, and accompanied by His disciples, the Lord Jesus began His public ministry with every necessary credential demonstrated. So, succinctly but convincingly, Mark's fast-moving, condensed, and selective introduction established the messianic character and divine nature of the Lord Jesus. From this point forward, as Mark begins the body of his gospel record, he will slow his pace to focus more intently on specific events from the ministry of the messianic King.

The history begins in verse 21 with the inspired recounting of an incident in which Jesus demonstrated His authority over the demonic realm. Mark has already highlighted Christ's authority over Satan, sin, and sinners in verses 12–20. In this section (vv. 21–28) he continues that theme, specifically focusing on a dramatic showdown one Sabbath day between Jesus and a demon. Once again, the cosmic authority of Jesus is vividly put on display, leaving no doubt about the King's ability to dominate demons and to obliterate the satanic bondage that can hold sinners captive all the way to hell.

The passage itself reveals a striking contrast between the response of people to Jesus' authority and the response of demons. On the one hand, people were amazed at Jesus' power and authority (vv. 22, 27). They reacted with wonder, curiosity, and surprise because He taught as no one they had ever heard before. On the other hand, demons were terrified by Christ. They responded in horror, dread, and panic. Those divergent reactions lie at the heart of understanding the significance of this passage. Both the demons and the people were sinful. Yet, only the demons shrieked in fear. They understood Jesus was their Judge who would cast them into hell. The people certainly did not.

Ironically, in the first half of Mark's gospel, the only beings sure of Jesus' true identity were the demons. The Jewish leaders rejected Him (3:6, 22); the crowds were curious but largely uncommitted (6:5–6; cf. John 2:24); and even His disciples exhibited a lingering hard-heartedness (8:17). But the demons knew for certain. As Mark explains, "Whenever the unclean spirits saw Him, they would fall down before Him and shout, 'You are the Son of God!'" (3:11). Knowing exactly who Jesus was and what He had the power to do, they responded with terror—fearing He might cast them immediately into the abyss (Luke 8:31; cf. Rev. 9:1). As one unclean spirit cried out, "What business do we have with each other, Jesus, Son of the Most High God? I implore You by God, do not torment me!" (5:7). They had known the Son of God since He created them (Col. 1:16). Their ancient minds were full of the particulars about their heavenly rebellion, defeat, and expulsion; they understood the eternal punishment that yet awaits them in the lake of fire (Matt. 25:41). Understandably, the demons were utterly terrified in Jesus' presence. Now that the Son had come to earth to begin the establishment of His rule, the evil angels had every reason to be tormented by terror.

There is no salvation for fallen angels (Heb. 2:16). However, sinners who come to a true understanding of the authority of the Son of God, and are terrified by the threat of hell are invited to flee from wrath and run in holy fear to Christ for the forgiveness and grace of salvation. Yet the vast majority of sinners who hear the good news of heaven still refuse to fear hell and come to Christ for the gift of salvation. Such is the great irony depicted by this passage. The demons recognized who Jesus was, but have no possibility of salvation. The crowds were offered divine forgiveness, but they refused to recognize the One who alone can provide it. Put another way, the demons were terrified and could not be saved; the people were amazed and would not be saved. Consequently, the amazed people (who would not believe) and the terrified demons (who do "believe, and tremble"—James 2:19 KJV) will ultimately end up in the same eternal lake of fire (Rev. 20:10–15).

It is important to emphasize that during Jesus' ministry, the demons did not attack Him. They assaulted the souls of sinful people but never Jesus. In fact, whenever a confrontation occurred, it was Jesus who attacked them. His mere presence sent them into a frenzied panic. Though invisible to the naked eye, they were not invisible to Him. They might be able to hide from people—disguising themselves as angels of light (2 Cor. 11:14) and dwelling comfortably within the confines of apostate religion. But they could not hide from the omniscient gaze of Christ. In His presence, they blew their cover due to the constraining power of their fear.

Throughout His entire ministry, Jesus' dominance over the demons was absolute and uncontested—indicative of the fact that He possessed absolute power over the devil and the entire force of fallen angels in the "domain of darkness" (Col. 1:13). He is able to overwhelm Satan—the one who controls this world system (1 John 5:19), and who has blinded sinners (2 Cor. 4:3–4) and holds them captive (Heb. 2:14–15) —in order to set sinners free (John 8:36). As the apostle John explained, "The Son of God appeared for this purpose, to destroy the works of the devil" (1 John 3:8). The new King needed to demonstrate His power to dethrone Satan and rescue sinners from his grip. To be sure, the demons knew why the Son of God had come. They knew the King of salvation had arrived, and the prince of darkness needed his spiritual forces to do everything in their capacity to oppose Him. From the start of the Lord's ministry, it was apparent that they were no match for His unsurpassed sovereign authority. It was divine power that threw them out of heaven and would one day throw them into hell. In between those two events, during Jesus' earthly ministry, the Lord's invincibility over the satanic realm was vividly put on display in every encounter with a demon.

This passage (1:21–28) relates one of what must have been many such encounters. Here Jesus confronted a traumatized and exposed demon while teaching in the synagogue in Capernaum. In 1:23, Mark explains that the demon **cried out** to Jesus. The verb translated "cried out" (*anakrazō*) means to scream or shout with strong emotion and describes the shrieks of someone experiencing intense agony. The demon's screeching outcry was abrupt, disruptive, and startling. Mark relates the dark angel's panic to three aspects of Jesus' authority: the authority of His word, the authority of His judgment, and the authority of His power.

THE AUTHORITY OF HIS WORD

They went into Capernaum; and immediately on the Sabbath He entered the synagogue and began to teach. They were amazed at His teaching; for He was teaching them as one having authority, and not as the scribes. (1:21–22)

Although the demon's reaction is not recorded until verse 23, these two verses describe the initial reason for his outburst. His violent outcry came in immediate response to the authoritative teaching of Jesus. The words of Christ ignited flames of dread in his consciousness, which erupted loudly as exclamations of terror and anguish.

Mark introduced this episode by noting that **they** (meaning

Jesus and His recently called disciples) **went into Capernaum.** The name **Capernaum** means "village of Nahum." It was likely a reference to the hometown of the Old Testament prophet Nahum. But Nahum also means "compassion," perhaps indicating that the town was also named for its compassionate residents. Located on the northwest edge of the Sea of Galilee, Capernaum was a prosperous fishing town. It was here that Peter, Andrew, James, and John had their fishing operation, and where Matthew worked as a tax collector (Matt. 9:9). Built on a major Roman road, the Via Maris, Capernaum was an important commercial town. According to historians, it had a promenade that stretched nearly half-mile long and sat on top of an eight-foot seawall. From there, piers jutted approximately one hundred feet out into the water, giving fishing boats easy access to the city. It contained a Roman garrison and was located in the tetrarchy of Herod Antipas, on the border of his brother Philip's domain. After being rejected at Nazareth (Matt. 4:13; Luke 4:16–31), Jesus established His headquarters there during His Galilean ministry (cf. Mark 2:1).

Mark continued by explaining that **immediately on the Sabbath He entered the synagogue and began to teach.** That was not unusual, since it had always been Jesus' habit to attend the synagogue every Sabbath (cf. Luke 4:16). The Jewish system of synagogues had initially developed in the sixth century B.C. during the Babylonian exile. Prior to the exile, worship centered in one place, the temple in Jerusalem. When Solomon's temple was destroyed, and the Jews were in captivity for seventy years, the people began to meet together in small group gatherings. Even after the Jews returned to their homeland and rebuilt the temple, they continued to structure the community life of local villages and towns around what had become official synagogues (the Greek word translated synagogue means "gathering" or "assembly"). As a result, the synagogue became the center of Jewish community life—a place of local worship, a meeting hall, a school, and a courtroom. Traditionally, a synagogue could be formed in any place where there were at least ten Jewish men. Consequently, larger cities in the ancient world often contained numerous synagogues.

One of the primary functions fulfilled by the synagogue was the public reading and exposition of Scripture, a practice that went back at least to the time of Nehemiah. A policy known as "freedom of the syna-gogue" allowed any qualified man in the congregation to deliver the ex-position of the Old Testament passage. That privilege was often extended to visiting rabbis, as it was on this occasion to Jesus. The apostle Paul simi-larly used such opportunities to proclaim the gospel in various cities throughout the Roman Empire (cf. Acts 9:20; 13:5; 18:4; 19:8). Because the news about Jesus' miracles had already spread (cf. Luke 4:14), the atten-dees in Capernaum would have been eager to hear Him teach.

Mark does not detail the content of the message Jesus preached to the congregation that Saturday in Capernaum. Instead, he focused on the people's response. **They were amazed at His teaching; for He was teaching them as one having authority, and not as the scribes.** The people were shocked. Never before had they heard a rabbi speak with such power, precision, and gravitas.

The word **authority** (*exousia*) speaks of rule, dominion, jurisdic-tion, full right, power, privilege, and prerogative. Jesus taught with absolute conviction, objectivity, dominion, and clarity. He spoke the truth with the unwavering confidence of the divine King, and the people could only respond in wonder (cf. Matt. 7:28–29). What a contrast Jesus' profoundly piercing words were to the esoteric pontifications of the scribes, who loved to quote the multitudinous views of other rabbis. They often taught in ways that were mystical, muddled, and often focused on minutiae. But Jesus was clearly different. He did not derive His theology from the musings of other people, nor did He offer a variety of possible explanations. His teaching was absolute not arbitrary. It was logical and concrete, not evasive or esoteric. His arguments were reasonable, inescapable, and focused on essential matters.

Scribes were the primary teachers in first-century Jewish society. They traced their heritage back to Ezra who, according to Ezra 7:10 and Nehemiah 8:4–8, read the law and explained it to the people. Most people had only limited access to the Scriptures, copies of which were too expensive for ordinary, working-class people to own. Consequently, they would go to the synagogue to hear the Scriptures read and explained by the scribes. Because they handled the Scriptures, the scribes became so revered that they were given the title "rabbi," meaning "honored one." Over the centuries, from the time of Ezra to the time of

Christ, the teaching of the scribes grew less focused on the text of Scripture and more focused on what previous rabbis had said. By the first century, scribes prided themselves on being familiar with all possible views.
Rather than faithfully explaining the simple meaning of Scripture, they
delighted in complex musings, fanciful allegories, obscure insights, mystical notions, and the teachings of earlier rabbis.

When Jesus began to explain the biblical text perfectly with clarity, conviction, and authority, His listeners were stunned. They had never
heard anything like it. Their astonishment is bound up in the word
amazed (*ekplessō*), which literally means "to be struck out of one's self"
with awe and wonder. To use the vernacular, Jesus blew them out of their
minds. There are a number of New Testament words that can be translated "amazed" or "astonished." This is one of the strongest and most intense. Jesus' message was so riveting and powerful that His audience sat
in stunned silence, hanging on to every word He uttered (cf. Luke 19:48).

The silent awe would be violently interrupted by the screams
coming through the lips of a demon-possessed man. It was the demon
who was panicked by the truth of Jesus' preaching and could not remain
hidden in the man any longer. Mark introduces the demon in verse 23,
noting the immediacy of the evil spirit's reaction to Jesus' preaching.
Unable to restrain himself, the demon erupted in a fit of shrieking rage in
response to the truth the Son of God proclaimed.

It is not surprising to find this evil spirit hanging around the synagogue. The demons had developed a false system of hypocritical religion
that was highly successful in first-century Israel. As is their nature,
demons hide in the middle of false religion, disguising themselves as
angels of light (2 Cor. 11:14) and perpetuating error and deceit (cf. 1 Tim.
4:1). Like their leader Satan, they are liars and murderers who seek people's eternal destruction. In John 8:44–45, Jesus told the Pharisees, "You
are of your father the devil, and you want to do the desires of your father.
He was a murderer from the beginning, and does not stand in the truth
because there is no truth in him. Whenever he speaks a lie, he speaks
from his own nature, for he is a liar and the father of lies. But because I
speak the truth, you do not believe Me." Those verses summarize the
heart of the conflict. Satan and his hosts propagate lies for the purpose of
perpetuating spiritual death. But Jesus is the way, the truth, and the life

(John 14:6). When Jesus preached the truth on that Sabbath day, the demon who heard Him teach was involuntarily exposed. Confronted by the authority of Jesus' words, the fallen angel reacted with a terrified scream.

THE AUTHORITY OF HIS JUDGMENT

Just then there was a man in their synagogue with an unclean spirit; and he cried out, saying, "What business do we have with each other, Jesus of Nazareth? Have You come to destroy us? I know who You are—the Holy One of God!" (1:23–24)

Mark's use of the phrase **just then** (*euthus*) underscores the immediacy of the demon's reaction. It followed directly on the heels of Jesus' preaching. His shrieking outburst provided audible evidence that fallen angels tremble at the power of Christ's word. The content of his exclamation, which is recorded in verses 23–24, indicated that the demon was also terrified by the authority of Christ's judgment.

Demon possession—always present, usually hidden—was dramatically and uniquely exposed during the ministry of Jesus Christ. The rebellious angels were unable to remain concealed in His presence. In the Old Testament, outside of Genesis 6:1–2, there are no recorded instances of demon possession. In the book of Acts, there are only two (Acts 16:16–18; 19:13–16). The Gospels, however, abound with it (Matt. 4:24; 8:28; 9:33; 10:8; 12:22–27; Mark 1:23–27; 5:4–13; 9:25; Luke 4:41; 8:2, 28; 9:39; 13:11). Confronted by the glory of the Son of God Himself, the demons revealed their identities, often in violent and remarkable ways.

On this occasion, the demon-possessed man responded by screaming at the top of his lungs—the demon inside him borrowing the man's vocal chords to express pure terror. In a burst of dread mixed with rage, the demon asked, **"What business do we have with each other, Jesus of Nazareth? Have You come to destroy us? I know who You are—the Holy One of God!"** The use of plural pronouns (**we** and **us**) suggest that this particular demon was asking these questions on behalf of fallen angels everywhere. As those who had joined in Satan's failed coup (cf. Isa. 14:12–17; Ezek. 28:12–19), demons once served in the presence of God. They knew each member of the Trinity intimately and immediately recognized Jesus as God the Son whenever they found themselves in His presence. They knew He was **the Holy One of God,** the messianic King who had come to save the world from the power of Satan (Luke 4:41).

In speaking to Christ, this demonic spirit employed two different names—one of which expressed his antagonism, the other his fear. The first, **Jesus of Nazareth,** carried a tone of scornful disdain. Nazareth was an obscure town, held in low esteem by other Israelites (cf. John 1:46). The Jewish leaders, in particular, used the term as a pejorative, because they mocked the idea that the Messiah would come from such humble, Galilean origins (cf. John 7:41, 52). In referring to Jesus' hometown, the demon joined the scorn of the disbelieving crowds.

At the same time, the evil spirit knew exactly who Jesus was. Consequently, his scorn is mixed with terrified dread. As a wretched fallen angel, his response was one of enmity intermingled with fear. He called Jesus **the Holy One of God** because he was fully aware of Jesus' divine authority. This unclean spirit, a being characterized by ultimate depravity and incurable wickedness, cringed in the presence of perfect virtue and holiness.

The demons knew that "the Son of God appeared for this purpose, to destroy the works of the devil" (1 John 3:8). Fully aware they were irredeemable, and would one day be cast in the lake of fire (Matt. 25:41), they feared the hour of their final destruction had come. Later in Jesus' ministry, other demons asked almost the same question: "What business do we have with each other, Son of God? Have You come here to torment us before the time?" (Matt. 8:29). The demons recognized exactly who Jesus was. They knew He had full authority and power to cast them into eternal punishment on God's appointed judgment day. That is why they repeatedly responded with such panic and dismay (cf. James 2:19).

The impending reality of future judgment explains the demon's response to Jesus on that Sabbath day in Capernaum. As an operative of Satan, he would have undoubtedly preferred to remain undetected—hidden in the shadows of hypocritical religion. Instead, overwhelmed with dread and panic, he could only uncover himself in a dramatic outburst.

THE AUTHORITY OF HIS POWER

And Jesus rebuked him, saying, "Be quiet, and come out of him!" Throwing him into convulsions, the unclean spirit cried out with a loud voice and came out of him. They were all amazed, so that they debated among themselves, saying, "What is this? A new teaching with authority! He commands even the unclean spirits, and they obey Him." Immediately the news about Him spread everywhere into all the surrounding district of Galilee. (1:25–28)

Though the eschatological day of eternal judgment for Satan and his angels has not yet come (cf. Rev. 20:10), this demon was given a foretaste of Christ's absolute authority over him. He was cast out by the same power that will one day cast him into the lake of fire.

Unfazed by the demon's histrionics, **Jesus rebuked him.** As the divine King, He possessed the inherent authority to command this fallen angel. No dialogue, negotiation, or struggle was necessary. Attempted exorcisms involving various formulas and rituals were not uncommon among the Jews of New Testament times, though they produced no real success. But Jesus' success rate was perfect. He never failed to cast out the demons He confronted, nor did He rely on any special formulas or rituals to do so. He simply issued a command and the demons obeyed.

The Lord delegated that power to His apostles and they did the same (Luke 9:1). Apart from Jesus and the apostles, the New Testament never presents exorcism as a practice in which believers ought to engage. In fact, when nonapostles tried to usurp that kind of authority, the results were disastrous. The seven sons of Sceva learned that lesson painfully. When they tried to cast an evil spirit out of a man by the power of "Jesus whom Paul preaches, . . . the evil spirit answered and said to them, 'I recognize Jesus, and I know about Paul, but who are you?' And the man, in whom was the evil spirit, leaped on them and subdued all of them and overpowered them, so that they fled out of that house naked and wounded" (Acts 19:13–16). Rather than engaging in exorcisms, believers today are called to engage in evangelism. Whenever we bring the gospel to nonbelievers and they put their faith in the Lord Jesus

Christ, the Holy Spirit washes them clean, takes up residence, and the demons are evicted.

Jesus' rebuke came in the form of two short imperatives: **"Be quiet, and come out of him!"** The demon had no choice but to obey immediately. The first command silenced the demon; the second drove him out. Throughout Jesus' ministry, He repeatedly forbade the unclean spirits to testify about Him (cf. Mark 1:34). Though their identification of Jesus was accurate, He did not need any publicity from the agents of Satan. As it was, the religious leaders accused Him of casting "out demons only by Beelzebul the ruler of the demons" (Matt. 12:24). Permitting the demons to continue speaking about Him would only have added support to the sneering speculations of the Pharisees. So whenever they affirmed His identity, He shut them up (cf. Acts 16:16–19).

Jesus' second command, **come out of him,** resulted in the demon's violent departure. The unclean spirit preferred to remain to hold that man's soul captive for hell. But he was forced to go, unwillingly but not quietly. As Mark records, **Throwing him into convulsions, the unclean spirit cried out with a loud voice and came out of him.** With one dramatic final protest, causing the man's body to convulse, the demon let out a final scream as he departed.

The scene is reminiscent of another demon Jesus encountered, later in His ministry, the day after His transfiguration. Mark relates that story in Mark 9:25–27:

> When Jesus saw that a crowd was rapidly gathering, He rebuked the unclean spirit, saying to it, "You deaf and mute spirit, I command you, come out of him and do not enter him again." After crying out and throwing him into terrible convulsions, it came out; and the boy became so much like a corpse that most of them said, "He is dead!" But Jesus took him by the hand and raised him; and he got up.

Like the demon described in Mark 1:23, this demon showed his rebellious objection to Christ with a final, violent thrashing of his victim. But it was only a momentary frenzy. Like every other fallen angel, he was no match for the sovereign power of the divine King, and once he left, the boy whom he had tormented was healed. Though the demon-possessed man in the synagogue in Capernaum was similarly thrown into convulsions, the demon did no damage. As Luke explains in the parallel account: "When the demon had thrown him down in the midst of the people, he came out of him without doing him any harm" (Luke 4:35).

Neither Mark nor Luke provide any biographical information about the man who was delivered. But the lack of detail is intentional, because the focus is not on him. It is on the One who liberated him from demonic possession. Appropriately, the attention centers on the Son of God, who again publicly displayed His divine power. By His own authority He commanded the demon to flee. Only the divine King has the power necessary to break the bondage of Satan. He can destroy the devil, dismantle his forces, and deliver captive souls.

Jesus' power was unmistakable, so that those who sat in the synagogue, who had already been amazed by His teaching, **were all amazed** at His ability to deliver this demon-possessed man. They had no category for what they had just witnessed, **so that they debated among themselves, saying, "What is this? A new teaching with authority! He commands even the unclean spirits, and they obey Him."** The crowd began to buzz with excitement over what had transpired. They had been stunned by the authority of His teaching and then equally shocked by the power He exercised over the unclean spirits. The debate was not a formal one but rather the excited chatter of wonder expressed by those who were amazed. Eventually, however, that debate would grow more polarizing. While no one could deny His authority over demons, the religious leaders would begin to question the source of that authority (cf. Matt. 12:24).

In the meantime, word about Jesus began to get out. As Mark explains, **"Immediately the news about Him spread everywhere into all the surrounding district of Galilee."** This was just the beginning. Mark 1:39 reports that "He went into their synagogues throughout all Galilee preaching and casting out the demons." The divine King launched His public ministry by putting on displays of power over evil spirits unprecedented in Israel and the world (cf. Matt. 9:33). He taught like no one else and He possessed and used force that no one else had ever seen. Behind His power was Jesus' authority. The demons recognized Him and were terrified; the crowds witnessed Him and were amazed. The demons believed Him but could not be saved; the crowds refused to believe in Him and, therefore, would not be saved.

A combination of both responses is necessary for salvation. Sinners need to be both terrified and amazed: terrified by such a Judge and astonished by such a Savior. It is not enough simply to be amazed by Jesus Christ. He is not satisfied with mere curiosity, wonder, or astonishment. He wants sinners to fear Him as the Judge and then run to Him as the Savior.

The people who heard Jesus teach and witnessed His authority on that Sabbath day in Capernaum were left with no excuses. Yet, the population of that city ultimately rejected Him as their Lord and Savior (Matt. 11:23; Luke 10:15). Perhaps they considered Jesus a good teacher, a moral idealist, or a misunderstood social activist. None of those conclusions was adequate. They may have been amazed by Him in the moment, but unless they came to embrace Him in saving faith—worshiping Him as the Son of God, trusting in Him as the Savior of the world, and submitting to Him as the Lord over all—their amazement was ultimately worthless. It was no better than the trembling terror of the demons. So it is for all who reject the true person and work of Jesus Christ.

Kingdom Power
(Mark 1:29–39)

5

And immediately after they came out of the synagogue, they came into the house of Simon and Andrew, with James and John. Now Simon's mother-in-law was lying sick with a fever; and immediately they spoke to Jesus about her. And He came to her and raised her up, taking her by the hand, and the fever left her, and she waited on them. When evening came, after the sun had set, they began bringing to Him all who were ill and those who were demon-possessed. And the whole city had gathered at the door. And He healed many who were ill with various diseases, and cast out many demons; and He was not permitting the demons to speak, because they knew who He was. In the early morning, while it was still dark, Jesus got up, left the house, and went away to a secluded place, and was praying there. Simon and his companions searched for Him; they found Him, and said to Him, "Everyone is looking for You." He said to them, "Let us go somewhere else to the towns nearby, so that I may preach there also; for that is what I came for." And He went into their

synagogues throughout all Galilee, preaching and casting out the demons. (1:29–39)

We live in a world devoured by sickness, pain, and death. It was not always this way. As Moses explained in Genesis 1:31, after God made the universe, He "saw all that He had made, and behold, it was very good." The creation was without blemish or defect, a reflection of the flawless One who had spoken it into existence.

When Adam and Eve disobeyed God, everything changed. Sin entered the world and brought with it disease, decay, and death. The whole creation was cursed (Gen. 3:17–19; Rom. 8:20), and Adam and Eve were alienated from God and banished from Eden. Sickness, suffering, and the reality of death serve as painful reminders of the inescapable fact that we reside on a fallen planet.

Even all the advancements of modern science cannot remove the plagues our world suffers. Two thousand years ago, however, conditions were far worse. Medical technology was essentially nonexistent, meaning that people simply languished under the full effects of illness and injury.

Though Jesus Christ came that He might spiritually rescue sinners who were dead in their transgressions and facing the wrath of God (1 Tim. 1:15), He chose to demonstrate that power to save as well as His profound love and compassion by delivering people from their diseases and demons. Jesus' delivering ability also served as a preview of the conditions of His coming earthly kingdom, in which Satan and his demons will be bound (Rev. 20:1–3), the curse will be mitigated, and its effects greatly reduced until it is completely removed in the righteous perfection of the eternal state in heaven (Rev. 21:1–22:5).

The incident recorded in Mark 1:29–34 took place on the same day as the events recorded in verses 21–28, when a demon-possessed man was dramatically delivered in the synagogue. Shortly afterward, Jesus and His disciples traveled to Peter's house, where Jesus demonstrated His authority over the physical effects of sin. Together, the two passages highlight the supernatural nature of Jesus' sovereign power. Whenever He confronted either demons or disease, both fled at His command. That kind of dominion provides undeniable proof of Jesus' deity, corroborating Mark's thesis that Jesus is the messianic King, the Son of God (1:1).

As the Savior of the world, the Messiah had to be able to rescue souls from both sin and Satan. As the resurrection and the life (John 11:25), He had to have power over both the physical and spiritual effects of the curse. As the Redeemer, He had to be able to redeem both the soul that was lost and the body that was decaying (Rom. 8:23). Jesus consistently demonstrated necessary heavenly might by repeatedly casting out demons and healing diseases to exhibit His total dominion over both the spiritual and physical realms devastated by sin. By those miracles He demonstrated that He possessed the power to impart eternal life to souls and bodies, fitting them for resurrected glory in heaven.

In this section (vv. 29–39), Jesus continued to evidence that He was the divine, compassionate Son of God. The passage can be divided into three sections: the proof of His person (vv. 29–34), the power of His action (v. 35), and the priority of His mission (vv. 36–39).

THE PROOF OF HIS PERSON

And immediately after they came out of the synagogue, they came into the house of Simon and Andrew, with James and John. Now Simon's mother-in-law was lying sick with a fever; and immediately they spoke to Jesus about her. And He came to her and raised her up, taking her by the hand, and the fever left her, and she waited on them. When evening came, after the sun had set, they began bringing to Him all who were ill and those who were demon-possessed. And the whole city had gathered at the door. And He healed many who were ill with various diseases, and cast out many demons; and He was not permitting the demons to speak, because they knew who He was. (1:29–34)

A typical **synagogue** service ended around noon. Jesus' first four disciples, whom He called just a short time earlier (cf. Mark 1:16–20), would have attended the synagogue service with Him and, along with the crowds, been amazed by His preaching (v. 22) and astonished by His authority over the demon who confronted Him (v. 27). As the hubbub subsided, and the people were dismissed, the four former fishermen **came with Jesus out of the synagogue,** undoubtedly talking excitedly with one another about the spectacular deliverance they had just witnessed.

Immediately after exiting the synagogue, **they came into the house of Simon and Andrew, with James and John.** All four of these men had been in the fishing business along the Sea of Galilee. These were not unsophisticated simpletons, as sometimes has been imagined, but successful tradesmen who apparently had a fairly large operation headquartered in Capernaum. Fish was a staple meat in ancient times and the Sea of Galilee yielded enough to export its produce throughout that part of the Mediterranean world. These two sets of brothers had abandoned earthly pursuits to follow Jesus and pursue the kingdom of heaven (1:16–20). In the synagogue that morning, they were given a front row seat to observe His kingly authority. That would have been the subject of their conversation as they walked.

Simon, also called Peter (cf. Matt. 16:18; John 1:42), and Andrew were originally from Bethsaida, a town on the north shore of the Sea of Galilee (cf. John 1:44). They had relocated to Capernaum, no doubt for the sake of business. First Corinthians 9:5 indicates that Simon Peter was married and that his wife traveled with him on his later ministry journeys. Church tradition further suggests that Peter and his wife had at least one child, though the New Testament is silent on that point.

At this point, early in the ministry of Jesus, Peter lived in Capernaum with his extended family—including his wife and children, his mother-in-law, his brother Andrew, and Andrew's family. Archaeologists have unearthed the traditional site of Peter's house, only a short walk from the ancient synagogue ruins. One commentator describes it this way:

> Within a stone's throw of Capernaum synagogue lies a structure that can reasonably be identified as the house of Peter. The house is part of a large "insula" complex, in which doors and windows open to an interior court rather than outward to the street. The court, accessed by a gateway from the street, was the center of the lives of the dwellings around it, containing hearths, millstones for grain, hand-presses, and stairways to roofs of dwellings. The dwellings were constructed of heavy walls of black basalt over which a flat roof of wood and thatch

was placed. (James R. Edwards, *The Gospel according to Mark,* Pillar New Testament Commentary [Grand Rapids: Eerdmans, 2002], 59)

Upon entering Peter's residence, Jesus and His disciples would have found themselves in a large plaza courtyard surrounded by multiple dwellings. Clearly, Peter was more than just an unskilled laborer with a fishing rod. Significantly, archaeological investigations have discovered sacred devotional markings written on the stone and scratched into the plaster. The engravings indicate that Peter's house was an early gathering place for Christians, and most likely a church, dating back to the late-first or early-second century.

As disciples of Jesus, and as residents of Capernaum who lived near the synagogue, it would have been natural for Peter and Andrew to invite Jesus, along with James and John, to their home for the noontime meal. Peter also had a secondary motivation. As Mark explains, **"Now Simon's mother-in-law was lying sick with a fever; and immediately they spoke to Jesus about her."** Luke the physician provides the added detail that it was a high fever (Luke 4:38), suggesting that her condition was related to a severe infection. Her daughter and son-in-law were clearly concerned, so much so that, as soon as Jesus entered the house, the family "asked Him to help her" (Luke 4:38). Having just seen His power on display in the synagogue, and familiar with other miracles He had performed (cf. Luke 4:23), they appealed to Him to heal her.

The fever was high enough that she was in bed, too weak to get up and greet the guests who had come to her house. The demands of everyday life in the first century did not afford most people the luxury of staying in bed just because they did not feel well. That would have been especially true when guests had been invited. It is likely that she was extremely ill. Responding with compassion, Jesus **came to her** while she was lying down **and raised her up.** The severity of her sickness was irrelevant to Jesus, who rebuked the fever (Luke 4:39), and **taking her by the hand, the fever left her.** Earlier that morning, in the synagogue, He had rebuked the unclean spirit, and the demon departed. Whether in the spiritual realm or the physical, whenever Jesus issued a rebuke, the effects were immediate.

At the end of verse 31, Mark notes that after Peter's mother-in-law got up, **she waited on them.** She was completely healed. Her symptoms were gone. There was no recovery period. One moment, she had been too weak to do anything but lie down. The next, she was on her feet, full of energy, and ready to help prepare the Sabbath dinner. It was if she had never even been ill.

The healing miracles of Jesus, like this one, stand in stark contrast to the alleged healings of contemporary "faith healers" and charismatic televangelists. The world has always been plagued by false healers who prey on the physical suffering of desperate people in order to extort money from them. In spite of their brash claims, modern healers are nothing more than spiritual con artists. They may have the ability to manipulate crowds of susceptible people, but they do not possess the power to genuinely heal anyone.

The healings of Jesus could not be more different than the contemporary counterfeits. Unlike faith healers, who supposedly cure invisible ailments, Jesus healed people with undeniable organic diseases and physical disabilities, such as deafness, blindness, leprosy, and paralysis. On one occasion, Jesus reattached a missing ear, such that it was perfectly restored (Luke 22:50–51). He did the most extreme form of healing whenever He raised someone from the dead (Mark 5:42; Luke 7:14–15; John 11:43–44).

Jesus also healed instantly and completely. Those who experienced His healing power needed no time for recovery or recuperation. Peter's mother-in-law is a prime example of the immediacy of Jesus' healings. She did not need to wait to feel better. The Lord did not instruct her to take it easy for a few weeks in order for her body to recover. She went from languishing in bed to functioning in full strength.

Modern faith healers, to control the illusion, carefully prescreen the people they allow onstage. But Jesus healed indiscriminately. He healed everyone who came to Him, no matter the nature of their illness or infirmity. In the parallel passage of Luke 4:40, Luke explains that, "While the sun was setting, all those who had any who were sick with various diseases brought them to Him; and laying His hands on each one of them, He was healing them." As Luke points out, Jesus laid His hands on "each one of them," healing all who came. The healings of Jesus did not require the faith of the participant, since most of the people He healed were unbelievers. Though some of them came to faith as a result of the healing, like one of the ten lepers (Luke 17:17–19), most did not, like the other nine.

Significantly, Jesus performed His healing miracles in full public view, during the normal course of His daily ministry as He moved through crowds of people from place to place. He did not require a highly controlled environment in order to manipulate the crowds and the circumstances. Rather, He was able to heal anyone at any time in any place of any ailment. There were no categories of illness beyond His power. Not surprisingly, whenever He performed a miracle, word about Him quickly spread throughout the city or region where He was ministering. The healing of Peter's mother-in-law was no exception. It triggered a citywide response.

Mark describes what happened next: **When evening came, after the sun had set, they began bringing to Him all who were ill and those who were demon-possessed**. Having heard what happened, the people immediately determined to come and see Jesus. They had to wait until **after the sun had set** because Jewish law prohibited them from carrying anything or anyone on the Sabbath. According to the Jewish reckoning of time, the day ended at sunset (around 6:00 p.m.), as the sky began to darken and the first stars became visible. Once the sun went down, the residents of Capernaum rushed to transport their sick friends and relatives to Jesus. In fact, the crowd outside of Peter's house was so large that as Mark explains, **the whole city had gathered at the door.**

In spite of the steady stream of needy people (the imperfect tense of the verb translated **began bringing** indicates that they kept coming and coming), Jesus with infinite compassion laid His hands on each one of them and healed them (Luke 4:40). Mark's statement, that **He healed many,** does not imply that there were some who were not healed. Rather, it speaks to the fact that He healed a great number of people on that occasion. Many sick and suffering people came to see Him, and of the many who came all were healed (cf. Matt. 8:16).

Some **were ill with various diseases** and Jesus immediately made them completely whole. Others were demon-possessed, so Jesus **cast out many demons, and He was not permitting the demons to**

speak, because they knew who He was. Jesus prohibited the demons from speaking because, apparently, He did not want affirmation of His identity from the agents of Satan. Their testimony to Him would only have confused the issue. This is similar to the experience of Paul in Philippi, when a demon-possessed slave girl gave affirming testimony to the apostle.

> It happened that as we were going to the place of prayer, a slave-girl having a spirit of divination met us, who was bringing her masters much profit by fortune-telling. Following after Paul and us, she kept crying out, saying, "These men are bond-servants of the Most High God, who are proclaiming to you the way of salvation." She continued doing this for many days. But Paul was greatly annoyed, and turned and said to the spirit, "I command you in the name of Jesus Christ to come out of her!" And it came out at that very moment. (Acts 16:16–18)

Paul cast the demon out to stop the deception. Demons prefer to be disguised as angels of light (cf. 2 Cor. 11:14). On this occasion in Capernaum, Jesus knew their intent to affirm His identity and silenced them. Neither the devil himself nor his demons can as much as speak a word without the permission of the sovereign Lord.

Presumably hundreds of people were healed on this occasion. Yet, this was only one night in the life of our Lord. Jesus would continue to display this type of divine power throughout His three-year ministry. In fact, there are some ninety gospel texts that feature the healings of Christ. During Jesus' ministry, there was an unparalleled healing explosion that virtually banished disease from Israel. Nothing like it has ever occurred, in all the centuries before Jesus' earthly ministry or since.

Modern faith healers may claim that the kind of healings Jesus performed have always occurred throughout history and are still happening today. Nothing could be further from the truth. Jesus' miracles were unique and undeniable, and the people who witnessed them responded in utter shock. As the crowds stated in Mark 2:12 after Jesus healed a paralyzed man, "We have never seen anything like this." A similar response is recorded in Matthew 9:33, after Jesus delivered a mute man who was demon-possessed: "Nothing like this has ever been seen in Israel." Though Jesus delegated His miraculous power to the apostles in order to authenticate their ministries (Mark 6:7–13; Acts 3:1–10; 2 Cor.

12:12; Heb. 2:3–4), supernatural gifts of healing and miracle working passed away when the apostolic age ended.

Jesus performed miracles, not to provide free health care but to affirm the true gospel and to validate His claim to be the messianic King, the Son of God, and the Savior of the world (cf. John 10:38). His miracles leave no reasonable doubt about His authority over demons and disease, over both the spiritual and physical creation. They showcased His power to conquer sin and Satan, and confirmed His ability both to rescue souls from sin, death, and hell and to raise bodies from the grave for eternal life.

In Matthew's parallel account, he concluded these events by making a reference to Isaiah 53:4. Matthew writes, "This was to fulfill what was spoken through Isaiah the prophet: 'He Himself took our infirmities and carried away our diseases'" (8:17). Jesus fulfilled this passage in at least three ways. First, He sympathized with the pain and sickness of those whom He healed, since He knew perfectly the agony of their hearts (John 2:25; Heb. 4:15). The gospel writers repeatedly tell of Jesus' compassion for those who experienced His healing touch (Matt. 9:36; 15:32; Mark 1:41; Luke 10:33). He bore the weight of human suffering by commiserating with those who experienced it. Second, He grieved over the destructive power that causes physical suffering—sin itself. When Jesus wept at Lazarus's tomb, it was not because His friend had died, since He knew Lazarus would soon be raised to life. Rather, it was due to the reality of sin, that brings suffering and death to every person (Rom. 5:12). He could not witness the pain of sickness and death without simultaneously being saddened by the effects of the curse. Third, and most importantly, Jesus took our infirmities and carried away our diseases by conquering sin so completely that, ultimately, all sickness and suffering will be eliminated. The King provided a foreshadowing of the glorious nature of His eternal kingdom, from which all sorrow and disease will be banished forever.

In order to redeem men and women from the devastating effects of sin, Jesus Himself would have to suffer and die. Sickness, sorrow, and death could not be permanently removed until sin itself was defeated. Through His death, Jesus paid the penalty for sin, and through His resurrection, He conquered death. Thus, by dying and rising again, the Lord Jesus defeated both sin and death for all who would put their faith in Him.

Christ's work of redemption will ultimately be fulfilled for believers in the future, when they receive their resurrection bodies (cf. Rom. 8:22–25; 13:11). On that glorious day, all who have trusted in Christ will be given physical bodies that are forever free from sin, disease, and the threat of death. Though that hope is yet future for those on this side of the grave, Jesus proved that He is able to fulfill that promise by what He did throughout His ministry.

THE POWER OF HIS ACTION

In the early morning, while it was still dark, Jesus got up, left the house, and went away to a secluded place, and was praying there. (1:35)

Given the massive crowds that had gathered in front of Peter's house just after sunset, Jesus' ministry to the sick and infirm must have lasted well into the night. It was likely long past midnight before the last of the people had left. After such an exhausting day of ministry, Jesus needed more refreshment than mere sleep could provide.

So **in the early morning, while it was still dark, Jesus got up, left the house, and went away to a secluded place, and was praying there.** The proof of His person had been demonstrated in His miracles, but the power behind His action was prayer. He was subject to the will of the Father and operating in the power of the Spirit. Consequently, a time of private communion with His Father was critical. Before the sun even came up, **Jesus got up,** which suggests that He had been sleeping—even if it had only been for a few short hours—and He **went away to a secluded place** in order to enjoy fellowship with His Father. The word translated **secluded place** (*erēmos*) is the same word translated "wilderness" earlier in Mark 1 (vv. 3, 4, 12, 13).

The Gospels record several occasions when Jesus went to an isolated place in order to pray (cf. Matt. 14:23; Mark 1:35; Luke 4:42; John 6:15). Of course, those were not the only times that He prayed. His entire ministry was marked by continual communication with His Father. Jesus prayed before His baptism (Luke 3:21), before calling the Twelve (Luke

6:12–13), before feeding the multitude (John 6:11), at His transfiguration (Luke 9:28–29), before He raised Lazarus (John 11:41–42), in the upper room (Matt. 26:26–27), in Gethsemane (Matt. 26:36–46), and even while hanging on the cross (Matt. 27:46). The perfect unity that existed between Jesus and the Father is highlighted in John 17:1–26, where an extended prayer of Christ is recorded. He always prayed that all those things that were in the will of God would be accomplished (cf. Matt. 26:39, 42), and He taught His disciples to do the same (Matt. 6:10).

Jesus' prayer life was more than just a model for His disciples to follow. It was an essential part of His obedience and submission. In the incarnation, the Son of God set aside the independent use of His divine attributes (cf. Phil. 2:6–7). He humbled Himself in becoming human, relying fully on the plan of the Father and the power of the Spirit. That is why He repeatedly explained that He only did what the Father told Him to do, and that even His miracles were performed through the power of the Holy Spirit. At every point, He was fully dependent on the Father and the Spirit. He relied on them completely for the means to fulfill His mission. It was because He was always fully submissive and totally dependent that He prayed.

The Priority of His Mission

Simon and his companions searched for Him; they found Him, and said to Him, "Everyone is looking for You." He said to them, "Let us go somewhere else to the towns nearby, so that I may preach there also; for that is what I came for." And He went into their synagogues throughout all Galilee, preaching and casting out the demons. (1:36–39)

Simon Peter woke up the next morning to realize that Jesus was gone. Apparently, large crowds had again assembled near Peter's house, in the hope that Jesus would continue His healing ministry from the previous day. When they realized He wasn't there, the people began looking for Him (cf. Luke 4:42). Peter **and his companions** (likely including Andrew, James, and John) joined the hunt and **searched for Him.**

When the search party eventually **found Him,** Peter **said to Him, "Everyone is looking for You."** The entire population of Capernaum joined the hunt to locate Jesus (Luke 4:42). But, like the crowds who hoped for a free breakfast the morning after Jesus fed the thousands (cf. John 6:24–26), and so many others (cf. John 2:24–25), these crowds had nothing more than a superficial self-interest in Jesus.

Jesus had come to preach the good news of His coming kingdom (cf. Mark 1:14–15). His ultimate purpose was not to deliver people from temporal ailments but to save them from sin and eternal judgment. Meeting people's physical needs was a demonstration of divine compassion and power, but He came to redeem sinners. With that in view, it was time to go and preach the gospel in the neighboring towns and regions. Jesus answered Peter and the other disciples in a way that probably surprised them. Instead of capitalizing on His newfound popularity in Capernaum, Jesus decided to leave. **He said to them, "Let us go somewhere else to the towns nearby, so that I may preach there also; for that is what I came for."** Though He compassionately healed the sick and fed the hungry, Jesus defined His mission in these words, "I have not come to call the righteous but sinners to repentance" (Luke 5:32). On another occasion, He similarly told His listeners, "The Son of Man came to seek and to save the lost" (Luke 19:10 ESV). The Lord sought out lost sinners and called them to repentance through the preaching of the gospel. As Mark earlier explained, "Jesus came into Galilee, preaching the gospel of God, and saying, 'The time is fulfilled, and the kingdom of God is at hand; repent and believe in the gospel'" (1:14–15). Jesus' miracles validated His gospel message, but miracles themselves could not save anyone. Salvation came only when people responded in repentant faith to gospel preaching.

In keeping with that priority, Jesus chose not to go back to Capernaum that day. Rather, **He went into their synagogues throughout all Galilee, preaching and casting out the demons** (v. 39). In that single verse, Mark summarizes weeks if not months of time as Jesus continued doing exactly what He had done in Capernaum—preaching the good news and overpowering the demons. In this way, Jesus both validated His identity as the messianic King, while also proclaiming that salvation can be found only through faith in His name (cf. Acts 4:12). When He taught throughout the synagogues of Galilee, His emphasis was on gospel proclamation. The apostle Paul would later articulate the importance of such preaching in Romans 10:13–15:

> For "Whoever will call on the name of the Lord will be saved." How then will they call on Him in whom they have not believed? How will they believe in Him whom they have not heard? And how will they hear without a preacher? How will they preach unless they are sent? Just as it is written, "How beautiful are the feet of those who bring good news of good things!"

In this section (1:29–39), Mark succinctly pulls together three core elements of Jesus' earthly ministry. The proof of His divine kingship was in His miracles. The power that sustained His ministry came from His prayer life, as He submitted to the Father and depended on the Spirit. The priority of His ministry was to preach the gospel to the lost, so that through Him they might have everlasting life.

The Lord and the Leper (Mark 1:40–45)

6

And a leper came to Jesus, beseeching Him and falling on his knees before Him, and saying, "If You are willing, You can make me clean." Moved with compassion, Jesus stretched out His hand and touched him, and said to him, "I am willing; be cleansed." Immediately the leprosy left him and he was cleansed. And He sternly warned him and immediately sent him away, and He said to him, "See that you say nothing to anyone; but go, show yourself to the priest and offer for your cleansing what Moses commanded, as a testimony to them." But he went out and began to proclaim it freely and to spread the news around, to such an extent that Jesus could no longer publicly enter a city, but stayed out in unpopulated areas; and they were coming to Him from everywhere. (1:40–45)

The Gospels do not come close to recording every healing miracle that Jesus performed. John suggests that such a full record would be impossible. As he explained at the end of his gospel, "There are also many other things which Jesus did, which if they were written in detail, I suppose that even the world itself would not contain the books that would be written" (John 21:25; cf. 20:30). The extent of Christ's healing ministry is perhaps best captured in the words of Luke 6:19, "And *all the people* were trying to touch Him, for power was coming from Him and healing *them all*" (emphasis added). On just that one day, Jesus healed all who came to Him, meaning that His healing miracles likely numbered in the hundreds or even thousands. The gospel writers provide only a sampling of the supernatural signs He performed.

As noted in the previous chapters of this volume, the purpose of Jesus' miracles was to validate the fact that He truly is who He claimed to be: the messianic King, the Son of God, and the Savior of the world. Each miracle—from walking on water to casting out demons to healing the sick—demonstrated His supernatural authority, whether over nature, Satan, disease, or sin and death. His miracles authenticated the truthfulness of His claim and message. The priority in His ministry was not performing miracles but preaching the gospel (Mark 1:38). He came to call sinners to repentance and saving faith (1:15).

As Jesus traveled from place to place preaching the gospel of the kingdom, He validated that preaching by countless divine power displays. The scope of His miracle-working ministry was so extensive that He essentially banished illness and demon possession from the land of Israel during the three-and-a-half years of His public ministry (see Matt. 4:23–24; 8:16–17; 9:35; 14:14; 15:30; 19:2; 21:14). It was a massive unleashing of divine power with no parallel in history. It made the Jewish leaders take notice.

Significantly, though those leaders never denied any of His miracles, they did attempt to shift the source of His power from God to the devil. Rather than acknowledging that He was operating through the power of the Holy Spirit, they openly accused Him of being empowered by Satan (Matt. 12:24). That was not only a ridiculous accusation given His perfect, sinless character and behavior but an irrational one since He was continually casting out Satan's demons. He exposed their unreasonable blindness by the single axiom in Matthew 12:25–26: "Any kingdom divided against itself is laid waste; and any city or house divided against itself will not stand. If Satan casts out Satan, he is divided against himself; how then will his kingdom stand?" There was no valid excuse for refusing to believe His message (cf. John 10:38; 14:31). The rejection of the Pharisees and Sadducees was not due to a lack of evidence but only to their own sinful hard-heartedness. With every miracle they rejected, their hearts became more calloused and they were further indicted. In the end, they refused to believe in spite of the overwhelming proof of His resurrection.

Given the extent of Jesus' healing ministry, it is likely that He healed many lepers (cf. Matt. 11:5; Luke 7:22). Yet, the New Testament Gospels detail only two specific occasions in which lepers were miraculously restored by Jesus. This passage recounts one of those (Mark 1:40–45; cf. Matt. 8:1–4; Luke 5:12–16). The other involved ten leprous men, all of whom were healed, but only one of whom returned to give thanks (Luke 17:12–19). The Gospels also mention a man named Simon the leper (Matt. 26:6; Mark 14:3); he may have been healed by Jesus, though the Gospels do not explicitly make that connection. Still, Mark 1:40–45 should be seen as representative of other occasions on which Jesus encountered lepers and cured them of their debilitating and alienating disease.

But what makes this account so significant that three gospel writers would choose to include it in their records of Jesus' life and ministry? Part of the answer to that question is found in the effect this healing had on Jesus' public ministry. His popularity skyrocketed as a result of this particular miracle, so that He "could no longer publicly enter a city, but stayed out in unpopulated areas" (Mark 1:45; cf. Luke 5:15). But there is another reason this account is so important: it serves as a powerful analogy to the truth of salvation, illustrating the spiritual restoration sinners experience when they respond in faith to the gospel. On the one hand, the leper was an outcast who was forced to stay in isolated places. But he ventured into the city, met Jesus, and was miraculously healed. On the other hand Jesus, who was initially in the city, after healing the leper, relocated to the isolated places. In order to heal this man of his leprosy, the Lord had to trade places with him. The Savior was willing to become an outsider so that an untouchable leper, the ultimate outsider, could be rescued and restored. Therein is pictured the reality of the gospel—Jesus traded places with sinners in order to deliver them from sin. On the cross, outside the city, Jesus was treated as an outcast so that those who truly were outcasts might be reconciled to God and accepted as citizens of His heavenly city.

The passage divides easily into three major features: the leper's predicament (v. 40), the Lord's provision (vv. 41–44), and the Lord's predicament (v. 45).

THE LEPER'S PREDICAMENT

And a leper came to Jesus, beseeching Him and falling on his knees before Him, and saying, "If You are willing, You can make me clean." (1:40)

Mark gives no details about the man who **came to Jesus,** except to explain that he was **a leper.** Luke adds that he was "covered with leprosy" (Luke 5:12). As such, his condition would have been obvious to anyone who saw him, rendering him a pariah in ancient Israel. The word "leprosy" is derived from the Greek word *lepros* ("scale") and refers to the scaly appearance of a leper's skin.

In the ancient Near East, any number of skin disorders could have given the skin a scaly appearance (from chronic inflammations like eczema to fungal scalp infections). The Hebrew word *tzaraath* (usually translated as "leprosy" in the Old Testament) is broad enough to encompass various types of skin maladies, some more serious than others. But the most serious type of leprosy in Bible times likely consisted of what is known today as Hansen's disease, a devastating bacterial infection that disfigured a person's appearance and debilitated his nervous system, often leading to death.

Medical historians believe Hansen's disease may have originated in Egypt, since the bacteria that causes it has been discovered in at least one Egyptian mummy. One of the most feared diseases in the ancient world, it was a communicable infection that could be spread both through the air and through physical touch. Even today, there is no cure for the disease, though it can be controlled with medication. Symptoms included spongy, tumorlike swellings that appeared on the face and body. As the bacteria became systemic, it began to affect internal organs while also causing bones to start deteriorating. It also weakened the victim's immune system, making lepers susceptible to other diseases, like tuberculosis.

The Lord gave specific instructions and strict regulations regarding leprosy in order to protect His chosen people (cf. Lev. 13). Anyone suspected of having the disease had to be examined by a priest. If the condition seemed like more than a superficial skin problem, the person was quarantined for seven days. If the symptoms worsened, another week of isolation was required. After fourteen days, the priest would pronounce the person to be either clean or unclean—depending on whether or not the rash had continued to spread. In some cases the symptoms were so obvious that a waiting time was not required, and the person would be declared unclean. Leviticus 13:12–17 also describes a less serious form of leprosy that caused the entire skin to turn white. In such cases, the person was declared clean after he or she was no longer infectious. This lesser form of leprosy likely consisted of psoriasis, eczema, vitiligo, tuberculoid leprosy, or possibly a condition known now as leukodermia. But when a person was diagnosed with the serious form of leprosy (i.e., Hansen's disease), the ramifications were immediate and severe.

According to Leviticus 13:45–46, lepers had to isolate themselves from society:

> As for the leper who has the infection, his clothes shall be torn, and the hair of his head shall be uncovered, and he shall cover his mustache and cry, "Unclean! Unclean!" He shall remain unclean all the days during which he has the infection; he is unclean. He shall live alone; his dwelling shall be outside the camp.

In order to avoid infecting others, lepers were quarantined, legally forbidden to live in any Israelite municipality (cf. Num. 5:2). According to the Talmud, the closest a leper could come to someone without the disease was six feet. On windy days, the distance was extended to 150 feet. The mandatory exile made the disease particularly grievous for those who contracted leprosy because it compounded the physical suffering with social isolation from all but other lepers.

According to medical experts who have studied modern cases

of Hansen's disease, leprosy usually begins with pain and is followed by numbness as the disease progressively attacks the nervous system. The skin in those areas loses its color, becoming scaly and thick, and eventually turns into sores. The effects are especially noticeable on the face, where eyebrows and lashes fall out while the skin swells and bunches up, especially around the eyes and ears. The disease also causes those it infects to emit a foul odor, making leprosy repulsive both to the sight and to the smell (cf. William Hendriksen, *The Exposition of the Gospel according to Matthew*, New Testament Commentary [Grand Rapids: Baker, 1973], 388). It is little wonder that it was one of the most dreaded diseases of the ancient world.

Since leprosy numbs its victims, making them incapable of feeling pain, they unintentionally destroy their own tissue because they are unable to feel the damage they are doing. As one author explains:

> Hansen's disease's numbing quality is precisely the reason such fabled destruction and decay of tissue occurs. For thousands of years people thought HD caused the ulcers on hands and feet and face which eventually led to rotting flesh and loss of limbs.... [Through modern medical] research, it has been established that in 99 percent of the cases, HD only numbs the extremities. The destruction follows solely because the warning system of pain is gone.
>
> How does the decay happen? In villages of Africa and Asia, a person with HD has been known to reach directly into a charcoal fire to retrieve a dropped potato. Nothing in his body told him not to. Patients at Brand's hospital in India would work all day gripping a shovel with a protruding nail, or extinguish a burning wick with their bare hands, or walk on splintered glass.... The daily routines of life ground away at the HD patient's hands and feet, but no warning system alerted him. If an ankle turned, tearing tendon and muscle, he would adjust and walk crooked. If a rat chewed off a finger in the night, he would not discover it missing until the next morning. (Philip Yancey, *Where Are You God When It Hurts?* [Grand Rapids: Zondervan, 1977], 32–34)

Not only were lepers physically disfigured and socially despised, they were religiously defiled. They could not go to the temple to worship or offer sacrifices. They were not even allowed to enter Jerusalem or any other walled city (cf. 2 Kings 7:3). Cut off from everyone and everything, they lived without family, friends, occupations, or hope. Their pitiful plight was permanent, as there were no cures in the ancient world.

In light of the stigmas attached to leprosy, the fact that this **leper came to Jesus** in a public setting would have been shocking to all who were there. Driven by his desperation and violating all the necessary standards of exclusion, he made his way to the Great Physician, **beseeching Him and falling on his knees before Him.** His actions may have been socially unacceptable, but his attitude toward Jesus was both respectful and reverential (cf. Matt. 8:2). Luke 5:12 notes that "he fell on his face." He flattened himself in humble adoration before Jesus. Recognizing his own unworthiness, the leper called Jesus "Lord" (Luke 5:12), and entrusted himself to the Savior's sovereign prerogative and well-known power, **saying, "If You are willing, You can make me clean."**

The leper saw himself not only as being despised by men but also cursed by God (cf. 2 Chron. 26:17–21). Because the common theology said physical sickness was a consequence for sin, this leper surely considered himself to be a sinner. And so, in desperation, he came to Jesus to beg for deliverance. He knew he could not presume on Jesus' mercy—hence the preface, **"If You are willing."** Yet, his request also exuded bold faith based on what he knew Jesus had done. He had no doubt about Jesus' power, so he confidently affirmed, **"You can make me clean."**

One can only imagine the people's reaction as they watched the dramatic scene unfold. Horror mixed with indignation must have swept through the crowd of onlookers. Some probably shrank back in startled fear, covering their mouths as they quickly retreated. Perhaps others glanced around for stones and sticks to drive away the unwanted outcast. Others surely stood watching in stunned silence, wondering how Jesus Himself would respond.

THE LORD'S PROVISION

Moved with compassion, Jesus stretched out His hand and touched him, and said to him, "I am willing; be cleansed." Immediately the leprosy left him and he was cleansed. And He sternly warned him and immediately sent him away, and He said to him, "See that you say nothing to anyone; but go, show yourself to the

priest and offer for your cleansing what Moses commanded, as a testimony to them." (1:41–44)

From the perspective of first-century Judaism, Jesus had every right to be outraged by the leper's behavior. The man had disregarded public health, social norms, and even the stipulations of the Mosaic law. But the Lord did not grow angry. Instead, He was **moved with compassion.** He sympathized with the man's plight, felt the agony of his isolation and distress, and grieved at the effects of sin in this world (cf. John 11:34). Motivated by genuine compassion, **Jesus stretched out His hand and touched him.** Ever since this man had been diagnosed with leprosy, no one had touched him. Yet here, in a moment of total vulnerability, as he lay in the dust begging for deliverance, the Son of God Himself reached out and healed him with a touch.

In Leviticus 5:3, the Mosaic law included a regulation forbidding the Jews from defiling themselves by touching anything or anybody that was unclean, including a leper. But Jesus could not be defiled by anything. Certainly He could have healed him with a simple word. The Lord wanted to make a point—one that would have left a lasting impression. The infinite compassion of Christ was dramatically illustrated in that profound act of kindness. His love was such that He was willing to touch those whom no one else would even come near. He touched this untouchable man, **and said to him, "I am willing; be cleansed."**

The healing was instantaneous. **Immediately the leprosy left him and he was cleansed.** There was no period of recovery or rehabilitation. He who had come disfigured, defiled, and despicable was instantly transformed into a man in full health, completely cured, and ready to be restored to society. His sores were gone. His limbs were made whole. His skin looked like new. His face was smooth and unscarred. Even in an age of modern medical marvels, nothing can compare to this kind of miraculous healing. Though medical advancements have made it possible to control the symptoms of leprosy, they cannot cure the disease or reverse its effects. Jesus could and He did so instantly.

The former leper was not only fully relieved of the disease, he was physically fit. Considering the fact that leprosy had racked his entire body, considerable damage must have been done, not only to his external appearance, but also internally. When Jesus healed him, however, the man was made completely well. That his recovery was immediate is evident because Jesus instructed him to go to Jerusalem (roughly a one hundred-mile walk) in order to be pronounced clean by the priest.

Jesus followed His healing work with specific instruction. **He sternly warned him and immediately sent him away, and He said to him, "See that you say nothing to anyone; but go, show yourself to the priest and offer for your cleansing what Moses commanded, as a testimony to them."** The test of true faith is always obedience, so as soon as Jesus healed this man, He gave him these two specific stipulations to follow. First, Jesus **sternly warned him** with these words, **"See that you say nothing to anyone."** This was not a suggestion, it was a command. Jesus probably issued warnings like this (cf. Mark 5:43; 7:36; 8:26) in order to avoid adding more fuel to the fire of the messianic hysteria that had already been sparked by His healing miracles (cf. John 6:14–15).

Second, Jesus **immediately sent him away,** telling him to **"Go, show yourself to the priest and offer for your cleansing what Moses commanded, as a testimony to them."** Before resuming his place in society, this man needed to fulfill the requirements of the Mosaic law regarding contagious skin diseases as outlined in Leviticus 14. The prescription required taking two birds and killing one of them in an earthenware vessel over running water. The other bird, along with cedar wood, a scarlet string, and hyssop, was then dipped in the blood of the bird that had been slain. The former leper was sprinkled seven times and pronounced clean by the priest, and the live bird was set free in an open field. The person was subsequently required to wash his clothes, shave off all his hair (including eyebrows), and bathe himself in water. After remaining outside of his tent for seven days, he would bring appropriate offerings to the priest on the eighth day. Then, upon offering the needed sacrifices, he would be anointed with oil by the priest, signifying he was clean.

Jesus' final statement, that this would be **a testimony to them,** was primarily directed at the priests serving in the temple. Any priests involved in pronouncing this former leper clean would have been confronted with the reality of Christ's undeniable healing power. While they may have seen some skin diseases remedy themselves, and so have been familiar with such a required ritual, this demonstration of Jesus' miraculous healing power would be shocking to the priests. Thus, this healing in Galilee would serve as a powerful testimony in Jerusalem. Jesus' words also served as a testimony to any onlookers that He did not disregard Old Testament requirements. While He detested the hypocrisy of Pharisaical tradition-laden religion, Jesus always upheld the Old Testament.

THE LORD'S PREDICAMENT

But he went out and began to proclaim it freely and to spread the news around, to such an extent that Jesus could no longer publicly enter a city, but stayed out in unpopulated areas; and they were coming to Him from everywhere. (1:45)

Though the Lord's instruction had been clear and unambiguous, the former leper proved disobedient. Although he had demonstrated humility and submission to Christ in making his request for healing, in his euphoric excitement **he went out and began to proclaim it freely and to spread the news around.** That was precisely the opposite of what Jesus had commanded him to do.

Before being healed, the leper was an outsider forced to live in isolated places away from the population centers of Israel. Now, through his disobedience, the former outcast put the One who healed him in a somewhat similar predicament. By his public testimony of what had happened to him, the healed man added to the crowd frenzy surrounding Jesus **to such an extent that Jesus could no longer publicly enter a city, but stayed out in unpopulated areas.**

The first-century Jewish historian Josephus reported that there were about 240 towns and villages in Galilee. Jesus had wanted to go to all of them in order to preach the gospel (Mark 1:38–39). The increasingly overwhelming response of the people made that impossible. The thronging crowds had become so large and demanding that Jesus could not publicly enter a town.

Consequently, the Lord began to minister in isolated areas,

whether in the wilderness or by the shore of the Sea of Galilee. Whenever He ventured back into places like Capernaum, the crushing crowds were waiting (Mark 2:2) and He was compelled to retreat to the less populated areas (2:13). Jesus was well aware that His popularity was the result of superficial and temporal desires and expectations (cf. John 2:24–25). The crowds got excited about His healing and His miracles, but they were largely uninterested in the message of the gospel (cf. John 6:66)—a reality that would ultimately culminate in His crucifixion, as they turned on Him in a deadly way in spite of His miracles.

Even when Jesus stayed away from the towns and villages of Galilee, the people did not stay away from Him. In fact, **they were coming to Him from everywhere.** Though He remained in the wilderness, the demanding crowds sought Him out and followed Him wherever He went. As Mark records later in his gospel, "Jesus withdrew to the sea with His disciples; and a great multitude from Galilee followed; and also from Judea, and from Jerusalem, and from Idumea, and beyond the Jordan, and the vicinity of Tyre and Sidon, a great number of people heard of all that He was doing and came to Him" (Mark 3:7–8).

Before leaving this passage, it is important to consider the juxtaposition of Jesus and the man whom He healed. The leper started in the wilderness in isolation. After meeting Jesus, he was able to mingle freely in the city. Conversely, Jesus started in the city. After meeting the leper, He was isolated to the wilderness. In that sense, Jesus took the leper's place. As one commentator explains:

> Mark began this story with Jesus on the inside and the leper on the outside. At the end of the story, Jesus is "outside in lonely places." Jesus and the leper have traded places. Early in his ministry Jesus is already an outsider in human society. Mark casts him in the role of the Servant of the Lord who bears the iniquities of others (Isa 53:11) and whose bearing of them causes him to be "numbered with the transgressors" (Isa 53:12). (James R. Edwards, *The Gospel according to Mark*, Pillar New Testament Commentary [Grand Rapids: Eerdmans, 2002], 72)

The account of the leper thus provides a wonderful metaphor for what Jesus did at the cross. As sinners, believers were once spiritual lepers who lived in alienation and isolation from God. God provided a way of salvation through His Son, Jesus Christ. In order to accomplish that plan of redemption, the Son left the presence of God and went into isolation. On the cross, Jesus was forsaken. He was rejected by men and even forsaken by the Father (Matt. 27:46). Yet, because He was treated as an outcast, believers have been accepted and welcomed into the presence of God.

It was on account of mankind's disobedience that He suffered. Yet, for those who come to Him in humble faith, recognizing their own unworthiness and asking for mercy, He offers full cleansing. To the spiritual leper who cries out in faith, "If You are willing, You can make me clean," (Mark 1:40) the Lord's compassionate reply is always the same: "I am willing, be cleansed" (v. 41).

Jesus' Authority to Forgive Sin (Mark 2:1–12)

7

When He had come back to Capernaum several days afterward, it was heard that He was at home. And many were gathered together, so that there was no longer room, not even near the door; and He was speaking the word to them. And they came, bringing to Him a paralytic, carried by four men. Being unable to get to Him because of the crowd, they removed the roof above Him; and when they had dug an opening, they let down the pallet on which the paralytic was lying. And Jesus seeing their faith said to the paralytic, "Son, your sins are forgiven." But some of the scribes were sitting there and reasoning in their hearts, "Why does this man speak that way? He is blaspheming; who can forgive sins but God alone?" Immediately Jesus, aware in His spirit that they were reasoning that way within themselves, said to them, "Why are you reasoning about these things in your hearts? Which is easier, to say to the paralytic, 'Your sins are forgiven'; or to say, 'Get up, and pick up your pallet and walk'? But so that you may know that the Son of Man has authority on earth to forgive

sins"—He said to the paralytic, "I say to you, get up, pick up your
pallet and go home." And he got up and immediately picked up
the pallet and went out in the sight of everyone, so that they were
all amazed and were glorifying God, saying, "We have never seen
anything like this." (2:1–12)

The most distinctive benefit that Christianity offers the world is
not sacrificial love for others, a high standard of morality, or a sense of
purpose and satisfaction in life. All of those virtues are by-products of
biblical Christianity, but they are far from Christianity's greatest gift to
humanity. The gospel offers one surpassing benefit that transcends all
others and is provided by no other religion. It corresponds directly to
mankind's greatest need. Only Christianity provides a solution for
humanity's fundamental and far-reaching problem—namely, the reality
that sinners stand guilty before holy God, who has justly condemned
them to eternal hell because of their rebellion and lawlessness.

Ultimately, God does not send people to hell because of sin but
because of unforgiven sin. Hell is populated by people whose sins were
never forgiven. The difference between those who look forward to eternal life in heaven and those who will experience everlasting punishment
in hell is not a matter of personal goodness, as other religions teach, but
is bound up entirely in one word: forgiveness. Since "all have sinned"
(Rom. 3:23), both eternal destinations are inhabited by people who were
sinners in this life. Only those in heaven were granted divine forgiveness
and the accompanying imputed righteousness that is appropriated by
grace through faith in Jesus Christ (cf. Rom. 5:9, 19). Simply stated, every
person's greatest need is the forgiveness of sin. Consequently, the greatest
benefit of the gospel is its offer of divine pardon to those who believe. No
other religion provides the means for full forgiveness; consequently, all
other religions are actually collecting souls for hell.

Both divine judgment and divine forgiveness are consistent with
God's nature. While His righteousness demands that every sin be punished (cf. Ex. 23:7; Deut. 7:10; Job 10:14; Nah. 1:3), His mercy patiently stays
His wrath and makes provision for sinners to be pardoned (cf. Num.
14:18; Deut. 4:31; Pss. 86:15; 103:8–12; 108:4; 145:8; Isa. 43:25; Joel 2:13). The
justice and mercy of God are repeatedly juxtaposed throughout Scrip-

ture, and there is no sense in which they represent irreconcilable truths (cf. Rom. 9:14–24). In Exodus 34:6–7, God introduced Himself with these words,

> The Lord, the Lord God, compassionate and gracious, slow to anger, and abounding in lovingkindness and truth; who keeps lovingkindness for thousands, who forgives iniquity, transgression and sin; yet He will by no means leave the guilty unpunished, visiting the iniquity of fathers on the children and on the grandchildren to the third and fourth generations.

Nehemiah 9 reiterates that same refrain: "You are a God of forgiveness, gracious and compassionate, slow to anger and abounding in loving-kindness.... However, You are just in all that has come upon us; for You have dealt faithfully, but we have acted wickedly" (vv. 17, 33). In Romans 2:4–5, Paul emphasizes both the mercy and justice of God when he warns unbelievers what will happen if they do not repent: "Do you think lightly of the riches of His kindness and tolerance and patience, not knowing that the kindness of God leads you to repentance? But because of your stubbornness and unrepentant heart you are storing up wrath for yourself in the day of wrath and revelation of the righteous judgment of God." On the one hand, there is nothing more offensive to God's holiness than sin. Unforgiven sinners will be punished by divine wrath. On the other hand, in His mercy, God finds glory in offering to all the forgiveness and absolution of sin through the gospel.

God can both uphold justice and forgive sinners because His justice has been satisfied by His Son, who died as a substitute for sinners (2 Cor. 5:20–21; Col. 2:13–14). Therein lies the heart of the Christian message: the Son of God became a man and died for sinners so that God's justice was satisfied and sinful men might be reconciled to God (cf. Heb. 2:14–18). The sacrifice of Christ is the sole means by which God offers forgiveness to the world (John 3:16; 14:6). The apostle Paul said it this way in Acts 13:38–39, "Therefore let it be known to you, brethren, that through Him forgiveness of sins is proclaimed to you and it is granted to all those who believe." Ephesians 1:7–8 echoes those words, "In Him we have redemption through His blood, the forgiveness of our trespasses according to the riches of His grace which He lavished on us." The good news of

MARK

salvation is that God eagerly forgives all who truly believe in the person and work of the Lord Jesus Christ.

The second chapter of Mark opens with a story about forgiveness. In the first chapter, Mark emphasized the divine authority of Jesus in several ways. His proclamation of the gospel was authoritative, as He called His disciples to leave everything and follow Him (1:14–20). His teaching was authoritative, such that it astonished those who heard Him (1:27). His healings were authoritative, as He displayed supernatural power over both demons and disease (1:25, 31, 34, 42). In this passage (2:1–12), Mark highlights the most necessary aspect of Jesus' divine privilege, the authority to forgive sins. That emphasis is at the heart of this unforgettable miracle.

The account centers on four different characters: the curious spectators, the crippled sinner, the compassionate Savior, and the calloused scribes. After tracking each of these, Mark concludes this account by returning to the crowd of onlookers and noting their surprise at everything they had just witnessed.

THE CURIOUS SPECTATORS

When He had come back to Capernaum several days afterward, it was heard that He was at home. And many were gathered together, so that there was no longer room, not even near the door; and He was speaking the word to them. (2:1–2)

Earlier, when Jesus left Capernaum, He went to preach the gospel in the surrounding towns and villages (1:38). After He healed the man with leprosy, the word about Him spread to such an extent that He "could no longer publicly enter a city, but stayed out in unpopulated areas; and they were coming to Him from everywhere" (1:45). Mark's comment that it was **several days afterward** is a very broad phrase that encompasses an indefinite period of time (cf. Luke 5:17). However long it had been (possibly weeks or even months), **when** Jesus came **back to Capernaum,** He must have done so quietly. The need for a discreet entrance into Capernaum is indicated by Mark 1:45. It was not long, however, before **it was heard that He was at home.** Though He **had come back** secretly, His presence became very public and eager crowds began to gather. The reference to Jesus' **home** was in keeping with His decision to make Capernaum His base of operations during His Galilean ministry. While in Capernaum, He likely stayed at the house of Peter and Andrew (cf. 1:29).

The last time He had been at Peter's home, the residents of Capernaum gathered en masse outside the house as Jesus healed all the sick who were brought to Him (1:33–34). As usual, on this occasion word spread that Jesus was there and a crowd immediately began to form. Mark's comment that **many were gathered together** is an understatement. People were crammed in so tightly **that there was no longer room, not even near the door.**

As always, the crowds primarily consisted of inquisitive onlookers and miracle seekers (Matt. 16:4), more interested in pursuing their own desires (John 6:26) than in mourning over and repenting from sin, thereby seeking salvation from Christ. There were, of course, some genuine followers and true believers, but they represented a small minority. For the most part, the multitudes remained spiritually indifferent to Jesus—drawn by their curiosity and fascination with His supernatural works, but ultimately unwilling to embrace His saving words (Mark 8:34–38; John 6:66). Despite such spiritual apathy and ambivalence, the Lord continued to preach to the throngs, knowing that the Father would draw out the elect from among them (John 6:37, 44). On this occasion in the house in Capernaum, as was His custom, **He was speaking the word to them.**

The crowd included a number of Pharisees (Luke 5:17), who were the primary guardians and advocates of the legalistic traditions and rituals that permeated first-century Judaism. The name "Pharisee," meaning "separated one," defined the philosophy behind the movement. Those who joined the sect, which numbered around six thousand, diligently avoided any interaction with Gentiles, tax collectors, or people whom they regarded as "sinners" (cf. Luke 7:39). Even their attitude toward the common Jewish people was one of disdain and condescension (cf. John 7:49). They considered themselves to be the most holy of all Israelites, but their "holiness" was entirely external and superficial (cf.

Matt. 23:28). It mainly consisted of adherence to their own man-made rules and regulations—stipulations they had added through the years to the law of Moses (cf. Matt. 15:2–9).

The precise origin of the Pharisees is not known. It is likely that their sect formed sometime before the middle of the second century B.C. By the time of Jesus' ministry, they comprised the dominant religious group in Israel. Fervently devoted to keeping the people loyal to both the Old Testament law, and more importantly, the complex set of extrabiblical traditions they had developed around the law, they were highly esteemed for their apparent spirituality and scriptural fidelity.

Within the sect there were scribes (2:6, 16), also referred to as "lawyers" (cf. Luke 10:25), who were professional theologians and Old Testament scholars. They traced their history back to the time of Ezra and Nehemiah, when the Israelites returned to their homeland after the Babylonian captivity. An ancient Jewish tradition asserted that God gave the law to angels, who gave it to Moses and Joshua, who gave it to the elders, who gave it to the prophets, who gave it to the scribes in order to lead and teach in the synagogues. The scribes were responsible both to copy and preserve the Scriptures, as well as interpret them in order to instruct the people. Because there were no more Old Testament prophets after Malachi, the scribes fulfilled the foundational teaching role in Israel. Scribes could be found in various Jewish sects (such as the Sadducees or Essenes), but most scribes in Jesus' day were associated with the Pharisees.

Though a few Pharisees would come to believe in Jesus (cf. John 19:39; Acts 15:5), collectively they appear openly opposed to Him. The scribes and Pharisees who intermingled in the crowd this day were not there to support Jesus' ministry or learn from Him. Rather, they were present because they saw Jesus as a growing threat. Most of them were not even from Capernaum but from other cities around Galilee and even from Jerusalem (Luke 5:17). They had embedded themselves in the crowd of curious spectators to hear what Jesus had to say for the sole purpose of finding fault with Him, in order to discredit and eventually eliminate Him.

THE CRIPPLED SINNER

And they came, bringing to Him a paralytic, carried by four men. Being unable to get to Him because of the crowd, they removed the roof above Him; and when they had dug an opening, they let down the pallet on which the paralytic was lying. (2:3–4)

The account moves from the crowd of curious spectators to focus on **a paralytic, carried by four men.** His condition had made him completely dependent on others. Unlike lepers (cf. 1:40–45), those who suffered from paralysis were not shunned by Israelite society, since their condition was not contagious. Nonetheless, because disease and disability in general were assumed to be the immediate consequence of sin (cf. John 9:2), this man was likely stigmatized by many in his community.

According to Matthew 4:24, Jesus healed many who suffered from paralysis. Yet, all three Synoptic Gospels draw attention to this particular man (cf. Matt. 9:1–8; Luke 5:17–26). His story is noteworthy not only because of the undaunted determination displayed by him and his friends to get to Jesus, but more importantly because of what Jesus did for him beyond healing his body.

Upon arrival, the five were confronted with an overflowing throng of people so tightly packed in and around the house that they were **unable to get to** Jesus **because of the crowd.** According to Luke 5:18, the four friends made an unsuccessful effort to get in through the door. Refusing to give up, they devised an aggressive and extreme plan for reaching Jesus. As Luke explains, "Not finding any way to bring him in because of the crowd, they went up on the roof" (5:19). Once there, **they removed the roof above** Jesus; **and when they had dug an opening, they let down the pallet on which the paralytic was lying.**

Jewish houses were typically one story with a flat patio roof accessible by an external staircase. The typical roof was constructed using large wooden beams with smaller pieces of wood in between, covered by a thatch consisting of grain, twigs, straw, and mud. Tiles would then be installed on top of the thatch. The four men carried their friend around the crowd and up the stairs to the roof. After determining where Jesus was located in the room below, they began removing the roof—

tiles, mud, and thatch—in their effort to create an opening large enough to lower the **pallet.**

The strategy was effective, though it must have been incredibly disruptive. Jesus was, no doubt, teaching in the large central room of the house with people pressed around Him, when debris suddenly started falling from the ceiling onto the heads below. One can easily imagine the shock and dismay as the opening grew bigger and bigger, until it was finally large enough to lower the stretcher. Carefully, **they let down the pallet on which the paralytic was lying.** According to Luke 5:19, the four men had calculated well because their friend came down directly in front of Jesus.

THE COMPASSIONATE SAVIOR

And Jesus seeing their faith said to the paralytic, "Son, your sins are forgiven." (2:5)

As the man was lowered in front of Jesus and the stunned onlookers, the reason for the gaping hole in the ceiling became obvious—the man had been brought in order to be healed. Everyone else in the room could see the man's physical need, but only Jesus perceived the deeper, more significant problem—the paralytic's need for forgiveness. Obviously, the man wanted physical restoration. Jesus knew he longed for more than that; He addressed the more serious issue first. His words to the paralytic must have stunned everyone in the room. **Seeing** the **faith** of both the desperate man and his friends, **Jesus said to the paralytic, "Son, your sins are forgiven."** As shocking as the man's dramatic entrance through the roof had been, Jesus' statement was even more astonishing.

Sinful mankind has no greater need than forgiveness. It is the only means for reconciliation to God, bringing blessing in this life and eternal life in the next. The reason Jesus came is so that He might "save His people from their sins" (Matt. 1:21), and that through Him sinners might be reconciled to God (2 Cor. 5:18–19). As Peter told Cornelius, speaking of Jesus, "Of Him all the prophets bear witness that through His name everyone who believes in Him receives forgiveness of sins" (Acts

10:43; cf. 5:31; 26:18; Eph. 1:7; 4:32; Col. 1:14; 2:13–14; 3:13; 1 John 1:9; 2:12; Rev. 1:5). Divine forgiveness, by grace alone apart from works, is distinctive to the Christian gospel. It distinguishes the true message of salvation from every false system of self-righteousness and merit-based religion.

The statement **seeing their faith** seems to indicate more than just a belief in Jesus' ability to heal (cf. John 2:23–24). The forgiveness that the Lord granted indicates a genuine, repentant faith. This man (along with his friends) must have believed that Jesus was the One who offered salvation to those who repent (1:15). The Lord, recognizing his true faith, said to him, **"Son, your sins are forgiven."** The crippled man saw himself as a guilty sinner, spiritually disabled and in need of forgiveness, like the penitent tax collector in Luke 18:13–14 who cried out, "God, be merciful to me the sinner!" Like the tax collector of Luke 18, this man went home justified. Through faith in Christ, he received forgiveness. The same is true for every sinner who believes. Salvation is received by grace through faith in Christ (John 14:6; Acts 4:12; 17:30–31; Rom. 3:26; 1 Tim. 2:5).

Recognizing the man's genuine faith and desire for salvation, Jesus compassionately and authoritatively forgave him of his sin. The Greek word rendered **are forgiven** refers to the idea of sending or driving away (Ps. 103:12; Jer. 31:34; Mic. 7:19). Complete pardon was granted by divine grace, apart from any merit or works-righteousness on the part of the paralyzed man. Jesus obliterated his guilt, and in that very moment, the crippled sinner was delivered from a future in everlasting hell to one in eternal heaven.

THE CALLOUSED SCRIBES

But some of the scribes were sitting there and reasoning in their hearts, "Why does this man speak that way? He is blaspheming; who can forgive sins but God alone?" Immediately Jesus, aware in His spirit that they were reasoning that way within themselves, said to them, "Why are you reasoning about these things in your hearts? Which is easier, to say to the paralytic, 'Your sins are forgiven'; or to say, 'Get up, and pick up your pallet and walk'? But

so that you may know that the Son of Man has authority on earth to forgive sins"—He said to the paralytic, "I say to you, get up, pick up your pallet and go home." (2:6–11)

Jesus' declaration of forgiveness gave the hostile religious leaders all the ammunition they were looking for to attack Him. When they heard what Jesus said, **some of the scribes were sitting there and reasoning in their hearts, "Why does this man speak that way? He is blaspheming; who can forgive sins but God alone?"** Their premise, that only God can grant full forgiveness of sins, was absolutely correct. The justification of sinners is a prerogative that belongs to God alone. As the supreme Judge, only He can grant eternal pardon to wicked people. Since every sin is ultimately an act of rebellion against Him and His law (Ps. 51:4), the right to forgive, as well as the right to condemn, belongs to God alone.

Because He claimed a level of authority that belongs only to God (cf. Matt. 26:65; John 10:33), the scribes saw Jesus as a blasphemer. From the perspective of the Jews, blasphemy was the most horrendous crime a person could commit. The first-century Jews identified three levels of blasphemy. First, a person was charged with blasphemy if he spoke evil of the law of God. Stephen (Acts 6:13) and Paul (Acts 21:27–28) were each wrongly accused of doing this. A second, more serious, type of blasphemy occurred when a person spoke evil of God directly (cf. Ex. 20:7). Cursing the name of the Lord, for example, was a crime punishable by death (Lev. 24:10–16). A third form of blasphemy, even more heinous than the other two, took place when a sinful human being claimed to possess divine authority and equality with God. For a mere mortal to act as if he were God was the most egregious offense of all. It was this form of blasphemy that the Jewish religious leaders charged Jesus with committing (cf. John 5:18; 8:58–59; 10:33). Eventually, they would use these same accusations to justify His murder (John 19:7; cf. Lev. 24:23).

In the face of their allegations of blasphemy, Jesus demonstrated His deity in three important ways. First, He read their minds. **Immediately Jesus** was **aware in His spirit that they were reasoning that way within themselves.** The fact that He knew their thoughts proved His deity, since only God is omniscient (1 Sam. 16:7; 1 Kings 8:39; 1 Chron.

28:9; Jer. 17:10; Ezek. 11:5). Jesus did not need them to verbalize their thoughts,"for He Himself knew what was in man"(John 2:25).

Second, He did not argue against their basic theological premise, that only God can forgive sins. Rather, He affirmed that truth. Jesus knew that the religious leaders were accusing Him of the blasphemy of claiming equality with God. That was His whole point. His claim to be able to forgive sins was nothing less than a claim that He was God.

Third, He backed up His claim by demonstrating divine power. Having unmasked their thoughts, Jesus **said to them, "Why are you reasoning about these things in your hearts? Which is easier, to say to the paralytic, 'Your sins are forgiven'; or to say, 'Get up, and pick up your pallet and walk'?"** Jesus was not asking which is easier to do, since both are beyond human ability. Rather, He was asking **which is easier** to claim as a convincing reality. Obviously, it is easier **to say** that someone's **sins are forgiven** since there is no empirical way to confirm or deny the reality of that claim. Conversely, telling a paralyzed man to **get up** and **walk** is something that can be immediately tested.

Jesus purposely waited to heal the paralyzed man until after He declared His authority to forgive sins. Disease and disability are consequences of living in a fallen world, meaning that sin's permeating effects are the root cause of all sickness and suffering. By healing the paralyzed man, in demonstration of His power over sin's effects, Jesus proved His authority over sin itself. The Lord thus performed the undeniable miracle of physical healing so that everyone watching **may know that the Son of Man** had **authority on earth to forgive sins.** The title **Son of Man** was one of Jesus' favorite self-designations. He used it more than eighty times in the Gospels (with fourteen of those occurrences in the book of Mark). Not only did the title humbly identify His humanity, it also had messianic implications (cf. Dan. 7:13–14).

Looking with compassion at the man still lying on the stretcher, **He said to the paralytic, "I say to you, get up, pick up your pallet and go home."** This miracle would prove whether or not Jesus had power over sin and its effects. More to the point, it would demonstrate whether or not He truly had the divine authority He claimed to possess. The scribes accused Jesus of being a blasphemer, but blasphemers are not able to read minds. They cannot forgive sins, and they cannot validate their claims by healing people who are paralyzed. By performing this miracle, Jesus proved for all to see that He was not a blasphemer. If He was not a blasphemer, then He was God as He claimed.

THE CROWD'S SURPRISE

And he got up and immediately picked up the pallet and went out in the sight of everyone, so that they were all amazed and were glorifying God, saying, "We have never seen anything like this." (2:12)

Jesus dramatically put His lofty claims to the test by telling the paralyzed man to get up and walk. Verification came instantly. The man **got up and immediately picked up the pallet and went out in the sight of everyone.** Whenever Jesus healed anyone, the person experienced a complete and immediate recovery. No recuperation period was needed, nor were there any lingering effects of the infirmity. This man was no exception. The moment the words left Jesus mouth, the man regained feeling, function, and full strength in every part of his body. He did not need months of physical therapy to relearn how to stand or walk. Instead, he stood right up, picked up his stretcher, and walked home. This time the crowd, utterly amazed by all that had just transpired, parted to let him pass. According to Luke 5:25, the former cripple went home "glorifying God" that not only had his body been healed but his sins had been forgiven.

Unlike the calloused scribes and Pharisees, who continued to reject Christ in spite of the undeniable signs He performed (cf. Luke 6:11; 11:15, 53; 13:17; 15:1–2; 19:47; John 5:36; 10:37–38), the crowds responded with surprise and astonishment. As Mark explains, **they were all amazed and were glorifying God, saying, "We have never seen anything like this."** The Greek word for **amazed** means to be astonished, confused, or even to lose one's mind. The people were absolutely dumbfounded by what they had just seen. Luke adds, "They were filled with fear, saying, 'We have seen remarkable things today'" (Luke 5:26). The word Luke uses for fear is *phobos,* which, in this context, describes the awestruck reverence that comes from being exposed to the person, presence, and power of God (cf. Luke 1:12, 65; 2:9; 7:16; 8:37; 21:26; Matt. 14:26; 28:4, 8; Mark 4:41; Acts 2:43; 5:5, 11; 9:31; 19:17). They responded by **glorifying** God, surely by offering familiar expressions of praise.

For most in the crowd, this response was still reflective of a superficial faith. Matthew 9:8 records their reaction to this very miracle with these words, "But when the crowds saw this, they were awestruck, and glorified God, who had given such authority to men." Though they were awestruck, and though they glorified God, they still viewed Jesus as just a man to whom God had granted authority. In spite of the obvious miracle and the unprecedented demonstration of divine power, many remained unconvinced of Christ's deity. They witnessed His supernatural works, but they refused to believe in His divinity. As John explained, "But though He had performed so many signs before them, yet they were not believing in Him" (John 12:37; cf. 1 Cor. 1:22).

Jesus' miracles functioned as signs validating His claim that He possessed divine authority to forgive sinners. Moreover, Jesus not only had the power to forgive sinners, He became the perfect sacrifice on which divine forgiveness is based. The words Jesus spoke to that paralyzed man two millennia ago are the same words He still speaks to all who come to Him in genuine faith: "Your sins are forgiven." The greatest benefit Christianity offers to the world is the forgiveness of sins. Jesus Christ made forgiveness possible through His death on the cross. He offers that forgiveness to all who are willing to repent of their sin and believe in His name (cf. Rom. 10:9–10).

The Scandal of Grace (Mark 2:13–17)

8

And He went out again by the seashore; and all the people were coming to Him, and He was teaching them. As He passed by, He saw Levi the son of Alphaeus sitting in the tax booth, and He said to him, "Follow Me!" And he got up and followed Him. And it happened that He was reclining at the table in his house, and many tax collectors and sinners were dining with Jesus and His disciples; for there were many of them, and they were following Him. When the scribes of the Pharisees saw that He was eating with the sinners and tax collectors, they said to His disciples, "Why is He eating and drinking with tax collectors and sinners?" And hearing this, Jesus said to them, "It is not those who are healthy who need a physician, but those who are sick; I did not come to call the righteous, but sinners." (2:13–17)

The Bible is clear that salvation cannot be earned through good works, personal merits, or any form of self-righteousness (cf. Titus 3:5–7). Human achievement cannot obtain salvation, since even the best deeds of unredeemed people "are like a filthy garment" before a holy God (Isa. 64:6). Only the power of divine accomplishment can provide forgiveness for sin and the hope of eternal life in heaven (cf. Rom. 1:16). What sinful human beings could never do through their own efforts, God did by sending His Son "as an offering for sin" (Rom. 8:3). The gospel message centers on the truth that "Christ died for our sins according to the Scriptures" (1 Cor. 15:3; cf. Gal. 1:4; Eph. 1:7; 5:2; 1 Peter 2:24; 3:18; 1 John 2:2; Rev. 1:5), so "that whoever believes in Him shall not perish, but have eternal life" (John 3:16; cf. 11:25–26; 20:31; Acts 16:31; Rom. 10:9). Through His death on the cross, the Lord Jesus paid the penalty for sin for all who would believe in Him, so that they might be reconciled to God. He who was entirely without sin became the bearer of sin "so that we might become the righteousness of God in Him" (2 Cor. 5:21). The sins of the redeemed were imputed to Christ at the cross, where He suffered for them as a substitutionary sacrifice (cf. 1 Peter 2:24). Conversely, through faith, the righteousness of Christ is imputed to the redeemed, so that they are declared righteous by God Himself (cf. Rom. 4:5–6; 5:19). Believers have been "justified as a gift by His grace through the redemption which is in Christ Jesus" (Rom. 3:24). Thus, salvation is entirely "by grace . . . through faith; and that not of yourselves, it is the gift of God; not as a result of works, so that no one may boast" (Eph. 2:8–9; cf. 2 Tim. 1:9).

Though the message of salvation is clearly set forth in Scripture, many false teachers throughout history (beginning with early legalists like the Judaizers—cf. Acts 15:1, 5) have attempted to add human works to the gospel of grace. Self-righteous works are not compatible with God's gracious work of divine pardon. As Paul explained in Romans 11:6, referring to salvation: "If it is by grace, it is no longer on the basis of works, otherwise grace is no longer grace." Those who distort the gospel by insisting that good works are necessary for justification place themselves outside of biblical orthodoxy. Responding to such people, Paul warned the Galatians:

> I am amazed that you are so quickly deserting Him who called you by the grace of Christ, for a different gospel; which is really not another; only there are some who are disturbing you and want to distort the gospel of Christ. But even if we, or an angel from heaven, should preach to you a gospel contrary to what we have preached to you, he is to be

accursed! As we have said before, so I say again now, if any man is preaching to you a gospel contrary to what you received, he is to be accursed! (Gal. 1:6–9)

Put simply, a gospel based on human achievement and self-righteous efforts is a false gospel. Salvation comes only from the justifying righteousness of God, made available through the all-sufficient work of Christ on the cross.

The scribes and Pharisees represented the epitome of legalistic self-righteousness in Jesus' day. Largely as a result of their influence, the religion of first-century Israel had deteriorated into a works-based system obsessed with observing external rituals and keeping man-made traditions. The apostate religious leaders taught that a righteous standing before God had to be earned through one's own effort. The apostle Paul, himself a former Pharisee, lamented that reality in Romans 9:31–32: "Israel, pursuing a law of righteousness, did not arrive at that law. Why? Because they did not pursue it by faith, but as though it were by works." Confident in their self-righteousness, Israel's religious elite refused to recognize their precarious spiritual condition—that they suffered from spiritual bankruptcy, bondage, and blindness (cf. Luke 4:18).

The irony of self-righteousness is that it condemns true righteousness. Nowhere was that principle more clearly illustrated than in the Pharisees' denunciation of Jesus. They measured spirituality not only in terms of one's external adherence to Old Testament law but also to man-made traditions (Mark 10:20). When Jesus showed no interest in conforming to nonbiblical rules and restrictions, the scribes and Pharisees accused Him of not being holy (cf. Matt. 12:22–24). To make their point, they scornfully referred to Him as "a friend of tax collectors and sinners" (Matt. 11:19; Luke 7:34; cf. 15:1–2). No epithet could have been more derisive. As those who defined their holiness in terms of separation from sinners, the Pharisees considered anyone who befriended sinful people to be the enemy of God (cf. Luke 7:39). They rejected Jesus, then, because He was not afraid to associate with those whom they considered unclean and unsavory. What the Pharisees regarded as a scandal was, in reality, the ultimate demonstration of God's grace toward utterly undeserving sinners. The Lord compassionately pursued the repentant unrighteous while simultaneously rejecting the impenitent righteousness of the Pharisees.

In rejecting Jesus as the friend of sinners, the scribes and Pharisees demonstrated their willful ignorance regarding the Messiah's mission, which was to seek and save the lost (Luke 19:10). The Lord did not approve of sinful actions or attitudes. He did not befriend sinners in order to endorse their lawless deeds or encourage their rebellious desires. Rather, He came to deliver sinful people from spiritual bondage and death. His purpose was not to condone sin but rather to rescue people from it.

Jesus identified all people as sinners, especially the scribes and Pharisees (cf. Matt. 23). Blinded by their self-righteousness, the religious leaders were unwilling to acknowledge their true condition. Holding tightly to the notion that they were righteous, they denied their need for a Savior and subsequently rejected the Messiah. By contrast, the gospel message is for those who recognize and admit that they are not righteous. That is why Jesus' ministry focused on those who were well aware of their own desperate condition. The "tax collectors and sinners" of Jewish society made no claims to be righteous. They knew they fell far short of God's law. Consequently, they were ripe for the gospel (cf. 1 Cor. 1:26–31).

The glory of the gospel is that God receives unworthy sinners. Forgiveness is not granted to people who are good enough to earn it but to those who know they are not, repent, and believe in the Lord Jesus Christ. The scandal of grace is that God saves those who do not deserve it (cf. Rom. 5:6–11). Systems of works-righteousness require people to earn divine favor through their own efforts. But that is an impossible task (cf. Phil. 3:4–9). The true gospel declares that sinners can do nothing to merit forgiveness or earn eternal life. All they can do is cry out to God for mercy, and by grace alone, He saves them (cf. Luke 18:13–14). The kingdom of salvation opens its doors to those who mourn over their sin and hunger and thirst after the righteousness they know they do not possess (cf. Matt. 5:3–6).

In 2:1–12, Mark recounted the story of the paralyzed man who was healed by Jesus in a house in Capernaum. That healing miracle validated the authority of Jesus to forgive sinners (v. 10). This section (2:13–17) reveals the people to whom Jesus extends that forgiveness—namely, repentant sinners. The dramatic incident recorded in these verses illustrates the fact that no sinner is beyond the reach of God's grace. Jesus was willing to save even the lowest of the low, a hated tax collector. Mark's account of the call of Levi (Matthew) revolves around four main points: the call of a social outcast (vv. 13–14), the community of sinners (v. 15), the contempt of the self-righteous (v. 16), and the condemnation of the Savior (v. 17).

THE CALL OF A SOCIAL OUTCAST

And He went out again by the seashore; and all the people were coming to Him, and He was teaching them. As He passed by, He saw Levi the son of Alphaeus sitting in the tax booth, and He said to him, "Follow Me!" And he got up and followed Him. (2:13–14)

After Jesus healed the paralytic (2:1–12), **He went out** from the house in Capernaum and began teaching **again by the seashore.** Much of the Lord's teaching ministry took place outdoors because it was not possible to contain the massive throngs inside a house or building. Mark's earlier account of the paralyzed man illustrated that point, since the man and his four friends were "unable to get to [Jesus] because of the crowd" (v. 4). So Jesus left the house and went to a place where more people could hear Him teach. He did not leave to escape the crowds but in order that even larger crowds could have access to Him. As He traveled along the shore of the Sea of Galilee, **all the people were coming to Him, and He was teaching them.** Jesus often ministered near the shores of Galilee (cf. Matt. 13:1–52; Mark 3:7; 4:1; 5:21). On this occasion, the content of His teaching undoubtedly consisted of the message of the gospel. As Mark explained in 1:14–15, "Jesus came into Galilee, preaching the gospel of God, and saying, 'The time is fulfilled, and the kingdom of God is at hand; repent and believe in the gospel.'"

As Jesus made His way back into the city of Capernaum, after ministering along the shore, **He passed by** a toll station in which **He saw Levi the son of Alphaeus sitting in the tax booth, and He said to him, "Follow Me!"** Jesus' words must have sent shockwaves through the surrounding crowd. No reputable rabbi would speak invitingly to a tax collector. Any association with such a despised member of Israelite society would be scandalous. Self-respecting Jewish people, and especially religious leaders, would never want a tax collector as an associate or follower. But Jesus shattered all the stereotypes.

Levi, better known by his Greek name Matthew (cf. Matt. 9:9), was of Jewish descent, as both his name and the name of his father, **Alphaeus,** indicate. As a tax collector in Capernaum, the largest city on the Sea of Galilee and situated on a busy trade route, Matthew was part of a lucrative financial operation. What he gained in material wealth, he lacked in terms of social respectability. Tax collectors were among the most hated and despised people in first-century Israel. They were considered the dregs of society and the worst of sinners (cf. Matt. 18:17; 21:31; Luke 5:30; 7:34; 18:11). For Jesus to call a tax collector to follow Him was an unconscionable act of social impropriety, especially in the eyes of the religious elite.

Due to the Roman occupation of Israel, the Jewish people were required to pay taxes to Rome. In Galilee, the responsibility to collect those taxes fell to Herod Antipas, the tetrarch, who sold tax collection franchises to the highest bidder. Those who purchased a franchise were required to meet a minimum quota for Rome, while anything they collected beyond that was theirs to keep (cf. Luke 3:12–13). That arrangement made tax collecting a profitable business venture for anyone with high financial aspirations and low ethical standards. Tax collectors continually looked for ways to squeeze extra money out of people and were aided in their collection by thugs and low-life sorts. Beyond the poll tax, income tax (about 1 percent), and land tax (one-tenth of all grain, and one-fifth of all wine and fruit), taxes were levied on the transport of goods and produce, the use of roads, the crossing of bridges, and other miscellaneous activities. Those assorted duties and tariffs were especially prone to corruption, since they could be easily inflated and collected under threat of harm. Tax collectors were notorious for exploiting people, charging more than was necessary or reasonable and then, for those unable to pay, loaning money at exorbitant interest rates.

Worse, tax collectors were seen as traitors to their own people. They extorted money from their fellow Jews in order to support the corrupt infrastructure of foreign oppression as well as to line their own pockets. Consequently, they were considered unclean, barred from attending the synagogue, and prohibited from testifying in a Jewish court. In short, tax collectors were classed with robbers, turncoats, and liars—the most-debased sinners for whom repentance was deemed especially difficult. As one commentator explains:

> The Mishnah and Talmud (although written later) register scathing judgments of tax collectors, lumping them together with thieves and murderers. A Jew who collected taxes was disqualified as a judge or witness in court, expelled from the synagogue, and a cause of disgrace to his family (*b. Sanh.* 25b). The touch of a tax collector rendered a house unclean (*m. Teh.* 7:6; *m. Hag.* 3:6). Jews were forbidden to receive money and even alms from tax collectors since revenue from taxes was deemed robbery. Jewish contempt of tax collectors is epitomized in the ruling that Jews could lie to tax collectors with impunity (*m. Ned.* 3:4). (James R. Edwards, *The Gospel according to Mark*, Pillar New Testament Commentary [Grand Rapids: Eerdmans, 2002], 83)

According to the Talmud, there were two kinds of tax collectors. The *gabbai* were responsible to collect the more general taxes, like the poll, land, and income tax. More specialized taxes, like tolls for using roads and bridges, were collected by the *mokhes*. (See Alfred Edersheim, *The Life and Times of Jesus the Messiah* [Grand Rapids: Eerdmans, 1974], I:515–518.) A tax booth would be owned by a great *mokhes* who would employ a little *mokhes* to sit there and actually collect the taxes. From Mark's description, it is clear that Matthew was a little *mokhes*. Because he was in constant contact with the people, daily charging them as they passed his toll booth, Matthew would have been one of the most familiar and hated men in Capernaum. One commentator describes his occupation in these words:

> Levi is no tax baron but one who is stationed at an intersection of trade routes to collect tolls, tariffs, imposts and customs, probably for Herod Antipas. Toll collectors were renowned for their dishonesty and extortion. They habitually collected more than they were due, did not always post up the regulations, and made false valuations and accusations (see Luke 3:12–13). Tax officials were hardly choice candidates for discipleship since most Jews in Jesus' day would dismiss them as those who craved money more than respectability or righteousness. (David E. Garland, *Mark*, NIV Application Commentary [Grand Rapids: Zondervan, 1996], 103)

Matthew's booth appears to have been located near the shore, meaning that he likely collected tolls and tariffs from those involved in the city's bustling fishing trade.

Jesus was not deterred by the social stigma attached to Matthew's profession. Instead, stopping at the tax booth, Jesus looked at **Levi** and **said to him, "Follow Me."** The Lord had earlier issued that same imperative to call His first four disciples (Mark 1:16–20). Matthew must have been as shocked as those in the crowd who witnessed this invitation. Undoubtedly, Matthew knew who Jesus was. Jesus had made Capernaum His ministry headquarters (Matt. 4:13), and word about Him had spread throughout the entire region (Luke 4:37). What Matthew knew about Jesus paled in comparison to what Jesus knew about him (cf. John 2:25). The Lord saw an outcast who was wretched and miserable, deeply distressed by the weight of his guilt and ready to repent. That **Levi** was the very kind of person whom Jesus had come to save became apparent when he did not hesitate in responding to Jesus' call. Without delay, **he got up and followed Him.** His rapid response was miraculous, a reflection of the supernatural work of regeneration that had taken place in his heart. According to Luke 5:28, Matthew "left everything behind" to go with Jesus. He had been a man of the world, who had sold his soul for a lucrative career in a despised and dishonest profession. In that moment, Matthew was transformed from a tax-collecting lover of money into a Christ-following lover of God (cf. Matt. 6:24). Everything that controlled his life up to that point no longer had any meaning. The money, the power, the pleasures of the world all lost their grip on his heart. Under conviction, all he wanted was forgiveness and he knew Jesus was the only one who could provide it. He had a new heart, new longings, and new desires (cf. 2 Cor. 5:17). In contrast to the rich young ruler, who chose temporal riches over eternal life (cf. Mark 10:21–22), Matthew abandoned his toll booth, and the fortunes it made him, in order to follow the forgiving Son of God.

In leaving behind his career, Matthew understood there was no going back. Because his life of sin was connected to his profession, his repentance had significant implications. His livelihood could no longer come through the illicit collection of taxes. Like Paul, Matthew realized that "whatever things were gain to [him], those things [he] counted as loss for the sake of Christ. More than that, [he began to] count all things to be loss in view of the surpassing value of knowing Christ Jesus [his] Lord" (Phil. 3:7–8). The former extortionist, traitor, and outcast was transformed into a disciple. Though he lost a career, he gained an eternal reward and an "inheritance which is imperishable and undefiled and will not fade away, reserved in heaven" (1 Peter 1:4). He lost material possessions but gained spiritual life; lost earthly security but gained a heavenly future; lost financial reward but gained an unfading crown of glory (cf. 1 Peter 5:4). Matthew may have been barred from the synagogue, but he was accepted by God and granted salvation.

THE COMMUNITY OF SINNERS

And it happened that He was reclining at the table in his house, and many tax collectors and sinners were dining with Jesus and His disciples; for there were many of them, and they were following Him. (2:15)

Matthew's transformation led immediately to a celebration. Out of his gratitude, he held a large reception for Jesus in his home (cf. Luke 5:29), so that **many tax collectors and sinners were** there. In order to accommodate such a sizeable gathering, Matthew's house must have been large—indicative of the lucrative nature of his career as a tax collector. The celebration centered on a feast, at which Jesus was the guest of honor. The Lord **was reclining at the table in** Matthew's **house** surrounded by his sordid friends who **were dining with Jesus and His disciples.** Matthew's companions primarily consisted of fellow **tax collectors and sinners.** The group would have included known criminals, thieves, thugs, enforcers, and prostitutes—all part of the outcast network of which Matthew himself had been part. From the perspective of the self-righteous religious leaders, these people represented the dregs of society. From Jesus' viewpoint, they comprised the mission field. They were sinners and knew it—the very kinds of people He had come to seek and to save.

The fact that Jesus was **reclining at the table** with them suggests a prolonged meal at which there would have been ample time for conversation and discussion. No respectable rabbi would ever have broken bread with such a group of social miscreants and religious outcasts, let alone attended the event. In first-century Israel, sharing a meal together was a statement of social acceptance and friendship. For the Messiah to eat with these kinds of people was beyond outrageous in the minds of the religious leaders.

Verse 15 contains the first appearance of the word **disciple** (*mathētēs* in Greek) in Mark's gospel. The word means "learner" and can be applied specifically to the Twelve (cf. Matt. 10:1), or in a more general sense to all the followers of Jesus (cf. Matt. 8:21–22; John 6:66; 8:31). In this instance, it included Peter, Andrew, James, and John, whom Jesus called in 1:16–20, along with Matthew. There were also numerous others who were beginning to follow Jesus. Speaking of those dining with the Lord at the banquet, Mark explains that **there were many of them, and they were following Him.** Matthew's dramatic conversion was illustrative of many others who believed in Jesus that day. Like Matthew the tax collector, they lived at the fringe of society, comprising a ragamuffin community of sinners. Yet, by the grace of God, they were transferred from the kingdom of darkness into the kingdom of salvation (Col. 1:13).

The banquet at Matthew's house became a revival. It was a celebration held to honor Jesus and to proclaim the story of forgiveness, as Matthew shared his testimony and as the Lord personally interacted with Matthew's friends. The crowd of society's most unsavory characters, considered unsalvageable by the religious establishment, were befriended by Jesus for the purpose of saving them. They were sinners in need of God's grace. The Messiah Himself extended that grace to them, and many of them believed in Him.

THE CONTEMPT OF THE SELF-RIGHTEOUS

When the scribes of the Pharisees saw that He was eating with the sinners and tax collectors, they said to His disciples, "Why is He eating and drinking with tax collectors and sinners?" (2:16)

Having witnessed what happened at the tax booth (v. 14), **the Pharisees** followed Jesus as He and His disciples made their way to Matthew's house. They were careful to make sure that nothing He did escaped their scrutiny. Though they refused to defile themselves by going inside, they **saw that** Jesus **was eating with the sinners and tax collectors.** Unable to quell their indignation at such scandalous impropriety, they expressed their contempt from outside the house. Apparently waiting until the banquet was over, **the scribes of the Pharisees** cornered **His disciples** and "grumbling" (Luke 5:30) against them, asked, **"Why is He eating and drinking with tax collectors and sinners?"**

The **scribes of the Pharisees** were experts in both the Mosaic law and the countless man-made traditions their sect had developed through the centuries. (For background information on the scribes and Pharisees, see chapter 7 of this volume.) They claimed to be holy, but in reality they were only superficially moral. Their righteousness was not the result of the transformation of the heart by God but was an external, hypocritical righteousness consisting of nothing more than rule keeping, judgmentalism, and outward show. The Pharisees expected Jesus and His disciples to observe their legalistic prescriptions and extrabiblical regulations. When He did not, they reacted with anger and resentment.

Their question to the disciples was not born out of curiosity but contempt. Their tone was not inquisitive but accusatory and vindictive. It was clearly rhetorical, intended as a cutting rebuke for what they viewed as despicable behavior on the part of Jesus. **Eating and drinking** symbolized acceptance, welcome, and friendship. That Jesus would share a meal with such a disreputable group of unclean reprobates enraged their vindictive hearts. In fact, the Pharisees prided themselves on maintaining strict separation from all such people.

Ironically, their judgmental attitudes exposed the true nature of their hypocritical religion. They arrogantly considered themselves to be spiritually whole, when in reality they were spiritually blind and destitute. Many of those they condemned as sinners were, in fact, the ones who had received God's gift of salvation through faith in Christ. Devoid of grace, the Pharisees clung to a spiritually dead system of superficial legalism. In response, Jesus rejected their self-righteous apostasy and focused instead on people who humbly recognized their sin and repented of it.

THE CONDEMNATION OF THE SAVIOR

And hearing this, Jesus said to them, "It is not those who are healthy who need a physician, but those who are sick; I did not come to call the righteous, but sinners." (2:17)

Upon **hearing** the protest of the scribes and Pharisees, **Jesus** answered **them** with a stinging rebuke of His own. He **said to them, "It is not those who are healthy who need a physician, but those who are sick; I did not come to call the righteous, but sinners."** Luke notes that Jesus added the words "to repentance" (Luke 5:32) after the word "sinners." Matthew explains that Jesus also said, "But go and learn what this means: 'I desire compassion, and not sacrifice'" (Matt. 9:13). Putting the accounts from Matthew, Mark, and Luke together, it is evident that Jesus' answer consisted of three parts.

First, Jesus used a medical analogy to illustrate the compassionate nature of His ministry to sinful people. The Pharisees would have readily agreed that tax collectors and sinners like Matthew were spiritually **sick.** In light of their condition, such sinners were obviously in need of spiritual critical care. Who then could argue that the Great Physician should not attend to their desperate state? Jesus' illustration exposed the calloused hearts of the Pharisees, because they would have preferred that He shun sinners instead of helping them. The Lord's analogy also exposed the spiritual blindness of the Pharisees, by underscoring the self-evident fact that only **those who** recognize they **are sick** seek out the help of a **physician.** Those who think they **are healthy** see no reason to go to the doctor. Because the Pharisees had deluded themselves into thinking they enjoyed spiritual vitality, when in reality they were spiritually dead (cf. Eph. 2:1–3), they were unwilling to seek true life in Christ.

Second, Jesus answered the Pharisees from the Old Testament Scriptures. According to Matthew 9:13, He told the scribes to "go and learn what this means: 'I desire compassion, and not sacrifice.'" The phrase "go and learn" was a rabbinic expression used to rebuke foolish ignorance. The potency of that phrase would not have been lost on the scribes, who were rabbis themselves. The biblical quotation "I desire compassion, and not sacrifice" comes from Hosea 6:6, and establishes the truth that God is more concerned with a merciful heart than with the hard, hypocritical observance of external rites (cf. Prov. 21:3; Isa. 1:11–17; Amos 5:21–24; Mic. 6:8). As God told Samuel, "God sees not as man sees, for man looks at the outward appearance, but the Lord looks at the heart" (1 Sam. 16:7; cf. 15:22). Coldhearted legalism may look holy on the outside. But it does not please God who weighs thoughts and motives. In their unwillingness to show mercy to others, the Pharisees betrayed the corrupt condition of their stony hearts. Though they claimed to rigorously keep the law, the Lord's use of Hosea 6:6 exposed their failure to do so. They prided themselves on observing the letter of the law—by dutifully performing sacrifices and ceremonies. They had utterly neglected the spirit of the law, as demonstrated by their unwillingness to extend grace and mercy to those who needed it (cf. Matt. 5:7; Luke 6:36; James 2:13).

Third, Jesus reiterated the purpose of His ministry, by declaring, **"I did not come to call the righteous, but sinners."** In other words, the Lord's saving mission was not directed toward those who were self-righteous but rather toward those who knew they were not righteous. Jesus **did not come to call** hypocritical legalists into His kingdom. Rather, He came to save those who knew they were **sinners.** The Pharisees, of course, regarded themselves as **righteous.** Consequently, they arrogantly assumed they did not need to repent (cf. Luke 15:7). Their self-delusion resulted in a fatal misdiagnosis of their spiritual condition. In their own minds, they were holy. In reality, they were more lost than tax collectors who knew they were rejected by God. Jesus made that point abundantly clear throughout His ministry. On a different occasion,

> He also told this parable to some people who trusted in themselves that they were righteous, and viewed others with contempt: "Two men went up into the temple to pray, one a Pharisee and the other a tax collector. The Pharisee stood and was praying this to himself: 'God, I thank You that I am not like other people: swindlers, unjust, adulterers, or even like this tax collector. I fast twice a week; I pay tithes of all that I get.' But the tax collector, standing some distance away, was even unwilling to lift up his eyes to heaven, but was beating his breast, saying, 'God, be merciful to me, the sinner!' I tell you, this man went to his house justified rather than the other; for everyone who exalts himself will be humbled, but he who humbles himself will be exalted." (Luke 18:9–14)

God seeks those who, recognizing their sinfulness, cry out for mercy and depend fully on His grace. By contrast, the Pharisees were so far from God that, although they could identify other people as sinners, they were unable to recognize their own miserable condition.

Whereas the religious leaders had no mercy on those whom they regarded as less holy than themselves, the Lord Jesus extended God's grace to all who sincerely sought it in faith (cf. John 6:37). Because they thought they were righteous, the Pharisees refused to show compassion toward others. Because He truly is righteous, Jesus graciously demonstrated the mercy and love of God toward sinners. When He attended to the needs of the spiritually desperate, the scribes and Pharisees raged with hate against Him. Yet, despite their protests, the merciful Great Physician gladly extended forgiveness to repentant sinners and welcomed them into His kingdom of salvation. He still does so today (cf. 2 Cor. 6:2). With Jesus, where sin abounds, grace abounds much more.

The church of Jesus Christ consists not of perfect people but of forgiven people. Believers know they are not righteous and cannot by their own power become righteous. Rather, they have been granted the very righteousness of God as a gift of grace through faith in Christ (cf. Rom. 3:21–26; 4:5; 2 Cor. 5:21). On the basis of Jesus' finished work, they have been pardoned and accepted by God, being trophies of His grace for all of eternity (cf. Rom. 9:23). As Paul told the Christians in Corinth:

> Do you not know that the unrighteous will not inherit the kingdom of God? Do not be deceived; neither fornicators, nor idolaters, nor adulterers, nor effeminate, nor homosexuals, nor thieves, nor the covetous, nor drunkards, nor revilers, nor swindlers, will inherit the kingdom of God. Such were some of you; but you were washed, but you were sanctified, but you were justified in the name of the Lord Jesus Christ and in the Spirit of our God. (1 Cor. 6:9–11)

The Exclusive Distinctiveness of the Gospel (Mark 2:18–22)

9

John's disciples and the Pharisees were fasting; and they came and said to Him, "Why do John's disciples and the disciples of the Pharisees fast, but Your disciples do not fast?" And Jesus said to them, "While the bridegroom is with them, the attendants of the bridegroom cannot fast, can they? So long as they have the bridegroom with them, they cannot fast. But the days will come when the bridegroom is taken away from them, and then they will fast in that day. No one sews a patch of unshrunk cloth on an old garment; otherwise the patch pulls away from it, the new from the old, and a worse tear results. No one puts new wine into old wineskins; otherwise the wine will burst the skins, and the wine is lost and the skins as well; but one puts new wine into fresh wineskins." (2:18–22)

The gospel of the Lord Jesus Christ is unique, matchless, and exclusive. It cannot coexist with any alternative religious system. In the same way that water cannot be mixed with poison and still be safe to drink, so the message of the water of life (cf. John 4:14) cannot be blended with error and retain its saving character. The renowned nineteenth-century pastor Charles Spurgeon expressed the exclusivity of the gospel with these inimitable words:

> Did you ever notice the intolerance of God's religion? . . . A thousand errors may live in peace with one another, but truth is the hammer that breaks them all in pieces. A hundred lying religions may sleep peaceably in one bed, but wherever the Christian religion goes as the truth, it is like a fire-brand, and it abideth nothing that is not more substantial than the wood, the hay, and the stubble of carnal error. All the gods of the heathen, and all other religions are born of hell, and therefore, being children of the same father, it would seem amiss that they should fall out, and chide, and fight; but the religion of Christ is a thing of God's—its pedigree is from on high, and, therefore, when once it is thrust into the midst of an ungodly and gainsaying generation, it hath neither peace, nor parley, nor treaty with them, for it is truth, and cannot afford to be yoked with error: it stands upon its own rights, and gives to error its due, declaring that it hath no salvation, but that in the truth, and in the truth alone, is salvation to be found. (Charles Spurgeon, "The Way of Salvation," sermon no. 209, preached August 15, 1858)

The absolute exclusivity of the Christian gospel runs contrary to the pluralistic mindset of contemporary culture. Religious diversity, relativism, and ecumenism are celebrated by the world. Consequently, the people our society most likely will not tolerate are those courageous enough to declare that Christianity alone is true and all other religions are false.

Where society celebrates ambiguity, Scripture demands absolute certainty. The Bible is clear that there is only one God, one authoritative divine written revelation, and one way of salvation. Jesus Himself could not have stated it any more directly than He did in John 14:6. Speaking of salvation, He declared, "I am the way, and the truth, and the life; *no one comes to the Father but through Me*" (emphasis added). The apostle Peter echoed that truth in Acts 4:12, "There is salvation in no one else; for there is no other name under heaven that has been given among men by which we must be saved." Many other biblical texts underscore the singularity and exclusivity of the Christian gospel (cf. Acts 10:43; 1 Cor. 16:22; Gal. 1:9; 1 Tim. 2:5), including this section of the gospel of Mark (2:18–22). These verses provide an unambiguous statement of the narrowness of the gospel—most specifically against the backdrop of apostate Judaism, but by extension in contrast to every other false religious system.

In the previous section (2:13–17), the Lord's invitation to Levi (Matthew) constituted a baffling breach of cultural propriety and religious duty, at least as far as the scribes and Pharisees were concerned. They refused to have anything to do with tax collectors, whom they viewed as quislings and outcasts. The Pharisees espoused a religion of external separation and superficial holiness, making sure never to associate with those they deemed to be sinners. Yet Jesus ignored such legalistic stereotypes and artificial stipulations. He purposely reached out to the riffraff of society because, as He said, "It is not those who are healthy who need a physician, but those who are sick; I did not come to call the righteous, but sinners" (v. 17).

Jesus calling a tax collector to be His disciple produced a jarring impact, especially on the scribes and Pharisees. Since the Lord's invitation to Matthew was public, taking place while He walked past the tax booth where Matthew was sitting, it constituted a flagrant violation of proper rabbinic conduct, confirming in the minds of the Jewish religious leaders that Jesus represented a serious threat to their form of Judaism. Convinced their religion came from God, they alleged that He was empowered by Satan (cf. Matt. 12:24). Their perception could not have been more backward. The true religion of the Old Testament was fulfilled in the Lord Jesus Christ. The Judaism that rejected Him was a false religion. Yet, in spite of their self-deception and apostasy, the scribes and Pharisees rightly understood that the message Jesus preached was utterly incompatible with the system they promoted. In fact, they knew that Jesus was so adversarial toward them that they had to end His existence.

All three of the synoptic writers record this conversation between Jesus and those who questioned Him (cf. Matt. 9:14–17; Luke 5:33–39), and all three place it immediately after the call of Matthew. The chronological sequence is not accidental. Shortly before this, Jesus had stunned the crowds when He declared that He possessed the authority to forgive sins (Mark 2:10). He then demonstrated His eagerness to extend that forgiveness to sinners by calling a tax collector to follow Him as a disciple, and even sharing a meal at the tax collector's home with his consorts (vv. 13–17). Through His actions, Jesus made it crystal clear that the content of His preaching was diametrically opposed to everything the scribes and Pharisees represented. While they articulated a way of salvation through self-righteous effort and legalistic works, the gospel of Jesus Christ focused on divine grace being granted to those believing in Him, who humbly cried out for mercy and repented from sin (cf. Luke 18:9–14). Jesus' message of forgiveness and repentance was rebuffed by the self-righteous, who self-righteously assumed they did not need it. But it was readily received by those who knew they were not righteous. So, Jesus focused His ministry on being a friend to sinners (Matt. 11:19).

It is on the heels of those earlier episodes that Jesus explains just how incompatible His message was with apostate Judaism, and by extension with any system of man-made religion. The passage contains three simple elements: a critical accusation, a corrective answer, and some clarifying analogies.

A CRITICAL ACCUSATION

John's disciples and the Pharisees were fasting; and they came and said to Him, "Why do John's disciples and the disciples of the Pharisees fast, but Your disciples do not fast?" (2:18)

The conflict between the Pharisees and Jesus revolved around questions related to His teaching or behavior. Whenever He or His disciples said or did anything contrary to their traditions and rules, they were quick to launch their protest in the form of a question. On this occasion, the group of inquisitors also included a number of disciples of John the Baptist. The parallel account in Matthew focuses exclusively on the disciples of John (Matt. 9:14), while Luke's account centers on the Pharisees (Luke 5:33). As Mark explains, representatives from both groups participated in this encounter with Jesus.

The presence of **John's disciples** alongside **the Pharisees** is surprising in light of John's unwavering testimony regarding Jesus (cf. John 1:29; 3:28–30; 5:33). As the herald of the Messiah, John the Baptist boldly pointed his followers to Jesus (cf. Mark 1:7; John 1:36–37), and even baptized the Lord after faithfully proclaiming His arrival (1:9–11). On that occasion, the prophet saw the Holy Spirit descend and heard the affirmation of the Father's voice (Matt. 3:13–17). Moreover, John had not hesitated to confront the scribes and Pharisees (cf. Matt. 3:7). Why then would some of his followers join them in questioning Jesus on this occasion?

The answer probably involves a number of factors. Perhaps this group of disciples was ignorant of the fact that Jesus was the one whose coming John had foretold. John ministered to tens of thousands of people, as multitudes traveled from Jerusalem and all over Israel to hear him preach in the wilderness and to be baptized by him in the Jordan River (cf. 1:5). Not all of his followers would have been present when he baptized Jesus. Many would not have witnessed that miraculous event, nor heard John's clear testimony regarding Jesus on that day. Almost thirty years after Jesus' baptism, the apostle Paul encountered a group of John's disciples who still did not know that Jesus was the one to whom John's ministry pointed (Acts 19:1–7). It is also possible that these disciples were motivated by feelings of jealousy toward Jesus. Though John personally felt no rivalry toward Jesus (cf. John 3:30), some of his disciples were less enthusiastic about Jesus' growing popularity (John 3:26; 4:1). Perhaps similar feelings of contention motivated these followers of John. For his part, John the Baptist was already in prison (Luke 3:20), which meant he was not available to correct either the misguided ignorance or misplaced zeal of those loyal to him.

It should be noted that the baptism of John was a baptism of repentance signifying renewed spiritual commitment. Those who heeded John's message were testifying of a desire to turn away from their sin in preparation for the Messiah's coming. Having been baptized by John in the wilderness, they returned home more conscientious about spiritual matters and religious observances (like fasting). Thus, some would have naturally gravitated toward the scribes and Pharisees, who outwardly appeared to take religion seriously.

Whatever the specific reasons for their association with the religious leaders on this occasion, some disciples of John were present when the Pharisees came to ask Jesus a question. Both groups dutifully observed the religious traditions regarding **fasting**; and both groups became concerned when they noticed that Jesus' followers did not. That Jesus and His disciples had just attended a banquet at Matthew's house

(vv. 15–16) only heightened their consternation. To eat with tax collectors and sinners, when custom required a fast, did more than just raise a few eyebrows. It raised serious questions. It is possible, of course, that the disciples of John may have merely wanted to know why Jesus approved of such behavior on the part of His followers. The Pharisees who accompanied them were clearly driven by rigid animosity. Their question did not express a desire for information. Rather, it was intended as a stinging rebuke. Indignant, **they came and said to Him, "Why do John's disciples and the disciples of the Pharisees fast, but Your disciples do not fast?"**

Fasting, prayer, and almsgiving were common expressions of piety in Judaism. All three were performed publicly, providing the Pharisees with a platform to flaunt their ostentatious false devotion. Jesus had confronted directly such superficial spirituality in the Sermon on the Mount, where He taught that fasting, prayer, and almsgiving were to be done in secret, to honor God and not to impress others (cf. Matt. 6:2–6, 16–18).

Frequently flaunted fasting was another example of how the Pharisees added their own superficial traditions to the law of God. The Mosaic law commanded only one annual fast, yet the Pharisees proudly fasted twice a week (Luke 18:12), on Mondays and Thursdays. According to Leviticus 16:29–31, the Israelites were to "humble [their] souls" on the Day of Atonement. That act of self-denial included abstaining from food, making the Day of Atonement the only mandatory fast day delineated in the Old Testament. Because the Day of Atonement was set aside for mourning over sin, eating of any kind was deemed inappropriate. Additionally, the Old Testament mentions a number of other nonmandatory fasts (e.g., Judg. 20:26; 1 Sam. 7:6; 31:13; 2 Sam. 1:12; 12:16; 1 Kings 21:27; 2 Chron. 20:3; Ezra 8:21, 23; Neh. 1:4; 9:1; Est. 4:1–3; Ps. 69:10; Dan. 9:3; Joel 1:13–14; 2:12, 15), but they were voluntary, being associated with grief, sorrow over sin, and the sincere pursuit of communion with God. Fasts motivated out of proud self-righteousness or calloused ritualism were wholly rejected by God (cf. Isa. 58:3–4).

That the scribes and Pharisees had added their own superficial superstructure to God's law (cf. Matt. 15:9) was exposed by their question. The true source of their indignation was not that Jesus' disciples were violating God's law but that they were failing to observe man-made traditions and rules. It was hypocrisy and legalism, not holiness or love for God that motivated the religious leaders' confrontation.

A CORRECTIVE ANSWER

And Jesus said to them, "While the bridegroom is with them, the attendants of the bridegroom cannot fast, can they? So long as they have the bridegroom with them, they cannot fast. But the days will come when the bridegroom is taken away from them, and then they will fast in that day." (2:19–20)

The chiding question deserved an answer, which Jesus readily gave. Rather than apologizing for causing an offense, the Lord escalated the conflict in order to expose the spiritual condition of those who asked. His response simultaneously eliminated the ignorance that might have existed on the part of John's disciples and confronted the indignation that motivated the Pharisees and scribes. The Pharisees accused Jesus of being in conflict with the rules and rituals of Judaism. Jesus responded by pointing out that, in reality, they were the ones who were set in opposition to God's saving purposes. If they had recognized that Jesus was the Messiah, they never would have posed their question in the first place.

The Lord used the illustration of a wedding celebration to make His point. **And Jesus said to them, "While the bridegroom is with them, the attendants of the bridegroom cannot fast, can they?"** The rhetorical question underscored an incontrovertible spiritual truth. Fasting was for times of grief and sorrowful reflection, but a wedding was a joyful and festive event (cf. Matt. 9:15). The **attendants of the bridegroom,** the groom's closest friends, were responsible for the execution of the wedding plans. A typical ancient Jewish wedding lasted up to seven days, with the celebration starting once the bridegroom and his attendants arrived. To fast at a wedding would have been inappropriate and insulting, so much so that ancient rabbinic rules forbade the practice. Jesus' words were emphatic: **So long as they have the bridegroom**

with them, they cannot fast. For a member of the wedding party to mourn at such a joyous occasion would have been as ridiculous as it was rude. So, it was equally ludicrous to think that Jesus' disciples ought to fast and grieve while the Messiah was in their midst.

Jesus used the anticipation and elation that accompanies a wedding to illustrate the joy surrounding His own presence. While it may have been acceptable to fast in preparation and anticipation of the Messiah's arrival, it was not appropriate when He arrived. His long-awaited advent ought to be a time of celebration and rejoicing. Though the Old Testament never refers directly to the Messiah as the bridegroom, it does so indirectly, by referring to Israel as the bride of the Lord (cf. Isa. 62:4–5; Jer. 2:2; Hos. 2:16–20). Jesus was enriching that imagery in referring to Himself as the bridegroom (cf. Matt. 9:15; 25:1–13; Luke 5:34–35; John 3:29). The New Testament develops Jesus' imagery even further, depicting the church as the bride of Christ (cf. Eph. 5:32; Rev. 19:7; 21:2, 9; 22:17).

Jesus' statement about the joys of a wedding feast ends on a threatening note. **"But the days will come when the bridegroom is taken away from them, and then they will fast in that day."** The disciples' celebration would come to an abrupt end when the groom was unexpectedly snatched away. The verb *apairō* (**taken away**) conveys the idea of a sudden, violent removal and serves as a clear reference to Jesus' crucifixion (cf. Isa. 53:8). At that time, mourning and grief would be warranted. On the night before His death, Jesus told His disciples in the upper room:

> Truly, truly, I say to you, that you will weep and lament, but the world will rejoice; you will grieve, but your grief will be turned into joy. Whenever a woman is in labor she has pain, because her hour has come; but when she gives birth to the child, she no longer remembers the anguish because of the joy that a child has been born into the world. Therefore you too have grief now; but I will see you again, and your heart will rejoice, and no one will take your joy away from you. (John 16:20–22)

Their sadness at the cross was profound. It was transformed into immeasurable joy just three days later when Jesus rose from the grave. After Jesus' ascension into heaven, His disciples did fast, but only as a voluntary act of humble dependence on God (cf. Acts 13:2–3; 14:23).

The disciples did not initially understand Christ's predictions of

His suffering and death (cf. Mark 9:31–32), and this is the first such reference recorded in Mark's gospel. Yet, His substitutionary sacrifice on the cross was central to His earthly mission—an integral part of the gospel of forgiveness that He preached. As Paul explained in 1 Corinthians 15:1–4:

> Now I make known to you, brethren, the gospel which I preached to you, which also you received, in which also you stand, by which also you are saved.... For I delivered to you as of first importance what I also received, that Christ died for our sins according to the Scriptures, and that He was buried, and that He was raised on the third day according to the Scriptures.

The celebration experienced by those at the heavenly wedding feast is only possible because the bridegroom was willing to die for His friends (cf. John 10:11; Rom. 5:6–11).

Jesus' point to His questioners was simply this: Judaism at its most devout level, as exemplified by the scribes and Pharisees, was completely out of touch with God's plan of salvation. They were mourning when they should have been rejoicing, because they had rejected Jesus the Savior and clung to their own rules and regulations to earn salvation. Consequently, they had nothing in common with Him. They were consumed with self-righteousness; He preached divine grace. They denied they were sinners; He preached repentance from sin. They were proud of their religiosity; He preached humility. They embraced external ceremony and tradition; He preached a transformed heart. They loved the applause of men; He offered the approval of God. They had dead ritual; He offered a dynamic relationship. They promoted a system; He provided salvation.

SOME CLARIFYING ANALOGIES

"No one sews a patch of unshrunk cloth on an old garment; otherwise the patch pulls away from it, the new from the old, and a worse tear results. No one puts new wine into old wineskins; otherwise the wine will burst the skins, and the wine is lost and the skins as well; but one puts new wine into fresh wineskins." (2:21–22)

The Lord further illustrated His point through the use of several analogies or "parables" (Luke 5:36). Matthew (9:16–17) and Mark (2:21–22) record the first two of these metaphors, while Luke includes a third (cf. Luke 5:39). Together, they illustrate the absolute uniqueness of the gospel—demonstrating the fact that the true message of salvation is utterly incompatible with any false system of works-righteousness, including Judaistic legalism.

First, Jesus explained that **no one sews a patch of unshrunk cloth on an old garment; otherwise the patch pulls away from it, the new from the old, and a worse tear results.** Repairing an old tunic with a piece of new, unshrunk fabric would be ill-advised. Not only would the new cloth not match the faded color of the old (cf. Luke 5:36), it would shrink when washed and pull the garment, causing it to tear. Our Lord's point was that His gospel of repentance and forgiveness from sin could not be patched into the legalistic traditionalism of Pharisaic Judaism. The true gospel cannot be successfully attached to the tattered garment of superficial religion worn so proudly by the scribes and Pharisees. Apostate Judaism's rituals and ceremonies were like filthy rags (Isa. 64:6); they were beyond repair. Jesus did not come with a message to patch up their old system. He came to totally replace it.

It is important to note that the old garment to which Jesus alludes is neither the Mosaic law nor the Old Testament as a whole. Jesus did not come to destroy the law but to fulfill it (Matt. 5:17–19). Moreover, the apostle Paul explains that the law of God is righteous and good (Rom. 7:16). The Jewish leaders had added their own rabbinic stipulations and traditions to God's law to the degree that Judaism had more to do with keeping extrabiblical prescriptions than with honoring divine requirements. The old garment is the legalistic system of rabbinic tradition that had obscured the law of God (cf. Matt. 15:3–6). Jesus was not interested in mending the religion of the Pharisees. The good news of salvation by grace through faith in Him could not be combined with the works-righteousness of Judaism.

Jesus' second analogy echoed that same point. He told His listeners, **"No one puts new wine into old wineskins; otherwise the wine will burst the skins, and the wine is lost and the skins as well; but one puts new wine into fresh wineskins."** Just as an unshrunk piece of new cloth would destroy an old garment, so new wine would destroy old wineskins. Wine was stored in ancient Israel in containers made from animal skin (cf. Josh. 9:4, 13). Often goatskins would be used. The animal's hide would be uncut except at the legs and neck, and sometimes would be turned inside out. The leg openings would then be sealed shut, and the neck would be used as a spout, so that wine could easily be poured in or out. As new wine began to ferment, gas would be released, causing the leather skins to expand. An old wineskin, having lost its elasticity, could break during the process of fermentation. Consequently, the wine would spill and the flask would be destroyed. In order to avoid this, new wine had to be placed in new wineskins—containers that had the strength and flexibility to hold up as the wine fermented.

Like the first illustration, which demonstrated that the true gospel cannot be attached to a false system of works-righteousness, this analogy exemplified the fact that the legalism of Judaism could not contain the message of salvation by grace. In the same way that new wine was incompatible with old wineskins, the true gospel is antithetical to any system of salvation by works (Rom. 11:6; Gal. 5:4). Jesus' point was that the good news of salvation could not be poured into the brittle, cracked wineskins of apostate Judaism. Nor is it compatible with any other man-made or demonic religion.

Luke 5:39 records a third parable that Jesus shared on this occasion: "And no one, after drinking old wine wishes for new; for he says, 'The old is good enough.'" That final analogy depicted the lost condition of the scribes and Pharisees, whose sensibilities had been deadened by the inebriating effects of their false religion. Those who would reject the true gospel in favor of a system of works-righteousness are like spiritual drunkards—desensitized to the point that they no longer care about how the wine tastes. Drunk on their old ways, they had no desire for the new. They would rather savor the foul flavors of false religion than imbibe the fresh purity of the true gospel. The Jews with their ancient traditions, passed down from generation to generation, were so deeply ingrained in rituals and ceremonies that it was difficult for them to relinquish them. They had cultivated such a taste for their own superficial system that, when offered something far better, they simply were not interested.

Taken together, these three metaphors illustrate the exclusivity of the Christian gospel, and the tragedy that results when any attempt is made to syncretize the truth with a false religious system. The only true message of salvation is the gospel of Jesus Christ, that pardon from sin comes by grace alone through faith in Him. Anything else is a false gospel that leads not to heaven but to hell (cf. Gal. 1:6–9). In an age where relativism reigns, believers need to be reminded of the fact that truth is exclusive and absolute. Rather than trying to build bridges of artificial unity with false religions, Christians ought to heed the words of the apostle Paul in 2 Corinthians 6:14–18:

> Do not be bound together with unbelievers; for what partnership have righteousness and lawlessness, or what fellowship has light with darkness? Or what harmony has Christ with Belial, or what has a believer in common with an unbeliever? Or what agreement has the temple of God with idols? For we are the temple of the living God; just as God said,
>
> > "I will dwell in them and walk among them;
> > And I will be their God, and they shall be My people.
> > Therefore, come out from their midst and be separate," says the Lord.
> > "And do not touch what is unclean;
> > And I will welcome you.
> > And I will be a father to you,
> > And you shall be sons and daughters to Me,"
> > Says the Lord Almighty.

The Lord of the Sabbath—Part 1 (Mark 2:23–28)

10

And it happened that He was passing through the grainfields on the Sabbath, and His disciples began to make their way along while picking the heads of grain. The Pharisees were saying to Him, "Look, why are they doing what is not lawful on the Sabbath?" And He said to them, "Have you never read what David did when he was in need and he and his companions became hungry; how he entered the house of God in the time of Abiathar the high priest, and ate the consecrated bread, which is not lawful for anyone to eat except the priests, and he also gave it to those who were with him?" Jesus said to them, "The Sabbath was made for man, and not man for the Sabbath. So the Son of Man is Lord even of the Sabbath." (2:23–28)

The biblical Gospels are more than just historical accounts of the earthly life of the Lord Jesus. They are also christological treatises revealing the transcendence of His heavenly character. Written under the inspiration of the Holy Spirit, the four histories represent the perfect blending of biography and theology—a masterful combination of factual precision and doctrinal depth. Not only do they recount the story of Jesus' life and ministry with absolute accuracy, they simultaneously present the infinite glories of His divine person, so that their readers may come to know Him for who He really is: the Son of Man and the Son of God.

Like the other three writers, Mark's purpose was to reveal and declare the truth about the person and work of the Lord Jesus. He began his gospel by declaring Jesus to be the divine messianic King, introducing Him with a royal title: "Christ, the Son of God" (1:1). In the verses that follow, Jesus is identified as "the Lord" (1:3), the coming One (1:7), the One who baptizes with the Holy Spirit (1:8), the "beloved Son" of the Father (1:11), the One who offers the gospel of the kingdom (1:14), and "the Holy One of God" (1:24). By chapter 2, it is clear that Jesus possessed the sovereign power to authenticate such elevated titles as He demonstrated unsurpassed authority over Satan and temptation (1:12–13), demons and demon possession (1:25–26), sickness and disease (1:29–34), sin and its effects (2:5–12), and even the social stigmas of first-century Judaism (2:13–17). His works convincingly validated His words, proving beyond any legitimate doubt that He was the Son of God, worthy of every elevated title and glorious superlative that could ever be bestowed on Him.

In Mark 2:23–28, we are introduced to another of His titles—Lord of the Sabbath (v. 28). That designation, coming from Jesus' own lips, underscored His divine authority while again setting Him in direct conflict with the hypocritical religious leaders of Judaism. Conflict was inevitable whenever Jesus interacted with the Pharisees and scribes. He embodied the truth (John 14:6); they represented a system of superficial pretense and false religion. In the same way that light pierces the darkness, Christ's words illuminated Israel's corrupt religious establishment— disclosing the dead traditionalism that characterized its most ardent defenders. Jesus refused to mince words, exposing the Pharisees and scribes for who they really were: spiritually blind false teachers who turned their disciples into sons of hell (cf. Matt. 7:15–20; 15:14; 23:15). The Lord's dogmatic declarations left no room for ambiguity or ambivalence. Would His hearers remain trapped as slaves in a system of extrabiblical rules and regulations or be set free by the gospel of grace through faith in the Savior (cf. John 8:31–36)?

When Jesus declared Himself to be the Lord of the Sabbath, He struck a severe blow at the entire system of merit and works-righteousness that found its focal point in the Sabbath. The seventh day of every week had become the platform for showcasing Pharisaic legalism. The command to observe the Sabbath, like the other nine commandments, was intended to promote love toward God and other people (cf. Ex. 20:1–17; Mark 12:28–31). What God established as a day of reverence toward Him and refreshment from work, the Pharisees and scribes transformed into a day of stifling regulation and restriction. Just as Jesus confronted the Sadducees for making the temple a den of robbers (Matt. 21:13), He blasted the Pharisees for turning a day of weekly worship into a rigorous burden of extraneous rule keeping. By openly defying the man-made traditions regarding the Sabbath, Jesus put Himself in direct conflict with the religious leaders at their most sensitive point.

The religious leaders viewed Jesus as a serious threat to their religious system. He, conversely, rebuked them for being imposters. With righteous indignation, He condemned them for perpetuating a burdensome system of external ritualism. They considered themselves holy; He called them hypocrites (cf. Matt. 23). But rather than repenting, they hardened their hearts against Him. The more Jesus preached, the deeper their resentment toward Him grew. The fact that He openly associated with the outcasts of society, even calling a tax collector to be one of His closest disciples (2:14), only added to the tension. They mockingly called Him the friend of sinners (Matt. 11:19; Luke 7:34). He embraced the title, reminding them that He "did not come to call the righteous, but sinners" to repentance (Mark 2:17).

By claiming to be the Lord of the Sabbath, Jesus essentially declared His authority over the whole of Jewish religion, because Sabbath-day observance was its high point. The implications of Christ's claim struck deeply. The pattern for a day of rest was established at creation, when God Himself rested on the seventh day (Gen. 2:2). Furthermore, it was God who wrote in the tablets of stone in Exodus 20:8, "Remember the sabbath day, to keep it holy" (cf. Ex. 31:12–17; Deut. 5:12–15). God was the One who established the Sabbath. Thus, to claim to be the Lord of the

Sabbath was to claim deity, a reality was certainly not lost on the Pharisees and scribes, who became incensed by what they perceived to be
blasphemy.

John 5:9–18 recounts an event that occurred in Judea shortly
before the events recorded in Mark 2:23–28. (For a complete harmony of
the Gospels, see John MacArthur, *One Perfect Life* [Nashville: Thomas Nelson, 2012].) On that occasion, which took place on a Sabbath day, Jesus
healed a man who had been severely ill for thirty-eight years. The Pharisees, rather than responding with compassion, were outraged because
Jesus told the man to pick up his bed mat and walk home—an act that
violated rabbinic regulations for the Sabbath. As John explains,

> Immediately the man became well, and picked up his pallet and began
> to walk. Now it was the Sabbath on that day. So the Jews were saying to
> the man who was cured, "It is the Sabbath, and it is not permissible for
> you to carry your pallet." But he answered them, "He who made me well
> was the one who said to me, 'Pick up your pallet and walk.'" They asked
> him, "Who is the man who said to you, 'Pick up your pallet and walk'?"
> But the man who was healed did not know who it was, for Jesus had
> slipped away while there was a crowd in that place. Afterward Jesus
> found him in the temple and said to him, "Behold, you have become
> well; do not sin anymore, so that nothing worse happens to you." The
> man went away, and told the Jews that it was Jesus who had made him
> well. For this reason the Jews were persecuting Jesus, because He was
> doing these things on the Sabbath. But He answered them, "My Father
> is working until now, and I Myself am working." For this reason therefore
> the Jews were seeking all the more to kill Him, because He not only
> was breaking the Sabbath, but also was calling God His own Father,
> making Himself equal with God.

The Jewish religious leaders hated Jesus because He violated their man-
made Sabbath regulations. They detested Him all the more because, in
the process of ignoring their extrabiblical rules, He claimed equality
with God. When Jesus designated Himself the Lord of the Sabbath, He
was not getting sidetracked with peripheral issues. With that single
claim, Jesus directly assaulted apostate Judaism while simultaneously
declaring His divinity. He called Israel to return to the true purpose of
the Sabbath—the purpose He Himself had established for it when He
issued the fourth commandment to Moses centuries earlier (cf. John
5:46; 8:58).

The Sabbath was intended to be a day of worship and rest for God's people under the old covenant. The word "sabbath" itself is derived from the Hebrew term *shabbat,* meaning "to rest," "to cease," or "to desist." On the seventh day of each week, the Israelites were to refrain from working in order to focus their attention on honoring the Lord. Over the ensuing fifteen centuries, from the time of Moses to the ministry of Jesus, the Sabbath accumulated a vast number of additional rabbinic rules and restrictions, which made observing the seventh day an overpowering burden (cf. Matt. 15:6,9). No less than twenty-four chapters of the Talmud (the central text of rabbinic Judaism) focus on Sabbath regulations, meticulously detailing the almost innumerable specifics of what constituted acceptable behavior.

Almost no area of life was spared from the fastidious Sabbath regulations of the rabbis, which were designed to gain God's favor. There were laws about wine, honey, milk, spitting, writing, and getting dirt off of clothes. Anything that might be contrived as work was forbidden. Thus, on a Sabbath, scribes could not carry their pens, tailors their needles, or students their books. To do so might tempt them to work on the Sabbath. For that matter, carrying anything heavier than a dried fig was forbidden; and if the object in question had been picked up in a public place, it could only be set down in a private place. If the object were tossed into the air, it had to be caught with the same hand. To catch it with the other hand would constitute work, and therefore be a violation of the Sabbath. No insects could be killed. No candle or flame could be lit or extinguished. Nothing could be bought or sold. No bathing was allowed, since water might spill onto the floor and accidentally wash it. No furniture could be moved inside the house, since it might create ruts in the dirt floor and thereby constitute plowing. An egg could not be boiled even if all one did was place it in the hot desert sand. A radish could not be left in salt because it would become a pickle, and pickling constituted work. Sick people were only allowed enough treatment to keep them alive. Any medical treatment that improved their condition was considered work and therefore prohibited. It was not even permissible for women to look in a mirror, since they might be tempted to pull out any gray hairs they spotted. Nor were they allowed to wear jewelry, since jewelry weighs more than a dried fig.

Other activities that were banned on the Sabbath included washing clothes, dyeing wool, shearing sheep, spinning wool, tying or untying a knot, sowing seed, plowing a field, reaping a harvest, binding sheaves, threshing wheat, grinding flour, kneading dough, hunting a deer, or preparing its meat. One of the more interesting restrictions related to the distance people could travel on the Sabbath. A person was not allowed to travel more than 3,000 feet from home (or to take more than 1,999 steps). Due to practical concerns, the rabbis devised creative ways to get around this. If one placed food at the 3,000-foot point before the Sabbath began, that point was considered an extension of one's home, thereby enabling a person to travel another 3,000 feet. Or, if a rope or piece of wood was placed across a narrow street or alley, it was considered a doorway—making it part of one's home and allowing the 3,000 feet of travel to begin there. Even in modern times, Jewish neighborhoods connect houses together using cords and ropes (known as an "eruv"). Doing so, from the perspective of rabbinic law, creates a single home out of every connected building—allowing people to move freely within the defined area without being limited to the 3,000-foot restriction, and to carry certain household items like keys, medicine, strollers, canes, and babies. (For a detailed discussion of the rabbinic Sabbath restrictions, see Alfred Edersheim, "The Ordinances and Law of the Sabbath as Laid Down in the Mishnah and the Jerusalem Talmud," appendix XVII in, *The Life and Times of Jesus the Messiah* [Grand Rapids: Eerdmans, 1974], 2:777–87.)

The man-made traditions perpetuated by the Pharisees and scribes clearly placed a crushing weight on the people (cf. Matt. 15:3; 23:4; Luke 11:46; Acts 15:10). In contrast, Jesus welcomed His hearers with liberating words of true refreshment: "Come to Me, all who are weary and heavy-laden, and I will give you rest. Take My yoke upon you and learn from Me, for I am gentle and humble in heart, and you will find rest for your souls. For My yoke is easy and My burden is light" (Matt. 11:28–30). The Lord was not talking about relieving physical labor. Rather, He was offering freedom to those under the burden of an oppressive, sabbatarian legalism from which they could get no relief and which could not gain them salvation

As a side note, it is important to understand that observing the

Sabbath is not required of believers in the church age (Col. 2:16; cf. Rom. 14:5–6; Gal. 4:9–10). The early church set aside Sunday, the first day of the week, as the day on which it gathered for worship, instruction, and fellowship (cf. Acts 20:7; 1 Cor. 16:2). However, it is not accurate to equate the "Lord's Day" (Sunday) with the Old Testament Sabbath, since the New Testament abrogates the Sabbath completely. Still this instruction by our Lord regarding that day (in Mark 2:23–28) contains rich christological truths for the church.

In this passage, Mark records the first of two incidents in which Christ directly challenged the Pharisees' false understanding of the Sabbath. The second incident (recorded in Mark 3:1–6) took place in the synagogue. This incident (2:23–28), which probably happened one week earlier as Jesus and His disciples were walking through some grain fields, can be understood under four headings: the Sabbath incident (v. 23), the scornful indictment (v. 24), the scriptural illustration (vv. 25–26), and the sovereign interpreter (vv. 27–28).

THE SABBATH INCIDENT

And it happened that He was passing through the grainfields on the Sabbath, and His disciples began to make their way along while picking the heads of grain. (2:23)

On this particular Sabbath, Jesus and His disciples were walking through fields where grain was growing. The Pharisees were dogging His steps carefully. As **He was passing through the grainfields on the Sabbath,** some of **His disciples** became hungry (Matt. 12:1). And so, they **began to make their way along while picking the heads of grain.** Luke adds that they were "rubbing them in their hands, and eating the grain" (Luke 6:1). The crop being grown in these particular fields was probably wheat or barley. In Israel, grain ripens from April to August, indicating that this event likely took place in spring or summer.

In the ancient world, it was normal for pathways to crisscross fields, so travelers traversed through crops routinely. Roads were scarce, especially in rural places, so travel usually took place on wide paths that stretched from one town to the next, passing through fields and pastures. As they journeyed on their way, people walked alongside the crops that lined both sides of the path. In light of this, God had prescribed a provision for His people. According to Deuteronomy 23:25, "When you enter your neighbor's standing grain, then you may pluck the heads with your hand, but you shall not wield a sickle in your neighbor's standing grain." To harvest someone else's grain (with a sickle) was not permitted for obvious reasons. To pluck a few heads of grain while walking beside a ripened field of wheat or barley was a provision made by God Himself.

Jesus' disciples were doing exactly what the Old Testament permitted them to do. When they picked off the heads of grain, rubbed the heads in their hands to remove the husk and shell, and then ate the kernel, their actions were perfectly allowable within the purposes of God, but not in the minds of religious Jews.

THE SCORNFUL INDICTMENT

The Pharisees were saying to Him, "Look, why are they doing what is not lawful on the Sabbath?" (2:24)

It is hard to imagine how the Pharisees could have followed Jesus through the grain fields while staying within 3,000 feet of their homes. Whatever the justification for their own transgressions, they observed Jesus' disciples violating rabbinic law and became incensed. They charged the disciples with **doing what is not lawful.** As noted, Jesus and His followers had not transgressed any biblical law. The Pharisees had elevated their own man-made tradition over Scripture (cf. Matt. 15:3, 6). They established themselves as the authority over Sabbath-day observances, usurping the rightful position of the only true Lord of the Sabbath—as Jesus would soon make clear.

When the Pharisees saw what the disciples were doing, they were outraged. Offended that Jesus would allow His followers to commit such a blatant violation, they **were saying to Him, "Look, why are they doing what is not lawful on the Sabbath?"** According to Luke 6:2, they did not limit their attack only to the disciples but targeted Jesus as well. The only law being transgressed was that of the Pharisees. By rabbinic standards, the disciples were guilty of several forbidden actions: reaping (by picking the grain), sifting (by removing the husks and shell), threshing (by rubbing the heads of grain), winnowing (by throwing the chaff in the air), and preparing a meal (by eating the grain after they had cleaned it). None of those activities were permitted on the Sabbath.

Not concerned about the hunger or well-being of Jesus' disciples, the Pharisees' only interest was in protecting the petty regulations that made up their hypocritical system of external religion. They followed Jesus to scrutinize His behavior, solely to find something for which to indict Him. The heart attitude behind their question was one of hatred toward Jesus, because He and His followers lived in such open defiance of their system of religion, in which the Sabbath was central.

THE SCRIPTURAL ILLUSTRATION

And He said to them, "Have you never read what David did when he was in need and he and his companions became hungry; how he entered the house of God in the time of Abiathar the high priest, and ate the consecrated bread, which is not lawful for anyone to eat except the priests, and he also gave it to those who were with him?" (2:25–26)

Without any apology, Jesus responded by challenging their authority and exposing their ignorance of the Old Testament. **He said to them, "Have you never read what David did when he was in need and he and his companions became hungry; how he entered the house of God in the time of Abiathar the high priest, and ate the consecrated bread, which is not lawful for anyone to eat except the priests, and he also gave it to those who were with him?"** Obviously, the Pharisees had read the story about David. But Jesus' words highlighted the fact that, even though they knew the facts of the story, they were ignorant of its true meaning. Thus, He responded to their question with one of His own: **Have you never read?** The rhetorical question exposed the inexcusable ignorance of those who were the self-proclaimed experts on Scripture and the teachers of Israel (cf. Matt. 19:4; 21:42; 22:31; Mark 12:10; John 3:10). In effect, Jesus was asking them, "If you are such fastidious students of Scripture, why don't you know what it says?"

The account to which Jesus referred is found in 1 Samuel 21:1–6. David, fleeing empty-handed from Gibeah to escape Saul, came to the tabernacle that was located at Nob, about a mile north of Jerusalem. Hungry and without proper provisions, David asked Ahimelech, the priest, for food.

> The priest answered David and said, "There is no ordinary bread on hand, but there is consecrated bread; if only the young men have kept themselves from women." David answered the priest and said to him, "Surely women have been kept from us as previously when I set out and the vessels of the young men were holy, though it was an ordinary journey; how much more then today will their vessels be holy?" So the priest gave him consecrated bread; for there was no bread there but the bread of the Presence which was removed from before the Lord, in order to put hot bread in its place when it was taken away. (1 Sam. 21:4–6)

The only bread at the tabernacle was "the bread of the Presence" (Ex. 25:30). Every Sabbath, twelve loaves of consecrated bread were baked and set on the gold table in the Holy Place. After the fresh loaves were placed, the priests were allowed to eat the week-old bread, but no one else was permitted to eat it (Lev. 24:9). Recognizing their need, Ahimelech showed compassion to David and his men by making an exception and giving them the consecrated bread. His only condition was that "the young men [must] have kept themselves from women" so that they would be ceremonially clean. Significantly, God did not punish either Ahimelech or David for their actions. He allowed a ceremonial law to be violated for the sake of meeting an urgent human need. In fact, the only person offended by Ahimelech's act of kindness was the volatile King Saul (1 Sam. 22:11–18).

Jesus' point, as illustrated by the Old Testament account, was that showing compassion, in God's sight, always trumped strict adherence to ritual and ceremony. His illustration employed the familiar rabbinic style of arguing from the lesser to the greater. If it was permissible for Ahimelech, a human priest, to make an exception to God's ceremonial law in order to aid David and his men, it was surely appropriate for the Son of God to disregard unbiblical rabbinic tradition in order to meet the needs of His disciples. The religious leaders were far more concerned with preserving their own authority than with the needs of anyone else. In a similar way to Saul's pursuit of David to kill him, the Pharisees were already seeking to put the Son of David to death.

According to Matthew's account (12:5–6), Jesus also told the Pharisees, "Or have you not read in the Law, that on the Sabbath the priests in the temple break the Sabbath and are innocent? But I say to you that something greater than the temple is here." By pointing to the example of the priests, Jesus demonstrated the inconsistency of the Pharisees' own legalistic standard. Each Sabbath, the ministering priests were required to light fires for the altar and slaughter animals for sacrifice (cf. Num. 28:9–10; cf. Lev. 24:8–9). These activities clearly violated the rabbinic restrictions for what was permissible on the Sabbath. Yet, the Pharisees exonerated the priests of any wrongdoing. Even under the Pharisees' own hyperlegalistic standard, some Sabbath violations were allowable and even considered necessary.

The Lord's statement that "something greater than the temple is here" was nothing less than a statement of His deity. The only One greater than the temple (which symbolized the presence of God among His people) was God Himself. As the One greater than the temple, Jesus wielded the divine authority to condemn the practices of the Pharisees.

THE SOVEREIGN INTERPRETER

Jesus said to them, "The Sabbath was made for man, and not man for the Sabbath. So the Son of Man is Lord even of the Sabbath." (2:27–28)

God never intended ceremony, ritual, and tradition to stand in the way of mercy, kindness, and goodness toward others. Thus, Jesus explained to the Pharisees that even originally **the Sabbath was made for man, and not man for the Sabbath.** God's purpose for the Sabbath day was to give His people a weekly rest. But the Pharisees had turned a divine blessing into a dreaded burden.

Matthew 12:7 notes that Jesus also told the Pharisees, "But if you had known what this means, 'I desire compassion, and not a sacrifice,' you would not have condemned the innocent." Quoting from a portion of Hosea 6:6, Jesus reminded His hearers that God designed the Sabbath to be a merciful day of spiritual reflection and physical recuperation for the people. By turning it into a burdensome day of restrictive observance, the Pharisees obscured its true purpose. The reality was that they were the real violators of the Sabbath. Their indifference to the needs of Jesus' disciples, and their feigned indignation over the fact that their customs had been violated, demonstrated the bankruptcy and ungodliness of their religion.

The conflict was already at a fevered pitch when Jesus escalated the matter even higher. In verse 28, He declared to them, **"So the Son of Man is Lord even of the Sabbath."** Without caveat or apology, Jesus claimed to be the sovereign ruler over the Sabbath. If there had been any ambiguity about His earlier claim, that "something greater than the temple is here" (Matt. 12:6), it was gone. Jesus was clearly claiming to be God, the Creator, and the One who designated the Sabbath in the first place and the sovereign over it (cf. John 1:1–3). He was the **Son of Man,** a messianic title from Daniel 7:13–14, the divine King who created the Sabbath and defined its parameters. The Pharisees prided themselves on being the authoritative interpreters of God's Word and will. In their midst stood the One whose interpretation was infinitely more authoritative: the Son of God Himself.

As God in human flesh, He condemned their self-righteous attempts to please God. He was characterized by grace; they prided themselves on their works. He demonstrated mercy and compassion to people; they cared only about protecting their petty customs. He exemplified the true purpose of the Sabbath; they twisted a divine blessing into a dismal day of drudgery.

For the Pharisees, the Sabbath belonged to them. For centuries they had been working out its rules. When Jesus elevated Himself far above them and their rules by declaring Himself to be the Lord of the Sabbath, their hostility and hatred could not be satisfied until they had Him murdered.

The Lord of the Sabbath—Part 2 (Mark 3:1–6)

11

He entered again into a synagogue; and a man was there whose hand was withered. They were watching Him to see if He would heal him on the Sabbath, so that they might accuse Him. He said to the man with the withered hand, "Get up and come forward!" And He said to them, "Is it lawful to do good or to do harm on the Sabbath, to save a life or to kill?" But they kept silent. After looking around at them with anger, grieved at their hardness of heart, He said to the man, "Stretch out your hand." And he stretched it out, and his hand was restored. The Pharisees went out and immediately began conspiring with the Herodians against Him, as to how they might destroy Him. (3:1–6)

For centuries, the nation of Israel had eagerly awaited the coming of the Messiah. His advent was anticipated at the beginning and end of the Old Testament (Gen. 3:15; 49:10; Mal. 3:1–6; cf. 4:5–6), and many places in between (cf. Pss. 2:1–12; 16:7–11; 22:1–31; 110:1–6; 118:22–23; Isa. 7:14; 9:6–7; 11:1–10; 42:1–9; 49:1–7; 50:4–10; 52:13–53:12; Dan. 9:24–27;

Mic. 5:2; Zech. 9:9; 12:10–13:1). Yet, when the long-anticipated Messiah arrived, Israel rejected Him. As the apostle John explains, "He came to His own, and those who were His own did not receive Him" (John 1:11). Rather than embracing their long-awaited deliverer, the people turned against Him—eventually crying out for His public execution (Matt. 27:22–23).

Perhaps most surprisingly, those leading the campaign against the Messiah were none other than Israel's religious leaders, the self-proclaimed experts on the promised, Anointed One. In spite of the indisputable miracles Jesus performed, the leaders only grew more and more resentful toward Him. They hated Him, not because He healed people or cast out demons but because He challenged their authority, violated their customs, and claimed to be the Son of God. They were especially infuriated by His claim to deity—an assertion they regarded as blasphemous and worthy of punishment by death. John 10:31–33 records their reaction to Jesus on one such occasion:

> The Jews picked up stones again to stone Him. Jesus answered them, "I showed you many good works from the Father; for which of them are you stoning Me?" The Jews answered Him, "For a good work we do not stone You, but for blasphemy; and because You, being a man, make Yourself out to be God."

Yet, Jesus validated His claim to be God by repeatedly demonstrating His divine power for all to see. As He told the Jews in John 10, "If I do not do the works of My Father, do not believe Me; but if I do them, though you do not believe Me, believe the works, so that you may know and understand that the Father is in Me, and I in the Father" (vv. 37–38).

The Old Testament also established the necessity for Jesus' lofty claim by indicating that the Messiah would be divine (cf. Pss. 2:7–12; 110:1; Prov. 30:4; Dan. 7:13–14; Jer. 23:5–6; Mic. 5:2). Isaiah 9:6 asserts His deity without qualification: "For a child will be born to us, a son will be given to us; and the government will rest on His shoulders; and His name will be called Wonderful Counselor, Mighty God, Eternal Father, Prince of Peace." Yet, blinded by their own traditions and hardness of heart, the Jewish guardians of Scripture refused to accept what was right in front of them (cf. John 5:39–40). Rather than acknowledging Jesus' miracles as signs of His deity, they explained them away in the most extreme fashion by suggesting that He was actually empowered by Satan (Matt. 12:24).

The message Jesus proclaimed was "the gospel of God" (Mark 1:14), the good news from heaven of forgiveness, salvation, and eternal life by divine grace. It brought sight to the spiritually blind, life to the spiritually dead, and freedom to those in spiritual bondage (cf. Luke 4:18). No invitation could be better: the kingdom of God was open to all who would repent and believe in the Lord Jesus. It was the best news the world has ever received. Yet it caused the religious leaders of Israel to recoil.

Jesus preached salvation bestowed by God's grace on sinners whom He justified even though they had done nothing to merit His favor (cf. Luke 18:9–14). The concept of justification by grace through faith, apart from works, ran contrary to apostate Judaism. The religion of the Pharisees centered on their own ability to become worthy of entering the kingdom of God by means of their own meticulous legalism. Jesus attacked such spiritual pride, explaining that eternal life actually comes only to those who humble themselves, confess their unworthiness, and turn from their sin (cf. Matt. 5:3–10). When tax collectors, prostitutes, criminals, and other social outcasts embraced the gospel Jesus preached, it only made the religious leaders more resentful (cf. Matt. 9:10–11; 11:19; Luke 15:1–2).

On the outside, the Pharisees and scribes—along with those who followed them—did maintain superficial adherence to the Mosaic law. They avoided outward acts of idolatry, murder, and adultery. Yet, on the inside, they were full of sin and conceit (cf. Matt. 23:27). In their hearts, they had violated all of the Ten Commandments, which is why Jesus' words in the Sermon on the Mount struck such a severe blow to their trust in externalism:

> "For I say to you that unless your righteousness surpasses that of the scribes and Pharisees, you will not enter the kingdom of heaven. You have heard that the ancients were told, 'You shall not commit murder' and 'Whoever commits murder shall be liable to the court.' But I say to you that everyone who is angry with his brother shall be guilty before the court; and whoever says to his brother, 'You good-for-nothing,' shall be guilty before the supreme court; and whoever says, 'You fool,' shall be guilty enough to go into the fiery hell. . . . You have heard that it was said, 'You shall not commit adultery'; but I say to you that everyone who

looks at a woman with lust for her has already committed adultery with her in his heart." (Matt. 5:20–22, 27–28)

The Lord's point was that true righteousness starts on the inside. Outward conformity to the law is not sufficient to save.

Before his conversion on the road to Damascus, the apostle Paul had been a devoted and fastidious Pharisee. In terms of external adherence to the law, he declared that he was blameless (Phil. 3:6). Yet, internally, he was full of covetousness, spiritual pride, and misplaced anger (Acts 9:1; Rom. 7:8; Phil. 3:4). Only after God transformed his heart did Paul come to realize that true righteousness came not from his own religious achievements but as a gift from God through faith in Christ. As he made clear to the Philippians:

> More than that, I count all things to be loss in view of the surpassing value of knowing Christ Jesus my Lord, for whom I have suffered the loss of all things, and count them but rubbish so that I may gain Christ, and may be found in Him, not having a righteousness of my own derived from the Law, but that which is through faith in Christ, the righteousness which comes from God on the basis of faith, that I may know Him and the power of His resurrection and the fellowship of His sufferings, being conformed to His death; in order that I may attain to the resurrection from the dead. (Phil. 3:8–11).

The Pharisees hated Jesus because He exposed them as hypocrites and denounced them as frauds. They were false shepherds, leading the people astray (cf. Ezek. 34:1–10). As the true Shepherd (Ezek. 34:11–25; John 10:7–16), He repudiated them and the spiritual façade they propagated. They were advocates of spiritual darkness (John 3:19). As the light of the world (John 8:12), He shone the spotlight of truth on their egregious errors.

The zenith of the Pharisees' manifestation of spiritual pride and hypocrisy was on the Sabbath. On that day, all of their self-righteous externalism peaked. The problem was not with the Sabbath itself. God had established the Sabbath as a day of worship and rest for Israel in the fourth commandment (Ex. 20:8–11). But over the centuries, the rabbis had developed hundreds of extrabiblical rules for Sabbath conduct. They overlaid laws upon laws, rituals upon routines, rules upon restrictions, and requirements upon restraints. Oozing with sanctimonious pride, the Pharisees used the Sabbath as a day to parade their own self-righteousness. They elevated themselves above the common people by flaunting their strict adherence to rabbinic traditions. Meanwhile, the people were smothered under the crushing burden of Pharisaic legalism. The rabbinic web of extrabiblical stipulations and meticulous details made the Sabbath an unbearable burden (cf. Matt. 23:4). They took a day designed for rest and refreshment and turned it into day of drudgery and oppression. (For more on the rabbinic rules and restrictions regarding the Sabbath, see chapter 10 in this volume.)

Since their distorted version of the Sabbath was central to their religious system, Jesus had to address the corrupted seventh day to expose the spiritual bankruptcy and error of the Pharisees and scribes. And that is exactly what He did, both in word and in deed. He publicly defied the unbiblical rules and artificial regulations invented by the rabbis, and the religious leaders resented Him deeply for it.

This section (Mark 3:1–6) continues the theme of the previous passage (Mark 2:23–28). Both focus on the conflict that ensued between Jesus and the Pharisees regarding acceptable behavior on the Sabbath. In the first passage, Jesus' disciples were seen violating rabbinic rules. When the Pharisees protested, Jesus declared Himself to be the Lord of the Sabbath (v. 28), which was a claim to be God. As John explains, speaking of an earlier occasion in the ministry of Christ, "For this reason therefore the Jews were seeking all the more to kill Him, because He not only was breaking the Sabbath, but also was calling God His own Father, making Himself equal with God" (John 5:18). The Pharisees and scribes were livid with Jesus, but He spoke the truth. As God in human flesh, He was the Lord of the Sabbath. And as the Lord of the Sabbath, He was determined to demonstrate proper Sabbath observance ordered in Scripture, while denouncing man-made rules.

Since these two events (from Mark 2:23–28 and 3:1–6) are connected in all three of the Synoptic Gospels (Matt. 12:1–14; Luke 6:1–11), it is possible that they occurred in close proximity to each other, perhaps on two subsequent Sabbaths. The first took place in the countryside, the second in the synagogue. This incident (Mark 3:1–6) can be divided into three parts: the context, the confrontation, and the conspiracy.

The Context

He entered again into a synagogue; and a man was there whose hand was withered. They were watching Him to see if He would heal him on the Sabbath, so that they might accuse Him. (3:1–2)

In an unspecified Galilean city, Jesus **entered again into a synagogue** where, according to Luke 6:6, He "was teaching" as He always did (cf. Mark 1:21; 2:2). The crowds were continually amazed by the teaching of Christ (Matt. 7:29; Mark 1:22; Luke 4:32), and this occasion would have been no exception. He taught with authority, unlike the scribes and Pharisees who were more interested in citing the opinions of other rabbis than in clearly expounding the biblical text (cf. Matt. 7:29). Moreover, the content of His message was unlike anything the people had ever heard. He emphasized repentance, humility, faith, and true righteousness. How different that was from the esoteric and allegorical ramblings of the rabbis. It is no wonder that, whenever Jesus preached, "all the people were hanging on to every word He said" (Luke 19:48).

In the midst of the congregation gathered at the synagogue that day, **a man was there whose hand was withered.** Luke, the physician, notes that it was his right hand (Luke 6:6). Given that most people are right handed, this condition would have been debilitating. The text does not explain what caused this man's affliction—whether it was an accident or a disease. The Greek word translated **withered** (*xerainō*) is a term that refers to atrophy. It is used of dead plants that have dried up and wasted away, suggesting that his hand was neurologically lifeless or incapacitated.

Since even normal manual tasks would have been extremely difficult to perform, it is likely that this man was unable to earn a living. An old tradition suggests that he was a stonemason who had lost the ability to work and been reduced to begging. However unlikely that tradition, this man was experiencing a severe limitation. At the same time, however, the man's condition was not life-threatening. Jesus could have waited until after the Sabbath to heal him, but the Lord was intent on making a spiritual point. He deliberately chose not to postpone the man's healing, because He wanted to confront the unbiblical restrictions contrived by the rabbis. As on other occasions, He intentionally healed this man on the Sabbath (Luke 4:31–35; 13:10–17; 14:1–6; John 5:1–9; 9:1–14).

The Pharisees and scribes, well aware of Jesus' antagonism toward their religious system, **were watching Him to see if He would heal him on the Sabbath, so that they might accuse Him.** This was no casual observation. It was intensive, sinister scrutiny. Perhaps they had even arranged for the injured man to be in attendance at the synagogue that day, hoping to trap Jesus in the act of violating the Sabbath. Outwardly, they pretended to protect the Sabbath. Inwardly, they desperately wanted Jesus to break their Sabbath traditions so that they could discredit Him.

The Pharisees and scribes knew what the Old Testament specified. Over the centuries, they had developed additional rules and traditions—including restrictions on what level of care could be given to those who were sick or injured. Unless a person's life was at stake, the rabbis determined that doing anything to improve someone's physical condition constituted work. The most a physician or relative was permitted to do on the Sabbath was keep the sick person alive, or maintain the status quo of their condition, until the following day. Anything more than that was regarded as work, and therefore a violation.

On that basis, if Jesus healed the man, He would be violating Sabbath restrictions. They obviously did not care about the physical well-being of the disabled man. Nor did they care about the unprecedented, supernatural power that Jesus would display by healing the man's hand. Their only concern was with whether or not Jesus would break their petty traditions. If He did, they could indict Him as a Sabbath violator—an irreligious blasphemer who deserved to be condemned. Jesus, of course, perceived the hostility of their hearts. According to Luke 6:8, "He knew what they were thinking." He recognized that this was a trap. But rather than avoiding the conflict, He sought it.

THE CONFRONTATION

He said to the man with the withered hand, "Get up and come forward!" And He said to them, "Is it lawful to do good or to do harm on the Sabbath, to save a life or to kill?" But they kept

silent. After looking around at them with anger, grieved at their hardness of heart, He said to the man, "Stretch out your hand." And he stretched it out, and his hand was restored. (3:3–5)

Knowing what the Pharisees were secretly plotting, Jesus initiated the showdown. He did not shy away or back down. He was in complete control of the situation. Not only was He the Lord of the Sabbath in a general sense (2:28), He was the Lord of that particular Sabbath and everything that would transpire that very day.

Significantly, the man with the withered hand did not initiate contact with Jesus. In fact, there is no record that the man ever said anything to the Lord. There is no indication that he asked to be healed. Rather, it was Jesus who called him out of the crowd. **He said to the man with the withered hand, "Get up and come forward!"** As He finished His teaching, Jesus commanded the injured man to come to the front of the synagogue. The man, perhaps startled by the unexpected invitation, obeyed.

According to Matthew's account, it was the Pharisees who began asking Jesus about what He intended to do:

> And they questioned Jesus, asking, "Is it lawful to heal on the Sabbath?"—so that they might accuse Him. And He said to them, "What man is there among you who has a sheep, and if it falls into a pit on the Sabbath, will he not take hold of it and lift it out? How much more valuable then is a man than a sheep! So then, it is lawful to do good on the Sabbath." (Matt. 12:10–12)

Jesus responded to their question with a general analogy, arguing from the lesser to the greater. If it is permissible to help a sheep on the Sabbath, how could it be wrong to help a human being, whose worth far exceeds that of an animal? No Pharisee would have argued that sheep were more valuable than people, since human beings were created in the image of God (Gen. 1:26–27). Yet, in practice, the Pharisees treated their livestock with more compassion than they treated other people. Incredibly, they would sooner suspend their religious traditions to help an animal than aid another person.

Recognizing the duplicity of their question, Jesus turned it back on His interrogators. **He said to them, "Is it lawful to do good or to**

do harm on the Sabbath, to save a life or to kill?" The question was a powerful charge against them on at least three levels. First, it exposed the unlawful nature of their extrabiblical restrictions and traditions. Clearly, the Old Testament law encouraged people to do good and prohibited them from doing harm. But the rabbinic regulations of the Pharisees caused harm to those trying to follow them. As such, it was the Pharisees and not Jesus who were violating God's law. Second, the question exposed their calloused attitude toward suffering and pain. They were more interested in bringing harm on Jesus than they were in helping the suffering man. Finally, the question targeted the Pharisees' plot against the Lord. How ironic that the self-professed protectors of the Sabbath secretly wanted the Messiah Himself to violate their rabbinic restrictions so that they could one day put Him to death.

The revelation from God made it clear that He was more concerned with His people doing good and showing compassion to others than with their fastidious observance of religious ceremonies and rituals. Isaiah 1:11–17 makes that point unmistakable:

> "What are your multiplied sacrifices to Me?"
> Says the Lord.
> "I have had enough of burnt offerings of rams
> And the fat of fed cattle;
> And I take no pleasure in the blood of bulls, lambs or goats.
> When you come to appear before Me,
> Who requires of you this trampling of My courts?
> Bring your worthless offerings no longer,
> Incense is an abomination to Me.
> New moon and sabbath, the calling of assemblies—
> I cannot endure iniquity and the solemn assembly.
> I hate your new moon festivals and your appointed feasts,
> They have become a burden to Me;
> I am weary of bearing them.
> So when you spread out your hands in prayer,
> I will hide My eyes from you;
> Yes, even though you multiply prayers,
> I will not listen.
> Your hands are covered with blood.
> Wash yourselves, make yourselves clean;
> Remove the evil of your deeds from My sight.
> Cease to do evil,
> Learn to do good;

Seek justice,
Reprove the ruthless,
Defend the orphan,
Plead for the widow."

God took no pleasure in the sacrifices or Sabbaths of His people when they refused to do good or show kindness to others (cf. Isa. 58:6–14).

Jesus' question put His enemies on the horns of a dilemma. What could they say? If they agreed that it was lawful to do good and save a life, then they would be unable to accuse Jesus of any wrongdoing. Acknowledging that truth would have contradicted their rabbinic traditions while simultaneously affirming His act of healing as acceptable. On the other hand, if they claimed that it was lawful to do evil and to kill, they would have put themselves squarely at odds with the Old Testament. Moreover, they would have publicly admitted their own merciless wickedness. They found themselves caught in a logical contradiction resulting from their own unbiblical customs. In the end, they did the only thing they could do. **They kept silent.**

By framing the extremes, Jesus forced the Pharisees to shut their mouths. They knew what the Old Testament said. They knew the intent of the Sabbath was for good and not harm. The Lord's question forced them to grapple with the real issue. Who was honoring God? Was it the One who desired to show mercy and compassion toward people? Or was it those who ignored the suffering of others in order to maintain strict adherence to their own man-made regulations?

Having cornered them, Jesus underscored His point with a dramatic act. He paused and stared His enemies down, **looking around at them with anger.** As their silence filled the room, their consciences must have burned under the weight of His piercing gaze. There was no mistaking His point. Nor could they have missed the righteous indignation that filled His heart and flooded His countenance. Though Jesus was certainly angry at other times (cf. Matt. 21:12–13; John 2:15–17), this is the only place in the four Gospels where the text specifically states that Jesus was angry. In the same way that the Lord God was angry at the hard-heartedness of Israel in the Old Testament (cf. Num. 11:10; Josh. 7:1; Ps. 2:1–6), Jesus became angry toward the calloused unbelief of the Pharisees. In particular, He was **grieved at their hardness of heart.** He was filled with wrath toward their coldhearted unbelief. Yet, His wrath was inter-mingled with sorrow and sadness because of the necessary condemnation He knew would come upon them. Even in His anger toward them, Jesus was filled with pity, knowing the eternal destruction that awaited them on account of their stubborn rebellion (cf. Matt. 23:37–38; Luke 19:41–44).

Out of His grief at the Pharisees' unbelief, Jesus **said to the man, "Stretch out your hand."** The man complied. **And he stretched it out, and his hand was restored.** A buzz of excitement must have shot through the congregation, most of whom would have known the man with the withered hand. Not only were they amazed at Jesus' preaching and His willingness to openly defy the Pharisees, but He also performed an undeniable miracle (cf. Mark 1:27). In that moment, feeling surged back into the man's right hand. His strength returned and his grip was as good as it had ever been.

THE CONSPIRACY

The Pharisees went out and immediately began conspiring with the Herodians against Him, as to how they might destroy Him. (3:6)

One would think that even the Pharisees would have responded in faith after witnessing a supernatural healing like that. At the very least, it should have given them pause. Instead, their fury against Jesus escalated. According to Luke 6:11, "They themselves were filled with rage, and discussed together what they might do to Jesus." Fuming, because their authority had been publicly challenged, and unwilling to tolerate any such threat, they acted quickly: **the Pharisees went out and immediately began conspiring with the Herodians against Him, as to how they might destroy Him.**

The Pharisees, unmoved by the power of Jesus, refused to be convinced. Having placed their confidence in their self-righteous works and rabbinic traditions, they shut their hearts to both the Word of God and the Son of God. Unable to refute Jesus' arguments, and unable to deny the reality of His healing power, they **went out** from the synagogue embarrassed and outraged. In all likelihood, they would have tried to kill Jesus on the spot were it not for His popularity with the people. Moreover, Roman law prohibited them from exercising capital punishment on their own (cf. John 18:31). They were nonetheless determined to find a way to eliminate Jesus.

In their quest to kill the Messiah, **the Pharisees** found an interesting ally in **the Herodians.** The Herodians were an irreligious and worldly political group that supported the dynasty of Herod the Great and, by extension, Rome. These secular Jews were viewed by their fellow countrymen as loyal to Greco-Roman culture and traitors to their own religious heritage. They could not have been more different than the Pharisees, whom they normally regarded as their archenemies. These two groups found a common enemy in Jesus. The Pharisees hated Jesus because He openly opposed their hypocritical system of works-righteousness. The Herodians hated Jesus because His popularity with the people made Him a potential threat to the power of Herod and of Rome (cf. John 6:15; 19:12), which they supported. Consequently, both rejected God's Son.

The mercy Jesus displayed toward that man in the synagogue stands in stark contrast to the hatred displayed by the Pharisees toward their own Messiah. So intense was their fury toward Him that they joined forces with their religious enemies in order to plot His demise. They were willing to do whatever it took to get rid of Jesus. According to Matthew 12:15, the Lord knew what they were plotting: "But Jesus, aware of this, withdrew from there." Nonetheless, storm clouds had begun to gather on the horizon. They would soon break on Him on a hillside outside Jerusalem called Golgotha where He would give His life. Even in death, Jesus Christ would triumph, paying the penalty for sin and rising from the dead in victory. Because of that sacrifice, the Lord of the Sabbath offers heavenly rest to all who believe in Him (Heb. 4:9).

Mark's Sweeping Summary of Jesus' Ministry (Mark 3:7–19)

12

Jesus withdrew to the sea with His disciples; and a great multitude from Galilee followed; and also from Judea, and from Jerusalem, and from Idumea, and beyond the Jordan, and the vicinity of Tyre and Sidon, a great number of people heard of all that He was doing and came to Him. And He told His disciples that a boat should stand ready for Him because of the crowd, so that they would not crowd Him; for He had healed many, with the result that all those who had afflictions pressed around Him in order to touch Him. Whenever the unclean spirits saw Him, they would fall down before Him and shout, "You are the Son of God!" And He earnestly warned them not to tell who He was. And He went up on the mountain and summoned those whom He Himself wanted, and they came to Him. And He appointed twelve, so that they would be with Him and that He could send them out to preach, and to have authority to cast out the demons. And He appointed the twelve: Simon (to whom He gave the name Peter), and James, the son of Zebedee, and John the brother of James (to

them He gave the name Boanerges, which means, "Sons of Thunder"); and Andrew, and Philip, and Bartholomew, and Matthew, and Thomas, and James the son of Alphaeus, and Thaddaeus, and Simon the Zealot; and Judas Iscariot, who betrayed Him. (3:7–19)

Mark introduced his gospel history by identifying Jesus Christ as the Son of God (1:1). That declaration was affirmed by testimony from the Old Testament prophets (1:2–3), John the Baptist (1:4–9), and even God Himself (1:10–11). It was further validated by the miraculous works that Jesus performed. Throughout the course of His ministry, Jesus repeatedly demonstrated His deity through visible displays of divine power: over Satan (1:12–13), demons (1:23–27), disease (1:30–34), sin (2:5–12), and the Sabbath (2:23–3:6). Even His disciples immediately left everything to obey His summons (1:18, 20; 2:14). Time after time, as Jesus exercised His divine power, He gave incontrovertible proof that He is who He claimed to be: the incarnate Son of God and Savior of the world.

In this section (3:7–19), Mark offers a sweeping summary of Jesus' ministry—highlighting in succinct fashion key themes he has already articulated. Specifically, these verses focus on three facets of the Lord's ministry: His popular appeal with the crowds (vv. 7–9), His power and authority over the demons (vv. 10–12), and His personal appointing of the Twelve (vv. 13–19). These three themes revolve around and add weight to the central theological truth of verse 11, which says of Jesus, "You are the Son of God."

POPULAR APPEAL

Jesus withdrew to the sea with His disciples; and a great multitude from Galilee followed; and also from Judea, and from Jerusalem, and from Idumea, and beyond the Jordan, and the vicinity of Tyre and Sidon, a great number of people heard of all that He was doing and came to Him. And He told His disciples that a boat should stand ready for Him because of the crowd, so that they would not crowd Him; (3:7–9)

After Jesus' showdown with the Pharisees in the synagogue, Mark 3:6 explains: "The Pharisees went out and immediately began conspiring with the Herodians against Him, as to how they might destroy Him." Fully aware of their plot, Jesus **withdrew to the sea with His disciples,** knowing it was not yet God's time for Him to be arrested and crucified (cf. John 7:8, 30; 12:23). In order to avoid His enemies, He distanced Himself from them by traveling along the north end of the Sea of Galilee to an isolated place.

At this point, **His disciples** consisted of an unknown number of followers. The Greek word *mathētēs* (disciple) means "learner" or "student" and refers to those who had moved beyond an initial interest in Jesus and desired to follow Him as their teacher. During His earthly ministry, Jesus had numerous disciples, many of whom were superficial and would not remain with Him (cf. John 2:23–25; 6:66). Yet, scattered among this crowd were those men who later became the twelve apostles. Jesus had already called Peter, Andrew, James, John, Philip, Nathaniel, and Matthew to be His disciples (1:16–20; 2:13–14; John 1:35–51). Soon, Thomas, James the son of Alphaeus, Thaddaeus, Simon the Zealot, and Judas Iscariot would be added to that list (3:18–19).

By leaving the city, Jesus escaped His enemies for the time being. But He did not escape the relentless crowds. In fact, **a great multitude from Galilee followed; and also from Judea, and from Jerusalem, and from Idumea, and beyond the Jordan, and the vicinity of Tyre and Sidon, a great number of people heard of all that He was doing and came to Him.** The double use of **great** likely indicates thousands if not tens of thousands of people. The size of the **multitude** was indicative of the fact that Jesus' fame had been spreading over the small region of Galilee and throughout Israel (cf. 1:28). His popularity made it difficult for Him to minister publicly in urban areas (1:45). Consequently, He often taught by the Sea of Galilee (2:13), away from the population centers. Even so, such crowds found Him.

Mark underscores the scope of Jesus' popularity by noting the various geographical regions represented in the throng of people who pressed to see Him. Some were from the south—**from Judea, from Jerusalem,** and even farther south, **from Idumea.** Others came from the east, from **beyond the Jordan.** Still more traveled from the northwestern **vicinity**

of Tyre and Sidon, a predominantly Gentile area, to join with the fasci-
nated masses **from Galilee.** Jesus' popularity had no equal in the history
of Israel. Even King Herod was intrigued by the news about Him (Luke
23:8; cf. Matt. 14:1–2).

Those who ventured out to see Jesus experienced miraculous
displays unlike anything in history. The blind were given sight, the crippled walked, the deaf heard, the sick were made well, and the leprous
cleansed. It was wonder upon wonder, beyond what anyone could have
ever imagined. In an era nearly two thousand years before the development of modern medicine in the nineteenth century, Jesus banished disease and its effects from the land of Israel for the duration of His ministry.
With nothing more than a word and a touch, He brought immediate,
complete healing and restoration to those who suffered from even the
most debilitating defects, diseases, and disabilities. In addition, demon-
possessed souls were delivered instantly.

People from every region around Israel, even the bordering Gentile areas, flooded into Galilee, bringing sick family members and desperate friends to Jesus. The Lord's miracles were public and undeniable,
which is why the people kept coming. No one questioned His miracles.
There is no record of any effort to deny any of them. Even His enemies,
who would have strongly desired to discredit the reality of His miracles,
never suggested they were not factual. Yet, they refused to believe in Him.
Unable to deny Jesus' power, these stubborn unbelievers attempted to discredit His person by attributing the source of His power to Satan (3:22).

Despite such sinister accusations, the religious leaders could not
keep the people away from Jesus. At times the crowds were so dense that
Jesus **told His disciples that a boat should stand ready for Him
because of the crowd, so that they would not crowd Him.** In order
to avoid being crushed by the swarms of people, all of whom were pressing to be close to Him, Jesus would sometimes get into a small boat and
be pushed out away from the shore. Mark 4:1 records such an incident,
"He began to teach again by the sea. And such a very large crowd gathered to Him that He got into a boat in the sea and sat down; and the
whole crowd was by the sea on the land." On such occasions, the separation allowed Him to accomplish His priority of preaching the good news
of the kingdom.

Most of the people who comprised the swarming crowds were eager to experience Jesus' miracles. Though they were attracted by His powerful works, they were simultaneously offended by His piercing words. Even many of His disciples ultimately rejected His message and permanently deserted Him (cf. John 6:60–69). Sadly, in the end, Jesus Himself would pronounce judgment on the unbelief of the vast majority who had experienced His miracles and heard Him preach the truth of God (cf. Matt. 7:13–14, 21–23; 11:21–24).

POWER AND AUTHORITY

For He had healed many, with the result that all those who had afflictions pressed around Him in order to touch Him. Whenever the unclean spirits saw Him, they would fall down before Him and shout, "You are the Son of God!" And He earnestly warned them not to tell who He was. (3:10–12)

Jesus' popular appeal with the people was fueled by His miracles, though popularity was not His goal. As manifestations of His divine power, His supernatural works were signs that authenticated His salvation message (cf. John 5:36; 10:38) as the divine messianic King. Most of the miracles Jesus performed were acts of healing (cf. Matt. 8:5–13; 9:32–33; Mark 1:30–31, 40–44; 2:3–12; 5:25–34; 8:22–26; 9:17–29; 10:46–52; Luke 13:10–17; 14:1–4; 17:11–19; 22:50–51; John 4:46–54; 5:1–15; 9:1–41). Those creative miracles required the instant reversal of disease and decay and the immediate restoration of the human body. For Jesus, the Creator of the universe (John 1:3), no sickness or disability proved too difficult to heal. He instantly created new limbs and organs—restoring eyes, ears, hands, feet, and bodies to full health and function.

The result was **that all those who had afflictions pressed around Him in order to touch Him.** The Greek word translated **afflictions** (*mastix*) literally refers to a scourge or a whip. Used figuratively, it was employed by the Jews to speak of a calamity or misfortune sent by God as a punishment. In first-century Judaism, it was common to interpret disease and disability as the judgment of God (Luke 13:2; John 9:2;

Acts 28:4). Many of those suffering from physical ailments interpreted their hardship as God's displeasure toward them. That notion made some particularly receptive to the good news of salvation. Jesus not only offered them physical healing but also spiritual healing—forgiveness from sin, reconciliation with God, and the hope of eternal life (cf. 2:1–12).

The people **pressed** tightly around Jesus, hoping just **to touch Him** in order to be healed (cf. 1:41). As Mark 6:56 reports regarding a later point in Jesus' ministry: "Wherever He entered villages, or cities, or countryside, they were laying the sick in the market places, and imploring Him that they might just touch the fringe of His cloak; and as many as touched it were being cured." They had learned that Jesus' power was so available and effective that merely putting a hand on Him could produce instant and total healing.

Along with healing diseases, Jesus also cast out demons. **Whenever the unclean spirits saw Him, they would fall down before Him and shout, "You are the Son of God!" And He earnestly warned them not to tell who He was.** The agents of Satan were everywhere, as always covertly working to destroy the souls of those under their influence. Though demons prefer to hide, masquerading as angels of light (cf. 2 Cor. 11:14), they were unable to conceal themselves from Jesus. In His presence, they panicked, falling **down before Him and** blurting out His identity (Mark 1:24; cf. James 2:19): **"You are the Son of God!"** They fearfully recognized Him for who He truly was, the Sovereign of the universe (cf. Mark 6:6–7). Though their declaration of His identity was theologically correct, Jesus was not looking for publicity from demons (cf. Acts 16:16–18). He desired no promotion or testimony from the realm of Satan, so **He earnestly warned them not to tell who He was.** Jesus' authority over demons underscores His divine nature. Not only did they recognize Him as the Son of God, but when He cast them out, they fled under His authority. When He told them to be quiet, they obeyed. Though they were His most vicious enemies, they were constrained to submit to His commands.

Jesus' unparalleled, unheard of power over the demons caused the people to wonder who He was (cf. 1:27). Who possessed such authority? Who could banish both demons and disease? Who was this Man? Mark's history has repeatedly answered such queries: He is none other than the Son of God. The Father declared that reality at His baptism (1:11), and even the demons could not help but acknowledge it when He confronted them (3:11). Eventually, Jesus' closest disciples would come to understand that same truth (8:29). The nation of Israel as a whole never did. Under the influence of their apostate religious leaders, the people rejected Jesus, refusing to confess Him as divine Messiah and King.

Personal Appointments

And He went up on the mountain and summoned those whom He Himself wanted, and they came to Him. And He appointed twelve, so that they would be with Him and that He could send them out to preach, and to have authority to cast out the demons. And He appointed the twelve: Simon (to whom He gave the name Peter), and James, the son of Zebedee, and John the brother of James (to them He gave the name Boanerges, which means, "Sons of Thunder"); and Andrew, and Philip, and Bartholomew, and Matthew, and Thomas, and James the son of Alphaeus, and Thaddaeus, and Simon the Zealot; and Judas Iscariot, who betrayed Him. (3:13–19)

Mark transitions from the popularity and power of Jesus to focus on a select group of His disciples. These twelve men, some of whom Mark has already introduced (1:16–20; 2:14–15), were personally chosen by Jesus as His apostles, who would be His legal representatives and royal ambassadors, even after He was gone.

When Jesus selected the Twelve, He was making a statement of judgment on Israel's unbelief. The caretakers of apostate Judaism had totally rejected Him. The Sadducees resented Him for cleansing the temple and exposing their system of greed and corruption (John 2:14–18). The Pharisees and scribes wanted Him dead for opposing their Sabbath observances and for claiming equality with God (John 5:18). Even the secularist Herodians agreed that Jesus was an agitator who had be eliminated (Mark 3:6). When the leaders of Israel rejected God's Son, God rejected them. The Pharisees and scribes, along with the Sadducees, had demonstrated their unworthiness as the shepherds of Israel (cf. Ezek. 34:1–10). The religious nobility and rabbinic academy of Judaism was altogether unqualified to represent God. They misrepresented the Old Testament, corrupted the people, and produced sons of hell (Matt. 23:15). They thought they were enlightened about God, but in reality they were "blind leaders of the blind" (Matt. 15:14 KJV). They perceived themselves to be the protectors and purveyors of God's Word, when in truth, they had substituted the traditions of men for the commandments of God (Mark 7:6–13). Though they convinced themselves that they were pleasing the God of their fathers, they were actually children "of [their] father, the devil" (John 8:44). It was not Jesus who was of Satan but them.

Clearly, they needed to be removed. That Jesus did so by selecting a group of twelve nondescript laymen, none of whom came out of the religious establishment, was a rebuke to the entire system. The number twelve was not arbitrary or accidental. It represented the fact that, in the messianic kingdom, these twelve men would be given the responsibility to rule over each of Israel's twelve tribes (cf. Luke 22:28–30; Rev. 21:12–14). By selecting twelve apostles, Jesus was sending an unmistakable message to the leaders of Israel that they were spiritually disqualified, and therefore shut out of His kingdom. He confronted them directly, publicly, and repeatedly with such denunciations. Instead of repenting, their determination to kill Him increased.

Jesus knew their hatred would eventually lead to His death, as the Father had planned (Acts 2:23–24; 4:27–28). The cross was looming nearer. As Jesus set His face toward Calvary, He also made preparations for what would happen after His death. Who would carry on the message of the gospel to the world after He, the Messiah, had been killed? The answer to that question started with these twelve men.

None of the Twelve turned in an application or submitted a résumé. Even if they had, their credentials would have been utterly unimpressive. Religiously, educationally, socially, they were unqualified commoners, but they were the ones Jesus Himself selected. Thus, His sovereign power and glory are displayed, not only through His miracles but also in the lowly men whom He chose, trained, and empowered to preach the gospel and establish the church (cf. 1 Cor. 1:26–31). As Mark notes, **He went up on the mountain and summoned those whom He Himself wanted.** Knowing the importance of this selection process, Jesus isolated Himself **up on the mountain** and, according to Luke 6:12, "spent the whole night in prayer to God." Only after a full night of communion with His Father did Jesus summon **those whom He Himself wanted.** In much the same way that He had earlier called Peter, Andrew, James, John (1:16–20), and Matthew (2:14–15), Jesus now commissioned those five men, along with seven others, to be His apostles. It was not that they volunteered, though they did not come unwillingly (cf. John 6:37). Rather, He took the initiative in pursuing them and selected them according to His sovereign prerogative. As Jesus would later remind His disciples, "You did not choose Me but I chose you, and appointed you that you would go and bear fruit, and that your fruit would remain, so that whatever you ask of the Father in My name He may give to you" (John 15:16). Up to this point, these twelve men had followed Jesus as part of His larger group of disciples (cf. 2:7). It was time for them to be pulled in closer to Jesus from the larger group. Over the preceding months, Jesus focused much of His time on the crowds. Moving forward, He would increasingly concentrate His attention on the training of these twelve men.

Mark articulates two reasons why **He appointed** the **twelve.** The first was simply **so that they would be with Him.** By constantly spending intimate time with Jesus, the Twelve would be personally mentored by the Messiah Himself. They would be trained as His apprentices. These twelve men would be responsible for the spread of the gospel and the establishment of sound doctrine, laying the foundation of the church (Eph. 2:20). For the remainder of His earthly ministry, Jesus intensely invested Himself in preparing them. Second, Jesus appointed these men so **that He could send them out to preach.** They were trained to be the first generation of heralds of the good news of salvation, following in the footsteps of their Lord, who Himself proclaimed the gospel of God (1:14). Jesus was a preacher, as was John the Baptist and the Old Testament prophets before Him. The disciples were to follow in that legacy of preaching the truth of the gospel.

Their calling would not be easy (cf. Matt. 10:24–38). The religious establishment of Israel had only disdain for them and persecuted them.

Even they often lacked the faith necessary for such a vital task (cf. Matt. 8:25–26; 14:31; 16:8; John 20:30–31). Yet, these twelve men would have a greater impact on the world than any group in history. On the day of Pentecost when Peter stood up to preach, three thousand people came to saving faith in Jesus (Acts 2:41). In the subsequent weeks and months, under their preaching tens of thousands more embraced the Savior. The only explanation for such immediate and widespread influence is that they had been with Christ and His Spirit empowered them (cf. Acts 4:13).

The twelve men chosen by Jesus would be given the responsibility of being His witnesses "in Jerusalem, and in all Judea and Samaria, and even to the remotest part of the earth" (Acts 1:8). He would commission them, as an initial generation of missionaries, to go "and make disciples of all nations" (Matt. 28:19 ESV). The church itself would be "built upon the foundation of the apostles and prophets, Christ Jesus himself being the corner stone" (Eph. 2:20 KJV). They would accomplish this task through the power of the Holy Spirit, who would remind them of Jesus' teachings (cf. John 14:26) and impart to them new revelation from their Lord (cf. John 16:12–15; Acts 2:42). Through them, the doctrine of the new covenant was proclaimed, articulated, and written in the divine words of New Testament Scripture for all subsequent generations.

The Twelve did not start out as preachers. As many as seven of them were fishermen. One was a tax collector, another a freedom fighter. None of them had received a formal theological education. Yet when Jesus was done with them, those who started out as learners, or disciples, became sent ones, or apostles. They were His ambassadors, His representatives, and His heralds. He sovereignly selected them; He personally discipled them; He radically transformed them; and He empowered them with His Spirit. As the Son of God, Jesus possessed absolute authority over all things. When He selected His twelve apostles, He delegated His authority to them. In Jewish thinking, an apostle was considered a proxy of the one who sent him. As the emissaries of Christ, these men were endowed with the delegated authority of the Messiah Himself. They were elevated to act on His behalf in the exercise of His authority and for the benefit of His kingdom by proclaiming His words.

In keeping with their role as His delegates, Jesus also gave them **authority to cast out the demons.** Matthew 10:1 adds that they were also given the power "to heal every kind of disease and every kind of sickness." In order to authenticate their position as His representatives, Jesus gave them authority in both the physical realm (over disease) and the spiritual realm (over demons). Like Jesus Himself, their message was confirmed by the supernatural signs that they performed by His power (cf. John 3:2; 2 Cor. 12:11–12). Speaking of the message of salvation, the author of Hebrews explains: "After it was at the first spoken through the Lord, it was confirmed to us by those who heard [i.e., the apostles], God also testifying with them, both by signs and wonders and by various miracles and by gifts of the Holy Spirit according to His own will" (Heb. 2:3–4). Like their Master, their words were validated by the supernatural works that they performed through the power of the Holy Spirit.

The names of the Twelve are recorded in four places in the New Testament (Matt. 10:2–4; Mark 3:16–19; Luke 6:13–16; Acts 1:13; cf. v. 26). In each list, their names are organized into the same three subgroups of four, arranged in order of decreasing intimacy with Christ. The first group was comprised of two sets of brothers: Peter and Andrew, and James and John. The second included Philip, Nathaniel, Matthew, and Thomas. The third consisted of James the son of Alphaeus, Thaddeus, Simon the Zealot, and Judas Iscariot (who was replaced by Matthias in Acts 1:26). Though the order of the names changes slightly from list to list, they always remain in the same subgroup. Moreover, the name that starts each subgroup is also consistent: Peter always heads group one, Philip group two, and James the son of Alphaeus group three. This suggests that each of these subgroups had its own leader. Though a great deal is known about the men in the first group, there is increasingly less information about those who made up the second and third groups.

A closer examination of each member of the Twelve highlights the diverse makeup of this motley team. (For a thorough study of these twelve men, see chapters 11–17 in *Matthew 8–15*, MacArthur New Testament Commentary [Chicago: Moody, 1987]; and also chapters 2–8 in *Luke 6–10*, MacArthur New Testament Commentary [Chicago: Moody, 2011]; see also, *Twelve Ordinary Men* [Nashville: Thomas Nelson, 2006].) In each list of the twelve apostles, **Simon** Peter is always named first, indicating that he was the spokesman for the other eleven. An impulsive man of action, Peter often spoke before thinking—a habit that got him into trouble on more than one occasion (Matt. 16:22–23; 26:33–35). Yet, the Lord would transform Peter into the grounded, steadfast leader of the apostles. That is why **Jesus gave** him **the name Peter,** which means "rock" (cf. Matt. 16:18; John 1:42). When Jesus first met Peter, he was anything but a rock, but he would become the dominant preacher among the apostles (cf. Acts 2:15–36; 3:12–26; 5:29–32) and a pillar of the early church (Gal. 2:9). It is likely that his preaching served as the basis for Mark's account of Jesus' life and ministry. (For more on that point, see the section on "Authorship" in the introduction to this volume.) Peter's letters demonstrate the profound love for Christ that came to characterize him as a seasoned pastor and theological stalwart. According to tradition, Peter was executed as a martyr in Rome—being crucified upside down by his request because he felt unworthy to be crucified in the same manner as his Lord. Like Peter, **James, the son of Zebedee, and John the brother of James** would have their lives completely transformed by Jesus. The Lord also **gave** them a nickname, **the name Boanerges, which means, "Sons of Thunder."** In Peter's case, his nickname indicated what Jesus wanted him to become. But in the case of James and John, their moniker depicted a hotheaded and judgmental attitude toward others that they needed to forsake (cf. Luke 9:54). By calling them "Sons of Thunder," Jesus reminded them of an unrighteous attitude they needed to avoid. Along with Peter, James and John were both present at the transfiguration of Jesus (Mark 9:2). They were also there on the day of Pentecost, gathered with 120 believers, including the other apostles, when the church was born (Acts 1–2). James was martyred early in church history, being beheaded by Herod Agrippa I in the mid-40s (Acts 12:2). John, by contrast, was the longest surviving member of the Twelve. He lived until approximately A.D. 100, penning five books of the New Testament and being exiled near the end of his life. That a major theme of his epistles is love (cf. 1 John 3:14–20; 4:7–21; 5:1; 2 John 6) underscores the radical change wrought in the life of a former "Son of Thunder." **Andrew** was the final member of this first group. The brother of Peter, Andrew had been a disciple of John the Baptist who began following Jesus early in the Lord's public ministry (cf. John 1:40). The few times Andrew is highlighted in the Gospels, he is often seen bringing people to Jesus—whether it was his brother Peter (John 1:41–42), a boy with five loaves and two fish (John 6:8–10), or a group of Greeks who wanted to see the Lord (John 12:20–22). According to tradition, Andrew died shortly after introducing the wife of a provincial governor to the gospel of Jesus Christ. When she refused to recant her faith, her angry husband had Andrew crucified on an X-shaped cross. He reportedly hung there for two days, preaching the gospel to anyone passing by until he died.

Philip was the leader of the second group. According to John 1:44, he was from Bethsaida, the same hometown as Peter and Andrew. Before the feeding of the five thousand, Philip openly wondered where they could buy bread for so many people (John 6:5). In the upper room, it was Philip who said to Jesus, "Lord, show us the Father, and it is enough for us" (John 14:8). In response, "Jesus said to him, 'Have I been so long with you, and yet you have not come to know Me, Philip? He who has seen Me has seen the Father; how can you say, "Show us the Father"?'" (vv. 9–10). Philip's thickheadedness on both of those occasions was typical of all the disciples, who only came to fully understand the truth about Jesus after His resurrection. **Bartholomew** began to follow Jesus through the influence of Philip (John 1:45). His name means "Son of Tolmai" and was, in reality, a surname. His first name was Nathaniel, which means "Given of God." It was to Nathaniel that Jesus said, "Behold, an Israelite indeed, in whom there is no deceit!" (John 1:47). **Matthew,** the former tax collector, was introduced by Mark in 2:14–15. Like all who collected taxes for Rome, he was a despised man who was elevated by the Savior to the privilege of penning the opening gospel. **Thomas** rounds out the second group. According to John 11:16, his nickname was Didymus, which, in Greek, means "twin." It is in that same verse that Thomas courageously, albeit pessimistically, told the other disciples, "Let us also go [with Jesus to Jerusalem], so that we may die with Him." That pessimism surfaced again, after the resurrection, when Thomas refused to believe the other apostles that Jesus was alive (John 20:24–29). But when he witnessed the risen Christ, Thomas's response was definitive: "My Lord and my God!" (v. 28). Strong tradition from church history indicates that Thomas took the gospel to India, where he was martyred.

James the son of Alphaeus leads off the third group. Not much is known about either James or his father, Alphaeus. According to Mark 15:40, he was also called James the Less. He had a mother named Mary who also followed Jesus (cf. 16:1; Luke 24:10). **Thaddaeus** was also called Judas the son of James (Luke 6:16; Acts 1:13) or Judas "not Iscariot" (cf. John 14:22). Very little is known about Thaddaeus. Though some commentators have suggested that he is the author of the epistle of Jude, it is best to assign that letter to Jude the half brother of Jesus (cf. Mark 6:3). **Simon the Zealot,** as his name suggests, was an anti-Roman revolutionary. The fact that he and Matthew, a former tax collector for Rome, were both members of the Twelve illustrates the diversity of this group. Before meeting Jesus, Simon would have undoubtedly had no qualms about killing someone like Matthew to advance his anti-Roman cause. The ignominious **Judas Iscariot** is always mentioned last in the lists of the apostles because he **betrayed Jesus.** The defection of Judas may have been a surprise to everyone else, but Jesus was not deceived by Judas Iscariot's treachery. As the Lord told His disciples in John 6:70, "Did I Myself not choose you, the twelve, and yet one of you is a devil?" Jesus knew all along that he would betray Him. In fact, that defection was part of God's plan (cf. Acts 1:15–26).

From a human standpoint, these twelve men were odd choices, because they were uneducated, untrained, and uninfluential. Yet, from God's standpoint, they were the perfect choice—weak and imperfect instruments through whom His power would be gloriously displayed (cf. 1 Cor. 1:26–31). Before their lives were over, they had been used to turn the world upside down (cf. Acts 17:6). That our Lord could use such ordinary vessels to accomplish His great purposes underscores the supernatural purpose of His sovereign power. As Mark's sweeping summary has shown, that power was demonstrated in the miracles Jesus performed. It was also evidenced in the men whom He chose. He took a dozen ordinary men and transformed them into the powerful foundation stones of His church (cf. Eph. 2:20; Rev. 21:14).

Jesus Christ: Liar, Lunatic, or Lord?
13
(Mark 3:20–35)

And He came home, and the crowd gathered again, to such an extent that they could not even eat a meal. When His own people heard of this, they went out to take custody of Him; for they were saying, "He has lost His senses." The scribes who came down from Jerusalem were saying, "He is possessed by Beelzebul," and "He casts out the demons by the ruler of the demons." And He called them to Himself and began speaking to them in parables, "How can Satan cast out Satan? If a kingdom is divided against itself, that kingdom cannot stand. If a house is divided against itself, that house will not be able to stand. If Satan has risen up against himself and is divided, he cannot stand, but he is finished! But no one can enter the strong man's house and plunder his property unless he first binds the strong man, and then he will plunder his house. Truly I say to you, all sins shall be forgiven the sons of men, and whatever blasphemies they utter; but whoever blasphemes against the Holy Spirit never has forgiveness, but is guilty of an eternal sin"—because they were saying, "He has an unclean spirit."

Then His mother and His brothers arrived, and standing outside they sent word to Him and called Him. A crowd was sitting around Him, and they said to Him, "Behold, Your mother and Your brothers are outside looking for You." Answering them, He said, "Who are My mother and My brothers?" Looking about at those who were sitting around Him, He said, "Behold My mother and My brothers! For whoever does the will of God, he is My brother and sister and mother." (3:20–35)

Born in 1898, Clive Staples Lewis became one of the most widely known literary figures of the twentieth century. Though raised in a Protestant Irish home, Lewis abandoned his childhood faith and embraced atheism when he was only fifteen years old. He thought he was done with God, being paradoxically "very angry at God for not existing" (C. S. Lewis, *Surprised by Joy* [London: Harvest Books, 1966], 115). But God was not finished with him. Years later, while teaching at Oxford University, Lewis found himself in the company of Christian friends who challenged his atheism. The Lord used their influence to draw Lewis to Himself. Reflecting on his conversion, the former atheist compared himself to the prodigal son, pursued by God in spite of his own attempts to resist. He wrote:

> You must picture me alone in that room in Magdalen, night after night, feeling, whenever my mind lifted even for a second from my work, the steady, unrelenting approach of Him whom I so earnestly desired not to meet. That which I greatly feared had at last come upon me. In the Trinity Term of 1929 I gave in, and admitted that God was God, and knelt and prayed: perhaps, that night, the most dejected and reluctant convert in all England. (Ibid., 228–29)

As a Christian thinker, apologist, and author, C. S. Lewis would go on to have widespread influence through fictional works like *The Chronicles of Narnia* and *The Screwtape Letters,* and through apologetic writings like *The Problem of Pain* and *Mere Christianity.*

One of Lewis's most well-known contributions to the field of Christian apologetics was the "trilemma" he proposed regarding the claims of Jesus Christ. Though not invented by Lewis, he gave the "trilemma" its most popular expression. In response to anyone who might suggest that Jesus was a good teacher but not divine, Lewis explained why such an opinion was not logically tenable:

> I am trying here to prevent anyone saying the really foolish thing that
> people often say about Him: I'm ready to accept Jesus as a great moral
> teacher, but I don't accept his claim to be God. That is the one thing we
> must not say. A man who was merely a man and said the sort of things
> Jesus said would not be a great moral teacher. He would either be a
> lunatic—on the level with the man who says he is a poached egg—or
> else he would be the Devil of Hell. You must make your choice. Either
> this man was, and is, the Son of God, or else a madman or something
> worse. You can shut him up for a fool, you can spit at him and kill him
> as a demon or you can fall at his feet and call him Lord and God, but
> let us not come with any patronising nonsense about his being a great
> human teacher. He has not left that open to us. He did not intend to....
> Now it seems to me obvious that He was neither a lunatic nor a fiend:
> and consequently, however strange or terrifying or unlikely it may
> seem, I have to accept the view that He was and is God. (C. S. Lewis,
> *Mere Christianity* [London: Collins, 1952], 54–56)

By claiming to be God (Mark 2:5–10; 14:61–62; John 1:1; 5:18; 8:58; 10:30,
33, 36; 14:9; cf. Matt. 1:23; Luke 7:16), Jesus Christ left His hearers with only
three options. They could discount Him as delusional, denounce Him as
demonic, or declare Him to be divine. There was no middle ground
(Matt. 12:30; Mark 9:40; Luke 11:23). The crowds that flocked to hear Him
would either embrace Him as the Son of God and the Savior of the world
(Mark 8:29; John 6:69; 20:28), or they would reject Him as a dangerous
and possibly insane megalomaniac who must be silenced (Mark 3:6;
John 11:53).

The New Testament Gospels were written to demonstrate to any
reader that Jesus Christ was neither a lunatic nor a liar. Lunatics cannot
heal sick people or raise the dead. Frauds cannot perform undeniable
miracles, nor would someone empowered by evil spirits use that power
to cast out demons (cf. Matt. 12:26–28; John 10:21). The Bible leaves its
readers with only one alternative. The Lord Jesus is the messianic King,
"the Son of the living God" (Mark 1:1; cf. Matt. 16:16). He is the Lord and
Savior whom God the Father raised "from the dead [having] seated Him
at His right hand in the heavenly places, far above all rule and authority
and power and dominion, and every name that is named, not only in this
age but also in the one to come" (Eph. 1:20–21).

Despite the massive evidence to confirm Jesus' deity (from His astonishing teaching to His spectacular miracles to His authority over demons), and despite the clear testimony of others that authenticated Him (from the Old Testament prophets to John the Baptist to God the Father—cf. Mark 1:2–11; John 5:33–46), there were many who stubbornly refused to believe in Him (cf. John 12:37). Some thought He was demented, especially when they heard Him express the cost of being His disciple (cf. Luke 9:57–62; John 6:66); others flatly accused Him of being demon-possessed (John 10:20). In this passage (Mark 3:20–35), we find both of those wrong responses to Jesus Christ. Members of His own family suggested He had lost His senses and was acting like a lunatic (vv. 20–21). Meanwhile, the religious leaders alleged that He was a liar whose undeniable powers came from Satan, not God (vv. 22–30). Nonetheless, there were those who genuinely followed Jesus—eagerly obeying the will of the Father by listening to the Son (vv. 31–35). These true believers rightly understood that Jesus is both Lord and God.

LUNATIC: THE ASSUMPTION OF JESUS' FAMILY

And He came home, and the crowd gathered again, to such an extent that they could not even eat a meal. When His own people heard of this, they went out to take custody of Him; for they were saying, "He has lost His senses." (3:20–21)

It is difficult to imagine that anyone could think that Jesus had lost His mind. His reason was the most perfect; His logic the most pure; and His preaching the most profound. No one ever spoke like He spoke—with such clarity or depth. Whenever He taught, the reaction of the people was always the same: "all the people were hanging on to every word He said" (Luke 19:48). But in spite of His popular reception by the crowds who flocked to hear Him, certain members of Jesus' family thought He had gone mad.

After Jesus appointed the Twelve (Mark 3:13–19), **He came** back **home** to Capernaum, His ministry headquarters. The phrase **He came home** literally means "He came to a house," and may refer to the home of Peter and Andrew (1:29; cf. 2:1). As normally happened when Jesus entered the city (1:32, 37, 45; 2:1–2), **the crowd gathered again, to such an extent that they**—meaning Jesus and His disciples—**could not even eat a meal.** Throngs of people pressed into the house where Jesus was staying. His ministry of healing was unlike anything the multitudes had ever seen (cf. Matt. 9:33), drawing people in droves from all around Israel to witness His supernatural power and hear His extraordinary teaching (Mark 3:7–12). It was not uncommon for leading rabbis to have a small band of followers, but no one had ever come close to rivaling the massive popularity of Jesus.

The size of the crowds often created unique logistical challenges. On more than one occasion, Jesus miraculously created food to satisfy the hunger of thousands who followed Him (Matt. 14:13–21; Mark 8:1–10). At other times, as people mobbed Him along the shores of the Sea of Galilee, Jesus entered a small boat so that He could escape the crush and address them away from the shore (Luke 5:1–3; Mark 3:9). Earlier in Capernaum, the crowd overflowed the house where Jesus was teaching, forcing the friends of a paralyzed man to dig a hole in the roof just to get an audience with Christ (Mark 2:4). Jesus' miracles—like the healing of that paralyzed man—only heightened the fervor of the eager throngs, who openly wondered if Jesus was the Messiah (cf. Matt. 12:22–23). On this occasion, the multitude was again pressing into the house, **to such an extent that** Jesus and His disciples **could not even eat a meal.** The throng was so overwhelming that Jesus and His disciples were unable to perform even the basic functions of life, like eating.

When news about the situation reached Nazareth, Jesus' family was shocked and concerned by what they heard. As Mark explains, **when His own people heard of this, they went out to take custody of Him.** That the phrase **His own people** refers to His immediate family is confirmed by verse 31, which notes that His mother and His half brothers traveled to Capernaum to find Him. Given the oppressive nature of the crowds, the concern of Jesus' family for His safety is understandable. Fearful that He might be in danger, they had left Nazareth and traveled the nearly thirty miles to Capernaum in order **to take custody of Him.** The verb translated **to take custody** means "to seize." Of the fifteen times it is used in Mark, eight refer to Jesus being seized, including His arrest. It is also used of the seizure of John the Baptist when he was arrested and imprisoned (Mark 6:17). Jesus' family was intent on rescuing Him, by force if necessary, from the oppressive multitudes that threatened to smother Him, as well as from Himself.

The family's desire to protect Jesus from self-imposed danger is reflected in their conclusions about Him, **for they were saying, "He has lost His senses."** Mary, of course, did not think that. Before Jesus was born, Mary had been told by the angel, "Behold, you will conceive in your womb and bear a son, and you shall name Him Jesus. He will be great and will be called the Son of the Most High; and the Lord God will give Him the throne of His father David; and He will reign over the house of Jacob forever, and His kingdom will have no end" (Luke 1:31–33). So she knew exactly who He was (cf. Luke 2:19, 51).

Jesus' brothers did not yet believe in Him (cf. John 7:5). Undoubtedly, they had been told by Mary and Joseph about their older half brother. For the first thirty years of His life, while Jesus lived in Nazareth, His siblings observed Him day after day. Everything He did was perfect (cf. Heb. 4:15)—a reality that validated His identity but may have frustrated His younger brothers and sisters (who could never match up to His impeccable standard). The biblical record implies that He did not begin performing miracles until after His public ministry started (John 2:11). Outside of astonishing the religious scholars in Jerusalem when He was twelve years old (Luke 2:46–47), Jesus appeared like other Jewish young men (cf. vv. 51–52).

The names of Jesus' half brothers are listed in Mark 6:3: James, Joses, Judas, and Simon. That verse also indicates that He had more than one half sister, meaning that Jesus was one of at least seven children born to Mary. (It might be noted that the Roman Catholic doctrine of Mary's perpetual virginity is a fabrication clearly rejected by the New Testament record—cf. Matt. 1:25; 13:55–56.) Growing up in the same family as Jesus, His siblings had witnessed His perfect obedience, but because of the seemingly ordinary nature of His childhood, they did not yet believe Him to be the Messiah.

When Jesus left the family in Nazareth around the age of thirty, and embarked on His public ministry, His siblings must have wondered what He was doing. When Jesus came back to Nazareth and rebuked His former neighbors so sharply that they tried to kill Him (Luke 4:16–29),

His brothers and sisters undoubtedly watched in shock. As Jesus' reputation spread, and news about Him reached Nazareth, their curiosity was probably matched by a growing consternation and concern. Having heard about the oppressive nature of the crowds, they decided to wait no longer. It was time to rescue their older brother from Himself.

The phrase **lost His senses** translates a single Greek term (*existēmi*), meaning to lose one's mind, to be beside oneself, or to be insane. Members of Jesus' own family were convinced that He was no longer in control of His rational senses. In reality, the only thing irrational about Jesus was what they had mistakenly concluded about Him. Though His brothers did not believe in Him yet, their unbelief was only temporary. They would come to embrace Him in faith after His resurrection (Acts 1:14; 1 Cor. 15:7). In fact, Jesus' brother James would become a leader in the Jerusalem church (cf. Acts 15:13–35; Gal. 1:19), and both James and Judas (Jude) would pen epistles in the New Testament. At this time, however, out of concern for Him perhaps mixed with a sense of pity and family duty, they determined to go to Capernaum to bring Him safely back to Nazareth.

LIAR: THE ACCUSATION OF JESUS' FOES

The scribes who came down from Jerusalem were saying, "He is possessed by Beelzebul," and "He casts out the demons by the ruler of the demons." And He called them to Himself and began speaking to them in parables, "How can Satan cast out Satan? If a kingdom is divided against itself, that kingdom cannot stand. If a house is divided against itself, that house will not be able to stand. If Satan has risen up against himself and is divided, he cannot stand, but he is finished! But no one can enter the strong man's house and plunder his property unless he first binds the strong man, and then he will plunder his house. Truly I say to you, all sins shall be forgiven the sons of men, and whatever blasphemies they utter; but whoever blasphemes against the Holy Spirit never has forgiveness, but is guilty of an eternal sin"— because they were saying, "He has an unclean spirit." (3:22–30)

The members of Jesus' immediate family were not the only ones who journeyed to Capernaum looking for Jesus. Israel's religious elite—**scribes who came down from Jerusalem**—also had a keen interest in finding Jesus, though not with the intent of saving His life. Their short-term strategy was to slander Jesus in order to turn public opinion against Him; ultimately, they wanted Him dead (Mark 3:6). Knowing they could not deny the reality of His miraculous, supernatural power, they devised a smear campaign that would call into question the source of it.

According to Matthew 12:22–23, the parallel passage to Mark 3:22–30, the response of **the scribes** and Pharisees was specifically related to a healing miracle performed by Jesus. Matthew writes, "Then a demon-possessed man who was blind and mute was brought to Jesus, and He healed him, so that the mute man spoke and saw. And all the crowds were amazed, and were saying, 'This man cannot be the Son of David, can he?'" As He had done many times before, Jesus demonstrated His authority over both the spiritual realm of demons and the physical realm of disease in this one dramatic act of healing. The results were immediate, complete, and undeniable. A formerly blind, mute, and demon-possessed man was instantly cured. The crowd, astonished by the display of supernatural deliverance, could not help but pose the obvious question—openly wondering if Jesus was indeed the messianic "Son of David" (cf. 2 Sam. 7:12–16; Ps. 89:3; Isa. 9:6–7). Their reaction soon reached the ears of the ever-vigilant religious leaders. "When the Pharisees heard it, they said, 'This man casts out demons only by Beelzebul the ruler of the demons'" (Matt. 12:24). Unable to deny what Jesus had just done, the apostate religious leaders attempted to discredit Jesus by attributing His power to Satan.

Mark picks up the story at that point, noting that these **scribes** had **come down from Jerusalem.** Though Capernaum was north of Judea, the Galilean town sat at a much lower elevation (almost 700 feet below sea level) than Jerusalem (about 2,550 feet above sea level), meaning that the route to Capernaum required traveling **down from Jerusalem.** Aware of Jesus' popularity, and looking for opportunities to undermine His credibility, a delegation of **scribes** journeyed from Israel's capital city to keep an eye on Jesus' ministry. Their willingness to make the trek of more than a hundred miles (traveling around Samaria) demonstrates the deep-seated antagonism that motivated their opposition to Jesus. His unprecedented popularity (cf. Mark 3:7–10, 20) made Him an ever-increasing threat to their own authority. So they came to Capernaum intent on destroying Jesus, dogging His steps in order to build their case against Him (v. 6).

Hearing the crowds seriously consider the possibility that Jesus might be the Messiah, the **scribes** and Pharisees panicked. Trapped in a dilemma of their own creation, they resorted to making preposterous personal attacks, **saying, "He is possessed by Beelzebul," and "He casts out the demons by the ruler of the demons."** Such odious accusations—oozing with loathsome malevolence—were designed to dissuade the crowds from believing in Jesus. If they could position Him as a representative of Satan, the religious leaders knew they could poison the multitudes against Him (cf. Matt. 27:20–23; John 19:14). The Pharisees and scribes, blinded by their own arrogance, hated Jesus because He openly denounced their hypocritical system of man-made tradition and works-righteousness. Considering themselves the guardians of Jewish doctrinal purity, they could not imagine that Israel's long-awaited Deliverer would vigorously oppose them. Thus, even when the evidence of Jesus' messiahship was obvious for all to see, they willfully rejected Him, adamantly insisting that He was **possessed by** Satan.

In answer to the question posed by the multitudes, Jesus' enemies insisted that He was actually the antithesis of the Son of David. He was not the Christ, they said, but a servant of **Beelzebul** the **ruler of the demons.** The name **Beelzebul** originally referred to Baal-Zebul (meaning, "Baal, the prince"), the chief deity of the Philistine city of Ekron. Expressing their disdain, the Israelites mockingly called him Baal-Zebub, meaning "Lord of Flies" (cf. 2 Kings 1:2). By the first century, **Beelzebul** (or Beelzebub) had become a name for Satan, which is what the Pharisees intended when they associated that name with Jesus (cf. Matt. 10:25; Luke 11:15). Jesus' power could only be explained as coming from one of two sources: God or Satan. When Jesus claimed to be from God (cf. John 10:30; 17:21), the leaders called Him a liar—whose power belonged instead to the prince of darkness. Though they claimed to be authoritative spokesmen for God, in reality they were the ones under Satan's power (John 8:41, 44).

Knowing what the Pharisees were saying about Him (cf. Matt. 12:25), Jesus **called** the crowd **to Himself and began speaking to them in parables.** The Lord often used **parables** (extended analogies used to make a specific spiritual point) to obscure the truth from unbelievers (cf. Matt. 13:11–12). On this occasion, however, Jesus' analogies were clear for all to understand, exposing the ludicrous nature of His enemies' accusations. **"How can Satan cast out Satan?"** He asked rhetorically. **"If a kingdom is divided against itself, that kingdom cannot stand. If a house is divided against itself, that house will not be able to stand. If Satan has risen up against himself and is divided, he cannot stand, but he is finished!"** The allegation of the scribes was a logical absurdity. It is axiomatic that any **kingdom** or royal **house** at war **against itself** is destined for collapse. Applied to the spiritual realm, the principle holds equally true. If **Satan** were casting out his own agents or destroying his own works, then his kingdom would be hopelessly **divided.** Jesus' point was obvious: though the kingdom of darkness is inherently chaotic and disorderly, the devil does not deploy his agents to fight against each other. The fact that Jesus spent His earthly ministry exposing, confronting, rebuking, and casting out demons (cf. Matt. 8:29; 10:1; 12:22; Mark 3:11; 9:29; Luke 8:2; 11:14) provided self-evident proof that He was not empowered by **Satan.** Everything Jesus did, from His healing miracles to His gospel preaching, was opposed to Satan's interests—since the very reason He came was to destroy the works of the devil (1 John 3:8; cf. Luke 10:18). Obviously, **Satan** never would have authorized or empowered such a cataclysmic attack on his own **kingdom.** For the Pharisees and scribes to make that claim was ridiculous.

The true explanation for Jesus' authority over demons was not that He was empowered by Satan but rather that He had power over Satan. As Jesus told the multitudes, **"No one can enter the strong man's house and plunder his property unless he first binds the strong man, and then he will plunder his house."** Jesus' analogy may reflect the words of Isaiah 49:24–25:

> "Can the prey be taken from the mighty man,
> Or the captives of a tyrant be rescued?" Surely, thus says the Lord,

> "Even the captives of the mighty man will be taken away,
> And the prey of the tyrant will be rescued;
> For I will contend with the one who contends with you,
> And I will save your sons."

Whether He had that Old Testament text in mind or not, the point of Jesus' illustration would have been obvious to His listeners. If anyone wished to take the **property** of a warrior or tyrant, he must first overpower him. In Jesus' analogy, the **strong man** represents Satan and his **property** consists of both the demonic forces and oppressed human beings under his control. Only someone stronger than Satan could enter his domain, bind him, disperse his agents, and liberate his captives from the kingdom of darkness (Col. 1:13–14; cf. Eph. 2:1–4). That Jesus wielded such power (cf. Rom. 16:20; Heb. 2:14–15) proved that He is from God, since God alone possesses that kind of absolute authority.

For the Pharisees and scribes to attribute the power of Jesus to Satan rather than the Holy Spirit was the highest form of blasphemy and placed them in eternal jeopardy. Jesus' warning was solemn and severe: **"Truly I say to you, all sins shall be forgiven the sons of men, and whatever blasphemies they utter; but whoever blasphemes against the Holy Spirit never has forgiveness, but is guilty of an eternal sin."** Any sin is forgivable, including irreverent words spoken against God and the Lord Jesus (cf. Matt. 12:32; 1 Tim. 1:13–14), with one notable exception: blasphemy **against the Holy Spirit.**

Though these verses have been the source of much unnecessary confusion, the context makes it clear that Jesus had a specific offense in mind when He warned His listeners about blasphemy **against the Holy Spirit.** In His incarnation, Jesus was perfectly submissive to His Father (John 4:34; 5:19–30) and wholly empowered by the Holy Spirit (Matt. 4:1; Mark 1:12; Luke 4:1, 18; John 3:34; Acts 1:2; 10:38; Rom. 1:4). At every point of Jesus' ministry, the Spirit was actively at work: His birth (Luke 1:35), His baptism (Mark 1:10), His temptation (Mark 1:12), His ministry (Luke 4:14), His miracles (Matt. 12:28; Acts 10:38), His death (Heb. 9:14), and His resurrection (Rom. 1:4). He always operated under the Spirit's full control, as He walked in perfect obedience to His Father. (For more on this point, see chapter 2 in this volume.)

Those who had seen the overwhelming evidence of the Spirit's power in Jesus' ministry, yet remained utterly unwilling to accept Jesus as the Son of God—choosing instead to attribute the Spirit's empowering work to Satan—were guilty of blasphemy of **the Holy Spirit.** Though they had witnessed Him heal all kinds of diseases, cast out scores of demons, and proclaim a gospel of divine forgiveness, Jesus' enemies nonetheless accused Him of being a demon-possessed deceiver. **They were saying, "He has an unclean spirit."** In the face of every possible evidence of the Spirit's working through Jesus, they stubbornly refused to believe. They had permanently hardened their hearts against their own Messiah. Consequently, because their rejection was final in the face of sufficient evidence, there was no possibility of forgiveness. As one commentator explains:

> For penitence they substitute hardening, for confession plotting. Thus, by means of their own criminal and completely inexcusable callousness, they are dooming themselves. Their sin is unpardonable because they are unwilling to tread the path that leads to pardon. For a thief, an adulterer, and a murderer there is hope. The message of the gospel may cause him to cry out, "O God be merciful to me, the sinner." But when a man has become hardened, so that he has made up his mind not to pay any attention to the promptings of the Spirit, not even to listen to His pleading and warning voice, he has placed himself on the road that leads to perdition. (William Hendriksen, *The Exposition of the Gospel according to Matthew* [Grand Rapids: Baker, 1973], 529)

For the religious leaders of Israel to conclude that the Messiah was a demon-possessed counterfeit constituted the ultimate act of apostasy. Because it was their final conclusion about Jesus, they were **guilty of an eternal sin.** (Even after this occasion, in spite of Jesus' warning, the religious leaders continued to maintain that He was empowered by Satan—cf. Matt. 10:25; Luke 11:15 John 10:20.) Those who blasphemed **against the Holy Spirit** cut themselves off from God's saving grace through their own hard-hearted unbelief.

Approximately forty years later, the author of Hebrews gave a similarly stern warning to those who knew the truth about Jesus and yet deliberately chose to reject it: "How shall we escape if we neglect so great a salvation? After it was at the first spoken through the Lord, it was confirmed to us by those who heard [that is, the apostles], God also testifying witness with them, both by signs and wonders and by various miracles and by gifts of the Holy Spirit according to His own will" (Heb. 2:3–4). A few chapters later, the writer issued an even more severe warning to those who might fall away and apostatize: "For in the case of those who have once been enlightened and have tasted of the heavenly gift and have been made partakers of the Holy Spirit, and have tasted the good word of God and the powers of the age to come, and then have fallen away, it is impossible to renew them again to repentance, since they again crucify to themselves the Son of God, and put Him to open shame" (Heb. 6:4–6). (For a detailed discussion of that important passage, see John MacArthur, *Hebrews,* MacArthur New Testament Commentary [Chicago: Moody, 1983].) Apostates, like the unbelieving religious leaders of Jesus' day, are those who have been fully exposed to the truth of the gospel and yet walk away from Christ in spite of the overwhelming evidence they have been given. At its heart, apostasy is a willful repudiation of the Holy Spirit's testimony to the person and work of Jesus Christ. Blasphemy **against the Holy Spirit,** then, describes the apostate heart that with full knowledge has irrevocably rejected the One to whom the Spirit points. That is why it is **an eternal sin**—because no forgiveness is possible for those who refuse to stop rejecting Christ.

LORD: THE ACKNOWLEDGMENT OF JESUS' FOLLOWERS

Then His mother and His brothers arrived, and standing outside they sent word to Him and called Him. A crowd was sitting around Him, and they said to Him, "Behold, Your mother and Your brothers are outside looking for You." Answering them, He said, "Who are My mother and My brothers?" Looking about at those who were sitting around Him, He said, "Behold My mother and My brothers! For whoever does the will of God, he is My brother and sister and mother." (3:31–35)

Having left Nazareth to find Jesus (v. 21), Jesus' **mother and His brothers** finally **arrived** in Capernaum. In light of the fact that Mary believed in Jesus, her coming was likely motivated by a desire to protect the Son of God. Jesus' half brothers, however, were convinced He had lost

His mind. They came to rescue Jesus from the massive crowds that threatened to smother Him—likely intent on taking Him back to Nazareth with them.

From outside the house, **they sent word to Him and called Him.** Inside, Jesus was addressing a **crowd** that **was sitting around Him,** when **they said to Him, "Behold, Your mother and Your brothers are outside looking for You."** Accepting the interruption, Jesus responded in a way that was utterly unexpected and must have surprised those who heard Him speak. **Answering them, He said, "Who are My mother and My brothers?"** Jesus' question was not born out of ignorance, since He obviously knew the identity of His earthly family members. Nor did it intend any level of disrespect or antagonism toward His **mother** and **brothers,** whom He clearly loved (cf. John 19:26–27). Jesus simply used this real-life interruption to teach a transcendent spiritual truth to His followers who were gathered **around Him.**

Answering His own question, Jesus looked **about at those who were sitting around Him** and **said, "Behold My mother and My brothers! For whoever does the will of God, he is My brother and sister and mother."** The Lord's point was that the only relationship to Him that matters eternally is not physical but spiritual. His spiritual family is comprised of those who have a saving relationship with Him through faith (cf. John 1:12; Rom. 8:14–17; 1 John 3:1–2). As He earlier explained to Nicodemus, it is not earthly birth that makes one part of the family of God but being born from above (John 3:3–8). Unlike the scribes and Pharisees, who resisted and blasphemed the Holy Spirit by rejecting the Son of God, genuine disciples are careful to do **the will of God** by honoring Jesus Christ as Savior and Lord (cf. 1 Cor. 12:3). As Jesus explained in John 6:40, "This is the will of My Father, that everyone who beholds the Son and believes in Him will have eternal life, and I Myself will raise him up on the last day." On another occasion in Judea, when a woman exclaimed to Jesus, "Blessed is the womb that bore You and the breasts at which You nursed" (Luke 11:27), He responded similarly, "On the contrary, blessed are those who hear the word of God and observe it" (v. 28). Only those who heed God's word will be eternally blessed. That word begins with the testimony of the Father, "This is My beloved Son, with whom I am well-pleased; listen to Him" (Matt. 17:5).

As Mark has already noted (v. 21), some of Jesus' family members regarded Him as a lunatic. Meanwhile, members of the religious elite regarded Him as a liar, accusing Him of being in league with Satan. But the followers of Jesus, those who belonged to His spiritual family, embraced Him as their Lord. They obeyed the will of the Father, which is that sinners would believe in the Son to whom the Holy Spirit bears witness and receive eternal life (cf. John 3:16; 15:26; 16:13–15).

Those who truly recognize that Jesus is Lord respond with an eagerness to obey Him. True conversion has always been marked by obedience to the Word of God and submission to the authority of Christ. As Jesus explained in John 8:31, "If you continue in My word, then you are truly disciples of Mine." A few chapters later, He echoed that same truth: "If you love Me, you will keep My commandments" (John 14:15). By contrast, "The one who says, 'I have come to know Him,' and does not keep His commandments, is a liar, and the truth is not in him" (1 John 2:4; cf. 3:24). Embracing the lordship of Jesus Christ is more than mere lip service (cf. Matt. 7:21). It is the essence of the Christian life and a sure characteristic of those who are part of the family of God. As John R. W. Stott explains:

> In order to follow Christ we have to deny ourselves, to crucify ourselves, to lose ourselves. The full, inexorable demand of Jesus Christ is now laid bare. He does not call us to a sloppy half-heartedness, but to a vigorous, absolute commitment. He calls us to make him our Lord. The astonishing idea is current in some circles today that we can enjoy the benefits of Christ's salvation without accepting the challenge of his sovereign lordship. Such an unbalanced notion is not to be found in the New Testament. "Jesus is Lord" is the earliest known formulation of the creed of Christians. In days when imperial Rome was pressing its citizens to say "Caesar is Lord," these words had a dangerous flavour. But Christians did not flinch. They could not give Caesar their first allegiance, because they had already given it to the Emperor Jesus. God had exalted his Son Jesus far above all principality and power and invested him with a rank superior to every rank, that before him "every knee should bow ... and every tongue confess that Jesus Christ is Lord." (John R. W. Stott, *Basic Christianity* [London, Inter-Varsity Press, 1971], 112–13)

The eternal destiny of every sinner is determined by what that person does with Jesus Christ. Those who ultimately regard Him as either a lunatic or a liar will spend eternity apart from Him in hell. But those who do the will of God by embracing Jesus Christ as Lord and Savior are promised eternal life in heaven (Rom. 10:9). There, as members of the family of God, they will worship their risen King forever.

Of Soils and Souls
(Mark 4:1–20)

14

He began to teach again by the sea. And such a very large crowd gathered to Him that He got into a boat in the sea and sat down; and the whole crowd was by the sea on the land. And He was teaching them many things in parables, and was saying to them in His teaching, "Listen to this! Behold, the sower went out to sow; as he was sowing, some seed fell beside the road, and the birds came and ate it up. Other seed fell on the rocky ground where it did not have much soil; and immediately it sprang up because it had no depth of soil. And after the sun had risen, it was scorched; and because it had no root, it withered away. Other seed fell among the thorns, and the thorns came up and choked it, and it yielded no crop. Other seeds fell into the good soil, and as they grew up and increased, they yielded a crop and produced thirty, sixty, and a hundredfold." And He was saying, "He who has ears to hear, let him hear." As soon as He was alone, His followers, along with the twelve, began asking Him about the parables. And He was saying to them, "To you has been given the

mystery of the kingdom of God, but those who are outside get everything in parables, so that while seeing, they may see and not perceive, and while hearing, they may hear and not understand, otherwise they might return and be forgiven." And He said to them, "Do you not understand this parable? How will you understand all the parables? The sower sows the word. These are the ones who are beside the road where the word is sown; and when they hear, immediately Satan comes and takes away the word which has been sown in them. In a similar way these are the ones on whom seed was sown on the rocky places, who, when they hear the word, immediately receive it with joy; and they have no firm root in themselves, but are only temporary; then, when affliction or persecution arises because of the word, immediately they fall away. And others are the ones on whom seed was sown among the thorns; these are the ones who have heard the word, but the worries of the world, and the deceitfulness of riches, and the desires for other things enter in and choke the word, and it becomes unfruitful. And those are the ones on whom seed was sown on the good soil; and they hear the word and accept it and bear fruit, thirty, sixty, and a hundredfold." (4:1–20)

The nation of Israel, at the outset of the first century, was dominated by messianic expectation. The Jewish people envisioned a deliverer who would rescue them from Roman occupation, restoring to Israel's national glory everything that had been lost at the hands of foreign oppressors like the Assyrians, Babylonians, Greeks, and Romans.

As devoted readers of the Old Testament, they looked to the extensive promises of Messiah's kingdom with eager anticipation, convinced He would reestablish David's throne in Jerusalem and exalt Israel above all other nations. In New Testament times, the only royal dynasty in Israel was that of the Herods, who ruled by Rome's consent. But Herod the Great and his sons were Edomites, descendants of Esau, who repeatedly put their own interests above those of the Jews. Under Roman dominion, the people were required to pay burdensome taxes to Caesar (cf. Mark 2:13–17), a painful reminder of their wearying national bondage. Often the target of Roman brutality, in part because of their strict monotheism, the Jewish people became increasingly resentful of the imperial yoke they were forced to bear. As the weight of foreign oppression grew heavier, the flames of messianic anticipation burned ever brighter.

When John the Baptist began preaching in the wilderness, declaring himself to be the Messiah's forerunner (cf. Mark 1:2), the response of the people was enthusiastic. Multitudes from all over Israel journeyed into the wilderness to hear what John had to say. Brimming with anticipation, their hearts undoubtedly raced when John declared to them, "After me One is coming who is mightier than I, and I am not fit to stoop down and untie the thong of His sandals. I baptized you with water; but He will baptize you with the Holy Spirit" (1:7–8).

Yet, in tragic irony, when their long-awaited Messiah finally arrived, the nation rejected Him. The apostle John expressed that reality with these familiar words, "He came to His own, and those who were His own did not receive Him" (John 1:11). The very crowds who looked forward to His coming turned against Him, eventually crying out for His death. As Peter told a Jewish audience in the temple, "The God of Abraham, Isaac and Jacob, the God of our fathers, has glorified His servant Jesus, the one whom you delivered and disowned in the presence of Pilate, when he had decided to release Him. But you disowned the Holy and Righteous One and asked for a murderer to be granted to you, but put to death the Prince of life, the one whom God raised from the dead, a fact to which we are witnesses" (Acts 3:13–15). Unthinkably, Israel hated God's anointed One, the Messiah, even at a time when anticipation for His arrival had never been more fervent. Preoccupied with the political deliverance promised in the Old Testament, the Jewish people blindly overlooked the fact that the same Old Testament also foretold that the Messiah must first suffer and die (cf. Ps. 22:1–18; Isa. 52:13–53:12; Zech. 12:10). As Peter went on to explain, "The things which God announced beforehand by the mouth of all the prophets, that His Christ would suffer, He has thus fulfilled" (Acts 3:18).

The Lord Jesus will, of course, return in a future day to establish His glorious kingdom in Jerusalem (Rev. 19:11–20:6). At that time, all of the Old Testament promises to His people regarding His earthly reign will be perfectly fulfilled (e.g., Isa. 9:6–7; 11:4–5; 24:23; 33:17–22; 42:3–4;

49:22–23; 60:1–62:7; Jer. 33:14–21). But in His first coming, Jesus came as the final sacrificial Lamb who would bear the penalty for sin by dying on the cross (cf. Phil. 2:5–11; 1 Peter 2:21–25). Jesus Himself declared His mission with these words: "For even the Son of Man did not come to be served, but to serve, and to give His life a ransom for many" (Mark 10:45). Clearly, His role as the Suffering Servant did not correspond to the prevailing expectations of a warrior prince who would overthrow the Romans. Though there was a great deal of superficial interest in Jesus' miracles, the number of true disciples was comparatively small.

It must have been difficult for Jesus' disciples to understand why so few of the Jewish people, and especially the religious leaders, believed in Him. On numerous occasions, they had witnessed Jesus exercise divine power over demons, disease, and even death. They knew He was the Messiah (cf. Mark 8:29). Jesus referred to them as members of His spiritual family (Mark 3:34), because they obeyed the will of the Father by believing in the Son (John 6:40). But they were in the minority, comprising only a little flock (cf. John 10:27).

Israel's religious establishment worked tirelessly to discredit Jesus in the people's minds. They claimed, "He casts out the demons by the ruler of the demons" (Mark 3:22). The crowds who came to hear Jesus found themselves caught between a superficial curiosity in His miracles and a desire not to offend the religious leaders (cf. John 2:24–25). Even some of the Pharisees experienced this very tension: "Nevertheless many even of the rulers believed in Him, but because of the Pharisees they were not confessing Him, for fear that they would be put out of the synagogue; for they loved the approval of men rather than the approval of God" (John 12:42–43). The fear of man, along with the high cost of discipleship, caused many who were initially attracted to Jesus to eventually fall away (cf. John 6:66).

Why did this happen? How could the long-awaited Messiah be so widely rejected by His own people? Jesus' power was unmistakably divine. His teaching was authoritative; His miracles, wondrously supernatural; His life, sinless; His popularity, unprecedented. Yet, at the end of His earthly ministry, His band of followers only numbered about 500, likely in Galilee, and 120 in Jerusalem (cf. Acts 1:15; 1 Cor. 15:6). Why were there so few? An unnamed follower of Christ asked Him that very question in

Luke 13:23, "Lord, are there just a few who are being saved?" Jesus had already answered that question in the Sermon on the Mount. "Enter through the narrow gate; for the gate is wide and the way is broad that leads to destruction, and there are many who enter through it. For the gate is small and the way is narrow that leads to life, and there are few who find it" (Matt. 7:13–14). Clearly, Jesus emphasized the narrow exclusivity of the gospel. Even so, those who truly believed in Him must have wondered why the majority of their fellow countrymen rejected the Messiah—even after many had initially responded to Him with enthusiasm and fascination.

To help His disciples understand the cause of Israel's growing rejection, Jesus created an explanatory parable drawn directly from the agricultural world of the first century. In Mark 4:1–9, He simply described the reality of different types of soil to the listening crowds. He then articulated the purpose behind His parables in verses 10–13, but only to His followers. In verses 14–20, He explained to them that the point of this parable was to illustrate the basic reason for people's responses to the gospel.

THE PARABLE: A STORY ABOUT SOILS

He began to teach again by the sea. And such a very large crowd gathered to Him that He got into a boat in the sea and sat down; and the whole crowd was by the sea on the land. And He was teaching them many things in parables, and was saying to them in His teaching, "Listen to this! Behold, the sower went out to sow; as he was sowing, some seed fell beside the road, and the birds came and ate it up. Other seed fell on the rocky ground where it did not have much soil; and immediately it sprang up because it had no depth of soil. And after the sun had risen, it was scorched; and because it had no root, it withered away. Other seed fell among the thorns, and the thorns came up and choked it, and it yielded no crop. Other seeds fell into the good soil, and as they grew up and increased, they yielded a crop and produced thirty, sixty, and a hundredfold." (4:1–8)

After His family came to find Him in an apparent attempt to take Him with them back to Nazareth (Mark 3:21, 32), Jesus left the house where He had been ministering and retreated to the shores of the Sea of Galilee. There, still surrounded by throngs of people, **He began to teach again by the sea.** Earlier that same day (Matt. 13:1), after healing a blind and mute demoniac, Jesus had been accused by the unbelieving Pharisees of casting "out the demons by the ruler of the demons" (Mark 3:22). In response, the Lord warned them of the eternal danger of thus blaspheming the Holy Spirit who was at work through Him (vv. 28–29).

Though He had been rejected and repudiated by Israel's religious elite because of His words, Jesus remained popular with the common people because of His works. The massive multitudes compelled Him to spend prolonged periods of time in rural areas, away from the cities, in order to accommodate all who came to Him because of His miracles (cf. 1:45). On this occasion, as on others (cf. 3:9), **such a very large crowd gathered to Him that He got into a boat in the sea and sat down; and the whole crowd was by the sea on the land.** In order to address the entire multitude, Jesus put some space between Himself and the pressing mob by getting into **a boat**—likely a small fishing vessel— which was pushed just offshore. In typical rabbinic style, the Lord **sat down** to teach. Doing so also provided Him with stability due to the rocking of the boat. According to Matthew 13:2, the crowd listened while standing on the beach.

On this occasion, **He was teaching them many things in parables** (cf. Matt. 13:1–52). From this point on, **parables** would be Jesus' primary means of teaching the multitudes (cf. Matt. 13:34). The purpose of parables was to clarify truth to believers and hide it from unbelievers. In that sense they were both a blessing and a judgment. The term *parabolē* (parable) comes from two Greek words—*para*, meaning alongside of, and *ballō*, meaning to place or lay. The idea is that of making a comparison by placing something alongside something else for the sake of illustration or explanation. As analogies or extended short stories, **parables** used familiar practices or objects to elucidate unknown or complex spiritual truths. They represented a common form of rabbinic teaching, with the term appearing some forty-five times in the Septuagint (the Greek version of the Old Testament).

As Jesus introduced the parable of the soils, He began by **saying to them in His teaching, "Listen to this!"** The command to heed His words underscored the importance of what He was about to say. The Lord chose a well-known scene for the setting of the parable of the soils. Undoubtedly, many of His listeners were farmers themselves. They knew, from firsthand experience, what it meant for **the sower** to go **out to sow** his fields. Everyone in that predominantly agrarian society in first-century Israel was well acquainted with the analogy Jesus used. Grain fields covered the landscape of Galilee. A man hoisting a seed bag over his shoulder and scattering seed as he slowly traversed his furrowed field would have been a familiar sight.

Jesus' listeners were equally aware of the types of ground on which seed could fall **as** the sower **was sowing.** Scattering seed by hand meant that some of the seed inevitably fell on various kinds of poor soil. **Some seed** was bound to fall **beside the road,** a reference to the narrow paths that crisscrossed the Galilean landscape, separating fields and providing both farmers and travelers access through the countryside. Jesus and His disciples had earlier walked along such a **road** when the Pharisees confronted them for picking grain on the Sabbath (Mark 2:23–28). Such paths were dry and unprotected from the hot, arid climate. Due to repeated foot traffic, roads were hard packed, almost like pavement, making it nearly impossible for any seed that fell there to penetrate the ground and take root. Because **seed** that **fell beside the road** lay exposed alongside the dusty path, it was not long before **the birds came and ate it up.** They followed the sower, flying behind and waiting until the sower had moved on to another part of the field, in order to swoop down and eat the easily accessible seed. Whatever the birds missed would be "trampled under foot" (Luke 8:5) by travelers as they walked along the path.

Other seed fell on a second type of unproductive ground: **the rocky ground where it did not have much soil.** Israel is a very rocky land, with much of the rock invisibly lying beneath the surface. Though farmers always removed the loose rocks from their fields prior to planting, there were inevitably places where underlying bedrock, usually limestone, was covered by only a shallow layer of soil. When seed landed in these areas and germinated, **immediately** a plant **sprang up,** because the soil was warm and the underlying rock helped to trap moisture and nutrients. What initially looked good on the surface was only temporary. Though the plant initially sprouted, **because it had no depth of soil** due to the underlying rock, its roots were unable to develop properly. Consequently, **after the sun had risen, it was scorched** in the dry, desert heat. After the spring rains ended, the fledgling plant was subjected to the harsh conditions of the summer months. **Because it had no root, it** quickly **withered away.** Without an adequate root system, the plant could not get the moisture it needed to bear fruit (cf. Luke 8:6).

Still more **seed fell** on a third type of soil: **among the thorns.** Though this ground looked good after it had been tilled, it was actually infested with thorns—so that as the grain began to sprout, a crop of weeds grew up with it, overwhelming the good seed until its life was squeezed out. **The thorns** sucked water and nourishment away from the good plants **and choked** them so that they **yielded no crop.**

Finally, in contrast to the first three useless soils, **other seeds fell into the good soil.** This ground was not hard packed like the road, or shallow like the rocky soil, or weed-infested like the thorny ground. Rather, it was soft and deep, free from thorns, and rich in moisture and nutrients. When seeds landed on this soil, **they grew up and increased,** so that **they yielded a crop and produced thirty, sixty, and a hundredfold.** In ancient Israel, farmers could usually expect a six-to-eight-fold yield at harvesttime. A crop that yielded tenfold would have been well above average. When Jesus spoke of crops that produced harvests of **thirty, sixty,** or **a hundredfold**—percentages that were unthinkably high—His listeners would have been stunned. Those kind of results would have been unheard of.

THE PURPOSE: THE REASON FOR PARABLES

And He was saying, "He who has ears to hear, let him hear." As soon as He was alone, His followers, along with the twelve, began asking Him about the parables. And He was saying to them, "To you has been given the mystery of the kingdom of God, but those who are outside get everything in parables, so that while seeing,

they may see and not perceive, and while hearing, they may hear and not understand, otherwise they might return and be forgiven." And He said to them, "Do you not understand this parable? How will you understand all the parables? (4:9–13)

Jesus concluded His parable with a statement of warning and judgment. Not everyone who heard Him speak was able to understand the truth He was explaining. The meaning of the parable would only be revealed to those whose hearts were ready to receive it; for the rest it was an unsolvable riddle. Thus **He was saying, "He who has ears to hear, let him hear."** The religious leaders, along with many of the laypeople in the multitudes, had already rejected Jesus. The judgment on them was that their hearts and ears were closed to His teachings. Consequently, they were not given any interpretation of the parables. Yet, Jesus' statement served as an invitation to believers who were willing to listen. To them He gave the explanation.

As soon as He was alone, meaning the crowds had left and Jesus was surrounded only by His closest disciples, **His followers, along with the twelve, began asking Him about the parables.** According to Matthew 13:10, "The disciples came and said to Him, 'Why do You speak to them in parables?'" They did not understand why Jesus chose to address the crowds using unexplained analogies and spiritual enigmas. Why did He tell stories without explaining what they meant? In part, the disciples' consternation was motivated by their own lack of understanding (Mark 4:13). Even they did not know how to interpret the parable until the Lord explained the meaning to them.

Jesus offered a twofold explanation for using parables: to conceal truth from the hard-hearted while revealing it to those who believed. Thus, **He was saying to them, "To you** [who believe in Me] **has been given the mystery of the kingdom of God, but those who are outside** [who have rejected Me] **get everything in parables."** The followers of Christ possessed the ears to hear, and Jesus willingly disclosed the meaning to them. When Jesus told a parable to those who believed, it was a revelation of grace that made spiritual truth clear.

The word **mystery** (*musterion*) refers to spiritual truth that was previously hidden but now has been revealed. In modern times, the word "mystery" is often used to speak of unexplainable events, unsolved crimes, or the intriguing plot of a detective novel. In ancient Rome, members of pagan cults, called "mystery religions," developed clandestine rites and prided themselves on possessing secret knowledge. In Scripture, **mystery** does not refer to any of those ideas. New Testament mysteries consist of revelations and explanations of divine truth that were not fully understood by believers before the New Testament era.

In this context, the **mystery** is **the kingdom of God,** a reference to the realm of salvation. Though God reigns over everyone and everything, the kingdom of salvation consists only of those who belong to Him through saving faith. Because they have genuinely embraced Jesus Christ as Savior and Lord, believers have been rescued by God "from the domain of darkness, and transferred ... to the kingdom of His beloved Son, in whom we have redemption, the forgiveness of sins" (Col. 1:13–14). Moreover, they have been adopted into the family of God (Rom. 8:14–17). They no longer belong to this world system (cf. 1 John 2:16–17). Instead, they are citizens of heaven (Phil. 3:20), their true home.

Jesus' parables served an entirely different purpose for unbelievers: to hide the truth from them. For **those who** were **outside** the kingdom, like the religious leaders who had just declared Jesus to be demonic (Mark 3:22), the parables were left unexplained and therefore sounded like nothing more than riddles. The fact that, from this point forward, the people would **get everything in parables** was an act of divine judgment on their persistent unbelief (cf. Matt. 13:34–35). Jesus illustrated this point by referencing Isaiah 6:9–10: **so that while seeing, they may see and not perceive, and while hearing, they may hear and not understand, otherwise they might return and be forgiven.** Though written some seven centuries earlier, those words from Isaiah provided an apt description of the unbelieving Israelites in Jesus' day. During Isaiah's ministry, the people repeatedly ignored the prophet's warnings until their consciences were so seared, and their spiritual senses so dulled, that they no longer had any ability to understand or respond. God allowed them to harden their hearts to the point that they could no longer repent. Consequently, divine judgment on Israel, executed through the instrument of Nebuchadnezzar's invading armies, became inevitable. Jesus' parables represented a similar form of judgment on the intractable unbelief He encountered in the first century. Due to the people's repeated rejection of His clear teachings and undeniable miracles, from this point on Jesus would frame His teachings in a way they could not understand. Unable to comprehend the truth, they would never **return and be forgiven.** Thus, they would face God's wrath. Historically, divine judgment came upon the apostate nation of Israel in A.D. 70 when Jerusalem was destroyed by the Romans. Eternally, that judgment came when those who had rejected Jesus died and were cast into the everlasting torments of hell.

Both the curious crowds and the religious leaders had been given more than enough time and evidence to conclude that Jesus was the Messiah. Their unbelief persisted, growing increasingly resolute until it passed the point of no return (cf. Mark 3:28–30). Consequently, divine judgment had set in. Their willful rejection of the Son of God had led to God's judicial rejection of them. God confirmed them in their resolute hard-heartedness, allowing them to remain cemented in their own unbelief. Because their rejection was final, the time had come when they would no longer be given the message.

Jesus directed the focus back to His disciples when **He said to them, "Do you not understand this parable?"** Clearly they did not. He continued, **"How will you understand all the parables?"** By asking that second question, the Lord motivated them to listen carefully as He explained its meaning. As Jesus' words indicate, understanding the parable of the soils was key to interpreting any subsequent parables. If the disciples could not comprehend such fundamental truths about salvation and the gospel, they would not be able to grasp later truths that built on that foundation. On a practical level, it was critical for Jesus' disciples to understand why His message was being rejected by so many. They, too, would be heralds of the gospel who would experience similar treatment from unbelievers. Yet, their evangelistic efforts would not be in vain. Though not all would listen, some would, and those who responded in faith would bear abundant fruit.

THE POINT: THE MEANING OF THE PARABLE

The sower sows the word. These are the ones who are beside the road where the word is sown; and when they hear, immediately Satan comes and takes away the word which has been sown in them. In a similar way these are the ones on whom seed was sown on the rocky places, who, when they hear the word, immediately receive it with joy; and they have no firm root in themselves, but are only temporary; then, when affliction or persecution arises because of the word, immediately they fall away. And others are the ones on whom seed was sown among the thorns; these are the ones who have heard the word, but the worries of the world, and the deceitfulness of riches, and the desires for other things enter in and choke the word, and it becomes unfruitful. And those are the ones on whom seed was sown on the good soil; and they hear the word and accept it and bear fruit, thirty, sixty, and a hundred-fold." (4:14–20)

Although this parable is popularly known as the "parable of the sower," **the sower** is not at all the focus of Jesus' analogy. In fact, no details about **the sower** are given. The seed that is sown is **the word** of God, the biblical message of salvation (cf. Luke 8:11). In Matthew 13:37, while explaining the parable of the wheat and tares, Jesus noted that "The one who sows the good seed is the Son of Man." Jesus' mission was to preach "the gospel of God" (Mark 1:14), proclaiming the message of salvation (cf. 1:38). Paralleling that parable, it is obvious that the sower in the soils story refers to anyone who disseminates the message of the gospel.

Only mentioning the sower and the seed briefly, Jesus' main emphasis fell on the types of soil. According to Matthew's account, the soil represents the hearts of those who hear the gospel preached to them (13:19). The message of salvation is received differently by different people. Many may demonstrate a superficial and temporary interest in the gospel, but only those whom the Spirit of God has supernaturally prepared will respond in true faith and bear lasting fruit (cf. John 6:67). Jesus' words would have been both clarifying and encouraging to the disciples—those whom He would soon commission to preach the gospel to all nations (cf. Matt. 28:18–20). On the one hand, this parable prepared the disciples for their evangelistic task by equipping them to expect some to respond positively to the gospel while others reject. On the other hand, it encouraged them with the knowledge that God was already at work in the hearts of His elect—cultivating the soil so that it would be ready to receive the seed of the gospel.

The Lord was preparing His disciples, and all subsequent generations of Christian evangelists, to expect four basic responses to the preaching of the gospel: the unresponsive, the superficial, the worldly, and the receptive.

THE UNRESPONSIVE, ROADSIDE SOIL

These are the ones who are beside the road where the word is sown; and when they hear, immediately Satan comes and takes away the word which has been sown in them. (4:15)

The hard, uncultivated dirt that covered the pathways throughout Galilee provided the perfect analogy for a hard, unreceptive heart. **The ones who are beside the road where the word is sown** are so calloused by their unbelief that the seed of the gospel is unable to penetrate at all. The same sun that gives life to the seed planted in good soil hardens the clay of unbelief in the hearts of these rejecters. The reason such people fail to receive the gospel is not due to any deficiency in either the skill of the sower or the power of the seed but rather to their own willful unbelief. Having continually resisted the truth about Christ, their hearts have become hard like pavement. Their calloused animosity toward the truth is so great that, **when they hear, immediately Satan comes and takes away the word which has been sown in them.** Refusing to believe, they remain enslaved to the prince of darkness (Eph. 2:1–2).

Satan (the "evil one," Matt. 13:19) is "the god of this world [who] has blinded the minds of the unbelieving, that they might not see the light of the gospel of the glory of Christ, who is the image of God" (2 Cor. 4:4). In his efforts to thwart the advance of the gospel, **Satan** may use any number of means to take **away the word which has been sown.** During the ministry of Jesus, the primary stumbling block to belief came from Israel's religious establishment. The Pharisees and Sadducees, who disguised themselves as angels of light (cf. 2 Cor. 11:14), were in reality agents of Satan (John 8:44). They openly opposed Jesus and denied His authority (cf. Mark 2:7; 3:22). They promoted an external system of works righteousness that was diametrically opposed to the true gospel of grace (cf. Matt. 23:1–39). Moreover, they used their influence to pressure people into following their lead (cf. John 7:13; 12:42). In the centuries since, Satan has continued to use false teachers, hypocritical religion, and the fear of men to keep the gospel from penetrating unbelieving hearts.

THE SUPERFICIAL, STONY SOIL

In a similar way these are the ones on whom seed was sown on the rocky places, who, when they hear the word, immediately receive it with joy; and they have no firm root in themselves, but are only temporary; then, when affliction or persecution arises because of the word, immediately they fall away. (4:16–17)

When the seed fell on the stony ground, it penetrated the soil and even sprouted quickly but soon died. The stony soil, then, represents people who, in spite of their initial excitement, ultimately reject the gospel. Because their faith is not genuine, Jesus compared them **in a similar way** to those described by the roadside soil. The only difference is that their hard-heartedness is not initially apparent, being buried beneath the surface.

At first, the stony soil looks good. As Jesus explained, **these are the ones on whom seed was sown on the rocky places, who, when they hear the word, immediately receive it with joy.** The initial response of some to the gospel is emotional and dramatic. Every external indication seems to indicate genuine faith. In reality, however, their faith is shallow and temporary. Their feelings were affected, but their hearts were not transformed. Consequently, **they have no firm root in themselves, but are only temporary.** Beneath the thin veneer of outward enthusiasm lies an impenetrable layer of unrepentant unbelief, like a ribbon of bedrock that is not immediately visible.

The superficiality of their commitment is evidenced **when affliction or persecution arises because of the word.** Forced to count the cost of following Christ, the true nature of their interest in the gospel becomes evident. Rather than enduring suffering for the sake of the gospel, their faith collapses at the first sign of self-sacrifice and trouble. Unable to persevere, because their faith in the gospel does not go deeper than the surface, **immediately they fall away** under the pressure of hardship.

The phrase **fall away** translates a form of the Greek word *skandalizō*, meaning to offend or cause to stumble, from which the English word "scandalize" is derived. When their faith is put to the test (cf. John 8:31; 1 John 2:19), these false believers stumble, fall, and are scandalized on account of the persecution they face. Because their faith in Christ lacks a genuine sorrow over sin, a sincere repentance, a heartfelt hunger for righteousness, and a deep love for the Savior, it has never truly taken root. Inevitably, when the going gets tough, they abandon their superficial commitment to the Lord. True believers, by contrast, possess a faith that endures persecution and even martyrdom for the sake of following Christ (cf. Luke 9:23–25; 2 Tim. 3:12).

THE WORLDLY, THORNY SOIL

And others are the ones on whom seed was sown among the thorns; these are the ones who have heard the word, but the worries of the world, and the deceitfulness of riches, and the desires for other things enter in and choke the word, and it becomes unfruitful. (4:18–19)

The ones on whom seed was sown among the thorns, like the rocky soil, look good on the surface, but underneath the ground is contaminated by dormant thorns and weeds. The word **thorns** (*akantha*) refers to a thorny bramble common to the land of Israel and frequently found in cultivated soil. (This same word is used in Matt. 27:29 to refer to the crown of thorns placed on Jesus' head at His crucifixion.) When the seed begins to grow, a thorny weed sprouts alongside it, eventually choking out the good plant so that it cannot bear fruit. The weed-infested soil represents **the ones who have heard the word, but the worries of the world, and the deceitfulness of riches, and the desires for other things enter in and choke the word, and it becomes unfruitful.** Unlike the hard-hearted resistance of the roadside soil or the shallow emotionalism of the rocky soil, those represented by the thorny soil are double minded. Rather than possessing a singular love for Christ, their hearts remain captivated by a love for the world. Their preoccupation with the **worries of the world, and the deceitfulness of riches, and the desires for other things** exposes the true allegiance of their hearts. As Jesus explained in the Sermon on the Mount,

> Do not store up for yourselves treasures on earth, where moth and rust destroy, and where thieves break in and steal. But store up for yourselves treasures in heaven, where neither moth nor rust destroys, and where thieves do not break in or steal; for where your treasure is, there your heart will be also. . . . No one can serve two masters; for either he will hate the one and love the other, or he will be devoted to one and despise the other. You cannot serve God and wealth. (Matt. 6:19–21, 24; cf. Mark 10:25; 1 Tim. 6:17)

Few barriers to the gospel are more deceptive or deadly than worldliness and the love of money. The apostle Paul warned that "the love of money is a root of all sorts of evil, and some by longing for it have wandered away from the faith, and pierced themselves with many griefs" (1 Tim. 6:10). The apostle John issued a similar admonition:

> Do not love the world nor the things in the world. If anyone loves the world, the love of the Father is not in him. For all that is in the world, the lust of the flesh and the lust of the eyes and the boastful pride of life, is not from the Father, but is from the world. The world is passing away, and also its lusts; but the one who does the will of God lives forever. (1 John 2:15–17)

A love for the world and a love for **the word** are incompatible and mutually exclusive; the one will **choke** out the other. Those who truly love Christ will forsake the world. Conversely, those who love the world will forsake Christ and thus be spiritually **unfruitful.**

THE GOOD, RECEPTIVE SOIL

And those are the ones on whom seed was sown on the good soil; and they hear the word and accept it and bear fruit, thirty, sixty, and a hundredfold. (4:20)

Jesus contrasts the three types of poor soil with the soft, clean, and fertile soil of true belief. He describes genuine disciples as **the ones on whom seed was sown on the good soil.** Their hearts have been prepared by God Himself (cf. John 6:44, 65), cultivated and tilled by the Holy Spirit (cf. John 16:8–11), so that **when they hear the word,** they **accept it** (cf. Paul's words in 1 Thess. 2:13: "For this reason we also constantly thank God that when you received the word of God which you heard from us, you accepted it not as the word of men, but for what it really is, the word of God, which also performs its work in you who believe"). The truth of God's Word takes deep root in them. Neither Satan nor the world can thwart the saving effect of the gospel when it is deposited in a heart prepared by God to receive it. By including **the good soil** in His parable, Jesus sought to encourage His disciples and, by extension, all other believers who proclaim the truth of His gospel. Though many hearers will reject the gospel—due to hardness, shallowness, and worldliness—there will always be some whom God has prepared to receive the good news of salvation (cf. Isa. 6:8–13).

True believers, those characterized by **the good soil,** do not merely **accept** the gospel mentally, they are transformed by it through the power of the Holy Spirit. Consequently, they inevitably and necessarily **bear fruit.** As Jesus explained to His disciples in John 15:5–8, using a different agricultural metaphor:

> I am the vine, you are the branches; he who abides in Me and I in him, he bears much fruit, for apart from Me you can do nothing. If anyone does not abide in Me, he is thrown away as a branch and dries up; and they gather them, and cast them into the fire and they are burned.... My Father is glorified by this, that you bear much fruit, and so prove to be My disciples.

As Jesus' words indicate, fruit-bearing is the ultimate mark of those who genuinely believe (John 8:31; 14:15). Having been made alive by the Spirit of God (cf. Eph. 2:4–5), they produce "fruit in keeping with repentance" (Matt. 3:8), "the fruit of righteousness" (Phil. 1:11; cf. Col. 1:6), and "the fruit of the Spirit" (Gal. 5:22–23). Though believers are not saved by doing good works (Eph. 2:8–9), those who are truly saved will give evidence of their new life in Christ through the fruit of obedience (Eph. 2:10; cf. Matt. 7:16–20; 2 Cor. 5:17).

Jesus often included a surprising element in His parables. The harvest He described here, of **thirty, sixty, and a hundredfold,** went far beyond anything farmers in the first century experienced. Those figures represent yields of 3,000, 6,000, and 10,000 percent. As noted above, natural yields were less than eightfold, and a crop that produced tenfold would have been extraordinary. Yet, the fields of which Jesus spoke were exponentially more productive. When the gospel goes forth, empowered by the Spirit of God, the results are supernatural.

All believers are called to be witnesses to the gospel of Jesus Christ (cf. Matt. 28:18–20). They are not to tamper with the seed, nor can they cultivate the soil. Rather, they are to faithfully cast the gospel message. As they do, they can expect the responses they receive to fall into one of these categories. Some will reject outright, due to hard-heartedness. Others will demonstrate a superficial interest, only to fall away when hardship comes. Still others will profess a love for Christ while simultaneously nurturing a deadly affection for the world. Finally, there will be some who genuinely receive the gospel. They will humbly turn from their sins and wholeheartedly embrace the Lord Jesus as their Savior and King. The genuineness of their profession will be demonstrated by the abundant fruit of their transformed lives, as they walk in obedience and faith.

On the one hand, knowing that many will reject the gospel enables believers to approach evangelism with proper expectations. On the other hand, knowing that some will truly believe ought to serve as a great encouragement. In evangelism, Christians are privileged to participate in an enterprise that cannot fail. Those whom God is sovereignly drawing to Himself will be saved. If He has prepared the soil of their hearts, the seed will invariably take root and bear abundant fruit.

Although there can be many explanations for why people reject the message of salvation, true repentance is only explainable as a supernatural work of God (cf. 2 Tim. 2:25). All sinners are born with hearts that are hard, shallow, and worldly. Speaking of their preconversion state, Paul told the Ephesians,

> And you were dead in your trespasses and sins, in which you formerly walked according to the course of this world, according to the prince of the power of the air, of the spirit that is now working in the sons of disobedience. Among them we too all formerly lived in the lusts of our flesh, indulging the desires of the flesh and of the mind, and were by nature children of wrath, even as the rest. (Eph. 2:1–3)

The unredeemed heart is incapable of making itself ready to receive the gospel. Only God can transform that which is cold, calloused, and dead into something vibrant, receptive, and full of life. As Paul went on to say, "But God, being rich in mercy, because of His great love with which He loved us, even when we were dead in our transgressions, made us alive together with Christ (by grace you have been saved)" (vv. 4–5).

What a comfort it is to know that soil preparation is God's work. He supplies both the seed of His Word and the power of His Spirit. He readies the soil, working in the hearts of those whom He is drawing to Himself. The task of the evangelist is simply this: to disseminate the seed through the faithful proclamation of the gospel. Having fulfilled that responsibility, believers can rest in the sovereignty of God, knowing that His Word will bear fruit in the hearts and lives of those whom He has called.

Fruitful Hearers (Mark 4:21–34)

15

And He was saying to them, "A lamp is not brought to be put under a basket, is it, or under a bed? Is it not brought to be put on the lampstand? For nothing is hidden, except to be revealed; nor has anything been secret, but that it would come to light. If anyone has ears to hear, let him hear." And He was saying to them, "Take care what you listen to. By your standard of measure it will be measured to you; and more will be given you besides. For whoever has, to him more shall be given; and whoever does not have, even what he has shall be taken away from him." And He was saying, "The kingdom of God is like a man who casts seed upon the soil; and he goes to bed at night and gets up by day, and the seed sprouts and grows—how, he himself does not know. The soil produces crops by itself; first the blade, then the head, then the mature grain in the head. But when the crop permits, he immediately puts in the sickle, because the harvest has come." And He said, "How shall we picture the kingdom of God, or by what parable shall we present it? It is like a mustard seed, which,

when sown upon the soil, though it is smaller than all the seeds that are upon the soil, yet when it is sown, it grows up and becomes larger than all the garden plants and forms large branches; so that the birds of the air can nest under its shade." With many such parables He was speaking the word to them, so far as they were able to hear it; and He did not speak to them without a parable; but He was explaining everything privately to His own disciples. (4:21–34)

Nothing remotely compares to the wonder of the good news that God gave His Son to die as a sin offering so that unworthy rebels might be reconciled to Him through Christ (2 Cor. 5:18–21). The fact that salvation is entirely a work of God's grace apart from any self-righteous effort only adds to the wonder. As the apostle Paul explained in Ephesians 2:8–9, "For by grace you have been saved through faith; and that not of yourselves, it is the gift of God; not as a result of works, so that no one may boast." John Chrysostom, the fourth-century preacher, compared that remarkable reality to a dream that was so amazing it seemed too good to be true. As he explained:

> For as people, on receiving some great good, ask themselves if it is not a dream, as not believing it; so it is with respect to the gifts of God. What then was it that was thought incredible? That those who were enemies and sinners, justified by neither law nor works, should immediately through faith alone be advanced to the highest favor, . . . [and] that a person who had misspent all his former life in vain and wicked actions should afterwards be saved by his faith alone. (John Chrysostom, *Homily on 1 Timothy 1:15–16*, cited in Joel C. Elowsky, *We Believe in the Holy Spirit* [Downers Grove, IL: InterVarsity, 2009], 98)

Such is the magnificent nature of the gospel. The utterly underserving are elevated to a position of highest privilege through no merit of their own (cf. Eph. 2:4–7). God rescues former slaves of sin from the kingdom of darkness and transfers them "to the kingdom of His beloved Son" (Col. 1:13). They become citizens of heaven (Phil. 3:20), heirs of eternal life (Titus 3:7), and the adopted and beloved children of God Himself (Rom. 8:14–17).

Given that no news can compare to the good news of salvation, the fact that most refuse to embrace it is both shocking and tragic. Jesus Himself illustrated that truth by telling the parable of the soils (Mark 4:3–20). Some people reject the gospel as soon as they hear it. Jesus compared their hardness of heart to the impenetrable, pavementlike soil by the road (v. 15). Others respond with superficial exuberance. When times of hardship and persecution arise, and the initial emotionalism fades, they fall away. The Lord likened such individuals to shallow, rocky ground, in which true faith never takes root (vv. 16–17). A third type of soil also looks good on the surface but is actually infested with thorns. The people in this category also react to the gospel with initial interest. But the cares of the world and the pursuit of riches, like suffocating weeds, choke out a genuine love for Christ (vv. 18–19). By contrast, the good soil represents those who embrace the gospel and bear varied amounts of fruit, "thirty, sixty, and a hundredfold" (v. 20).

In differentiating the good soil from the bad, Jesus highlighted a critical difference between the two. The good soil is comprised of those who "hear the word and accept it and bear fruit" (v. 20). In other words, those who truly hear the gospel are those who accept it and bear fruit. Many may profess to "hear" the message of salvation, but true hearers are invariably characterized by fruitful obedience. The theme of hearing runs throughout the parables recounted in Mark 4:1–34. In verse 9, Jesus told His audience, "He who has ears to hear, let him hear." He underscored the importance of that phrase by repeating it in verse 23. His point was simple: true disciples listen eagerly and obediently. As those whose hearts and minds have been opened to the truth by the Holy Spirit, genuine disciples of Jesus love to hear and obey His Word (John 8:32; cf. 10:3–4, 27). Divine truth has found a home in their hearts. They delight in it, submit to it, and bear fruit by putting it into practice and by proclaiming it to others.

The parable of the soils emphasized the importance of being a fruitful hearer by distinguishing the good soil from the bad. In this passage (4:21–34), Jesus articulated three additional parables that expand on that theme. The Lord indicated that understanding the parable of the soils was key to understanding these later parables (v. 13). These parables, then, should not be regarded as disconnected stories. Rather, they are interrelated illustrations carefully arranged by Jesus to make a divine truth clear. Having identified His disciples as those who are both able to perceive divine truth and equipped to proclaim that truth to others, Jesus used these parables to identify four characteristics of fruitful hearers: they witness obediently, work expectantly, wait dependently, and walk confidently.

FRUITFUL HEARERS WITNESS OBEDIENTLY

And He was saying to them, "A lamp is not brought to be put under a basket, is it, or under a bed? Is it not brought to be put on the lampstand? For nothing is hidden, except to be revealed; nor has anything been secret, but that it would come to light. If anyone has ears to hear, let him hear." (4:21–23)

In the parable of the soils, Jesus used good soil to represent believers who hear the gospel, receive it, and consequently bear lasting fruit. Christians demonstrate spiritual life by repenting and turning from sin (Matt. 3:8) to live in obedience to God through the power of the Holy Spirit (Eph. 5:18). Paul delineated the elements of spiritual attitudes in his letter to the Galatians, "The fruit of the Spirit is love, joy, peace, patience, kindness, goodness, faithfulness, gentleness, self-control; against such things there is no law" (5:22–23). The apostle similarly addressed the behavior of believers in his command to the Colossians: "Walk in a manner worthy of the Lord, to please Him in all respects, bearing fruit in every good work and increasing in the knowledge of God" (Col. 1:10). Jesus Himself taught that those who abide in His love and submit to His Word will be fruitful (John 15:4–10). Though it can take many forms, spiritual fruit always consists of both joyful attitudes and acts of obedience to the Lord (cf. John 1:16; Eph. 1:3–8; 2:7–10; Phil. 1:11).

In this passage, the Lord's specific emphasis was on the fruit that comes from being a faithful witness to Him. The parable of the soils focused on the recipients of the gospel, distinguishing between those who would ultimately reject the message and those who would genuinely embrace it. By contrast, these subsequent parables (in vv. 21–32) highlight the responsibility of the faithful hearer as an evangelist. As those who had received the gospel and accepted it, Jesus' disciples would now be called to bear fruit by obediently proclaiming the message of salvation to others (cf. Rom. 1:13; Col. 1:3–6).

The Lord used a simple analogy to make this point. **He was saying to them, "A lamp is not to be put under a basket, is it, or under a bed? Is it not brought to be put on the lampstand?"** Terracotta lamps consisted of a small pitcher or saucer with a handle on one end. The pitcher would be filled with oil and a floating wick would be placed atop the oil. In order to maximize their radiance, lamps were set on lampstands or on shelves protruding from the wall, where their glow could radiate throughout the room unobstructed. For obvious reasons, no one would place a lamp **under a basket** or **under a bed,** thereby negating its purpose.

The point of Jesus' analogy is clear: Those who have received the light of the gospel are not to conceal it; rather they are to let is shine for others to see. Throughout Scripture, light is variously used as a metaphor for truth (Pss. 36:9; 119:105, 130; Prov. 6:23; Acts 26:23; Eph. 5:9; 1 Thess. 5:5), holiness (Rom. 13:12), and spiritual life in Christ (John 1:4). In this analogy, however, Jesus used light to illustrate the message of the gospel. Faithful hearers have an obligation, beyond heeding the gospel themselves, to proclaim it to the world of sinners. Those who have been transformed by the good news are themselves to present that truth to others (cf. Rom. 1:8; 16:19; 1 Thess. 1:8). As Jesus explained in the Sermon on the Mount,

> You are the light of the world. A city set on a hill cannot be hidden; nor does anyone light a lamp and put it under a basket, but on the lampstand, and it gives light to all who are in the house. Let your light shine before men in such a way that they may see your good works, and glorify your Father who is in heaven. (Matt. 5:14–16)

The Lord's words served as a mandate for the disciples, who may have wondered if the proclamation of the gospel was still part of Jesus' strategy for reaching the world. Though Jesus had earlier gone throughout Galilee plainly preaching the gospel (cf. Mark 1:14, 38), He was now speaking in parables. As He told His disciples, "To you has been given the mystery of the kingdom of God, but those who are outside get everything in parables, so that while seeing, they may see and not perceive, and while hearing, they may hear and not understand, otherwise they might return and be forgiven" (4:11–12). As noted earlier, Jesus' parables were an act of divine judgment against the obstinate unbelief of the people, including the outlandish claim made by the religious leaders that He was empowered by Satan (3:22; cf. John 10:20). Recognizing the finality of their rejection, Jesus cut them off from any further truth by speaking to them in unexplained riddles and enigmas.

Perhaps the disciples, observing the shift in Jesus' preaching strategy, wondered if they were also to obscure the gospel message as a judgment on Israel's unbelief. That was not what the Lord planned for them to do. In a short time, He would send them out in pairs to preach the gospel (Mark 6:7–13; cf. Luke 9:1–6). Such was part of the preparation for their full commissioning after His resurrection (Matt. 28:18–20). As Jesus told His disciples before He ascended, "You will receive power when the Holy Spirit has come upon you; and you shall be My witnesses both in Jerusalem, and in all Judea and Samaria, and even to the remotest part of the earth" (Acts 1:8).

That the Lord did not intend for the gospel to be permanently obscured is made clear from verse 22. As the Lord told His disciples, **"For nothing is hidden, except to be revealed; nor has anything been secret, but that it would come to light."** In other words, there was an occasion when the truth was hidden and obscured from some obstinate rejecters; there was coming an era when the **hidden** things were to be revealed, and the **secret** things disclosed to the world. That era of unveiling mysteries would commence with the preaching ministry of the apostles (starting while Jesus was still with them—cf. Matt. 10:26), continue on the other side of the Great Commission, and last until His return (Matt. 24:14).

Jesus' words in verse 22 may have also included an admonition about the reality of spiritual hypocrisy. In Luke 12:1–2, Jesus used this same expression as a warning against the hypocrisy of the Pharisees: "Beware of the leaven of the Pharisees, which is hypocrisy. But there is nothing covered up that will not be revealed, and hidden that will not be known." In the parable of the soils, Jesus described two types of people who initially respond enthusiastically to the gospel but later prove to be false converts. The Lord compared those individuals to soil that was either rocky or infested with thorns. As the disciples considered their evangelistic task, they may have wondered how they would be able to distinguish between spiritual hypocrites and genuine believers. Jesus' words assured them that, given enough time, the truth would come to light. In the short term, false converts might be undetected, but eventually the hidden reality of their hearts would become evident.

Whatever the response to their gospel proclamation, the disciples were to faithfully disseminate the message. The seed of saving faith in their hearts was to produce the fruit of gospel witness. That evangelistic mandate did not end with the apostles. It began with them and has fallen on all believers, in every generation of church history. Christians are called to eagerly "proclaim the excellencies of Him who has called [them] out of darkness into His marvelous light" (1 Peter 2:9). Jesus' statement, **"If anyone has ears to hear, let him hear,"** repeated the truth of Mark 4:9 and underscored the importance of what He had just said. It was imperative that the disciples carefully consider the implications of being a diligent and, therefore, fruitful hearer.

FRUITFUL HEARERS WORK EXPECTANTLY

And He was saying to them, "Take care what you listen to. By your standard of measure it will be measured to you; and more will be given you besides. For whoever has, to him more shall be given; and whoever does not have, even what he has shall be taken away from him." (4:24–25)

Pressing the theme of being attentive hearers, Jesus **was saying to them, "Take care what you listen to."** Another way to say that is, "Pay close attention to what you hear." The truths He was explaining to them were to be established in their minds.

Having articulated their evangelistic responsibility, Jesus highlighted the importance of serious dedication to the task because of the promise of eternal reward for their faithfulness. As He explained to His followers, **"By your standard of measure it will be measured to**

you; and more will be given you besides." At harvesttime, the farmer could expect to get back from his field only what he had put into it. He would reap what he had sown (cf. 2 Cor. 9:6; Gal. 6:7). If he had been lazy or negligent, his harvest would be minimal. If he had been diligent and faithful to the task, he could expect a fruitful crop. His efforts as a sower would be rewarded by the size of his harvest.

Jesus' point was that those who faithfully preach the gospel can similarly expect to be rewarded eternally by God for their diligent efforts. Eternal rewards are privileges that last forever (cf. 1 Cor. 9:24–25; 1 Thess. 2:19–20; 2 Tim. 4:8; Rev. 22:12). What incomparable motivation that should be for all believers. Jesus promised that God would bless their work, not only in accordance with their level of effort (their **standard of measure**) but even far beyond (**more will be given you besides**). As they scatter the seed of the gospel, all believers work expectantly, knowing that their faithfulness to the task will be fruitful and abundantly rewarded in heaven (cf. Luke 6:38).

Driven by an eagerness to please their heavenly Master (cf. 2 Cor. 5:9–10), fruitful hearers put forth enduring effort, knowing that **whoever has, to him more shall be given.** The parallel account of Matthew 13:12 adds the phrase "and he will have an abundance." As believers dispense truth to others, God blesses them with more power, joy, satisfaction, and reward.

False disciples, by contrast, are characterized by fruitlessness (John 15:2, 6). As Jesus warned His listeners, **"Whoever does not have, even what he has shall be taken away from him."** The parallel statement in Luke 8:18 makes the intent of Jesus' statement clear: "Whoever does not have, even what he thinks he has shall be taken away from him." False converts (as illustrated by the rocky and weedy soils) may claim to have spiritual life, but in reality they do not possess it. They may profess to know God, but through their works they deny Him (Titus 1:16). On the day of judgment, with no foundation, their house will come crashing down (Matt. 7:26–27; cf. Phil. 3:8). The emptiness of their superficial faith will be exposed (cf. James 2:19), and the Lord will say to them "I never knew you; depart from Me, you who practice lawlessness" (Matt. 7:23).

Jesus' words also served as a warning to false teachers, those who scatter corrupted seed. Just as there are false disciples, there are also false evangelists. Both will be judged by God. Conversely, genuine believers delight in proclaiming the truth of the gospel to others, knowing that such obedience brings divine blessing both in this world and in heaven.

FRUITFUL HEARERS WAIT DEPENDENTLY

And He was saying, "The kingdom of God is like a man who casts seed upon the soil; and he goes to bed at night and gets up by day, and the seed sprouts and grows—how, he himself does not know. The soil produces crops by itself; first the blade, then the head, then the mature grain in the head. But when the crop permits, he immediately puts in the sickle, because the harvest has come." (4:26–29)

A third characteristic of fruitful hearers is that they have learned to wait dependently on God, who alone can bring results. Though believers are called to witness obediently and work expectantly, they cannot produce life. Only God can give spiritual life (cf. John 3:3–8; 2 Cor. 4:5–7).

Jesus drew another analogy from farming to illustrate His point. This brief parable, unique to Mark's gospel, complements the illustration of planting in the parable of the soils (cf. Mark 4:2–20) by looking at the way the seed grows. In it, Jesus compared **the kingdom of God,** a reference to the sphere of salvation, which is advanced through the proclamation of the gospel, to **a man who casts seed upon the soil.** After he finishes sowing the seed, he goes to bed at night and sleeps. The farmer cannot cause the seed to sprout or new life to form. For that matter, he cannot even fully understand how it comes to life. Yet he plants the seed and waits. And while he waits, entirely apart from his involvement, the seed in the ground comes to life. As the days and weeks pass, while the farmer sleeps at night and **gets up by day** and goes about his normal routine, little green shoots begin to break through the soil. **The seed sprouts and grows—how, he himself does not know. The soil produces crops by itself; first the blade, then the head, then the mature grain in the head.** The sower is not involved in the mysterious process by which the dormant seed is transformed into a living plant.

In the spiritual realm, the evangelist (represented by the sower) distributes the message of the gospel (the seed). Some of the hearers (the good soil) respond to the gospel in saving faith and exhibit spiritual life. This regeneration and spiritual transformation is the work of the Holy Spirit (John 3:5–8). Clearly, it does not depend on the evangelist but only on God, who imparts life through the power of the gospel (cf. John 6:37–44; Rom. 1:16; 1 Thess. 1:5; 1 Peter 1:23). Human ingenuity, emotional manipulation, man-centered techniques, and market-driven strategies cannot create new life in the heart of a sinner. Regeneration is only by the Spirit of God (cf. Eph. 2:1–4; Titus 3:5). Though believers are all called to faithfully proclaim the message, they can take no credit when unbelievers respond in repentant faith (cf. 1 Cor. 3:6–7).

The point of this parable is simple: in the same way that the farmer is not the power behind the regeneration of the seed, so also the evangelist is not the power behind the regeneration of souls. What a comfort this must have been for Jesus' disciples to hear. Perhaps they were concerned that the task of saving sinners rested on their shoulders. Jesus countered that notion by reminding them that only God can change the human heart. Their responsibility was to faithfully preach the message. Having done so, they could trust God with the results. The diligent evangelist, whose message corresponds to the true gospel, can sleep soundly at night, knowing that it is God who causes the growth (1 Cor. 3:6). All the evangelist can do is proclaim the Word (cf. Rom. 10:13–17). The rest is God's work, and believers can fully trust in His sovereign prerogative.

Jesus concluded this illuminating analogy by pointing out that even though the sower did not cause the growth of the grain, he still rejoices in the harvest (cf. 2 Tim. 2:6). **When the crop permits, he immediately puts in the sickle, because the harvest has come.** In a similar manner, although the human messenger plays no role in the actual work of regeneration, he is still given the privileged blessing of enjoying the spiritual harvest. One primary aspect of that blessing is the added fellowship that comes every time a new believer is added to the body of Christ (cf. 2 Cor. 4:15; 1 Thess. 2:19). The riches of that fellowship will last for all of eternity, as the glorified saints—as one great spiritual harvest—gather around the throne to worship their Savior and King.

FRUITFUL HEARERS WALK CONFIDENTLY

And He said, "How shall we picture the kingdom of God, or by what parable shall we present it? It is like a mustard seed, which, when sown upon the soil, though it is smaller than all the seeds that are upon the soil, yet when it is sown, it grows up and becomes larger than all the garden plants and forms large branches; so that the birds of the air can nest under its shade." With many such parables He was speaking the word to them, so far as they were able to hear it; and He did not speak to them without a parable; but He was explaining everything privately to His own disciples. (4:30–34)

A fourth characteristic of fruitful hearers is that they proclaim the gospel with confidence. Because God is the one who blesses His Word and creates spiritual life, believers can fulfill their evangelistic calling with the certainty of knowing that they are part of an enterprise that cannot fail (cf. Matt. 16:18). With this final parable, Jesus assured His disciples that the work in which they would engage would produce an abundant harvest far beyond anything they could ever imagine (Eph. 3:20). Speaking of the spread of the gospel, **He said, "How shall we picture the kingdom of God, or by what parable shall we present it?"** To the disciples, who were still being trained as preachers, the task may have seemed overwhelming, given such seemingly humble beginnings. But Jesus wanted them to be confident in the final outcome.

To illustrate that point, the Lord gave them another agrarian picture. **It is like a mustard seed, which, when sown upon the soil, though it is smaller than all the seeds that are upon the soil, yet when it is sown, it grows up and becomes larger than all the garden plants and forms large branches; so that the birds of the air can nest under its shade."** The Lord Jesus compared the advance of the gospel to a **mustard seed** that is **sown upon the soil,** which starts small but grows into a mighty, treelike bush.

When Jesus said that **it is smaller than all the seeds that are upon the soil,** He was not saying that mustard seeds are the smallest seeds on planet earth. Wild orchids, for example, have a seed much smaller than that of the mustard plant. Rather, Jesus was limiting His statement to that with which His audience would have been familiar. Of the plants grown in first-century Israel for agricultural purposes, the mustard plant had the smallest seeds. Moreover, using the **mustard seed** as a way to refer to things that were very small was a common proverbial expression (cf. Matt. 17:20), one that those listening to Jesus would have immediately recognized. Even though the mustard seed is very small, **yet when it is sown, it grows up and becomes larger than all the garden plants and forms large branches.** Mustard plants in Israel grew to a height of fifteen feet, larger than other garden plants, with branches in which birds could nest.

The point of Jesus' parable would have been self-evident to the disciples: though the kingdom of heaven at that moment was tiny, like a mustard seed, it would grow to encompass the globe for generation after generation. The Messiah Himself had a humble upbringing—born in a stable, laid in a manger, and raised in an out-of-the-way town in Galilee (cf. John 1:46). None of the twelve disciples were highly educated or members of Israel's social or religious elite. Far from being spiritual leaders, the disciples were often fearful, slow to believe, and spiritually weak (cf. Matt. 8:26; 14:31; 16:8). When Jesus was arrested, they fled (Mark 14:50). Even after His resurrection and ascension, the group that gathered in Jerusalem numbered only about 120 followers (Acts 1:15), with another five hundred or so in Galilee (1 Cor. 15:6). Those small beginnings would soon grow. Three thousand souls were added to the 120 in Jerusalem on the day of Pentecost (Acts 2:41). Hundreds of millions more have been added since.

The parable of the mustard seed also anticipated the reality that the kingdom of God (a reference to the sphere of salvation) would bless the whole world. The mustard plant, fully grown, provided shelter to **the birds of the air** who **can nest under its shade.** In the Old Testament, the image of a tree providing safe haven to the birds was used to illustrate kingdoms that were so mighty they brought stability and blessing to nations around them (cf. Dan. 4:10–12, 20–22; Ezek. 31:3–6). Despite its small beginnings, the kingdom of God would become a mighty tree providing security and blessing to the whole earth.

In the church age, that blessing extends to the nations through the influence of Christians around the globe. When believers walk faith-fully, they are a blessing to those around them. The corporate influence of the church has benefited the world in many ways: spiritually, economi-cally, culturally, and morally. Yet, the implications of this parable go beyond the church age to Christ's future millennial kingdom (cf. Ezek. 17:23). During His glorious reign, the Lord Jesus will rule from Jerusalem over the whole world, extending unparalleled blessings to all the nations.

In spite of numbering so few and facing severe opposition, the disciples could proclaim the gospel in the confidence that they were instruments in building God's invincible kingdom. What to them seemed hopelessly small would spread in influence until it permeated the earth for centuries. That which was weak and frail, under divine power, was the beginning of the unstoppable and eternal completion of God's redemp-tive plan through the church to gather the elect to glory.

Mark concludes this section of Jesus' parables with a final sum-mary statement: **With many such parables He was speaking the word to them, so far as they were able to hear it; and He did not speak to them without a parable; but He was explaining every-thing privately to His own disciples.** The unbelief of the crowds was judged by Jesus as He obscured the truth and taught them only unex-plained riddles (cf. Matt. 13:3–52). Even their rejection was part of God's sovereign plan. The parallel passage of Matthew 13:35 explains that Jesus spoke in parables "to fulfill what was spoken through the prophet: 'I will open My mouth in parables; I will utter things hidden since the founda-tion of the world.'" Those words, written by the prophet Asaph (2 Chron. 29:30) in Psalm 78:2, anticipated both the rejection of the Messiah and His response.

John records similar judgment words from Jesus, drawn out of Isaiah 6:

> So Jesus said to them, "For a little while longer the Light is among you. Walk while you have the Light, so that darkness will not overtake you; he who walks in the darkness does not know where he goes. While you have the Light, believe in the Light, so that you may become sons of Light." These things Jesus spoke, and He went away and hid Himself from them. But though He had performed so many signs before them, yet they were not believing in Him. This was to fulfill the word of Isaiah the prophet which he spoke: "Lord, who has believed our report? And

to whom has the arm of the Lord been revealed?" For this reason they could not believe, for Isaiah said again, "He has blinded their eyes and He hardened their heart, so that they would not see with their eyes and perceive with their heart, and be converted and I heal them." (John 12:35–40)

Jesus' followers consisted of true hearers who embraced the gospel. What was hidden from the unbelievers, **He was explaining . . . privately to His own disciples.** Believers today share that same privilege of knowing the truth. Though the Lord Jesus has ascended to heaven, His Spirit indwells and illuminates the hearts of all who belong to Him (cf. 1 Cor. 2:10–14; 1 John 2:27). Thus, every Christian has the privilege of knowing and understanding the truth, a reality that enables them to be fruitful hearers.

Calming the Storm (Mark 4:35–41)

16

On that day, when evening came, He said to them, "Let us go over to the other side." Leaving the crowd, they took Him along with them in the boat, just as He was; and other boats were with Him. And there arose a fierce gale of wind, and the waves were breaking over the boat so much that the boat was already filling up. Jesus Himself was in the stern, asleep on the cushion; and they woke Him and said to Him, "Teacher, do You not care that we are perishing?" And He got up and rebuked the wind and said to the sea, "Hush, be still." And the wind died down and it became perfectly calm. And He said to them, "Why are you afraid? Do you still have no faith?" They became very much afraid and said to one another, "Who then is this, that even the wind and the sea obey Him?" (4:35–41)

The Scriptures boldly declare the deity of the Lord Jesus Christ. The apostle John explicitly states that truth at the outset of his gospel: "In the beginning was the Word, and the Word was with God, and the Word was God. He was in the beginning with God" (John 1:1–2; cf. v. 18). Seven centuries earlier, the prophet Isaiah declared of the Messiah, "His name will be called Wonderful, Counselor, Mighty God, Everlasting Father, Prince of Peace" (Isa. 9:6). In recounting the birth of Christ, Matthew cited the Old Testament to explain that "'they shall call His name Immanuel,' which translated means, 'God with us'" (Matt. 1:23). After Jesus' death and resurrection, upon seeing the risen Savior, Thomas enthusiastically addressed Him as, "My Lord and my God!" (John 20:28). The apostle Paul said of Jesus that "He is the image of the invisible God" (Col. 1:15) and "in Him dwells all the fullness of the Godhead bodily" (Col. 2:9 NKJV). Consequently, believers are those who eagerly await the return of "our great God and Savior, Christ Jesus" (Titus 2:13).

As the incarnate Word of God (cf. John 1:14), Jesus Himself repeatedly affirmed His divinity. He often referred to Himself as the "Son of Man" (cf. Matt. 8:20; Mark 2:28; Luke 6:22; John 9:35–37), a messianic title derived from Daniel 7:13–14 (NKJV), where the "one like the Son of Man" appears as an equal with "the Ancient of Days" (cf. Matt. 25:31; 26:64). He similarly described Himself as the "Son of God," a title clearly indicating His divine nature and eternal union with God the Father. As He explained in Matthew 11:27, "All things have been handed over to Me by My Father; and no one knows the Son except the Father; nor does anyone know the Father except the Son, and anyone to whom the Son wills to reveal Him." In John 5:25–26, speaking of His divine authority, He said, "Truly, truly, I say to you, an hour is coming and now is, when the dead will hear the voice of the Son of God, and those who hear will live. For just as the Father has life in Himself, even so He gave to the Son also to have life in Himself." After receiving word that Lazarus was seriously ill, Jesus told His disciples, "This sickness is not to end in death, but for the glory of God, so that the Son of God may be glorified by it" (John 11:4). At His trial, when His enemies asked Him, "Are You the Son of God, then?" Jesus replied, "Yes, I am" (Luke 22:70; cf. Mark 14:61–62).

Jesus similarly asserted that He was from above, having eternally preexisted in heaven before being born in Bethlehem. On the day after feeding the thousands in Galilee, He asked the crowds, "What then if you see the Son of Man ascending to where He was before?" (John 6:62). A short time later, He told His enemies, "You are from below, I am from above; you are of this world, I am not of this world" (John 8:23). In the upper room, He explained that same truth to His disciples, "I came forth from the Father and have come into the world; I am leaving the world again and going to the Father" (John 16:28). His high priestly prayer echoed that heavenly refrain: "Now, Father, glorify Me together with Yourself, with the glory which I had with You before the world was" (John 17:5).

As God in human flesh, Jesus gladly assumed the prerogatives of deity—claiming to do what only God can do. He maintained His absolute sovereignty over the eternal destiny of every human soul (John 8:24; cf. Luke 12:8–9; John 5:22, 27–29). He declared Himself to be Lord of the Sabbath (Matt 12:8; Mark 2:28; Luke 6:5), and claimed the power to answer prayer (John 14:13–14; cf. Acts 7:59; 9:10–17), the right to receive worship (Matt. 21:16; cf. John 5:23), and the authority to forgive sins (Mark 2:5–11). He referred to God's angels as His angels (Matt. 13:41; 24:30–31), God's elect as His elect (Matt. 24:30–31), and God's kingdom as His kingdom (Matt. 13:41; 16:28; cf. Luke 1:33; 2 Tim. 4:1). Jesus even took the covenant name for God (Yahweh or "I Am") and applied it to Himself. One such example is found in John 8:58, where He told an audience of hostile Jewish leaders, "Truly, truly, I say to you, before Abraham was born, I am" (cf. John 13:19; 18:5–8).

Jesus' enemies knew exactly what Jesus was claiming, which is why they attempted to stone Him for blasphemy (John 8:59; cf. 10:33). As the apostle John recorded, "The Jews sought all the more to kill Him, because He not only broke the Sabbath, but also said that God was His Father, making Himself equal with God" (John 5:18 NKJV). It was, in fact, His claim to be the Son of God that provided the religious leaders with the legal grounds for His execution. As they explained to Pilate, "We have a law, and by that law He ought to die because He made Himself out to be the Son of God" (John 19:7; cf. Matt. 27:43). In spite of His enemies' threats, Jesus never backed down from that claim or its implications. Because He was God in human flesh, He could boldly declare, "I and the Father are one" (John 10:30); "He who sees Me sees the One who sent Me" (12:45); and "He who has seen Me has seen the Father" (14:9–10).

Jesus not only declared His deity, He demonstrated it powerfully through His miracles. The supernatural works of Christ include turning water into wine (John 2:1–11), frequently casting out demons (Mark

1:21–27; Luke 4:31–36, etc.), arranging miraculous catches of fish (Luke 5:1–11; John 21:4–11), creating food for thousands of people (Matt. 14:13–21; Mark 6:30–44; Luke 9:10–17; John 6:1–15), walking on water (Matt. 14:22–33; Mark 6:45–52; John 6:16–21), causing a coin to appear in a fish's mouth (Matt. 17:24–27), and healing all kinds of sickness and disease (Matt. 8:16–17; Mark 1:32–34; Luke 4:40–41, etc.), from crippling paralysis (Matt. 9:1–8) to withered hands (Matt. 12:9–14; Mark 3:1–6; Luke 6:6–11) to blindness (Matt. 9:27–31; 20:29–34; John 9:1–12) to speech handicaps (Matt. 9:32–34) to deafness (Mark 7:31–37) to leprosy (Luke 17:11–19) to the reattachment of a severed ear (Luke 22:50–51). Jesus also raised dead people to life (Matt. 9:23–26; Mark 5:35–43; Luke 8:49–56; Luke 7:11–17; John 11:1–45). Incredibly, this list is only a representative sampling. In fact, Jesus performed so many miraculous signs that John concluded his gospel with these words: "There are also many other things which Jesus did, which if they were written in detail, I suppose that even the world itself would not contain the books that would be written" (John 21:25; cf. 20:30).

That kind of supernatural power over creation, repeatedly demonstrated by Jesus throughout His ministry, has only one explanation: it belongs to the Creator Himself. As the New Testament declares of Jesus Christ, "All things came into being through Him, and apart from Him nothing came into being that has come into being" (John 1:3). The apostle Paul echoed that truth in Colossians 1:16, where he said of Christ, "by Him all things were created, both in the heavens and on earth, visible and invisible, whether thrones or dominions or rulers or authorities—all things have been created through Him and for Him" (cf. 1 Cor. 8:6; Heb. 1:2). The miracles of Jesus were but a small glimpse at the infinite power He possesses as the Son of God.

This miracle (Mark 4:35–41) comprises another occasion on which the supernatural power of Jesus was dramatically displayed. Though His disciples had seen Jesus heal countless people, and though each healing was itself a vivid demonstration of His divine power, they had never before experienced anything of this magnitude. They knew He had authority over demons and disease. Yet, they were wholly unprepared for the show of unbridled omnipotence about to be manifest. The account may be divided into four parts: the calm before the storm, the calm during the storm, the calm after the storm, and the storm after the calm.

THE CALM BEFORE THE STORM

On that day, when evening came, He said to them, "Let us go over to the other side." Leaving the crowd, they took Him along with them in the boat, just as He was; and other boats were with Him. (4:35–36)

It had been a long day of preaching to vast throngs along the shores of the Sea of Galilee near the city of Capernaum. Jesus had been teaching in parables—using analogies about soil (vv. 3–20), lamps (vv. 21–22), and mustard seeds (vv. 30–32)—to illustrate powerful truths about the kingdom of God. Though the crowds were unable to understand the meaning of Jesus' parables, due to their unbelief (cf. v. 13), the Lord was careful to explain "everything privately to His own disciples" (v. 34).

On that day, when evening came, Jesus **said to** His disciples, **"Let us go over to the other side."** From the vicinity of Capernaum, on the northwest tip of the Sea of Galilee, Jesus and His followers headed for the eastern shore. The multitude that had gathered to hear Jesus preach earlier that day was so massive that, in order to effectively address them all, "He got into a boat in the sea and sat down; and the whole crowd was by the sea on the land" (Mark 4:1). As night began to fall, the Lord again used a boat to distance Himself from the throngs of people still assembled on the shore. Traveling to the eastern shores of the Sea of Galilee, where there were no major cities and thus fewer people, would allow Jesus and His disciples to get some reprieve from the massive multitudes. Yet, there was another reason Jesus intended to cross the lake. He had a divine appointment to keep in "the country of the Gerasenes" (Mark 5:1). There He would compassionately deliver a man possessed by a legion of demons (cf. 5:1–20). So, **leaving the crowd,** the disciples **took Him along with them in the boat, just as He was.**

The boat was likely a small, open fishing vessel owned by either Peter and Andrew or James and John. Though these two pairs of brothers had left fishing behind in order to follow Jesus (1:16–20), they retained their boats (cf. John 21:3) and used them to serve Jesus when He had need of them (cf. Mark 3:9). The boat was not large enough to transport all twelve apostles and others of Jesus' followers, so **other boats** were brought to accommodate those who **were with Him.**

It should be noted that the word "disciples" (*mathētēs*), used in 4:34, is a broad term that simply means follower, learner, or student. It encompasses all of those who had shown enough interest in Jesus to follow Him for a time. Though some of these disciples were genuine believers, most would eventually fall away (John 6:66; cf. Luke 9:57–62). Jesus used the illustration of rocky and thorny soil (Mark 4:16–19) to demonstrate that superficial interest in the gospel is not sufficient for salvation. The faith of genuine disciples, like the seed in good soil, takes root and produces lasting fruit, meaning that true believers' lives are characterized by obedience and perseverance. The Lord would later reiterate that point "to those Jews who had believed Him, 'If you continue in My word, then you are truly disciples of Mine'" (John 8:31). False disciples are those whose love for Jesus "will grow cold. But the one who endures to the end, he will be saved" (Matt 24:12–13). For these disciples who accompanied Him in the boats, Jesus was about to display His astonishing divine power designed to move them to genuine faith in Him.

The Sea of Galilee is known today as Yam Kinneret. In Scripture, it is variously referred to as the Lake of Gennesaret (Luke 5:1), the Sea of Chinnereth (Num. 34:11; Josh. 13:27) or Sea of Chinneroth (Josh. 12:3), and the Sea of Tiberias (John 6:1; 21:1), after the main city on its western shore, which was named after Tiberius Caesar Augustus. The sea is in reality a large freshwater lake, measuring approximately thirteen miles long by seven miles wide. Sitting at about 690 feet below sea level, it is both the lowest body of freshwater on earth and the most significant geographical feature of Galilee. Though partially fed through underground springs, the lake gets most of its water from the Jordan River, which runs from north to south—from its source near Mt. Hermon (at an elevation of 9,232 feet above sea level) and its terminus at the Dead Sea (at 1,400 feet below sea level). Even today, the pristine water of the lake not only provides drinking water for local residents, it also supports a thriving fishing industry.

Shaped like a harp, the Sea of Galilee sits roughly thirty miles east of the Mediterranean Sea. The Jordan Valley in which it is situated is part of the Great Rift Valley that runs some 4,500 miles from Syria through the Red Sea and down the east coast of the African continent to Mozambique. The steep hills and cliffs that encompass the Sea of Galilee make it vulnerable to high winds, which can cause sudden, violent storms to develop on the lake. As cooler air travels down from the northern Golan Heights, it collides with the warm air in the basin of the lake, creating turbulent conditions that are intensified as winds force their way through the ravines and canyons of the upper Jordan Valley. In 1992, one such storm generated ten-foot high waves on the lake, causing flooding and damage in the city of Tiberias.

When Jesus and the disciples began their journey, conditions on the lake were ideal. According to Luke 8:23, they "were sailing along," indicating that a steady breeze propelled the boats without anyone needing to row. Jesus, understandably exhausted after an arduous day of teaching and ministering, "fell asleep" (Luke 8:23) in the stern of the boat. Though He was fully God, Jesus was also fully human. He became hungry (Matt. 4:2; 21:18), thirsty (John 4:7; 19:28), and tired (John 4:6). That He needed to sleep is an indication of His true humanity. Yet, the Lord's yielding to sleep had a purpose beyond much-needed rest.

THE CALM DURING THE STORM

And there arose a fierce gale of wind, and the waves were breaking over the boat so much that the boat was already filling up. Jesus Himself was in the stern, asleep on the cushion; and they woke Him and said to Him, "Teacher, do You not care that we are perishing?" (4:37–38)

The tranquility of their journey across the lake ended when, suddenly, **there arose a fierce gale of wind.** *Lailaps* (**fierce gale**) describes the violent gusts of a powerful storm. Mark added the adjective *megas* ("great") to the noun *lailaps* in order to intensify His description of the hurricane-like tempest. Luke, in his account of this event, reported that the winds "descended" on the lake (8:23), to convey that they were racing down the slopes and whipping across the surface of the water. Matthew describes the violent shaking of the storm by using the word *seismos*, from which the English word "seismology" is derived (8:24). The ferocious winds quickly turned the surface of the lake into a raging, convulsive sea. **The waves were breaking over the boat so much that the boat was already filling up.** Though the disciples undoubtedly bailed out the water as fast as they could, "the boat was being covered with the waves" (Matt. 8:24) so that "they began to be swamped and to be in danger" (Luke 8:23).

In the midst of the violent tempest, **Jesus Himself was in the stern, asleep on a cushion.** As the storm raged around Him, He remained asleep. Not even the severe rocking of the boat, the thunderous roar of the wind, or the sloshing water in the boat awakened Him. Presumably soaked to the bone, Jesus slept soundly on the hard wooden planks with only a small cushion as a pillow for His head. Perhaps nowhere else in Scripture is the humanity of Christ more dramatically juxtaposed with His deity. The one sleeping in the stern of the boat, exhausted after a day of intense ministry, is the very one who would awaken to stop the massive storm with a word.

As many as seven of the disciples were fishermen—including Peter, Andrew, James, and John. They had spent their lives navigating the lake and were intimately familiar with what their boats could endure. That they were terrified by the wind and the waves underscores the extreme nature of this storm. To these seasoned fishermen experienced with the conditions on the lake, it became obvious that their own efforts were no match for the powerful tempest, and they panicked.

Frantic and afraid, they came to Jesus, **woke Him and said to Him, "Teacher, do You not care that we are perishing?"** Matthew notes that they called Jesus "Lord," and Luke records that they addressed Him as "Master." Such variations do not imply any contradiction between the gospel accounts. Rather, they reflect the pandemonium of the situation. As the frenzied disciples sought to awaken Jesus, trying to be heard over the roar of the howling wind and crashing waves, some cried out, "Master," others called Him, "Lord," and still others shouted, "Teacher." They were shocked, perplexed, and flustered that He was still asleep, seeming

not to **care** about the dire circumstances that threatened their lives. Reflecting on the disciples' question to Jesus, the Puritan commentator Matthew Henry remarked:

> Their address to Christ is here expressed very emphatically; *Master, carest thou not that we perish?* I confess this sounds somewhat harsh, rather like chiding him for sleeping than begging him to awake. I know no excuse for it, but the great familiarity which he was pleased to admit them into, and the freedom he allowed them; and the present distress they were in, which put them into such a fright, that they knew not what they said. *They* do Christ a deal of wrong, who suspect him to be *careless* of his people in distress. The matter is not so; he is not willing that any should perish, much less any of his little ones. (*Matthew Henry, An Exposition of the Old and New Testament,* 3 volumes [London: Joseph Ogle Robinson, 1828], 3:273, on Mark 4:38)

As Matthew Henry observed, the disciples had no legitimate reason to question Jesus' care for them or their situation. They had witnessed the divine power of Jesus and had followed Him long enough to know of His genuine love for them (cf. John 13:1). But, in their terror, their faith and steadfastness were replaced by fear and doubt.

In their despondency, the disciples would have done well to recall the promises of the Old Testament. A number of psalms are particularly relevant to their traumatic situation. In Psalm 65:5–7, David wrote:

> By awesome deeds You answer us in righteousness, O God of our salvation,
> You who are the trust of all the ends of the earth and of the farthest sea;
> Who establishes the mountains by His strength,
> Being girded with might;
> Who stills the roaring of the seas,
> The roaring of their waves,
> And the tumult of the peoples.

In Psalm 89:9, Ethan the Ezrahite similarly expressed:

> You rule the swelling of the sea;
> When its waves rise, You still them.

The unknown author of Psalm 107 offered these words of comfort and praise:

Those who go down to the sea in ships,
Who do business on great waters;
They have seen the works of the Lord,
And His wonders in the deep.
For He spoke and raised up a stormy wind,
Which lifted up the waves of the sea.
They rose up to the heavens, they went down to the depths;
Their soul melted away in their misery.
They reeled and staggered like a drunken man,
And were at their wits' end.
Then they cried to the Lord in their trouble,
And He brought them out of their distresses.
He caused the storm to be still,
So that the waves of the sea were hushed.
Then they were glad because they were quiet,
So He guided them to their desired haven.
Let them give thanks to the Lord for His lovingkindness,
And for His wonders to the sons of men! (vv. 23–31)

In response to the desperation of His disciples, Jesus was about to accomplish a literal fulfilment of those verses. That He cared about them and their circumstances would soon be made dramatically clear.

THE CALM AFTER THE STORM

And He got up and rebuked the wind and said to the sea, "Hush, be still." And the wind died down and it became perfectly calm. And He said to them, "Why are you afraid? Do you still have no faith?" (4:39–40)

Having heard the frantic cries of His disciples, Jesus **got up and rebuked the wind and said to the sea, "Hush, be still."** In Genesis 1, the pre-incarnate Christ established the boundaries of the seas with nothing more than a word (Gen. 1:9–10; cf. John 1:3; Col. 1:16). On this occasion, He similarly used a simple command to restrain the waves and restore calm on the lake. The word for **hush** comes from the same Greek word that Jesus used earlier when He commanded a demon to "be quiet and come out of him" (Mark 1:25). In the same way that Jesus rebuked spiritual powers, and they obeyed Him, so natural powers submitted to the authoritative command of their Creator.

The result was instantaneous. In a moment, **the wind died down and it became perfectly calm.** The towering waves vanished, the howling gusts were silenced, and the surface of the lake became like glass. As Charles Spurgeon expressed, "There was no trace of storm another moment after He had been awakened. The most blustering of the conflicting winds slept like a babe in its mother's bosom. The waves were as marble" (Charles Spurgeon, "Christ Asleep in the Vessel," sermon no. 1121, July 13, 1873). When Christ **rebuked the wind** and the waves, they did not subside gradually until calm was restored. Both disappeared immediately. The storm may have arisen suddenly, but it vanished even faster than it came. Mark's use of the word *megas* (meaning "great," translated **perfectly**) indicates the absolute stillness that now characterized the Sea of Galilee.

With the storm gone, Jesus turned to address the astonished disciples—who undoubtedly stared back at Him wide-eyed with mouths agape. The Lord **said to them, "Why are you afraid? Do you still have no faith?"** (cf. Matt. 6:30; 14:31; 16:8; 17:20; Luke 12:28). Having silenced the literal tempest, Jesus turned His attention to the winds of fear and the waves of faithlessness that had been raging in their hearts (cf. James. 1:6). The answer to Jesus' first question is implied by the second: the reason they were **afraid** (from the Greek word *deilos*, meaning cowardly or timid) was because they **still** had **no faith.** They knew He possessed divine power, having seen Him perform miraculous healing for many others. Yet, when their own lives were at stake, the inadequacy of their faith was exposed.

Clearly, Jesus intended to teach the disciples a critical lesson: that they could trust Him even in the most treacherous and helpless situations. Even after Jesus' ascension, they would need to be reminded of that truth. As the author of Hebrews reminded his readers, "He Himself has said, 'I will never desert you, nor will I ever forsake you,' so that we confidently say, 'The Lord is my helper, I will not be afraid. What will man do to me?'" (Heb. 13:5–6). The apostle Peter similarly encouraged believers to cast "all [their] anxiety on Him, because He cares for [them]" (1 Peter 5:7; cf. Ps. 55:22). Writing to the Romans, Paul expressed that same kind of confident trust in the permanence of divine love: "For I am convinced that neither death, nor life, nor angels, nor principalities, nor things present, nor things to come, nor powers, nor height, nor depth, nor any other created thing, will be able to separate us from the love of God, which is in Christ Jesus our Lord" (Rom. 8:38–39).

THE STORM AFTER THE CALM

They became very much afraid and said to one another, "Who then is this, that even the wind and the sea obey Him?" (4:41)

Understandably, the disciples marveled in extreme amazement (cf. Matt. 8:27). There was only one explanation for what they had just witnessed. The realization of that fact triggered a storm of wonder in their hearts that greatly overshadowed any momentary terror they had experienced during the storm on the lake. These men had encountered storms on the Sea of Galilee before. None of them had experienced the kind of supernatural power that Jesus displayed on that day. Mark's explanation that **they became very much afraid** could be literally translated, "they feared with a great fear," emphasizing the intensity of their astonishment. The realization that the Creator was in their boat was far more frightening than any terror they might face outside their boat.

They knew only God possessed such power. In their shock they asked **one another** a question to which they already knew the answer, **"Who then is this, that even the wind and the sea obey Him?"** Later in Jesus' ministry, after He miraculously walked on water, the disciples would articulate their answer: "Those who were in the boat worshiped Him, saying 'You are certainly God's Son'" (Matt. 14:33).

Fear is the natural response for sinful human beings to exhibit whenever they are in the presence of God. As Abraham acknowledged after speaking with the Lord, "I am but dust and ashes" (Gen. 18:27). Job responded similarly after witnessing God's power, "I have heard of You by the hearing of the ear; but now my eye sees You; therefore I retract, and I repent in dust and ashes" (Job 42:5–6). When Samson's father, Manoah, realized that the Angel of the Lord had appeared to him, he "said to his wife, 'We will surely die, for we have seen God'" (Judg. 13:22). Upon seeing a vision of God, the prophet Isaiah declared his own demise:

"Woe is me, for I am ruined!
Because I am a man of unclean lips,
And I live among a people of unclean lips;
For my eyes have seen the King, the Lord of hosts." (Isa. 6:5)

Ezekiel saw a vision of the glory of the Lord and "fell on [his] face" (Ezek. 1:28). Daniel similarly, "fell into a deep sleep on [his] face, with [his] face to the ground" (Dan. 10:9). In the New Testament, Peter "fell down at Jesus' feet, saying, 'Go away from me Lord, for I am a sinful man!'" (Luke 5:8). The apostle Paul, confronted by the risen Christ on the road to Damascus, "fell to the ground" and was temporarily blinded by His heavenly glory (Acts 9:4, 9). When the glorified Christ appeared to John on the isle of Patmos, the apostle "fell at His feet like a dead man" (Rev. 1:17). As these examples illustrate, even a small glimpse of the glory of God is overwhelming (cf. Ex. 33:19–21). When Jesus' disciples realized that God was present with them in the boat, they too were overcome with fear at the thought of His power and holiness.

Though this incident exemplifies the divine glory of Christ, as the Creator and controller of the natural world, it also reveals His compassionate care. In the midst of a frightening storm on the lake, and in spite of the disciples' failing faith, the sovereign Savior rescued His followers. Similarly and obviously, believers today can rest confidently in the fact that, through all of life's storms, the omnipotent Lord of creation is willing and able to deliver those who trust in Him. That does not mean Christians will never face trials (cf. James 1:2–3); but when they do they can rest confidently in the promise of Romans 8:28, "And we know that God causes all things to work together for good to those who love God, to those who are called according to His purpose." Armed with that faith-filled perspective, believers are able to obey the command of Philippians 4:6–7: "Be anxious for nothing, but in everything by prayer and supplication with thanksgiving let your requests be made known to God. And the peace of God, which surpasses all comprehension, will guard your hearts and your minds in Christ Jesus." The apostle Paul, who penned those words, endured the many trials of his ministry with that very confidence. Thus, even as his life came to a close, Paul could resolutely declare, "The

Lord will rescue me from every evil deed, and will bring me safely to His heavenly kingdom; to Him be the glory forever and ever. Amen" (2 Tim. 4:18). As the words of the hymn *Our Great Savior* (written by John Wilbur Chapman in 1910) so eloquently express:

> Jesus! What a help in sorrow! While the billows o'er me roll,
> Even when my heart is breaking, He, my comfort, helps my soul.
> Jesus! What a guide and keeper! While the tempest still is high,
> Storms about me, night o'ertakes me, He, my pilot, hears my cry.
> Hallelujah! What a Savior! Hallelujah! What a Friend!
> Saving, helping, keeping, loving, He is with me to the end.

Dominating Powers
(Mark 5:1–20)

17

They came to the other side of the sea, into the country of the Gerasenes. When He got out of the boat, immediately a man from the tombs with an unclean spirit met Him, and he had his dwelling among the tombs. And no one was able to bind him anymore, even with a chain; because he had often been bound with shackles and chains, and the chains had been torn apart by him and the shackles broken in pieces, and no one was strong enough to subdue him. Constantly, night and day, he was screaming among the tombs and in the mountains, and gashing himself with stones. Seeing Jesus from a distance, he ran up and bowed down before Him; and shouting with a loud voice, he said, "What business do we have with each other, Jesus, Son of the Most High God? I implore You by God, do not torment me!" For He had been saying to him, "Come out of the man, you unclean spirit!" And He was asking him, "What is your name?" And he said to Him, "My name is Legion; for we are many." And he began to implore Him earnestly not to send them out of the country. Now there was a

large herd of swine feeding nearby on the mountain. The demons implored Him, saying, "Send us into the swine so that we may enter them." Jesus gave them permission. And coming out, the unclean spirits entered the swine; and the herd rushed down the steep bank into the sea, about two thousand of them; and they were drowned in the sea. Their herdsmen ran away and reported it in the city and in the country. And the people came to see what it was that had happened. They came to Jesus and observed the man who had been demon-possessed sitting down, clothed and in his right mind, the very man who had had the "legion"; and they became frightened. Those who had seen it described to them how it had happened to the demon-possessed man, and all about the swine. And they began to implore Him to leave their region. As He was getting into the boat, the man who had been demon-possessed was imploring Him that he might accompany Him. And He did not let him, but He said to him, "Go home to your people and report to them what great things the Lord has done for you, and how He had mercy on you." And he went away and began to proclaim in Decapolis what great things Jesus had done for him; and everyone was amazed. (5:1–20)

Why did the Lord Jesus Christ come into this world? The apostle John answered that question with this succinct statement: "The Son of God appeared for this purpose, to destroy the works of the devil" (1 John 3:8). Thus, the Messiah came to vanquish Satan, the usurping prince of this world, in order to rescue sinners from spiritual bondage and usher them into the kingdom of God (cf. Mark 1:14–15; Luke 19:10; Eph. 2:1–10; Col. 1:13–14). As early as Genesis 3:15, in the aftermath of mankind's fall into sin, God had promised to send a deliverer who would one day crush the serpent's head. That promise was ultimately fulfilled at the cross, where Christ simultaneously defeated Satan, sin, and death (John 12:31–32; 16:11; Col. 2:14–15). The Lord Jesus died, not as a helpless victim but as the heroic victor, "that through death He might render powerless him who had the power of death, that is, the devil, and might free those who through fear of death were subject to slavery all their lives" (Heb. 2:14–15; cf. 1 Cor. 15:55–57). But the cross was not the only place where Jesus demonstrated sovereign power over Satan and his demon realm. At the outset of His ministry, when He was tempted by the devil in the wilderness, Jesus decisively defeated His archenemy (cf. Mark 1:13; Luke 4:1–13). The Lord subsequently went on the offensive against the powers of darkness (cf. Mark 1:32; Luke 10:19). His earthly ministry sparked an outburst of demonic activity unlike anything before or since, as fallen angels shrieked out in terror whenever they were in His presence (cf. Mark 3:11). Jesus dominated them wherever He found them. They did not attack Him; He attacked them, directly and forcefully, and compelled them to succumb to His commands. The power He exercised over them was absolute, so that in spite of their resistant hatred for Him, they were immediately bound to succumb to His demands.

Although some first-century Jews, like others throughout history, attempted to perform exorcisms through various rituals and formulas, they had no real success (cf. Acts 19:13–16). That Jesus commanded demons with such invincible power, and without failure, was a reality the people found astonishing. As the crowd exclaimed in Mark 1:27, "What is this? A new teaching with authority! He commands even the unclean spirits, and they obey Him." The apparent ease with which He drove out the forces of darkness from the possessed led His enemies to allege that He was actually in league with Satan (3:22). Jesus exposed the obvious folly of such accusations, explaining that His power came from God:

> Any kingdom divided against itself is laid waste; and a house divided against itself falls. If Satan also is divided against himself, how will his kingdom stand? . . . If I cast out demons by the finger of God, then the kingdom of God has come upon you. When a strong man, fully armed, guards his own house, his possessions are undisturbed. But when someone stronger than he attacks him and overpowers him, he takes away from him all his armor on which he had relied and distributes his plunder. (Luke 11:17–22)

Jesus' point was unmistakable: If He were in league with Satan, He would not be attacking Satan's kingdom. He cast out demons, not because He was colluding with Satan but because He was empowered by the only one stronger than Satan—namely, God Himself. In Matthew 12:28, He attributed this divine power specifically to the Spirit of God. It was because Jesus possessed divine power that He could exhibit such absolute authority over Satan's domain. (The "finger of God" was an Old Testament reference to God's power [cf. Ex. 8:19].) His ability to wield that kind of authority proved Him to be the messianic King and the Son of God (cf. Mark 1:1).

Of all the accounts where demons are confronted and cast out, the most dramatic is unquestionably the scene recorded in this passage (Mark 5:1–20; cf. Matt. 8:28–34; Luke 8:26–39). In the biblical record, not since God cast Satan and his rebellious angels out of heaven (cf. Rev. 12:7–12) had so many demons been simultaneously displaced by divine command. Perhaps nothing of this magnitude will occur again until Satan and his forces are bound for a thousand years and subsequently thrown into the lake of fire (Rev. 20:2, 7–10; cf. Isa. 24:21–23).

In the previous passage (Mark 4:35–41), Jesus demonstrated His power over the forces of the natural world by His complete control of the wind and waves. In this passage (5:1–20), He exercised His absolute sovereignty over the forces of the supernatural realm. The account illustrates three spiritual forces at work: the destructive power of demons, the delivering power of deity, and the damning power of depravity.

THE DESTRUCTIVE POWER OF DEMONS

They came to the other side of the sea, into the country of the Gerasenes. When He got out of the boat, immediately a man from the tombs with an unclean spirit met Him, and he had his dwelling among the tombs. And no one was able to bind him anymore, even with a chain; because he had often been bound with shackles and chains, and the chains had been torn apart by him and the shackles broken in pieces, and no one was strong enough to subdue him. Constantly, night and day, he was screaming among the tombs and in the mountains, and gashing himself with stones. Seeing Jesus from a distance, he ran up and bowed down before Him; and shouting with a loud voice, he said, "What business do we have with each other, Jesus, Son of the Most High God? I implore You by God, do not torment me!" (5:1–7)

It had been both an exhausting and exhilarating night for Jesus' disciples. When they set out in their boats from Capernaum the previous evening, they expected to sail quietly across the Sea of Galilee. Instead, they encountered the most unforgettable storm they had ever experienced. But it was not the force of the wind or magnitude of the waves that made their harrowing journey so memorable. In the midst of the tempest, Jesus "rebuked the wind and said to the sea, 'Hush, be still.' And the wind died down and it became perfectly calm" (4:39). The fury of the storm caused them momentary panic, but the sovereign omnipotence of Jesus produced a far more profound fear in their hearts. Astonished, they asked themselves a question to which they already knew the answer, "Who then is this, that even the wind and the sea obey Him?" (v. 41).

The disciples were undoubtedly still in a state of shock and awe when, early the next morning, **they came to the other side of the sea, into the country of the Gerasenes.** According to Luke, this predominantly Gentile region was "opposite Galilee" (Luke 8:26), running along the eastern shore of the lake. Both Mark and Luke called it **the country of the Gerasenes** (Mark 5:1; Luke 8:26), while Matthew referred to it as "the country of the Gadarenes" (Matt. 8:28). Both designations are correct. Mark and Luke were evidently referring to the small village of Khersa (or Gersa, modern-day Kursi), located by the Sea of Galilee near the place Jesus and His disciples landed, about six miles from Capernaum. Matthew was referencing the larger town of Gadara, situated to the southeast of Gersa, which gave the region its name and may have been its main city.

The disciples likely thought they had traveled across the lake as they had done before to find some reprieve from the relentless crowds. Jesus, however, knew He had a divine appointment to keep. **When He got out of the boat, immediately a man from the tombs with an unclean spirit met Him.** No sooner had the disciples reached the shore and docked their boats than a raging lunatic came racing down the slope to the edge of the lake to meet them. Matthew 8:28 indicates there were actually two such men. Though Mark and Luke chose to focus solely on the man with whom Jesus spoke, nothing in their accounts contradicts the material found in Matthew. (For an example of how the three Synoptic Gospels can be harmonized regarding this account, see John

MacArthur, *One Perfect Life* [Nashville: Thomas Nelson, 2012], 180–82.)

That the man had **an unclean spirit** indicates he was demon-possessed—a point reiterated in verse 15. When the New Testament speaks of those "with an unclean spirit" (cf. Mark 1:23; 7:25), those who "have a demon" (cf. Matt. 11:18; Mark 3:22, Luke 4:33; 7:33; 8:27; John 7:20; 8:48, 49, 52; 10:20), or those who are "demon-possessed" (cf. Matt. 4:24; 8:16, 28, 33; 9:32; 12:22; 15:22; Mark 1:32; 5:15–16, 18; Luke 8:36; John 10:21), it is describing people who were indwelt, and thus controlled and tormented by evil, fallen angels. It is because demons indwell their victims (cf. Luke 8:30) that Jesus cast them out thus liberating the afflicted person (Matt. 8:16; 9:33; 12:24, 28; Mark 1:34; cf. Matt. 8:32; Mark 5:8, 13). Though demons generally work in society through the promotion of error, lies, false religion (1 Tim. 4:1; cf. 1 Cor. 10:20–21), and apostasy (1 Tim. 4:1–3; cf. James 3:13–16), demon possession is an extreme form of individualized subjugation, wherein one or more evil spirits control a person's mind, body, and voice. While demon possession can cause physical symptoms (cf. Matt. 9:32; 12:22; 17:14–15; Mark 1:26; 5:5; Luke 8:27; 9:42), it is a supernatural phenomenon that goes beyond scientific, psychological, or medical explanation. It should be added that, when Scripture speaks of the power of fallen angels, it does so to demonstrate the infinitely greater power of God (cf. Eph. 1:21). This is especially true in the ministry of Jesus, where the emphasis is on Christ's power over the spirits of darkness. Those who belong to Jesus Christ are indwelt by the Holy Spirit. They need not fear demon possession because they are the temple of the Spirit of God (1 Cor. 6:19–20). And as the apostle John told his readers, "Greater is He that is in you than he who is in the world" (1 John 4:4).

In describing the demon-possessed man, Mark began by noting that **he had his dwelling among the tombs.** In ancient times, burial chambers were often carved out of the hillside, and a number of such tombs have been discovered near Khersa. The Jews generally avoided lingering near tombs for fear of becoming ceremonially unclean by touching a dead body (cf. Num. 19:11). Here, in a Gentile region was a demon-possessed man who was more comfortable among the dead than among the living. Luke adds that he "had not put on any clothing for a long time" (Luke 8:27). The man's nakedness not only indicated sexual perversion (cf. Lev. 18:16–19; 20:11, 17–21) and shame (cf. Gen. 3:7; Rev. 3:18), it also illustrated the physical torment he suffered at the hands of the demons who possessed him, since he was constantly exposed to the natural elements. The raucous approach of this Gentile madman, along with his frenetic companion, must have severely startled the disembarking disciples. After a traumatic night on the lake, they were once again shocked and alarmed by the sudden appearance of this dangerous lunatic and his friend.

Recognizing the obvious threat posed by the man, the local residents had tried repeatedly to restrain him, unsuccessfully. **No one was able to bind him anymore, even with a chain; because he had often been bound with shackles and chains, and the chains had been torn apart by him and the shackles broken in pieces, and no one was strong enough to subdue him. Constantly, night and day, he was screaming among the tombs and in the mountains, and gashing himself with stones.** Under demonic domination, the man was a supernaturally strong, raging, self-mutilating, deviant madman. To this startling description, Luke 8:29 adds that he had been "driven by the demon into the desert," and Matthew 8:28 notes that he and his companion were "so extremely violent that no one could pass by that way." Seated on their hillside perch, they watched as Jesus and His disciples reached the shore and began to disembark. Likely thinking they had new victims to terrify, the naked man and his companion raced down the slope toward the shore, screaming and yelling.

But waiting on the shore this time was the Son of God. **Seeing Jesus from a distance,** the demons who indwelt this man could sense the presence of the glorious King of the universe and they panicked. They verbalized their fear through the voice of the tortured soul, who screamed in terror (cf. Luke 8:28) as **he ran up and bowed down before Him.** The word for bow (*proskuneō*) means to worship. This reverence was not motivated by repentance (since demons cannot repent) but out of the horrifying recognition of their heavenly sovereign (cf. James. 2:19). Compelled by sheer dread, the demons were utterly subdued before their Judge. What no human being could tame, even through the use of ropes and chains, Jesus restrained with nothing more than His presence.

The demons addressed Jesus through the man's voice. **Shouting with a loud voice, he said, "What business do we have with each other, Jesus, Son of the Most High God? I implore You by God, do not torment me!"** As fallen angels who served God from their creation until they joined Satan's rebellion and were cast out of heaven, they knew exactly who Jesus was: the **Son of the Most High God.** The name **Most High God** is a glorious title used throughout Scripture to accentuate God's absolute sovereignty over all other powers (cf. Gen. 14:19; Deut. 32:8; 2 Sam. 22:14; Pss. 18:13; 21:7; 47:2; 57:2; 78:35, 56; 97:9; Lam. 3:38; Dan. 3:26; 5:18, 21; Acts 16:17; Heb. 7:1). That **Jesus** is the **Son of the Most High God** means that He possesses the same authority and essence or nature as His Father (cf. Luke 1:32, 35; John 10:30).

Trembling in the presence of their divine Judge, the demons feared Jesus might immediately cast them into the bottomless pit where other fallen angels were held captive (Luke 8:31; cf. 2 Peter 2:4; Jude 6; Rev. 9:1–12). But they also assumed that they were not destined for final incarceration until the end of human history (cf. Rev. 20:7–10). Aware of God's eschatological timetable and believing their appointed day of punishment to still be future, they blurted out, **"What business do we have with each other?"** and also, "Have You come here to torment us before the time?" (Matt. 8:29). As they groveled before Jesus, all they could do was plead for a little more time before being sentenced to the pit. Thus, one of the demons cried out on behalf of the whole host, **"I implore You by God, do not torment me!"** Though the time of final judgment for fallen angels has not yet come, their reign of terror on earth has its end. One day Satan and his entire host will be cast into the lake of fire, in which they will suffer eternal torment (cf. Matt. 25:41; Rev. 14:11).

THE DELIVERING POWER OF DEITY

For He had been saying to him, "Come out of the man, you unclean spirit!" And He was asking him, "What is your name?" And he said to Him, "My name is Legion; for we are many." And he began to implore Him earnestly not to send them out of the country. Now there was a large herd of swine feeding nearby on

the mountain. The demons implored Him, saying, "Send us into the swine so that we may enter them." Jesus gave them permission. And coming out, the unclean spirits entered the swine; and the herd rushed down the steep bank into the sea, about two thousand of them; and they were drowned in the sea. Their herdsmen ran away and reported it in the city and in the country. And the people came to see what it was that had happened. They came to Jesus and observed the man who had been demon-possessed sitting down, clothed and in his right mind, the very man who had had the "legion"; and they became frightened. Those who had seen it described to them how it had happened to the demon-possessed man, and all about the swine. (5:8–16)

The demons were fully acquainted with the Son of God and aware of their inability to resist His power. They had no option but to leave their human victim, **for Jesus had been saying to him** (namely, the fallen angel who in verse 7 had spoken on behalf of the entire demon host), **"Come out of the man, you unclean spirit!"** In the process of casting out the demon, Jesus paused to ask him, **"What is your name?" And he said to Him, "My name is Legion; for we are many."** That name, of course, was not the man's name but the title taken by the demon forces who indwelt the man. **Legion** is a military designation used to identify groups of soldiers. At that time, a Roman legion consisted of up to six thousand soldiers, demonstrating just how "many demons had entered him" (Luke 8:30; cf. Matt. 12:43–45). Jesus demanded the name of these demons for one simple reason: to demonstrate the extent of His power over the realm of Satan. He not only had the authority to cast out a solitary demon but even an entire horde. Fallen angels, whether they numbered few or many, were under the control of His will and incomparable power.

The spokesman for the demons, after divulging their name, **began to implore Him earnestly not to send them out of the country.** Luke 8:31 adds, "They were imploring Him not to command them to go away into the abyss." Jesus could have exiled them to any place He wanted. Their desire was to stay in that Gentile region, evidently to continue operating in and through the local culture and pagan religious practices. Noticing **a large herd of swine feeding nearby on the mountain,** they saw a possible escape. **The demons implored Him, saying, "Send us into the swine so that we may enter them."** The request of the demons was bizarre, reflecting the desperation caused by both their realization that they could not stay where they were and their recognition that they might be cast into the abyss if they did not come up with a quick alternative. If they could no longer wreak havoc through the man, they would do so through a herd of pigs. That would be temporary, they likely thought, until they could find other human victims.

It is important to note that, if it had been His desire, Jesus could have immediately sent these demons to the abyss. That He chose not to do so was neither a sign of compromise nor compassion toward these evil spirits. The Lord **Jesus** had another purpose for them to fulfill, and so He **gave them permission** to enter the swine. As powerful as they are, Satan and his demonic forces can do nothing outside of what God either commands or permits them to do (cf. Judg. 9:23; 1 Sam. 16:14; 1 Kings 22:19–23; Job 1:9–11; 2:3–6; Isa. 37:7; Luke 22:31; 2 Cor. 12:7–8; Rev. 20:1–3). Certainly, God is not the author of evil (James 1:13). Yet even the chaos and corruption produced by evil spirits fits within His sovereign plan (cf. Prov. 16:4; Isa. 45:7; Lam. 3:38)—in which all things work together both for His glory and for the spiritual good of those who belong to Him (cf. Rom. 8:28). By granting permission for these demons to go into the herd of pigs, Jesus was allowing them to put on display the true magnitude of their destructive and deadly force. In so doing, He also highlighted the glorious superiority of His own power.

With permission received, the demons did not hesitate to relocate. **And coming out, the unclean spirits entered the swine; and the herd rushed down the steep bank into the sea, about two thousand of them; and they were drowned in the sea.** The dramatic scene provided stunning, undeniable proof that the evil spirits had left the man. It similarly demonstrated their damaging power on a massive scale; the fact that roughly two thousand pigs were affected suggests that an equivalent number of demons were cast out of the man. More importantly, it demonstrated the extent of Jesus' authority over them. The demons had no choice but to comply with His sovereign command. Though fallen angels are exceptionally powerful beings (cf. 2 Kings 19:35;

Ps. 103:20; 2 Peter 2:11), they instantly submitted to the omnipotent authority of the divine Son.

Thus, the unclean spirits were cast into a herd of unclean animals (Lev. 11:7; Deut. 14:8); once there, they caused a massive stampede, as the pigs charged violently down a slope and drowned in the lake. Some people wonder why Jesus would allow so many animals to be killed in such dramatic fashion. Several points might be made in response. First, and most obviously, Jesus did not kill the pigs; the demons did. That God sovereignly permits Satan and his agents to act wickedly does not mean that God is responsible for their sinful actions (cf. James 1:13). Second, the Lord's focus was on rescuing the man. The loss of the pigs represented a relatively small sacrifice in comparison to the human life that was recovered when the demons were expelled. Third, all of the swine would have eventually been slaughtered anyway, since they were being raised for food. Though it hastened their deaths, the drowning of the swine did not destroy their meat. The herd's owners undoubtedly recovered much of it by retrieving the dead pigs from the water, butchering their meat and sending it to market. Finally, to become fixated on what happened to the pigs is to fall far below the point of this event, which is that the demon forces were so numerous and violent that, within moments of their expulsion from the man, they were able to occupy and drown a multitude of otherwise impersonal beasts. The only power that could control them was that of the Lord Jesus.

Understandably alarmed by what they had just witnessed, the **herdsmen ran away and reported it in the city and in the country. And the people came to see what it was that had happened.** According to Matthew 8:33, they "reported everything," indicating that even they realized the connection between the man's deliverance and the herd's traumatic demise. The alarming report—from the untamable madman bowing before Jesus to the pigs charging recklessly into the sea—piqued the curiosity of the local residents, who hurried to see what had happened. **They came to Jesus and observed the man who had been demon-possessed sitting down, clothed and in his right mind, the very man who had had the "legion."** When they arrived on the scene, they saw the former demon-possessed lunatic and local menace, not raging violently as always but **sitting down, clothed and**

in his right mind. What a startling evidence of the total transformation that had taken place in his life! Undoubtedly, Jesus had explained the gospel to him, so that he had been delivered not only from demons but also from sin and hell. If the townspeople were at all concerned about the pigs, they failed to mention anything about them. Instead, their focus was on Jesus and on the man who had been dramatically delivered from a demon horde.

Given the man's miraculous deliverance, one might expect the people to respond with relief, gratitude, and worship. In reality, they reacted with utter dread. Their fear had previously been directed toward the demon-possessed man who terrorized the countryside. But he was clearly no longer a threat. So what made them afraid? **They became frightened** as they heard **those who had seen it** explain **to them how it had happened to the demon-possessed man, and all about the swine. Frightened** translates a form of the Greek word *phobeō*, referring to extreme fear or terror (the related noun *phobos* is the root of the English word "phobia"). In the same way the disciples had been initially terrorized by the raging sea, only to experience a far greater fear when they realized they were in the presence of deity (Mark 4:40), so it was for these townspeople. Their fear of the man was gone; in its place was the terrifying dread that accompanies a recognition of being in the presence of God, who has power over spiritual beings. The disciples were frightened by the storm but more frightened by Jesus after He calmed the storm (cf. Luke 8:25). The next day, the local people were initially frightened by the demoniac, but they were far more fearful of Jesus when they became aware of His supernatural power.

THE DAMNING POWER OF DEPRAVITY

And they began to implore Him to leave their region. As He was getting into the boat, the man who had been demon-possessed was imploring Him that he might accompany Him. And He did not let him, but He said to him, "Go home to your people and report to them what great things the Lord has done for you, and how He had mercy on you." And he went away and began to pro-

claim in Decapolis what great things Jesus had done for him; and everyone was amazed. (5:17–20)

One would expect such a dramatic miracle to produce a spontaneous revival in that region. Instead, the response of the people was immediate rejection. Motivated by fear, **they began to implore Him to leave their region.** The word **implore** translates a form of the Greek verb *parakaleō*, meaning to entreat or beseech. In a tragic twist, the demons implored Jesus to let them stay in that country (v. 10) while the people implored Jesus to leave (v. 17). Their reaction revealed the calloused depravity of their lost condition (cf. John 3:19; 2 Cor. 4:4). They preferred the company of dangerous demons to that of the divine Deliverer.

In their rejection of the Lord Jesus, the people stand as an instructive illustration of the power of unbelief. The astonishing miracle Jesus performed did not lead them to faith in Him as Lord and Messiah. In fact, it had the opposite effect. No one could deny that He had displayed divine power. Nor did anyone doubt the transformation of the former demoniac. (Matt. 8:33 implies that his companion was also delivered.) Yet, in the face of such undeniable evidence, their hearts remained cold and impenetrable. Confronted with the presence of God the Son, and gripped with fear, they begged Him to leave their shores immediately. Earlier, Jesus had conceded the request of the terrified demons, allowing them to go into the pigs. Here He yielded to the wishes of the terrified residents, granting their wish for Him to depart.

Jesus and His disciples got back in their boats in order to return to Capernaum. **As He was getting into the boat, the man who had been demon-possessed was imploring Him that he might accompany Him.** In contrast to the unbelieving townspeople, the former demoniac did not want to live another day without Jesus. His tormented soul had been reborn, as clearly evidenced by his eagerness to leave everything behind to follow Christ. As a new believer, he begged the Lord to allow him to accompany Him. But Jesus had other plans for this man. Consequently, **He did not let him, but He said to him, "Go home to your people and report to them what great things the Lord has done for you, and how He had mercy on you."** Instead of bringing him back to Capernaum, the Lord commissioned this man to be a missionary where he was. As the Lord had earlier explained to His disciples, "A lamp is not brought to be put under a basket, is it, or under a bed? Is it not brought to be put on the lampstand?" (Mark 4:21). With his life dramatically transformed, the former demoniac known to all in the region would radiate the transforming glory of the gospel simply by being there and declaring what Christ had done for him.

Though he initially and understandably wanted to accompany Christ, the man faithfully submitted to Jesus' directive. **And he went away and began to proclaim in Decapolis what great things Jesus had done for him; and everyone was amazed.** Traveling throughout the Gentile region east of Galilee, the former demoniac spread the news about Jesus far and wide. It is important to recognize his impact. When Jesus again visited the region around Decapolis (Mark 7:31–8:9), a massive crowd came to hear Him teach—motivated, surely, by the reports from this man. The response to his testimony was that **everyone was amazed.** The word **amazed** (a form of the Greek verb *thaumazo*) means "to marvel" or "to admire with wonder." Undoubtedly many, like the disciples, found themselves asking the question, "Who is this man, that even the demons obey Him?" (cf. Mark 4:41).

The main point of this account, like the storm on the Sea of Galilee, is to underscore the divine authority of Jesus Christ. As God incarnate, He rules over both the natural and the supernatural realms. No angelic power is any match for His absolute sovereignty (cf. Eph. 1:21). Thus, those who love the Lord Jesus have nothing to fear from demonic powers (cf. Rom. 8:38). Secondly, this account also teaches an important lesson about the requirements necessary for being a faithful evangelist. The former demoniac had no formal theological training, yet he still had everything he needed to fulfill Christ's commission for him. Having been delivered and transformed by the Lord Jesus, he was given the simple responsibility of relating the wonder of his salvation transformation to others. That same responsibility is shared by all who belong to Jesus Christ. When believers tell others about how the Savior delivered them from sin and gave them eternal life, they similarly fulfill their God-given commission to the world (cf. Matt. 28:18–19).

The Power and Pity of Jesus (Mark 5:21–43)

18

When Jesus had crossed over again in the boat to the other side, a large crowd gathered around Him; and so He stayed by the seashore. One of the synagogue officials named Jairus came up, and on seeing Him, fell at His feet and implored Him earnestly, saying, "My little daughter is at the point of death; please come and lay Your hands on her, so that she will get well and live." And He went off with him; and a large crowd was following Him and pressing in on Him. A woman who had had a hemorrhage for twelve years, and had endured much at the hands of many physicians, and had spent all that she had and was not helped at all, but rather had grown worse—after hearing about Jesus, she came up in the crowd behind Him and touched His cloak. For she thought, "If I just touch His garments, I will get well." Immediately the flow of her blood was dried up; and she felt in her body that she was healed of her affliction. Immediately Jesus, perceiving in Himself that the power proceeding from Him had gone forth, turned around in the crowd and said, "Who touched My garments?" And His disciples said to Him, "You see the crowd pressing in on You, and You say, 'Who touched Me?'" And He looked around to see the woman who had done this. But the woman fearing and trembling, aware of what had happened to her, came and fell down before Him and told Him the whole truth. And He said to her, "Daughter, your faith has made you well; go in peace and be healed of your affliction." While He was still speaking, they came from the house of the synagogue official, saying, "Your daughter has died; why trouble the Teacher anymore?" But Jesus, overhearing what was being spoken, said to the synagogue official, "Do not be afraid any longer, only believe." And He allowed no one to accompany Him, except Peter and James and John the brother of James. They came to the house of the synagogue official; and He saw a commotion, and people loudly weeping and wailing. And entering in, He said to them, "Why make a commotion and weep? The child has not died, but is asleep." They began laughing at Him. But putting them all out, He took along the child's father and mother and His own companions, and entered the room where the child was. Taking the child by the hand, He said to her, "Talitha kum!" (which translated means, "Little girl, I say to you, get up!"). Immediately the girl got up and began to walk, for she was twelve years old. And immediately they were completely astounded. And He gave them strict orders that no one should know about this, and He said that something should be given her to eat. (5:21–43)

Like a deadly virus, sin is a devastating force that infects every human being (cf. Rom. 3:23). Its corrupting influence is pervasive and destructive—careening people into sickness, suffering, and ultimately death (cf. Rom. 6:23). Adam's disobedience in the garden of Eden first introduced death into the world (Rom. 5:12), and his descendants have all inherited his terminal condition.

The fear of death is a universal human reality (Heb. 2:15). Popular metaphors for death, from the grim reaper to the great unknown, reflect the apprehension that grips human hearts. The Bible, too, recognizes that people are afraid to die. Thus, Job 18:14 refers to death as "the king of terrors," and Psalm 55:4 similarly speaks of "the terrors of death." Throughout the millennia, people have tried to escape death but without success. Even advancements in modern medical science, as incredible as they are, can only prolong the inevitable.

The universal reality of death raises a critical question: In all of human history, has anyone conquered death and, in so doing, made it possible for others to triumph over it? The Bible answers that question with a resounding yes. There is a deliverer. He is none other than the Lord Jesus Christ, the Son of God (cf. Acts 4:12). As Jesus Himself said, "I am the resurrection and the life; he who believes in Me will live even if he dies, and everyone who lives and believes in Me will never die" (John 11:25–26). Elsewhere, Jesus reiterated that truth: "Everyone who beholds the Son and believes in Him will have eternal life, and I Myself will raise him up on the last day" (John 6:40); "I came that they may have life, and have it abundantly" (10:10); "I am the way, and the truth, and the life" (14:6); "Because I live, you will live also" (14:19).

The veracity of those claims was proven by Jesus when He personally defeated death by rising from the grave (cf. Acts 2:24–32; Rom. 1:4; 2 Tim. 1:10; Heb. 2:14; Rev. 1:18). The historicity of Christ's resurrection is detailed by each of the four Gospels (Matt. 28:1–8; Mark 16:1–8; Luke 24:1–8; John 20:1–10), a fact corroborated by eyewitnesses, including more than five hundred at one time (1 Cor. 15:6). The gospel proclaims the truth that, in His resurrection, the Lord Jesus conquered death not only for Himself but also for all who would believe in Him.

As a preview to His own resurrection, Jesus raised a number of people from dead during His earthly ministry, including the son of a widow from Nain (Luke 7:11–15), a man from Bethany named Lazarus (John 11:1–44), and the young woman mentioned in this passage (Mark 5:21–43). In so doing, He demonstrated His divine nature and power over death (cf. John 5:28–29). When the disciples of John the Baptist asked Him, "Are You the Expected One, or do we look for someone else?" (Luke 7:20) Jesus answered by pointing to His power over disease and death: "Go and report to John what you have seen and heard: the blind receive sight, the lame walk, the lepers are cleansed, and the deaf hear, the dead are raised up, [and] the poor have the gospel preached to them" (Luke 7:22).

The events recorded in this passage form two final vignettes in a series of stories that reveal the power of Jesus. In Mark 4:35–41, Jesus displayed His authority over the natural world when, with a word, He instantly calmed a storm on the Sea of Galilee. The next day, He displayed His sovereignty over supernatural forces by casting out a legion of demons (5:1–20). In this section (5:21–43), upon returning to Capernaum, Jesus exercised miraculous power over both disease and death. These verses relate a double miracle. Not only did He heal a woman from a twelve-year ailment, He also raised a twelve-year-old girl from the dead. Clearly, His creative power was without limits. As the Creator Himself (cf. John 1:1–3), He could restore just one part of the body and also bring an entire body back to life.

This passage not only showcases Jesus' incomparable might, it also highlights His mercy, gentleness, sensitivity, and loving-kindness. The greatness of His miraculous power is thus placed alongside the goodness of His personal ministry. The Son of God not only had the creative ability to heal and give life, He also had the desire to do so. As the miracle unfolds, four compelling facets of Jesus' compassion become distinguishable: in the crowd, He was accessible; in the commotion, He was interruptible; in the crisis, He was unflappable; and in the cure, He was charitable.

In the Crowd, Jesus Was Accessible

When Jesus had crossed over again in the boat to the other side, a large crowd gathered around Him; and so He stayed by the seashore. One of the synagogue officials named Jairus came up, and on seeing Him, fell at His feet and implored Him earnestly, saying, "My little daughter is at the point of death; please come and lay Your hands on her, so that she will get well and live." And He went off with him; and a large crowd was following Him and pressing in on Him. (5:21–24)

Unlike many religious leaders, including the rabbis of first-century Judaism, Jesus did not seclude Himself from people. His entire ministry was spent surrounded by the crowds, with only occasional retreats into isolation for the purpose of prayer, rest, and focused times of instruction with His disciples. Ministering among the multitudes was not easy; they relentlessly hounded (cf. 1:37, 45) and crowded (cf. 2:4; 3:9, 20) Him. Yet, He remained accessible to them.

In the previous section (5:1–20), Jesus cast a legion of demons out of a man on the eastern shore of the Sea of Galilee. The residents of the area, frightened by such a dramatic display of divine power and revealing their unbelieving indifference, begged the Lord to leave. Obliging their request, **Jesus** and His disciples **crossed over again in the boat to the other side,** traveling roughly six miles across the lake to the western shore near Capernaum. When they arrived, they were greeted by **a large crowd** that **gathered around Him** to the extent that **He stayed by the seashore.** According to Luke 8:40, "the people welcomed Him, for they had all been waiting for Him." This crowd was no doubt comprised of many who were suffering from various diseases and disabilities. Hoping to be healed, they had waited eagerly for Jesus' arrival.

Mark's account focuses on two individuals out of the massive multitude who desperately needed Jesus. They had little in common, other than the dire nature of their circumstances. One was a man, the other a woman; one wealthy, one poor; one respected, one rejected; one honored, one ashamed; one leading the synagogue, the other excommunicated from the synagogue; one with a twelve-year-old child, the other with a twelve-year-old malady. Though they had no obvious relationship to one another, in God's perfect providence their lives intersected that day in an unforgettable way.

The first of these individuals was **one of the synagogue officials,** a man **named Jairus.** Given the animosity Jesus had received from Israel's religious establishment (cf. 3:6, 22), the disciples must have been shocked when they saw a respected synagogue official making his way through the crowds to find Jesus. **The synagogue officials** were a group of men (usually numbering between three and seven) in each local synagogue who acted as the caretakers and administrators of synagogue life. They safeguarded the scrolls, cared for the facility, organized the synagogue school, and supervised the readers, teachers, and those who prayed. As such, Jairus would have been both religiously devout and highly respected in the community. None of the gospel writers identify Jairus as a member of the Pharisees. Even so, his position in the synagogue meant he was intimately connected with the Pharasaic establishment of Capernaum. He was undoubtedly aware of the hatred the religious leaders had toward Jesus. Yet, he was willing to very publicly seek His help.

As an official leader in Capernaum, Jairus would have been well aware of the miraculous works Jesus had performed there. It is possible that the synagogue in which Jesus cast out a demon (in Mark 1:21–28) was the place where Jairus served as an official. If so, he likely had personally witnessed the Lord's supernatural power. Jairus also would have heard of the many healing miracles Jesus performed, both in that city and in the surrounding regions. When the life of his daughter was at stake, he knew exactly whom to seek.

Making his way through the dense crowd to Jesus, Jairus **came up, and on seeing Him, fell at His feet.** Unlike Nicodemus, who secretly approached Jesus under the cover of darkness (John 3:2), Jairus came boldly and openly and upon arriving even **fell at His feet.** Matthew 9:18 says Jairus "bowed down" before Him. Significantly, Matthew used the Greek word *proskuneō*, which is often translated "worshiped" (cf. Matt. 4:10; John 4:21–24; 1 Cor. 14:25; Rev. 4:10). Compelled by both the urgency of his need and the hopefulness of his faith, this respected man prostrated himself before Jesus in an act of highest homage and reverence. That Jairus believed Jesus could heal his daughter is evidenced by his poignant request. He **implored Him earnestly, saying, "My little daughter is at the point of death; please come and lay Your hands on her, so that she will get well and live."** The authenticity of Jairus's faith in Christ is never questioned by any of the gospel writers. In fact, his faith was so strong that, according to Matthew 9:18, he believed Jesus could not only heal his daughter but, if necessary, even raise her from the dead.

According to verse 42, Jairus's **little daughter** was twelve years old, which according to Jewish custom meant she had entered the first year of womanhood. She was thus eligible to be married and ready to begin her life as an adult. Yet from Jairus's perspective, understandably, she was still his **little daughter.** What should have been the most anticipated time in this young girl's life, filled with joy and hope, was instead marked by suffering and grief. The sunshine of blossoming womanhood had been clouded by the shadow of death.

Gripped with grief and yet emboldened by faith, Jairus sought Jesus in the midst of the crowd. How grateful he must have been when the Lord not only listened to his heartfelt request but agreed to go with him to his home. The accessibility of Jesus is seen, not only in His willingness to intermingle with the crowds but also in His availability to go with one desperate man who needed Him. Because He was accessible, He could be contacted, spoken to, and reached in a moment of need; because He was available, He was willing to give of Himself to meet the need of one man. Consequently, **He went off with him. Though a large crowd was following Him and pressing in on Him,** Jesus began the journey through the streets of Capernaum to Jairus's house.

Despite the many demands He faced in His earthly ministry, the Creator walked with people and made Himself accessible to them. The King of creation, the Lord of hosts, and the Ruler of all was not too busy to graciously care for those in need. The Gospels are filled with the accounts of His merciful availability to individuals.

IN THE COMMOTION, JESUS WAS INTERRUPTIBLE

A woman who had had a hemorrhage for twelve years, and had endured much at the hands of many physicians, and had spent all that she had and was not helped at all, but rather had grown worse—after hearing about Jesus, she came up in the crowd behind Him and touched His cloak. For she thought, "If I just touch His garments, I will get well." Immediately the flow of her blood was dried up; and she felt in her body that she was healed of her affliction. Immediately Jesus, perceiving in Himself that the power proceeding from Him had gone forth, turned around in the crowd and said, "Who touched My garments?" And His disciples said to Him, "You see the crowd pressing in on You, and You say, 'Who touched Me?'" And He looked around to see the woman who had done this. But the woman fearing and trembling,

aware of what had happened to her, came and fell down before Him and told Him the whole truth. And He said to her, "Daughter, your faith has made you well; go in peace and be healed of your affliction." (5:25–34)

As he escorted Jesus back toward his house, Jairus's heart must have leaped with joy at the thought that his daughter would soon be healed. The concerned father undoubtedly did everything he could to speed the journey along. Yet, the congestion of the crowds (v. 24) made it impossible to walk quickly. At least they were heading in the right direction, making slow but steady progress.

Suddenly, to Jairus's certain dismay, their journey came to an abrupt halt. There, in the crowd, was **a woman who had had a hemorrhage for twelve years, and had endured much at the hands of many physicians, and had spent all that she had and was not helped at all, but rather had grown worse.** In some ways, this woman was the antithesis of Jairus. He was a highly respected leader of the synagogue. She was a social outcast who, due to her condition, had been ostracized from Jewish religious life. While Jairus had known twelve years of joy and happiness with his daughter, this woman had experienced twelve years of heartache and rejection due to her ailment. Yet, she and Jairus shared this in common: they both knew Jesus was their only hope.

The cause of the woman's **hemorrhage** of blood is not stated. Her repeated attempts to find an effective cure had clearly failed. No matter how many doctors she consulted, having **spent all that she had** trying to find a solution, her condition only worsened. The Jewish Talmud listed eleven possible remedies for such an infirmity. These included superstitious prescriptions like placing the ashes of an ostrich egg in a cloth sack, or carrying around a barleycorn kernel procured from female donkey dung. Undoubtedly, this desperate woman had tried every potential cure. Financially drained and emotionally exhausted, she suffered both the physical discomfort and the social humiliation caused by many years of continual bleeding.

There were even greater ramifications for someone in her condition. According to Leviticus 15:25–27, any such discharge rendered a woman ceremonially unclean. Women had to wait seven days after any bleeding stopped before they were permitted to offer the prescribed sacrifices (vv. 28–29). For more than a decade, this woman had experienced no reprieve, meaning she was not able to participate in either temple or synagogue worship during those years. She had been ostracized due to the perpetual state of her uncleanness. Her experience was almost like that of a leper; even her associations with family and friends had to be maintained from a distance.

After hearing about Jesus, she determined to find Him, believing He could deliver her from an otherwise incurable predicament (cf. Luke 8:43). She desperately pressed her way through the crowd—clearly violating the acceptable boundaries for those who were ceremonially unclean. Finding Jesus, **she came up in the crowd behind Him and touched His cloak. For she thought, "If I just touch His garments, I will get well."** Like Jairus, she was compelled to approach Jesus by both the urgency of her need and the strength of her faith. Yet, hoping to avoid notice, she came just close enough to touch "the fringe of His cloak" (Luke 8:44). In Numbers 15:37–41, the Israelites were instructed to sew tassels on the bottom of their cloaks as a visible symbol that they belonged to God (cf. Deut. 22:12). These tassels served a dual purpose. They reminded the Jews of their commitment to serve the Lord, while simultaneously testifying to the world that they were part of God's chosen people. Religious hypocrites, like the Pharisees, tried to exalt themselves by lengthening their tassels (Matt. 23:5). Jesus, by contrast, would have worn a robe with traditional tassels attached to the bottom.

Believing she would be healed, the woman reached out to grasp the tassels of the Lord's robe. Her faith was not in His clothing, as if His robe had magical power, but in Him. She knew about His miracles and therefore had no doubt that He could heal her infirmity. Her unwavering faith was instantly rewarded. As Mark records, **immediately the flow of her blood was dried up; and she felt in her body that she was healed of her affliction.** The very moment she touched His garment, her body was restored. What twelve years of medical appointments could not cure, the power of God healed in an instant.

Jesus had a purpose for this woman's life that went beyond her physical healing. She had come incognito, hoping to shrink back unnoticed into the crowd. But Jesus intended to bring her out in order to draw her to Himself. **Immediately Jesus, perceiving in Himself that the power proceeding from Him had gone forth, turned around in the crowd and said, "Who touched My garments?"** That Jesus perceived **the power proceeding from Him** reveals an important truth about the nature of God. Divine power is not an impersonal cosmic force somehow detached from its sovereign source. Rather, God is personally engaged in every act of power—from creation to redemption to the providential sustaining of the universe (cf. Heb. 1:3). He feels it all. For this woman, the personal expression of the Lord's power immediately healed her physical infirmity. Jesus knew her spiritual condition still needed to be addressed.

With that in mind, Jesus **turned around in the crowd and said, "Who touched My garments?"** His question was not motivated by ignorance (since He knew whom He had healed) but in order to pull the woman out of the crowd. True to form, His disciples did not understand what He was doing. Looking around, they **said to Him, "You see the crowd pressing in on You, and You say, 'Who touched Me?'"** The verb translated **pressing** (*sunthlibō*) means to compress or jam. It indicates Jesus was crammed in by the crowd, being touched and enclosed by the people on all sides. From a human point of view, the disciples (through their spokesman Peter—cf. Luke 8:45) asked an obvious question. There were so many people in close proximity to Jesus that it seemed impossible to single out just one. From the divine perspective, the Lord knew precisely to whom He was referring. **And He looked around to see the woman who had done this.** She had wanted to hide, but she knew Jesus was speaking directly to hear. And so, **the woman fearing and trembling, aware of what had happened to her, came and fell down before Him and told Him the whole truth.**

For the past twelve years, she had faced the fear of embarrassment and rejection. The **fearing and trembling** she felt in that moment was of a different kind altogether. Her heart was gripped with a holy fear as the reality **of what had** just **happened to her** began to sink in. Realizing she was in the presence of deity, she **came and fell down before Him** and publicly related **the whole truth** about both her malady and her healing (cf. Luke 8:47). The Lord responded to her public confession by affirming the authenticity of her faith. He said to her, **"Daughter, your faith has made you well; go in peace and be healed of your affliction."** The word **affliction** (*masti*) literally means "whip" or "scourge," illustrating the traumatic nature of the trial this woman had endured. But Jesus' words transcended her physical condition, indicating that this physical **daughter** of Abraham had become a spiritual **daughter** of God (cf. John 1:12). The common Greek word for physical healing was *iaomai*. That is the term Mark used when he wrote that the woman **was healed of her affliction.** Luke used a synonymous term, *therapeuō* (from which the English word "therapeutic" is derived), when he noted that this woman "could not be healed by anyone" (Luke 8:43). But the word used for being **made well** in verse 34 (cf. Matt. 9:21–22; Luke 8:48) is *sōzō*, a term usually used in the New Testament for being saved from sin.

The Gospels often use *sōzō* to demonstrate a connection between a person's faith and their salvation. For example, when a penitent prostitute washed Jesus' feet with her tears, He told her the same thing He told this woman, "Your faith has saved you" (Luke 7:50; cf. Mark 10:52; Luke 17:19). The Greek in both places is identical, though most English translations do not render them in the same way. While Jesus healed many people who did not exhibit genuine faith (and thus were made well only in a physical sense), there were also those who expressed saving faith in Him. In such cases, their bodies were not only delivered but also their souls. Jesus' response to this woman, connecting the word *sōzō* with her faith, suggests she was healed of more than just a physical affliction. Because she had been saved, she could now truly **go in peace.** Her bodily healing enabled her to be reunited with her family and restored to the synagogue. More importantly, her salvation meant she was now reconciled to God.

Though Jesus was on His way to Jairus's house, He was willing to be interrupted in order to help this woman. From a human perspective, He had more pressing needs to meet. Jairus's daughter was on death's doorstep, and this woman's medical condition was not life-threatening. The commotion of the crowd and the urgency of the moment made it difficult to stop. Yet, from the divine perspective, Jesus knew she was one of His elect (cf. John 6:37). Consequently, He welcomed the interruption, taking the necessary time to minister to her, not only by healing her body but also by saving her soul.

IN THE CRISIS, JESUS WAS UNFLAPPABLE

While He was still speaking, they came from the house of the synagogue official, saying, "Your daughter has died; why trouble the Teacher anymore?" But Jesus, overhearing what was being spoken, said to the synagogue official, "Do not be afraid any longer, only believe." And He allowed no one to accompany Him, except Peter and James and John the brother of James. They came to the house of the synagogue official; and He saw a commotion, and people loudly weeping and wailing. And entering in, He said to them, "Why make a commotion and weep? The child has not died, but is asleep." They began laughing at Him. But putting them all out, He took along the child's father and mother and His own companions, and entered the room where the child was. (5:35–40)

The gospel writers do not indicate how long Jesus' interaction with the woman took. Whatever the duration, it lasted long enough that **while He was still speaking** to the woman, messengers **came from the house of the synagogue official, saying, "Your daughter has died; why trouble the Teacher anymore?"** The delay, to the consternation and alarm of Jairus, had turned deadly. How his heart must have sunk as messengers from his house related the tragic news. The insinuation in their message was that Jesus had been wasting time, and now it was too late. Their hopelessness is reflected in their question, **"Why trouble the Teacher anymore?"** They wrongly assumed Jesus' power could do nothing once death arrived. Thus His involvement became pointless. Mary and Martha would later have a similar reaction when their brother Lazarus died (John 11:21,32).

Surrounded by panicky messengers, an anxious synagogue official, and a crushing crowd, the Lord continued to move steadily in the sovereign purposes of His Father. **Jesus, overhearing what was being spoken, said to the synagogue official, "Do not be afraid any longer, only believe."** Knowing Jairus would be tempted to doubt, Jesus directly addressed his fears. The Greek expression could be translated, "Stop being afraid and keep believing." According to Luke 8:50, Jesus added the promise, "And she will be made well." With tender compassion, rather than waiting until He arrived at Jairus's home, the Lord reassured this distraught man.

When they entered the house (cf. Luke 8:51), **He allowed no one to accompany Him, except Peter and James and John the brother of James.** For obvious reasons, Jesus did not allow the entire crowd to follow Him into Jairus's home. Neither did He take all the Twelve. Instead, He brought only His inner circle of **Peter and James and John the brother of James.** These three, along with Andrew, made up the most intimate group of Jesus' disciples. (For more on the Twelve and their relationship to Jesus, see chapter 12 of this volume.)

When Jesus, Jairus, and the three disciples **came to the house of the synagogue official,** they discovered that the funeral had already begun. The journey to the house, delayed by Jesus' interaction with the woman (vv. 25–34), had taken long enough for mourners to assemble. Consequently, as Jesus entered the home, **He saw a commotion, and people loudly weeping and wailing.** Though modern funerals in the Western world are generally solemn and quiet affairs, ancient Jewish funerals were nothing of the sort. Three distinctive elements characterized the first-century event. First, those who attended expressed their grief by tearing their clothes. Jewish tradition included thirty-nine regulations on how one's clothes were to be torn. For example, relatives of the deceased were required to rip their garments directly over the heart. The tear could be sewn up loosely, but it was to be worn over a thirty-day period as a sign of prolonged grief. Second, professional mourners were hired to vocalize and broadcast feelings of sadness. Agony was magnified, not shrouded in silence; these professionals had mastered the art of howling and groaning. Their sorrowful histrionics set the mood for everyone who attended. Third, the funeral included the hiring of musicians, most commonly flute-players (cf. Matt. 9:23). Like the mourners, they would play loud, dissonant sounds that symbolized the emotional discord and pain associated with death. According to Jewish tradition, even the poor were required to have at least two flute-players and one wailing woman. Clearly,such occasions were neither quiet nor subdued.

So, when Jesus arrived at Jairus's house, the scene was chaotic, loud, and depressing. In keeping with Jairus's position as a high-ranking synagogue official, the number of hired mourners and musicians was probably large. Though the cacophony produced by such a motley group would have been especially loud and boisterous, Jesus was unfazed by the mayhem. **Entering in, He said to them, "Why make a commotion and weep?"** According to the parallel accounts in Matthew and Luke,Jesus told the mourners to "stop weeping" (Luke 8:52) and to "leave" (Matt. 9:24). The unexpected interruption undoubtedly brought the funeral to a halt,as startled mourners shut their mouths and stunned musicians put down their flutes.The drama of the moment was intensified by the sudden silence.

Jesus broke the silence by making a shocking statement, **"The child has not died, but is asleep."** Jesus,of course,was well aware that Jairus's daughter had died. In John 11:11, Jesus responded similarly to the death of Lazarus, telling the disciples, "Our friend Lazarus has fallen asleep; but I go,that I may awaken him out of sleep." On that occasion,not even His disciples immediately understood the metaphor. As John explains:

> The disciples then said to Him, "Lord, if he has fallen asleep, he will recover." Now Jesus had spoken of his death, but they thought that He was speaking of literal sleep. So Jesus then said to them plainly, "Lazarus is dead, and I am glad for your sakes that I was not there, so that you may believe; but let us go to him." (John 11:12–15)

This incident similarly provided Jesus with an opportunity to display His life-giving power. By using the metaphor of sleep, the Lord redefined death as a temporary state. That same word picture is used throughout the New Testament to remind believers that death is not permanent and that future resurrection awaits (cf. Matt. 27:52; Acts 7:60; 1 Cor. 15:6,20,51; 1 Thess. 4:13–15; 5:10; 2 Peter 3:4).Though the body sleeps temporarily in death, the soul does not (cf. Luke 16:19–31; 23:43; 2 Cor. 5:8; Phil. 1:23; Rev. 6:9–11).

When the mourners heard what Jesus said, having missed His true intent, **they began laughing at Him.** Their supposed grief, which was clearly superficial, instantly turned into scornful mockery. They knew the girl was dead (cf. Luke 8:53) and found it ridiculous to claim she was only sleeping—thereby providing proof that this was a real resurrection. Undeterred by their scornful laughter, and **putting them all out** of the house, **He took along the child's father and mother and His own companions, and entered the room where the child was.** Once the mockers were removed, Jesus found Jairus and his wife and lovingly led them, along with His three disciples, to the place where their daughter's body was. That the house had multiple rooms suggests that Jairus was a prosperous man. Having restored order where there had been chaos, the Lord was about to restore life where there was death.

In the Cure, Jesus Was Charitable

Taking the child by the hand, He said to her, "Talitha kum!" (which translated means, "Little girl, I say to you, get up!"). Immediately the girl got up and began to walk, for she was twelve years old. And immediately they were completely astounded. And He gave them strict orders that no one should know about this, and He said that something should be given her to eat. (5:41–43)

Jesus had already demonstrated His kindness to Jairus in multiple ways. First, He granted him a personal audience in the midst of a crushing crowd. Second, He agreed to go with him to see his daughter. Third, He reassured Jairus even after his daughter died. Fourth, He took charge of the situation at Jairus's home—sending away the professional wailers and bringing calm to a chaotic scene. Fifth, the Lord led Jairus and his wife into the room where the girl's body lay. The most noteworthy expression of Jesus' compassion toward Jairus and his family came at the climax of this event: in the miracle and its immediate aftermath.

The Lord Jesus, who was always characterized by compassion toward people (cf. Matt. 9:36; 14:14; Mark 1:41; 8:2), demonstrated tender sensitivity in His treatment of this young woman and her family. He could easily have healed her from afar, without making the trek to her home. His personal presence and promise demonstrated the infinite compassion that motivated His ministry to people. With a touch, **taking the child by the hand, He said to her, "Talitha kum!" (which translated means, "Little girl, I say to you, get up!").** Only Mark's gospel records the original Aramaic, which was the daily language spoken by most Jews in the first century. **Talitha** means youth or lamb. In essence, Jesus referred to her as a "little lamb," an expression of endearment and kindness. Though culturally she had entered womanhood at the age of twelve, the Creator of the universe saw her as a little lamb, as her parents surely viewed her.

Then His miraculous power was unleashed. **Immediately** "her spirit returned" (Luke 8:55) and **the girl got up and began to walk, for she was twelve years old.** The young woman was dead one moment, and alive and full of energy the next. There was no time needed for recovery, rehabilitation, or physical therapy. As soon as Jesus gave her life, she stood up in full strength and began to traverse the room. Like all of Jesus' miracles, this was a creative work. Its effects were immediate, complete, and undeniable. The reaction from both the girl's parents and the three disciples was one of shock and awe. **Immediately they were completely astounded.** The verb **astounded** (*existēmi*) literally means to stand outside oneself or to be beside oneself with bewilderment (cf. Mark 3:21; 2 Cor. 5:13). There was no human explanation for what had just happened. For Jairus and his wife, grief was instantly transformed into joy and pain gave way to praise.

In the midst of the celebration, **He gave them strict orders that no one should know about this, and He said that something should be given her to eat.** The Lord's compassion is again evidenced in His continued concern for this young woman. In all the excitement, no one thought to give her something to eat. She had been miraculously resurrected, but she still needed food. Having suffered from a terminal disease, likely for a prolonged period of time, it may have been weeks or even months since her last full meal. Jesus graciously recognized her need for nourishment and instructed her parents accordingly.

The Lord also **gave them strict orders** that they were not to tell others what had happened. He issued similar commands on other occasions too (Matt. 8:4; 9:30; 12:16; 17:9; Mark 1:25, 34, 44; 3:12; 7:36; 8:26, 30; 9:9; Luke 4:41; 9:21). Why did He do this? There were times when Jesus insisted on silence because He knew the report would heighten the fanatical enthusiasm of the crowds, which would only hinder His ministry (cf. Mark 1:40–45; John 6:14–15). On other occasions, it was an act of judgment intended to obscure truth from those who had permanently rejected Him (cf. Luke 9:21). Those reasons are not the main reason Jesus repeatedly called for this kind of mandatory silence. Mark 8:30–31 reveals the primary purpose: "And He warned them to tell no one about Him. And He began to teach them that the Son of Man must suffer many things and be rejected by the elders and the chief priests and the scribes, and be killed, and after three days rise again." The Lord knew His earthly mission would not be finished until after His death and resurrection, and no one, including His own disciples (cf. Mark 9:32; Luke 9:45; 18:34; John 12:16), would fully understand His message until then. Jesus did not want to be known simply as a miracle worker or teacher. Those designations, while accurate, are incomplete because He came for a greater purpose (cf. Luke 19:10). He insisted on silence, then, because the story was not yet finished.

The full message about Jesus must include the fact that He is the crucified and risen Savior. His death and resurrection are essential to the good news of the gospel. As Paul explained to the Corinthians:

> Now I make known to you, brethren, the gospel which I preached to you, which also you received, in which also you stand, by which also you are saved, . . . For I delivered to you as of first importance what I also received, that Christ died for our sins according to the Scriptures, and that He was buried, and that He was raised on the third day according to the Scriptures. (1 Cor. 15:1–4)

Jesus knew that a miracle like the resurrection of Jairus's daughter could only be fully appreciated in light of the cross and the empty tomb. Ultimately, it was His own victory over sin and death that enabled Him not only to give temporary life to a dead girl but to offer eternal life to all those who believe in Him (cf. Rom. 8:11).

Mark's recounting of these two miracles highlights both the supernatural power and tender loving-kindness of Jesus. Seven centuries before Jesus' birth, the prophet Isaiah pictured the Messiah's compassion with these words, "A bruised reed He will not break and a dimly burning wick He will not extinguish" (Isa. 42:3). From an esteemed synagogue official to a poor social outcast to countless others, Jesus repeatedly demonstrated that kind of genuine care for suffering people. As God in human flesh, the greatness of His creative power was equaled only by the goodness of His compassion.

Amazing Unbelief (Mark 6:1–6)

19

Jesus went out from there and came into His hometown; and His disciples followed Him. When the Sabbath came, He began to teach in the synagogue; and the many listeners were astonished, saying, "Where did this man get these things, and what is this wisdom given to Him, and such miracles as these performed by His hands? Is not this the carpenter, the son of Mary, and brother of James and Joses and Judas and Simon? Are not His sisters here with us?" And they took offense at Him. Jesus said to them, "A prophet is not without honor except in his hometown and among his own relatives and in his own household." And He could do no miracle there except that He laid His hands on a few sick people and healed them. And He wondered at their unbelief. And He was going around the villages teaching. (6:1–6)

Though people were constantly astonished by Jesus, the New Testament relates only two times when He was amazed by people. Both involved faith. On the positive side, Jesus marveled at the strong faith expressed by a Roman centurion in Capernaum. According to Luke 7:9, "When Jesus heard this, He marveled at him, and turned and said to the crowd that was following Him, 'I say to you, not even in Israel have I found such great faith.'" Conversely, in His hometown of Nazareth, it was the utter absence of faith that caused the Lord to be amazed. As Mark explained in this passage, "He wondered at their unbelief" (Mark 6:6).

Unbelief is a powerful force with devastating ramifications, first in this life and then the next. In the garden of Eden, Satan tempted Eve to doubt God's clear instruction, and she ate from the forbidden tree (cf. Gen. 3:1–7; 1 Tim. 2:14). The people of Noah's day refused to believe his warning, and they were subsequently drowned in the flood (cf. Matt. 24:38–39; 2 Peter 2:5; 3:3–6). After the exodus from Egypt, the faithlessness of Aaron, embodied in the form of a golden calf, resulted in three thousand people being slaughtered (cf. Ex. 32:28, 35). The fear-laden doubt of the ten spies, representative of the nation of Israel, caused that entire generation to die in the wilderness (Num. 13:32; 14:20–23; cf. 1 Cor. 10:1–10). Achan's unbelief—expressed in greed, theft, and an attempted cover-up— brought about the execution of his entire family (Josh. 7:25). Even after settling in the Promised Land, the recurring apostasy and unbelief of the Israelites brought about God's repeated judgment (cf. Judg. 2:7–11).

Paradoxically, the Jewish religious leaders portrayed in the New Testament exhibited that same level of unbelief in their response to Jesus. As Stephen told the Sanhedrin,

> "You men who are stiff-necked and uncircumcised in heart and ears are always resisting the Holy Spirit; you are doing just as your fathers did. Which one of the prophets did your fathers not persecute? They killed those who had previously announced the coming of the Righteous One, whose betrayers and murderers you have now become; you who received the law as ordained by angels, and yet did not keep it." (Acts 7:51–53)

Like all other unbelievers, their hard-heartedness resulted in them dying in their sins and forfeiting heaven (cf. John 8:24). Unbelief in the Son of God activates divine wrath and catapults souls into eternal hell. In the familiar words of John 3:18, "He who believes in Him is not judged; he who does not believe has been judged already because he has not believed in the name of the only begotten Son of God" (cf. John 8:24).

This passage (Mark 6:1–6) comes on the heels of several signifi-cant miracles performed by Jesus. In Mark 4:35–41, He instantly calmed a violent storm on the Sea of Galilee. The next day, on the eastern shore of the lake, He cast a legion of demons into a herd of pigs (5:1–20). Return-ing to Capernaum (5:21–24), Jesus healed a woman who had suffered from incessant bleeding for more than a decade (5:25–34). He then raised the twelve-year-old daughter of Jairus back to life (5:35–43). Mes-merized by His teaching and astounded by His miracles, the crowds in Galilee generally responded to Jesus with an attitude of enthusiasm. Their astonished curiosity about Him, however, fell far short of saving faith (cf. John 2:24; 6:66).

Of course, the popular excitement of the crowds stood in stark contrast to the open hostility of the Pharisees and scribes, who hated Jesus and were already plotting to kill Him (Mark 3:6; cf. Matt. 12:14). Instead of attributing His supernatural power to God, they accused Him of being empowered by Satan (3:22). Jealous of His popularity, and incensed by His opposition to their hypocrisy and tradition, the Phari-sees hounded Him everywhere He went. They were even willing to join forces with their political enemies, the Herodians (3:6) and Sadducees (John 11:47–53), to bring about His death.

At this point in Jesus' ministry, the religious leaders' attitude of outright rejection was not shared by most of the people. As Jesus traveled throughout the cities and towns of Galilee (cf. Matt. 4:23; 9:35; Mark 1:39), He was generally received favorably. There was one notable exception: His own hometown of Nazareth. The residents of Nazareth knew Jesus only as a local carpenter who had grown up and lived in their small com-munity for the better part of three decades (cf. Mark 1:9, 24; 10:47; 14:67; 16:6). Joseph and Mary had moved to Nazareth after they returned from Egypt when Jesus was still a baby (cf. Matt. 2:23; Luke 2:39). He had grown up there, progressing through the stages of youth to adulthood (Luke 2:40). Though He had been catapulted onto the public scene after begin-ning His public ministry around age thirty, His former neighbors still viewed Him as nothing more than the oldest son of a familiar family from their village.

The trip to Nazareth recorded in this passage (6:1–6; cf. Matt. 13:54–58) was Jesus' second recorded visit to His hometown since the start of His public ministry. His first visit occurred shortly after His temptations in the wilderness (cf. Luke 4:1–13). As Luke records, "Jesus returned to Galilee in the power of the Spirit; … And He came to Nazareth, where He had been brought up; and as was His custom, He entered the synagogue on the Sabbath, and stood up to read" (Luke 4:14a, 16). Jesus would have been very familiar to the people attending the synagogue that day, since they had known Him since He was a child. To them, He was an ordinary member of their small-town community. Yet, that Sabbath day would prove to be far from ordinary.

It was customary for traveling rabbis to be invited to the local synagogue to read the Scriptures and address the congregation. Because word about Jesus had been spreading, the people of Nazareth were undoubtedly eager to hear Him preach. After reading a messianic passage from Isaiah 61:1–2, Jesus told His familiar friends and neighbors, "Today this Scripture has been fulfilled in your hearing" (Luke 4:21). The implication was clear. He was claiming to be the Messiah. Initially, the congregation's response seemed fairly positive: "All were speaking well of Him, and wondering at the gracious words which were falling from His lips; and they were saying, 'Is this not Joseph's son?'" (v. 22). But Jesus knew their hearts (cf. John 2:24). He recognized their response for what it was—a superficial desire to see Him perform miracles (cf. Luke 4:23). When Jesus rebuked their faithlessness and hypocrisy, comparing them to the apostate generation of Israelites who lived during the days of Elijah and Elisha (vv. 25–27), they reacted by revealing the true condition of their hearts. "All the people in the synagogue were filled with rage as they heard these things; and they got up and drove Him out of the city, and led Him to the brow of the hill on which their city had been built, in order to throw Him down the cliff" (vv. 28–29). After just one sermon, people who had known Jesus very well were so incensed by His message they turned into a mob, wanting to murder Him. But He escaped, as Luke reports, and "passing through their midst, He went His way" (v. 30).

Months passed before Jesus decided to return to Nazareth for a second and final time. Leaving Capernaum, **Jesus went out from there and came into His hometown.** Up to this point, Capernaum had been the headquarters of Jesus' Galilean ministry. From this point forward, that was no longer the case. The residents of the city had received more than enough revelation to believe and, therefore, to be responsible for rejecting Him (cf. Matt. 2:23). Moreover, the hostility of the Jewish religious leaders and the proximity of Herod's palace, situated in nearby Tiberias, made it too dangerous for Him to stay in Capernaum for prolonged periods of time.

Nazareth, located twenty-five miles southwest of Capernaum, was an insignificant village in Jesus' day with a population of around five hundred inhabitants. It was so obscure that it is never mentioned in either the Old Testament or the Jewish Talmud. Yet, it had been the Lord's **hometown** for almost three decades. The fact that **His disciples followed Him** indicates that this was not a private family visit but was intended for public ministry. As part of their own ministry training (cf. 6:7–13), the disciples would be exposed to the hard-hearted rejection that characterizes unbelievers.

The response of the Nazarenes to Jesus reveals four truths about the pernicious nature of unbelief: it obscures the obvious, elevates the irrelevant, assaults the messenger, and spurns the supernatural.

UNBELIEF OBSCURES THE OBVIOUS

When the Sabbath came, He began to teach in the synagogue; and the many listeners were astonished, saying, "Where did this man get these things, and what is this wisdom given to Him, and such miracles as these performed by His hands? (6:2)

Despite their violent response to Jesus during His previous visit, **when the Sabbath came** the residents of Nazareth invited Him **to teach in the synagogue.** His growing popularity throughout Galilee no doubt made them curious to hear Him again. On a human level, they knew Him very well. They also were fully aware that, since leaving Nazareth to begin preaching and performing miracles, He had caused wonder and amazement throughout Israel. Though they did not attempt to kill Jesus on this occasion, as they had on the first (cf. Luke 4:29), their unbelieving disposition toward Him had not changed.

As the Lord Jesus taught, **the many listeners were astonished.**

Unlike the meandering rambling of the rabbis, the Lord's teaching was authoritative (Matt. 7:28–29), knowledgeable (John 7:15–16), powerful (Luke 4:32 KJV), and unmatched (John 7:46). Understandably, the response of the congregation was utter amazement. The Greek word **astonished** (*ekplessō*) means "to strike" or "to blast." To use the vernacular, Jesus' teaching was "mind-blowing" for those who heard. (For more on the astonishing nature of the Lord's teaching, see chapter 4 in this volume.)

Yet, the amazement of the audience did not lead them to put their faith in Him as Lord and Messiah. Instead, they hardened their hearts in continued rejection. Rather than recognizing the obvious—that Jesus was empowered by God—the residents of Nazareth questioned the source of His supernatural wisdom and power, **saying, "Where did this man get these things, and what is this wisdom given to Him, and such miracles as these performed by His hands?"** The residents of Nazareth knew He had never been trained to become a rabbi (cf. John 7:15). Yet, His teaching was characterized by unparalleled clarity, veracity, and profundity so that it stunned even the most learned scribes of the day (cf. Mark 11:18; Luke 2:47). Their experience with Him left them dumbfounded.

In reality, the words (**wisdom**) and works (**miracles**) of Jesus proved objectively, beyond any reasonable doubt, that He was from God. The fact that His teaching captivated the hearts and minds of the people (cf. Matt. 7:28; 22:33; Mark 1:22; Luke 4:32) filled the proud, false religious leaders with envy and dismay. As Luke 19:47–48 reports, at a later point in Jesus' ministry: "He was teaching daily in the temple; but the chief priests and the scribes and the leading men among the people were trying to destroy Him, and they could not find anything that they might do, for all the people were hanging on to every word He said." Jesus' miracles, likewise, were undeniable manifestations of divine power, as He restored to full health those who were leprous (Mark 1:40), paralyzed (2:3), deaf (7:32), blind (10:46), demon-possessed (5:2), and even dead (5:35). Jesus' former neighbors had obviously heard of His many miracles, as reports about Him circulated throughout Galilee and the surrounding regions (cf. Matt. 4:24; 9:26, 31; 14:1; Mark 1:28, 45; 6:14; Luke 4:14, 37; 5:15). Such dramatic demonstrations of supernatural power confirmed His deity. As Nicodemus rightly observed, "No one can do these signs that You do unless God is with him" (John 3:2). The Lord Himself directed His critics to examine His miracles: "If I do not do the works of My Father, do not believe Me; but if I do them, though you do not believe Me, believe the works, so that you may know and understand that the Father is in Me, and I in the Father" (John 10:37–38). Earlier, He explained to the religious leaders in Jerusalem, "The testimony which I have is greater than the testimony of John; for the works which the Father has given Me to accomplish —the very works that I do—testify about Me, that the Father has sent Me" (John 5:36). Jesus' enemies knew they could not deny the reality of His miracles (cf. John 11:47). So, instead, they obstinately denied the divine source of His power, alleging that He was actually energized by Beelzebub (cf. Mark 3:22–30).

The residents of Nazareth did not accuse Jesus of being empowered by Satan, but neither were they willing to acknowledge that His power came from God. Their agnosticism and skepticism found its expression in the form of a question: **Where did this man get these things?** In order to maintain their disbelief, they looked for any explanation other than the obvious one. Like the compact ground alongside the road in the parable of the soils (Mark 4:15), their hearts were impenetrable and hard. They had been given more than enough evidence; yet they obstinately refused to believe in Him (cf. John 3:18–20).

Unbelief Elevates the Irrelevant

"Is not this the carpenter, the son of Mary, and brother of James and Joses and Judas and Simon? Are not His sisters here with us?" (6:3*a*)

Rather than embracing the obvious, Jesus' former neighbors focused on the irrelevant, throwing up a smoke screen of unrelated information to justify their unbelief. Though they were admittedly astonished by His teaching and amazed by the reports of His miracles, they refused to believe that Jesus was Lord and Savior. They were appalled that a homegrown laborer from their village—a common craftsman with no specialized theological education or religious credentials—would claim to be the long-awaited Messiah of God (cf. Luke 4:18–21).

In keeping with their attitude of incredulity, they raised issues that were irrelevant to the question at hand. It was true that Jesus was a carpenter by trade, the firstborn son of Mary, and the half brother of His siblings. But those details were not germane to the issue of His messiahship. While the first-century Jews had many misconceptions about the Messiah's coming, they nevertheless understood that He would be born as a man, growing up in a Jewish family somewhere in the land of Israel. Rather than embracing Jesus as that promised and proven Messiah, and praising God for choosing their obscure village for such an esteemed honor, the residents of Nazareth responded with resentment, derision, and disbelief.

Is not this the carpenter? they asked in bewilderment. According to Matthew 13:55, they also asked, "Is not this the carpenter's son?" It was usual for fathers to teach their children to follow their trade. Jesus learned to be a carpenter from Joseph and likely took over the family business after Joseph died. The word translated **carpenter** (*tektōn*) is a broad term meaning builder or craftsman. It could refer to a carpenter, stonemason, metalsmith, or shipbuilder. Some early church tradition suggests that Joseph and Jesus specialized in making yokes and plows. Growing up in Nazareth, Jesus had likely crafted many farming implements, and perhaps done other building projects, for His neighbors. Those same people found it hard to believe that a woodworker from their humble hometown who had not previously revealed His divine nature could suddenly exhibit such profundity and power. Though many legends about Jesus' childhood arose later in church history, claiming that He performed miracles as a boy in Nazareth, they are obviously fabrications. If any of that was factual, the residents of Nazareth would have responded to Him differently. But Jesus' growing up seemed so ordinary and natural to His neighbors and family friends that they found it impossible to think of Him as possessing divine wisdom and supernatural power.

Additionally, Jesus' former neighbors pointed out that He was **the Son of Mary.** This is the only place in the Gospels where Jesus was referred to by that title. The normal Jewish practice identified a son by His father's name. (In Jesus' case, they would have used the name of His

adopted father, Joseph—cf. Luke 4:22; John 6:42.) Perhaps they refer-
enced Mary because Joseph had already died while Mary was still living
in Nazareth. It is also possible that they intended this as an insult, implying that He had been born illegitimately (cf. John 8:41; 9:29); when a
man's father was unknown, he was called the son of his mother. This false
accusation is still proffered by some who reject the Lord Jesus Christ.

The people not only knew Jesus was Mary's oldest son, they also
knew He was the **brother of James and Joses and Judas and Simon.**
It is likely in that small village that they understood how Jesus' siblings
felt about Him. If so, it would have only added to their incredulity, since at
this point "not even His brothers were believing in Him" (John 7:5). His
siblings thought He had "lost His senses" (Mark 3:21); their fellow townspeople may have shared that same perspective. It was not until after
Jesus' death and resurrection that His half brothers were added to the
church (Acts 1:14; cf. 1 Cor. 15:7). **James** (whose name is literally Jacob)
became the leader of the Jerusalem church (cf. Acts 15:13) and wrote
the epistle of James. **Judas** was also influential in the early church, writing the epistle of Jude. Completing the family picture, the Nazarenes also
asked, **"Are not His sisters here with us?"** The fact that Jesus had multiple siblings exposes the lie of the Roman Catholic doctrine of Mary's
perpetual virginity (cf. Matt. 12:46–47; Luke 2:7; John 7:10; Acts 1:14). As
this passage indicates, Mary gave birth to at least six additional children
after Jesus was born.

By bringing up His occupation and His family, the people of
Nazareth turned irrelevant issues into stumbling blocks to defend their
unbelief. They diverted their attention away from the truth in order to justify their rejection of Jesus. They had only known Him as the son of a
local carpenter. Thus, they were unwilling to embrace Him for who He
truly was: the Son of God.

UNBELIEF ASSAULTS THE MESSENGER

**And they took offense at Him. Jesus said to them, "A prophet is
not without honor except in his hometown and among his own
relatives and in his own household." (6:3b–4)**

Unbelief soon soured the initial amazement of the crowd, **and they took offense at Him.** The word translated **offense** (a form of the Greek word *skandalizō*, from which the English word "scandalize" is derived) means "to snare" or "to cause to stumble" (cf. 1 Cor. 1:23). During His earlier visit to Nazareth, Jesus had similarly offended the people (cf. Luke 4:28) both by claiming to be the Messiah (v. 21) and by confronting their hypocrisy and unbelief (v. 23). On this occasion, the contents of His message in the synagogue are not recorded, but Jesus undoubtedly emphasized truths that were similar to what He taught the first time. Once again, the people were outraged. They could not move past the fact that someone as familiar to them as Jesus would dare to make such an exalted claim or to issue such stern rebukes.

The Lord responded to their anger and resentment by quoting the same well-known proverb He had cited on His previous visit (cf. Luke 4:24). **Jesus said to them, "A prophet is not without honor except in his hometown and among his own relatives and in his own household."** This axiomatic truth was the ancient parallel of the contemporary saying, "familiarity breeds contempt." Jesus used a progression of social circles, from the wider to the narrower, in order to make His point. At this point, no one in **his hometown** of Nazareth believed in Him. Even within His own family, both among **his own relatives and in his own household,** only His mother believed (cf. Luke 2:19), though as noted earlier His brothers would later come to saving faith. Many people outside of Nazareth regarded Him as a prophet (cf. Matt. 21:11, 46; Mark 6:15; Luke 7:16; 24:19; John 6:14; 7:40; 9:17), but **in his hometown** Jesus was rejected with hostility and antagonism. In essence, Jesus' former neighbors found themselves indignantly asking, "Who does this fellow think He is?" Admittedly, their curiosity was piqued when they heard about how popular He had become since leaving home. Yet, they could not believe their familiar neighbor had the audacity to return and confront them with rebukes while claiming to be the Messiah.

Jesus later warned His disciples that they would similarly face persecution for the sake of the gospel. In many cases, hostility begins at home. As He told them, "Beware of men, for they will hand you over to the courts and scourge you in their synagogues. . . . For I came to set a man against his father, and a daughter against her mother, and a daughter-in-law against her mother-in-law; and a man's enemies will be the members of his household" (Matt. 10:17, 35–36). On the night before His death, Jesus reiterated the fact that Christians ought to expect persecution: "If the world hates you, you know that it has hated Me before it hated you.... If they persecuted Me, they will also persecute you; if they kept My word, they will keep yours also" (John 15:18, 20).

When they cannot refute His message, unbelievers will not hesitate to attack Him and anyone who speaks for Him. Hemmed in by the truth, they strike back with ridicule, disdain, scorn, and sometimes even violent persecution. The Pharisees and Sadducees ultimately responded to Jesus by resorting to such tactics. Refusing to believe His teaching and miracles but unable to refute His wisdom and power, they devised a plan to silence Him permanently. As John 11:47–53 records,

> Therefore the chief priests and the Pharisees convened a council, and were saying, "What are we doing? For this man is performing many signs. If we let Him go on like this, all men will believe in Him, and the Romans will come and take away both our place and our nation." But one of them, Caiaphas, who was high priest that year, said to them, "You know nothing at all, nor do you take into account that it is expedient for you that one man die for the people, and that the whole nation not perish." Now he did not say this on his own initiative, but being high priest that year, he prophesied that Jesus was going to die for the nation, and not for the nation only, but in order that He might also gather together into one the children of God who are scattered abroad. So from that day on they planned together to kill Him.

UNBELIEF SPURNS THE SUPERNATURAL

And He could do no miracle there except that He laid His hands on a few sick people and healed them. And He wondered at their unbelief. And He was going around the villages teaching. (6:5–6)

In response to the people's unbelief, Jesus chose not to do any miracles in Nazareth, with the exception of a few healings. As Mark explains, **"And He could do no miracle there except that He laid His hands on a few sick people and healed them."** The issue was not that He lacked the supernatural power to perform miracles. Rather, there was no reason to do miracles there, since the purpose of His miracles was to attest to the truth and reveal Himself as the Lord and Messiah, and thus to lead sinners to saving faith. Because the people of Nazareth had already set their rejection in stone, miracles were unnecessary.

To remove any false conclusions that Jesus' ability to do miracles was dependent on the faith of people, He frequently healed people who did not express any faith in Him. For example, in Luke 17:11–19, only one of the ten lepers cured confessed faith in Him and was saved. The crippled man at the pool of Bethesda (John 5:13) did not even know Jesus' identity when he was healed; the man born blind (John 9:1, 7) did not speak of his faith in Jesus until after he was given sight (v. 38). The demoniacs whom Jesus delivered (cf. Mark 1:23–26; 5:1; cf. Matt. 12:22) also made no profession of faith before being liberated. When Jesus raised people from the dead, He obviously did so without first requiring faith from them (Luke 7:14; John 11:43). Moreover, the Lord healed multitudes of people, even though not all of them believed (cf. Matt. 9:35; 11:2–5; 12:15–21; 14:13–14, 34–36; 15:29–31; 19:2). Clearly, Jesus' power was not at all diminished by unbelief. Nonetheless, the hard-hearted rejection of Nazareth was such that there was no reason to do any miracles there.

On the one hand, Jesus' decision was merciful. If He had done additional miracles in Nazareth, their condemnation for rejecting Him would have only increased. Hell would have forever been worse for them. The people of Jesus' hometown would have been judged like the unrepentant cities of Chorazin, Bethsaida, and Capernaum. As Matthew explained:

> Then He began to denounce the cities in which most of His miracles were done, because they did not repent. "Woe to you, Chorazin! Woe to you, Bethsaida! For if the miracles had occurred in Tyre and Sidon which occurred in you, they would have repented long ago in sackcloth and ashes. Nevertheless I say to you, it will be more tolerable for Tyre and Sidon in the day of judgment than for you. And you, Capernaum, will not be exalted to heaven, will you? You will descend to Hades; for if the miracles had occurred in Sodom which occurred in you, it would have remained to this day. Nevertheless I say to you that it will be more tolerable for the land of Sodom in the day of judgment, than for you." (Matt. 11:20–24)

Still, the Lord's withholding more miracles was also a sign of judgment (cf. Matt. 7:6). The purpose of miracles was never to entertain the hard-hearted but to move those who were open to the gospel toward saving faith. As Jesus told the Pharisees, "An evil and adulterous generation craves for a sign; and yet no sign shall be given to it but the sign of Jonah the prophet" (Matt. 12:39). His miracles were of no spiritual benefit for those who refused to believe, and He had no interest in indulging ungodly curiosity (cf. Luke 23:8–9).

This shocking and calloused rejection by the people in Nazareth was so fixed that even Jesus **wondered at their unbelief.** The word **wondered** indicates that Jesus was jarred by the deep-rooted faithlessness and open hostility He encountered there. For all of His earthly life, He had been the most unique and amazing person in their midst. They did not know why Jesus was different, but they could not have missed the manifestations of His divine perfection. How could those who claimed to know all about Him stubbornly refuse to accept the only reasonable explanation regarding Him, that He was the Son of God? But such is the blinding power of unbelief (cf. 2 Cor. 4:3–4). Once it became clear that Nazareth had rejected Jesus, He rejected them. **And He was going around the villages teaching.** The Savior left and began a teaching tour in other, more receptive towns in Galilee. For the inhabitants of His hometown, the outcome was horribly and forever tragic. "Ichabod" was written on Nazareth: "the glory has departed" (1 Sam. 4:21–22).

Ordinary Men, Extraordinary Calling
(Mark 6:7–13)

20

And He summoned the twelve and began to send them out in pairs, and gave them authority over the unclean spirits; and He instructed them that they should take nothing for their journey, except a mere staff—no bread, no bag, no money in their belt—but to wear sandals; and He added, "Do not put on two tunics." And He said to them, "Wherever you enter a house, stay there until you leave town. Any place that does not receive you or listen to you, as you go out from there, shake the dust off the soles of your feet for a testimony against them." They went out and preached that men should repent. And they were casting out many demons and were anointing with oil many sick people and healing them. (6:7–13)

This section marks a turning point in the Lord's ministry. Before this, only Jesus preached the gospel message, healed diseases, performed miracles, and confronted the hard-hearted unbelief of Israel's religious establishment. That changed with the authorizing of the twelve apostles as official preachers. Knowing His remaining time in Galilee was limited (cf. Mark 10:1), Jesus strategically multiplied the extent of His ministry by sending the Twelve as His heralds throughout the region.

The dozen men selected by Jesus had already spent countless hours accompanying and learning from Him. Though already named as apostles, they had not yet been set apart from the larger group of Jesus' disciples for specific service. The Lord had earlier promised them that He would train them to be "fishers of men" (Mark 1:17). Now the time had come for their evangelistic ministries to begin. Though they would not be fully equipped and empowered for that task until the coming of the Holy Spirit (Acts 1:8), their ministry internship began here.

In all, there were five phases culminating in their final sending, of which this was the fourth. First, they were called to confess Jesus as Lord and Messiah (cf. John 1:35–51), being drawn by the Holy Spirit to believe in Him. Second, the Lord called them to follow Him permanently in full-time ministry and leave behind their trades, such as fishing and tax collecting (cf. Mark 1:16–20; 3:13–17; Luke 5:1–11). Third, He elevated these twelve to the level of preachers. They were not only called to follow but to be sent by Him as His apostolic delegates (cf. Luke 6:12–16). (For more on this aspect of their calling, see chapter 12 of the current volume.) Fourth, He prepared them for ministry by sending them out on a short-term preaching tour. It is this phase of their training that is described in these verses. Fifth, after His resurrection and before His ascension, Jesus finally commissioned them to do miracles and to preach the gospel throughout Jerusalem, Judea, Samaria, and the uttermost parts of the earth (cf. Acts 1:8). As Jesus commanded them in Matthew 28:19–20: "Go therefore and make disciples of all the nations, baptizing them in the name of the Father and the Son and the Holy Spirit, teaching them to observe all that I commanded you; and lo, I am with you always, even to the end of the age."

In addition to its evangelistic purpose, the selection of these twelve apostles also constituted an act of judgment on Jesus' part against Israel's apostasy and unbelief. Not one of the men chosen by the Messiah was from Israel's religious establishment. Christ's delegates were not priests, scribes, Pharisees, Sadducees, or rabbis. They were ordinary men (cf. 1 Cor. 1:26), comprising a group that consisted of fishermen, common laborers, a tax collector, and even an anti-Roman zealot. And it was no accident that Jesus selected twelve. Whereas the twelve tribes of Israel comprised the apostate nation, Jesus chose twelve emissaries to preach the true message of salvation. These men symbolized the new spiritual leadership of the nation, chosen by the Messiah Himself (cf. Luke 22:29–30).

Jesus, of course, had many more than just twelve followers. At a later point, He would select seventy others to go on a similar short-term mission (cf. Luke 10). The seventy, however, must be distinguished from the twelve apostles. Although the seventy were given temporary power for their mission (cf. Luke 10:9, 17), their ministry was not revelatory like that of the Twelve. The apostles of Jesus Christ filled a unique and unrepeated role in the history of the church (cf. Rev. 21:14). Authenticated by miracles, they were specifically authorized to deliver new canonical revelation to the church (cf. John 16:12–15), through which they laid the foundation of the church, with "Christ Jesus Himself being the cornerstone" (Eph. 2:20).

Significantly, Mark connects this account to his recounting of the death of John the Baptist (cf. Mark 6:14–29). When Herod heard of Jesus' growing popularity, in part due to the success of this apostolic preaching tour, he assumed that Jesus was actually John back from the dead (v. 16). Though the two accounts may initially appear disjointed, a number of important connections should be noted. First, John the Baptist was the last of the Old Testament prophets, while the apostles were called to be the first of the New Testament prophets. In a sense, the Old Testament prophets passed the baton of faithfulness to the apostles. Second, John was killed for steadfastly upholding the message of the kingdom and preaching against sin; the apostles faced similar persecution as they fulfilled the task Jesus had given them (cf. Matt. 10:16–38). Third, Herod's growing interest in Jesus meant that the Lord's time in Herod's territory was necessarily limited (cf. Mark 7:24, 31), since Herod would have detained Jesus and probably killed Him if given the opportunity (cf. Mark 3:6; Luke 13:31–32; 23:8).

In commissioning His twelve apostles, the Lord Jesus delegated His message and power to the first generation of gospel preachers. Though the miraculous elements included in this passage (such as the supernatural ability to heal, perform miracles, and cast out demons) were limited to the apostles (2 Cor. 12:12), the broader principles apply as examples to all who preach the gospel as ministers of Christ. In particular, six marks of faithful messengers are demonstrated in this passage: they proclaim salvation, manifest compassion, live dependently, exhibit contentment, exercise discernment, and respond in obedience.

FAITHFUL MESSENGERS PROCLAIM SALVATION

And He summoned the twelve and began to send them out in pairs (6:7a)

After leaving His unbelieving hometown of Nazareth, Jesus began to preach throughout the cities and villages of Galilee (v. 6). In order to multiply the extent of His ministry in the region, as well as to train His disciples for their future responsibilities, **He summoned the twelve and began to send them out in pairs.** He sent them, as His delegates, to take the message of the gospel to other places throughout the region of Galilee. That He **began to send them out** suggests that Jesus did not send them all at once but staggered their send-off over a brief period of time. It is likely they returned the same way (cf. v. 30). The Lord sent them out in pairs for obvious reasons: to provide mutual support and protection, to strengthen the impact of their individual capabilities, and to ensure that their message was confirmed by two witnesses (cf. Deut. 19:15).

According to Luke 9:2, "He sent them out to proclaim the kingdom of God and to perform healing." The word "proclaim" (*kērussō*) refers to the authoritative, public pronouncement of vital information by a herald or forerunner. In village after village, the Twelve functioned as Christ's personal heralds, emulating His example by publicly preaching the gospel of the kingdom of God (cf. Mark 1:14, 38; Luke 4:43; 8:1)—the good news that sinners could be reconciled to God and enter into His kingdom of blessing, hope, and salvation.

Mark explains later, in verse 12, that "they went out and preached that men should repent." Having announced that the kingdom of God was at hand, they stressed the need for their listeners to respond in repentant faith. In the same way that both John the Baptist (Mark 1:4; cf. Matt. 3:2) and Jesus (Mark 1:15; cf. Matt. 4:17) emphasized repentance, the apostles declared that sinners must turn from sin and believe the gospel (cf. Acts 3:19; 17:30). Only those who recognized the bankruptcy of their spiritual condition, penitently crying out to God for mercy and embracing His Son in faith, would be saved (cf. Luke 18:13–14; John 3:16; Acts 4:12).

The implication for contemporary ministers is clear: the faithful messenger accurately and urgently proclaims the good news of salvation to the lost. As the apostle Paul explained to the Corinthians, "We are ambassadors for Christ, as though God were making an appeal through us; we beg you on behalf of Christ, be reconciled to God" (2 Cor. 5:20). He reiterated the importance of evangelistic preaching in his letter to the Romans:

> "Whoever will call on the name of the Lord will be saved." How then will they call on Him in whom they have not believed? How will they believe in Him whom they have not heard? And how will they hear without a preacher? How will they preach unless they are sent? Just as it is written, "How beautiful are the feet of those who bring good news of good things!" (Rom. 10:13–15)

Proclaiming the true gospel, in which both faith and repentance are emphasized, is essential to the minister's calling (2 Tim. 4:5). To preach anything less constitutes a serious breach of the herald's divinely ordained responsibility (cf. Gal. 1:6–9; 2 Tim. 4:1–2), the repercussions for which are severe (cf. James 3:1).

FAITHFUL MESSENGERS MANIFEST COMPASSION

and gave them authority over the unclean spirits (6:7*b*)

As the apostles went out to preach, the Lord Jesus **gave them authority** (*exousia*) **over the unclean spirits.** This delegated supernatural authority authenticated them as true messengers who were empowered by God. Not only did they have power "over all demons"

(Luke 9:1), but according to Matthew 10:8, they were also given authority to heal the sick and raise the dead (cf. Mark 6:13). Speaking of the miraculous power given to the apostles, the author of Hebrews explained to his readers:

> How will we escape if we neglect so great a salvation? After it was at the first spoken through the Lord, it was confirmed to us by those who heard, God also testifying with them, both by signs and wonders and by various miracles and by gifts of the Holy Spirit according to His own will. (Heb. 2:3–4)

That they could perform the same kinds of signs as Jesus proved that He had sent them (cf. Mark 1:21–27; 32–34; 40–45; 2:1–12; 5:35–43). He used miracles to validate His message (cf. John 5:36; 10:37–38), and so would they (cf. 2 Cor. 12:12). With the end of the apostolic era and the canon of Scripture fully revealed, authenticating miraculous signs no longer exist. All who claim to speak the truth from God can be tested now according to the inerrant standard of the written Word of God (cf. 2 Tim. 3:16–17).

By the nature of the miracles they performed, the authenticating supernatural power given to the apostles also demonstrated the compassion and loving-kindness of God. Jesus could have demonstrated His divine power in many ways that would not have relieved human suffering (cf. Matt. 4:5–7), but He chose to do wonders that primarily delivered the sick and suffering, thereby reflecting God's compassion (cf. Job 36:5–6; Pss. 9:18; 12:5; 14:6; 35:10; 69:33; 140:12; Isa. 41:17). In contrast to the calloused legalism of the Jewish religious leaders (cf. Matt. 23:4), Jesus was continually sympathetic, tender, and compassionate (cf. Matt. 11:28–30). The Twelve were enabled to follow His example.

Scripture describes false teachers as merciless, brutal, and compassionless (Isa. 56:10–12; Jer. 23:1–2; 50:6; Lam. 4:13; Ezek. 22:25; Mic. 3:5, 11; Matt. 7:15; 23:2–4; Mark 12:38–40; John 10:8, 10; Acts 20:29; 2 Cor. 2:17; Rev. 2:20). They abuse people, taking advantage of the poor to enrich and elevate themselves by trampling on the necks of the weak (cf. Job 4:4–10; Amos 2:6; 4:1). Faithful ministers, by contrast, share the attitude of the apostle Paul, who explained to the Thessalonians:

For we never came with flattering speech, as you know, nor with a pretext for greed—God is witness—nor did we seek glory from men, either from you or from others, even though as apostles of Christ we might have asserted our authority. But we proved to be gentle among you, as a nursing mother tenderly cares for her own children. Having so fond an affection for you, we were well-pleased to impart to you not only the gospel of God but also our own lives, because you had become very dear to us. (1 Thess. 2:5–8)

That attribute of divine compassion ought to characterize all who represent the Lord Jesus Christ as His ministers.

FAITHFUL MINISTERS LIVE DEPENDENTLY

and He instructed them that they should take nothing for their journey, except a mere staff—no bread, no bag, no money in their belt—but to wear sandals; and He added, "Do not put on two tunics." (6:8–9)

Jesus continued by delineating a number of stipulations for the apostles' short-term ministry trip. When the Israelites left Egypt during the exodus, the Lord God commanded them to eat the Passover meal "with your loins girded, your sandals on your feet, and your staff in your hand; and you shall eat it in haste—it is the Lord's Passover" (Ex. 12:11). Jesus similarly instructed the apostles to take only one staff, along with the clothes and sandals they were already wearing. The parallel with the Passover may have been intended to demonstrate that a new era in redemptive history was about to begin, starting with an exodus of God's true people from apostasy.

Jesus **instructed them that they should take nothing for their journey, except a mere staff,** which served as both a walking stick and a means of self-defense against robbers and wild animals. According to the parallel account in Luke 9:3, Jesus said, "Take nothing for your journey, neither a staff." Though these passages may initially appear contradictory, they are not. Luke (as well as Matthew) emphasized Jesus' insistence that the disciples not take anything extra for their journey—whether it be an additional staff or an extra pair of sandals (cf.

Matt. 10:10). They were to be ready to leave at a moment's notice, without making any preparations or gathering additional provisions. All they could take with them was what they already had in their possession, including the staff in their hands, the clothes on their backs, and the sandals on their feet. Nothing more was to be taken on the journey. They were to take **no bread, no bag, no money in their belt—but to wear sandals.** Then **He added, "Do not put on two tunics."** Unable to prepare or bring provisions, they were forced to be entirely dependent on the Lord to provide.

Jesus insisted on this level of austerity in order to teach the Twelve the vital importance of trusting in God's faithfulness and seeing Him provide. They needed to know, from firsthand experience, the truth of Jesus' words from the Sermon on the Mount, "Do not worry then, saying, 'What will we eat?' or 'What will we drink?' or 'What will we wear for clothing?' For the Gentiles eagerly seek all these things; for your heavenly Father knows that you need all these things. But seek first His kingdom and His righteousness, and all these things will be added to you" (Matt. 6:31–33). As they preached the message of the kingdom, they could confidently depend on God to supply their needs.

It should be noted that these stringent stipulations were only temporary. They did not represent a permanent vow of poverty, as Jesus Himself later made clear. In the upper room, as He reflected on this event, the Lord explained to His disciples,

> "When I sent you out without money belt and bag and sandals, you did not lack anything, did you?" They said, "No, nothing." And He said to them, "But now, whoever has a money belt is to take it along, likewise also a bag, and whoever has no sword is to sell his coat and buy one. For I tell you that this which is written must be fulfilled in Me, 'And He was numbered with transgressors'; for that which refers to Me has its fulfillment." (Luke 22:35–37)

As Jesus' words indicate, the normal expectation for the apostles was that they would plan and prepare wisely for the future. By extension, that principle applies to pastors and evangelists throughout all of church history. Although the New Testament permits ministers to earn a reasonable living for their work in the church (cf. 1 Cor. 9:5–14), they must always remember to depend ultimately on the Lord who will keep His promise (cf. Heb. 13:5–6). That was the lesson Jesus wanted the apostles to learn on this occasion (cf. Matt. 6:25–34).

FAITHFUL MINISTERS DEMONSTRATE CONTENTMENT

And He said to them, "Wherever you enter a house, stay there until you leave town." (6:10)

In a day when inns were often sordid and even dangerous, travelers generally stayed in people's homes as they journeyed from one town to the next, and the Twelve were no exception. But Jesus added an important caveat in that regard: **wherever** they went, once they decided to **enter a house** for the purpose of lodging, they were to **stay there until** they left **town.** Given their power to heal diseases and cast out demons, they likely received invitations to upgrade their comfort by changing homes. But they were not to move from house to house, as if to receive money from more people. After they accepted one initial invitation, they were to decline all others.

Doing so would distinguish them from traveling false teachers, who made a career of going from house to house, seeking money and taking advantage of the resources of unsuspecting hosts. The apostle Paul warned Timothy about such men, "who enter into households and captivate weak women weighed down with sins" (2 Tim. 3:6). False teachers used their hypocritical religious positions as a means for material gain (cf. 1 Tim. 6:5). In contrast, Timothy was to avoid the love of money and be characterized by contentment:

> But godliness actually is a means of great gain when accompanied by contentment. For we have brought nothing into the world, so we cannot take anything out of it either. If we have food and covering, with these we shall be content. But those who want to get rich fall into temptation and a snare and many foolish and harmful desires which plunge men into ruin and destruction. For the love of money is a root of all sorts of evil, and some by longing for it have wandered away from the faith and pierced themselves with many griefs. (1 Tim. 6:6–10)

Speaking of his own contentment, made possible through the strength supplied by Christ, Paul told the Philippians,

> Not that I speak from want, for I have learned to be content in whatever circumstances I am. I know how to get along with humble means, and I also know how to live in prosperity; in any and every circumstance I have learned the secret of being filled and going hungry, both of having abundance and suffering need. I can do all things through Him who strengthens me. (Phil. 4:11–13)

The lesson for the Twelve was that they were to possess contentment. Once they settled in someone's house, they were not to seek nicer accommodations. According to Matthew 10:8–9, Jesus also forbade them from using their ministry to make money: "Freely you received, freely give. Do not acquire gold, or silver, or copper for your money belts." Again, in contrast to the false teachers, the disciples were not to put a price on their ministry. They had been given extraordinary power, but they were not to exploit it for personal gain.

FAITHFUL MINISTERS EXERCISE DISCERNMENT

"Any place that does not receive you or listen to you, as you go out from there, shake the dust off the soles of your feet for a testimony against them." (6:11)

As He finished His instruction, Jesus explained how the Twelve should respond to those who inevitably would reject them. If **any** town would **not receive** the apostles **or listen to** their message, they were to **go out from there** and **shake the dust off the soles of** their **feet as a testimony against** that place. Shaking the dust off one's feet was a traditional Jewish way of expressing scorn toward Gentiles. When travelers ventured outside of Israel, upon returning to Jewish soil they would shake the dust off their sandals as an act symbolizing that they were leaving the uncleanness and contamination of Gentile lands behind them. What the Jews understood as a symbolic protest against uncircumcised pagans, Jesus applied as a sign of judgment against Jews who rejected the gospel (cf. Acts 13:50–51). The Twelve were being sent to the "lost sheep of the house of Israel" (Matt. 10:6). But if the people to whom they ministered refused to receive their message, even after it was authenticated by miraculous signs, the apostles were to treat them as they did Gentiles. According to Matthew's parallel account, Jesus expanded on this point by telling the apostles:

> "Whatever city or village you enter, inquire who is worthy in it, and stay at his house until you leave that city. As you enter the house, give it your greeting. If the house is worthy, give it your blessing of peace. But if it is not worthy, take back your blessing of peace. Whoever does not receive you, nor heed your words, as you go out of that house or that city, shake the dust off your feet. Truly I say to you, it will be more tolerable for the land of Sodom and Gomorrah in the day of judgment than for that city." (Matt. 10:11–15)

Christ's words underscore the eternal consequences of rejecting the gospel (cf. 1 Cor. 16:22; 2 Thess. 1:6–9). Those who have been exposed to the truth of salvation, and knowingly reject it, will receive the severest form of eternal punishment (cf. Heb. 10:29).

The inevitable reality, of course, was that the apostles would be treated the same way that Jesus had been treated (cf. Matt. 10:16–39). Even in His hometown of Nazareth, the Lord was compelled to leave because He was repudiated by His former neighbors (Mark 6:1–6). Accordingly, the apostles would have to exercise discernment regarding how long they should stay in any given town or village. If the people rejected their message, the apostles were to move on to another place.

Earlier, in the Sermon on the Mount, Jesus explained this principle with these words: "Do not give what is holy to dogs, and do not throw your pearls before swine, or they will trample them under their feet, and turn and tear you to pieces" (Matt. 7:6). The Jews would rightly have been horrified at the thought of throwing to the dogs that which had been consecrated as holy to God. They would have been similarly disgusted at the notion of tossing valuable jewelry into a pen of unclean pigs. Jesus used that shocking double analogy to describe those who rejected the gospel and treated it as common and worthless. As the Twelve went throughout the region of Galilee, they would undoubtedly encounter those whom Christ described as spiritual dogs and pigs—hard-hearted Jewish hypocrites who smugly snubbed the sanctity and preciousness of the good news. When they came across such people, the apostles were to exercise discernment by recognizing the need to leave and preach to those who were receptive.

FAITHFUL MINISTERS RESPOND IN OBEDIENCE

They went out and preached that men should repent. And they were casting out many demons and were anointing with oil many sick people and healing them. (6:12–13)

Sent by Christ for this temporary assignment, the Twelve responded in obedience. They proclaimed the message they had been commanded to proclaim: **they went out and preached that men should repent.** And they performed the deeds they were instructed to perform: **and they were casting out many demons and were anointing with oil many sick people and healing them.** In both their words and their actions, they did exactly what Jesus told them to do.

Though they were not an illustrious group, humanly speaking, they were obedient to the Lord's commission. Their faithful compliance is especially remarkable in light of the opposition that Jesus promised they would face. In his parallel account, Matthew records the warning words of Jesus:

> "Behold, I send you out as sheep in the midst of wolves; so be shrewd as serpents and innocent as doves. But beware of men, for they will hand you over to the courts and scourge you in their synagogues; and you will even be brought before governors and kings for My sake, as a testimony to them and to the Gentiles. But when they hand you over, do not worry about how or what you are to say; for it will be given you in that hour what you are to say. For it is not you who speak, but it is the Spirit of your Father who speaks in you. Brother will betray brother to death, and a father his child; and children will rise up against parents and cause them to be put to death. You will be hated by all because of My name, but it is the one who has endured to the end who will be saved. But whenever they persecute you in one city, flee to the next; for truly I say to you, you will not finish going through the cities of Israel until the Son of Man comes. A disciple is not above his teacher, nor a slave above his master. It is enough for the disciple that he become like

his teacher, and the slave like his master. If they have called the head of the house Beelzebul, how much more will they malign the members of his household!" (Matt. 10:16–25)

In spite of the persecution they knew they would face, the apostles submissively obeyed. Consequently, the Lord used them powerfully (cf. 1 Cor. 1:20–31).

Mark notes that, as part of their healing ministry, the apostles **were anointing with oil many sick people and healing them.** The gospel records never indicate that Jesus anointed the sick with oil, yet the apostles did on at least this occasion. Though olive oil was sometimes used for medicinal purposes (cf. Luke 10:34), that was not its purpose here since the apostles healed the sick miraculously and not through the use of medicine (Matt. 10:8). Why then did they anoint the sick with oil? In the Old Testament, olive oil was used to symbolize God's presence and authority, especially in the anointing of priests and kings (cf. Ex. 30:22–33; 1 Sam. 16:13). The apostles, then, anointed the sick with oil to symbolize the fact that their authority came from God and not from themselves; they were not the source of their power but only channels for it. By using a simple symbol, familiar to the first-century Jews, the apostles passed the glory back to the Lord Himself. As God incarnate (cf. Col. 2:9), Jesus needed no such symbol when He healed.

At this point in the narrative, Mark stopped to focus on Herod's treatment of John the Baptist. Later in the chapter, however, he revisited the ministry of the Twelve in order to report on their return (v. 30). As they came back, they reported to Jesus "all that they had done and taught." Like every minister of Jesus Christ, they welcomed being accountable to the Lord for what they said and did on His behalf (cf. 2 Cor. 5:10; Heb. 13:17). (For further discussion of v. 30, see chapter 22 in this volume.) Though contemporary pastors and preachers have not been given miraculous power like that delegated to the apostles, the principles contained in this passage are clearly applicable to all who would seek to faithfully serve the Lord Jesus. They do so knowing, like the Twelve, that they will soon appear before Christ to give an account (cf. 1 Peter 5:4; cf. Rom. 14:11–13; 2 Cor. 10:5).

The Murder of the Greatest Prophet (Mark 6:14–29)

21

And King Herod heard of it, for His name had become well known; and people were saying, "John the Baptist has risen from the dead, and that is why these miraculous powers are at work in Him." But others were saying, "He is Elijah." And others were saying, "He is a prophet, like one of the prophets of old." But when Herod heard of it, he kept saying, "John, whom I beheaded, has risen!" For Herod himself had sent and had John arrested and bound in prison on account of Herodias, the wife of his brother Philip, because he had married her. For John had been saying to Herod, "It is not lawful for you to have your brother's wife." Herodias had a grudge against him and wanted to put him to death and could not do so; for Herod was afraid of John, knowing that he was a righteous and holy man, and he kept him safe. And when he heard him, he was very perplexed; but he used to enjoy listening to him. A strategic day came when Herod on his birthday gave a banquet for his lords and military commanders and the leading men of Galilee; and when the daughter of Herodias herself came

in and danced, she pleased Herod and his dinner guests; and the king said to the girl, "Ask me for whatever you want and I will give it to you." And he swore to her, "Whatever you ask of me, I will give it to you; up to half of my kingdom." And she went out and said to her mother, "What shall I ask for?" And she said, "The head of John the Baptist." Immediately she came in a hurry to the king and asked, saying, "I want you to give me at once the head of John the Baptist on a platter." And although the king was very sorry, yet because of his oaths and because of his dinner guests, he was unwilling to refuse her. Immediately the king sent an executioner and commanded him to bring back his head. And he went and had him beheaded in the prison, and brought his head on a platter, and gave it to the girl; and the girl gave it to her mother. When his disciples heard about this, they came and took away his body and laid it in a tomb. (6:14–29)

Even a brief survey of the Old Testament evidences the tragic way that God's people repeatedly rejected and mistreated His prophets. Early in Israel's history, prophets like Moses (cf. Deut. 34:10) and Samuel (cf. 1 Sam. 3:20) faced repeated criticism and grumbling from the people (cf. Ex. 15:24; 1 Sam. 8:4–6; 10:18–19; Acts 7:39). Later, during the period of the divided monarchy, many prophets endured even more intense forms of persecution. In the days of Elijah, evil Queen Jezebel killed many true prophets of the Lord (cf. 1 Kings 18:4). Though Elijah survived, he was constantly threatened by Jezebel and her husband, Ahab (cf. 1 Kings 18:17; 19:1–3). The prophet Micaiah was imprisoned (1 Kings 22:27); Elisha was mocked (2 Kings 2:23); Isaiah was likely sawn in half (cf. Heb. 11:37); Uriah was killed by the sword (Jer. 26:20–23); and Zechariah the son of Jehoiada was stoned to death in the court of the temple (2 Chron. 24:20–21). Other examples of mistreatment, persecution, and rejection could easily be multiplied. As the author of Hebrews recounts of the prophets, "They were stoned, they were sawn in two, they were tempted, they were put to death with the sword; they went about in sheepskins, in goatskins, being destitute, afflicted, ill-treated (men of whom the world was not worthy), wandering in deserts and mountains and caves and holes in the ground" (Heb. 11:37–38; cf. Acts 7:52). Perhaps no Old Testament figure better illustrates the constant persecution the prophets faced than Jeremiah, the weeping prophet (Jer. 9:1; 13:17; 14:17). During his prophetic ministry, he was threatened with death (11:18–23), beaten and put in stocks (20:2), arrested (26:7–24), imprisoned (37:15–16), placed in a pit to die (38:6–7), bound in chains (40:1), and publicly called a liar (43:2).

The religious leaders of Jesus' day claimed that if they had been alive in earlier generations, they would never have persecuted the prophets like their forefathers did. The obvious hypocrisy of that claim was seen in their rejection of both the Messiah (to whom all of the Old Testament prophets pointed) and His forerunner, John the Baptist. Jesus did not hesitate to expose their duplicity:

> "Woe to you, scribes and Pharisees, hypocrites! For you build the tombs of the prophets and adorn the monuments of the righteous, and say, 'If we had been living in the days of our fathers, we would not have been partners with them in shedding the blood of the prophets.' So you testify against yourselves, that you are sons of those who murdered the prophets. Fill up, then, the measure of the guilt of your fathers. You serpents, you brood of vipers, how will you escape the sentence of hell? Therefore, behold, I am sending you prophets and wise men and scribes; some of them you will kill and crucify, and some of them you will scourge in your synagogues, and persecute from city to city, so that upon you may fall the guilt of all the righteous blood shed on earth, from the blood of righteous Abel to the blood of Zechariah, the son of Berechiah, whom you murdered between the temple and the altar. Truly I say to you, all these things will come upon this generation." (Matt. 23:29–36)

The nation had been guilty of reviling and mistreating God's spokesmen throughout its entire history (cf. Acts 7:51–53). As Jesus' words indicate, the religious leaders of the first century would continue the hard-hearted legacy of their forefathers, by rejecting Him and persecuting the apostles and prophets whom He sent. He told a parable about a vinedresser to dramatically illustrate this malignant reality of rejection (Mark 12:1–11; cf. Matt. 21:33–44; Luke 20:9–18).

This section (Mark 6:14–29) recounts the execution of John the Baptist, the forerunner to the Messiah, the last Old Testament prophet, and the one of whom Jesus said, "Truly I say to you, among those born of women there has not arisen anyone greater than John the Baptist!" (Matt. 11:11). (For more on the ministry of John the Baptist, see chapter 1 in this volume.) John's preaching always pointed to Christ, whom he declared to be "the Lamb of God who takes away the sin of the world" (John 1:29; cf. 3:30). If the religious leaders had received John as a true prophet, they would have been compelled to receive the One of whom he spoke. Conversely, by rejecting Jesus, they rejected John as well. Given John's biting rebukes of their hypocrisy (cf. Matt. 3:7), they were undoubtedly happy to hear he had been permanently silenced. As a martyr, John prefigured the type of persecution Jesus' followers would face for their faithfulness to Him. The story of John's murder is as dramatic as any story in the New Testament, perhaps exceeded only by the account of Jesus' crucifixion. Though true, it reads like a bizarre soap opera of intrigue, heinous iniquity, and vengeful brutality.

At the center of the story is a regional monarch named Herod Antipas. His father, Herod the Great (cf. Matt. 2:1, 19), ruled the land of Israel under Rome for thirty-six years, during which he greatly enlarged the temple. Herod the Great was not a Jew but an Idumean (a descendant of the rejected twin, Esau). As such, he had little interest in Judaism beyond whatever superficial connection was necessary for the sake of political gain. The Jewish people resented his rule, not only because he was a Gentile overlord representing Roman oppression but also on account of his gross immorality and brutality. It was Herod the Great who slaughtered the male babies of Bethlehem in an attempt to kill Jesus (cf. Matt. 2:16). He also ordered the execution of the Sanhedrin when they opposed him and even murdered two of his own sons.

When he died (in 4 B.C.), his territory was divided among several of his surviving sons—one of whom was Herod Antipas (cf. Luke 3:1). The southern territories of Judea and Samaria were given to another son, Archelaus (cf. Matt. 2:22), who proved to be inept. In A.D. 6 he was deposed by Rome and replaced with a series of governors, one of whom was Pontius Pilate (who ruled from A.D. 26 to 36). The northern regions of Ituraea and Trachonitis were given to another son, Philip the Tetrarch, who was eventually succeeded by his nephew Herod Agrippa (cf. Acts 12:1–4, 20–23). The territory that included Galilee and Perea went to Herod Antipas. Of the sons who succeeded Herod the Great, Herod

Antipas survived the longest, holding his seat of power for forty-two years. The city of Tiberias, which he built, was named after Tiberius Caesar, a Roman emperor under whom he ruled.

Although the sons of Herod the Great did not inherit the level of power and prestige enjoyed by their father, they did inherit his character, so they were equally immoral and barbaric. They were not absolute monarchs but ruled as vassals of Rome. Consequently, they had little influence or power outside of the specific regions Rome let them govern. Yet, within their territories, they wielded the authority to use military force and exercise capital punishment, prerogatives they readily employed to maintain their sovereignty. As the primary antagonist, Herod Antipas plays a key role in this account. Considered from his perspective, the passage may be divided under three headings: Herod's fascination, fear, and folly.

HEROD'S FASCINATION

And King Herod heard of it, for His name had become well known; and people were saying, "John the Baptist has risen from the dead, and that is why these miraculous powers are at work in Him." But others were saying, "He is Elijah." And others were saying, "He is a prophet, like one of the prophets of old." (6:14–15)

As the apostles traveled through the cities and villages of Galilee, preaching the gospel and performing miracles (cf. Mark 3:7–13), news of their ministry spread so that even **King Herod heard of it.** Herod Antipas existed in the grip of lust, luxury, and laziness. For whatever reason, he only now began to take an interest in the impact of Jesus. Perhaps he had been traveling, or perhaps he had been indifferent since his palace was located in Tiberias, and Jesus apparently never visited that city, even though it was within walking distance of both Nazareth and Capernaum. Tiberias was a place where most first-century Jews refused to go; it was considered unclean from its start because it had been built atop a cemetery.

That Jesus' **name had become well known** indicates that the apostles, through their ministry, pointed the people to Him as the source of their power and the sole subject of their preaching. The explosion of miraculous power wrought through the apostles in Jesus' name had caused the curious crowds to recognize that He was no ordinary prophet. As word about Him began to circulate, some of the **people were saying, "John the Baptist has risen from the dead, and that is why these miraculous powers are at work in Him."** Given His supernatural power and growing popularity, and John's recent execution, some people speculated that Jesus might be John the Baptist in resurrected form.

But others were saying, "He is Elijah." They knew that before the arrival of Messiah, according to the book of Malachi (cf. Mal. 4:5; Luke 1:17), one like the prophet Elijah would come. Ironically, they failed to understand that it was John the Baptist who had already fulfilled that role (Matt. 11:13–14). **And others were saying, "He is a prophet, like one of the prophets of old."** Some likely equated Jesus with the prophet foretold by Moses in Deuteronomy 18:15. Others identified Him as merely being in line with miracle-working Old Testament preachers, like Elijah and Elisha. Though they struggled to identify Him correctly, the people clearly understood that Jesus' ministry was unique and supernatural.

As these reports reached Herod, he became fixated on Jesus. According to Luke 9:7–9:

> Now Herod the tetrarch heard of all that was happening; and he was greatly perplexed, because it was said by some that John had risen from the dead, and by some that Elijah had appeared, and by others that one of the prophets of old had risen again. Herod said, "I myself had John beheaded; but who is this man about whom I hear such things?" And he kept trying to see Him.

Though the king desperately wanted to see Jesus, unlike the crowds who flocked to Him out of curiosity or a desire for healing, Herod's fascination with Jesus was motivated by guilty fear.

HEROD'S FEAR

But when Herod heard of it, he kept saying, "John, whom I beheaded, has risen!" For Herod himself had sent and had John arrested and bound in prison on account of Herodias, the wife of his brother Philip, because he had married her. For John had been saying to Herod, "It is not lawful for you to have your brother's wife." Herodias had a grudge against him and wanted to put him to death and could not do so; for Herod was afraid of John, knowing that he was a righteous and holy man, and he kept him safe. And when he heard him, he was very perplexed; but he used to enjoy listening to him. (6:16–20)

Herod was understandably alarmed when he received the news about Jesus. **When Herod heard** the reports of the people, thinking John may have returned from the dead, he projected his own worst apprehensions, repeatedly **saying, "John, whom I beheaded, has risen!"** Herod's inner turmoil was the result of his own evil actions toward John the Baptist. Though he knew John was a righteous man, the wicked king imprisoned him for more than a year before beheading him in barbaric fashion. Haunted by dread and superstition, Herod now sought to see Jesus in order to know for certain whether He was actually John (cf. Luke 9:9). His attitude was not one of remorse but sinister trepidation. Because he viewed a resurrected John the Baptist as a potential threat to his power, Herod would have undoubtedly tried to kill Jesus if given the opportunity (cf. Luke 13:31).

Mark relates the story in the form of a flashback, briefly reviewing the details of John's arrest, imprisonment, and execution. That **Herod himself had sent and had John arrested and bound in prison** indicates that Herod's action against John was intensely personal. His anger toward the wilderness prophet was not merely motivated by political unrest, popular demand, or Roman decree; it stemmed from a deep-seated vendetta.

John had been baptizing in the Jordan River "in Aenon near Salim" (cf. John 3:22–24), where he preached a singular message of repentance in preparation for Messiah's coming (cf. Matt. 3:2). Multitudes traveled to hear him (cf. Matt. 3:5), and many confessed their sins, publicly demonstrating their desire to live righteously by being baptized. John's call for repentance from sin was an open indictment of the immoral, lecherous, and corrupt life of Herod Antipas. When the courageous prophet heard that the king was living in incest and adultery, **on account of Herodias, the wife of his brother Philip, because he had married her,** John did not hesitate to confront specifically the iniquity of the adulterous monarch. Not only was Herodias his niece (being the daughter of Aristobulus, the half brother of Herod Antipas), but she was already married to another of Herod's half brothers, Herod Philip I (or Herod II, not to be confused with Philip the Tetrarch). Moreover, Herod Antipas himself was already married to the daughter of King Aretas, who ruled Nabatean Arabia, to the southeast of the Dead Sea. Compounding his unlawful divorce with adultery and incest, Herod Antipas enticed his niece to divorce his half brother so that he could marry her. Herod's wickedness not only angered his former father-in-law, King Aretas, who brought an army against Herod and would have defeated him if Roman troops had not intervened; it also outraged John the Baptist who publicly rebuked the regional monarch for his blatant iniquity (cf. Lev. 18:16; 20:21).

Mark does not indicate how John first confronted Herod. In all likelihood, John began publicly preaching against Herod's actions, until the angry king responded by sending soldiers to arrest John and bring him back to the palace. Once there, John issued a scathing face-to-face rebuke, **saying to Herod, "It is not lawful for you to have your brother's wife."** That **John had been saying** these things indicates that he repeated this rebuke on multiple occasions, even after Herod threw him into prison. According to Matthew 4:12 and Mark 1:14, John's imprisonment took place shortly after Christ's baptism and subsequent temptation in the wilderness.

Over the next year or so, John was likely incarcerated in the dungeon at Herod's palace in Machaerus, near the northeastern end of the Dead Sea. The fortress was situated on a high hilltop, offering dramatic views of the surrounding countryside. Deep in the earth below, the dank dungeon offered no natural light or fresh air, and it was there that Herod held John captive. After living his entire life in the open expanses of the

Judean wilderness, John ended his days in the isolation of an intolerable dungeon. His only respite were the visits he received from his disciples (cf. Luke 7:18).

As a faithful prophet of God, John was fearless in his willingness to confront sin, even in the most powerful and threatening leaders. When the Jewish religious elite came to hear him preach, John openly rebuked their hypocrisy, comparing them to a brood of snakes (Matt. 3:7). His response to Herod was similarly characterized by holy boldness, born out of the conviction to speak for God rather than please men (cf. Acts 5:29). As a result of John's unflinching confrontations, **Herodias had a grudge against him and wanted to put him to death.** Yet she **could not do so; for Herod was afraid of John, knowing that he was a righteous and holy man, and he kept him safe.** Herod protected John from the jealous rage of his new wife, Herodias. According to Matthew 14:5, the king was motivated not only out of fear of John but also fear of the people because of John's popularity: "Although Herod wanted to put him to death, he feared the crowd, because they regarded John as a prophet." Herod's wicked mind, as vividly illustrated by this story, was dominated by fright and trepidation. Initially, he was afraid to kill John. Then, after he killed him, he became terrified that John had come back from the dead and would come for him in vengeance. Standing in stark contrast to Herod's terror over John was John's trust in the Lord.

Ironically, though John repeatedly blasted Herod on account of his immorality, the king's curiosity was piqued by his preaching. Consequently, **when** Herod **heard him, he was very perplexed; but he used to enjoy listening to him.** John was obviously a powerful communicator. On some superficial level, Herod was intrigued by the passionate oratory of his imprisoned guest. An erratic combination of curiosity and fear restrained Herod from taking John's life.

HEROD'S FOLLY

A strategic day came when Herod on his birthday gave a banquet for his lords and military commanders and the leading men of

Galilee; and when the daughter of Herodias herself came in and danced, she pleased Herod and his dinner guests; and the king said to the girl, "Ask me for whatever you want and I will give it to you." And he swore to her, "Whatever you ask of me, I will give it to you; up to half of my kingdom." And she went out and said to her mother, "What shall I ask for?" And she said, "The head of John the Baptist." Immediately she came in a hurry to the king and asked, saying, "I want you to give me at once the head of John the Baptist on a platter." And although the king was very sorry, yet because of his oaths and because of his dinner guests, he was unwilling to refuse her. Immediately the king sent an executioner and commanded him to bring back his head. And he went and had him beheaded in the prison, and brought his head on a platter, and gave it to the girl; and the girl gave it to her mother. When his disciples heard about this, they came and took away his body and laid it in a tomb. (6:21–29)

In spite of the king's curiosity and fear, John's imprisonment in Herod's fortress came to a forced and violent end. Mark recounts how it happened: **A strategic day came when Herod on his birthday gave a banquet for his lords and military commanders and the leading men of Galilee.** The Jews viewed birthday celebrations as pagan festivities that they generally avoided. But, for the Romans, birthday parties were excuses for uninhibited revelry, often characterized by overindulgence, gluttony, drunkenness, and sexual deviance. Such was certainly true of the orgiastic festival to which Herod invited his nobles, the political elite of Galilee. His dinner guests, limited to men only, included the most powerful people, from upper-level tax collectors to high-ranking military commanders to those whom Mark 3:6 identifies as Herodians (supporters of Herod and the Romans). The party itself was a lecherous affair as evidenced by the erotic entertainment that amused those in attendance.

The debauchery reached its low point when Herod invited his own stepdaughter, whose name according to Josephus was Salome, to dance for him and his friends. **When the daughter of Herodias herself came in and danced, she pleased Herod and his dinner**

guests. Salome's provocative dance was a highly suggestive, erotic per-
formance, comparable to a modern striptease. In their drunken stupor,
Herod and his friends were **pleased** (a euphemism for "sexually
aroused"), causing **the king** to foolishly promise **the girl, "Ask me for
whatever you want and I will give it to you." And he swore to her,
"Whatever you ask of me, I will give it to you; up to half of my
kingdom."** Herod's magnanimous offer was nothing more than sheer
braggadocio. In reality, he did not have anything to give, since he ruled his
territory only as a proxy of Rome. Motivated by foolish pride and sexual
perversion, Herod took an oath in the hearing of his guests and bound
himself to the fancies of his stepdaughter.

Before giving an answer, the girl knew just whom to seek. **She
went out and said to her mother, "What shall I ask for?"** Like a
New Testament Jezebel, Salome's mother, Herodias, was wicked, wily, and
vindictive. She resented John the Baptist for his tireless attack on her iniq-
uitous life, which not only stung her conscience but also stirred up dis-
sent among her husband's subjects. From the moment of John's arrest,
she wanted him put to death. Her hatred was so bitter that she permitted
her daughter to perform a lewd dance for Herod and his party guests,
just so she could claim her revenge. So, when Salome asked her mother
what she should ask for, Herodias did not hesitate. **She said, "The head
of John the Baptist."** To honor her mother's request, Salome rushed
back before her stepfather had an opportunity to sober up or change his
mind. **Immediately she came in a hurry to the king and asked, saying, "I want you to give me at once the head of John the Baptist
on a platter."**

Salome's request undoubtedly caught Herod off guard, but he
was stuck. He did not want to kill John the Baptist (for the reasons noted
above). Having made such a bold promise in front of his friends, to maintain his pride he had no choice. Thus, **although the king was very
sorry, yet because of his oaths and because of his dinner guests,
he was unwilling to refuse her.** Herod's motivation for keeping his
promise had nothing to do with personal integrity and everything to do
with keeping up appearances. In the ancient Near East, promises made
with an oath were regarded as especially binding and inviolable (cf.
Matt. 5:33). Having made such a promise in the presence of his dinner

guests—many of whom were political supporters and military dignities —Herod could not go back on his word without losing face. **Herod was very sorry,** yet his fear of embarrassment precluded him from doing what he knew to be right. He was filled with regret, but his sorrow had no connection to true repentance (cf. 2 Cor. 7:10). Though he realized that he had been trapped by his wife, Herod obliged the wicked request of his stepdaughter in order to avoid personal humiliation.

So, **immediately the king sent an executioner and commanded him to bring back his head.** Even though he was only a petty pseudo-king who functioned as no more than a servant under Roman oversight, Herod did have the authority to exercise the death penalty within his territory. Once the command was issued, it was carried out immediately. The executioner **went and had** John **beheaded in the prison, and brought his head on a platter, and gave it to the girl; and the girl gave it to her mother.** Though the setting of John's head on a platter was a presentation fit for cannibals, such an act was not uncommon in the barbaric world of antiquity because it guaranteed that the execution had been carried out. According to the ancient Roman historian Cassius Dio, when the head of Cicero (d. 43 B.C.) was brought to Mark Antony's wife, Fulvia, she pulled out his tongue and repeatedly stabbed it with her hairpin. Her violent assault on his tongue was intended as a poetic act of final vengeance against Cicero, because he had delivered powerful speeches that attacked Mark Antony. The fifth-century church father Jerome (d. 420) suggested that Herodias similarly mutilated the severed head of John the Baptist. Though such cannot be verified, it would certainly fit with the spiteful rage that characterized the vulgar queen.

Presumably, with one deft stroke of the executioner's blade, John the Baptist entered into his glorious eternal rest, to receive his full reward for uncompromising faithfulness to God. He was not only the greatest and last of the Old Testament prophets, he was also the first martyr for Jesus Christ. His entire life pointed to the coming Messiah. Even in death, he remained faithful to his God-given task. (For a biographical treatment of John the Baptist, see John MacArthur, *Twelve Unlikely Heroes* [Nashville: Thomas Nelson, 2012].)

When his disciples heard about this, they came and took away his body and laid it in a tomb. It is difficult to imagine the heartbreak that John's disciples must have endured as they gave his headless body a proper burial. He had been both their teacher from God and their leader. God had used John's fiery preaching in their lives to convict their hearts of sin and bring them to a place of repentance. He had also pointed them to the Messiah (cf. John 1:35–37). It is not surprising, then, that John's disciples came and reported what had happened to Jesus (Matt. 14:12).

As noted above, it was not until after John the Baptist was killed that Herod began to pay attention to the ministry of Christ. Fearful that John may have come back from the dead, Herod sought to see Jesus. But that meeting would not take place until just a few hours before the Lord's crucifixion. According to Luke, Pilate sent Jesus to Herod because Pilate could find no guilt in Him:

> When Pilate heard it, he asked whether the man was a Galilean. And when he learned that He belonged to Herod's jurisdiction, he sent Him to Herod, who himself also was in Jerusalem at that time. Now Herod was very glad when he saw Jesus; for he had wanted to see Him for a long time, because he had been hearing about Him and was hoping to see some sign performed by Him. And he questioned Him at some length; but He answered him nothing. And the chief priests and the scribes were standing there, accusing Him vehemently. And Herod with his soldiers, after treating Him with contempt and mocking Him, dressed Him in a gorgeous robe and sent Him back to Pilate. (Luke 23:6–11)

In the end, Herod saw Jesus. The king was undoubtedly relieved that He was not John risen from the grave. He was in truth far more, but to Herod Jesus seemed like far less—nothing more than a novelty whom he ridiculed and sent back to Pilate.

In his interactions with both John the Baptist and Jesus, Herod Antipas stands like Judas as a monumentally tragic figure in history. He had the greatest man who had ever lived, the most honored prophet of God in his hands, and he locked him in a dungeon until he had him executed. More importantly, he had an audience with the King of kings, and he mocked Him and turned Him away. Such wasted opportunity was the result of his insidious love for sin, his arrogant unwillingness to believe, and his cowardly fear of the truth. Herod claimed to rule over others, but in reality he was a man controlled by the fear of man. His fear of the people initially kept him from killing John. His fear of his friends finally compelled him to authorize John's execution. His fear of John made him anxious when he heard about Jesus. But his fear turned to scorn when he finally had an audience with the Son of God. Herod feared everyone except the Lord, and he lost his soul as a result.

Hours after that meeting with Herod, Jesus would be nailed to the cross. His death fulfilled the warning He had earlier issued to the Jewish religious leaders: "Jerusalem, Jerusalem, who kills the prophets and stones those who are sent to her! How often I wanted to gather your children together, the way a hen gathers her chicks under her wings, and you were unwilling. Behold, your house is being left to you desolate!" (Matt. 23:37–38). Having rejected the ministry of John, the religious leaders also rejected the Messiah to whom he and every other Old Testament prophet pointed. Consequently, they came under God's severe and everlasting judgment, along with the apostate nation they represented (cf. Rom. 11:25, 28).

The Creator Provides
(Mark 6:30–44)

22

The apostles gathered together with Jesus; and they reported to Him all that they had done and taught. And He said to them, "Come away by yourselves to a secluded place and rest a while." (For there were many people coming and going, and they did not even have time to eat.) They went away in the boat to a secluded place by themselves. The people saw them going, and many recognized them and ran there together on foot from all the cities, and got there ahead of them. When Jesus went ashore, He saw a large crowd, and He felt compassion for them because they were like sheep without a shepherd; and He began to teach them many things. When it was already quite late, His disciples came to Him and said, "This place is desolate and it is already quite late; send them away so that they may go into the surrounding countryside and villages and buy themselves something to eat." But He answered them, "You give them something to eat!" And they said to Him, "Shall we go and spend two hundred denarii on bread and give them something to eat?" And He said to them, "How

many loaves do you have? Go look!" And when they found out, they said, "Five, and two fish." And He commanded them all to sit down by groups on the green grass. They sat down in groups of hundreds and of fifties. And He took the five loaves and the two fish, and looking up toward heaven, He blessed the food and broke the loaves and He kept giving them to the disciples to set before them; and He divided up the two fish among them all. They all ate and were satisfied, and they picked up twelve full baskets of the broken pieces, and also of the fish. There were five thousand men who ate the loaves. (6:30–44)

Significantly, of the countless miracles that occurred during the ministry of Jesus (cf. John 21:25, only two are found in all four Gospels: Christ's resurrection and the event recorded in this passage (cf. Matt. 14:13–22; Luke 9:10–17; John 6:1–15). Commonly known as the feeding of the five thousand, this familiar miracle occurred near the end of Jesus' Galilean ministry and served as the climactic capstone to His time there. According to John 6:4, it took place shortly before the Passover (likely in March or early April A.D. 29).

Jesus was raised in Galilee (in the village of Nazareth), but that was not the primary reason for His extensive ministry in that region. By focusing His attention far away from Israel's religious establishment in Jerusalem, the Lord used geography to make a spiritual point. Other than through confrontation and condemnation, the Messiah would have nothing to do with the nation's apostate leadership. Still the Lord would not stay in Galilee indefinitely. Soon after performing this massive miracle, Jesus traveled with His disciples to the predominantly Gentile regions of Tyre and Sidon, and the Decapolis, before finally journeying south to Judea and Jerusalem. As opposition from the Pharisees and scribes increased (cf. Mark 3:6, 22), along with a growing interest from hostile King Herod (cf. Luke 9:9), Jesus began to spend less time preaching in public and more time instructing His disciples privately. During the final year of His ministry, in the looming shadow of the cross, His primary focus was training the Twelve for the mission He would give them after His resurrection (cf. Matt. 28:18–20).

In terms of visible scale, the feeding of the five thousand was

Jesus' most extensive miracle. Its name is somewhat misleading since, in reality, it encompassed far more than just five thousand people. As Matthew explains, "There were about five thousand men who ate, *besides women and children*" (Matt. 14:21, emphasis added). Assuming the number of women was approximately equal to the number of men, and that the number of children was at least the same as the number of adults, a crowd of twenty thousand or more was likely present on that Galilean spring day. To instantaneously create food for twenty to twenty-five thousand people was something only the Maker of the universe could do (cf. John 1:3).

This miracle was more than just an astounding display of Jesus' divine nature and creative power. It also demonstrated His merciful compassion and tender care. God the Son not only possessed the power to meet vast human needs, He also had the sincere desire to do so. Here is a picture of Jehovah-jireh (Gen. 22:14), an Old Testament name for God, meaning "the Lord who provides." Tragically, most of the people in the crowd that day would ultimately reject Jesus (cf. John 6:66). Yet He generously fed them anyway, thereby providing a vivid illustration of God's common grace, in which "He causes His sun to rise on the evil and the good, and sends rain on the righteous and the unrighteous" (Matt. 5:45). Thus, this section (Mark 6:30–44) highlights both the creative power and the compassionate provision of Jesus. As the passage unfolds, the Lord provides rest for the weary, truth for the wandering, and food for the wanting.

REST FOR THE WEARY

The apostles gathered together with Jesus; and they reported to Him all that they had done and taught. And He said to them, "Come away by yourselves to a secluded place and rest a while." (For there were many people coming and going, and they did not even have time to eat.) They went away in the boat to a secluded place by themselves. (6:30–32)

Earlier, Jesus had delegated His power to the Twelve and instructed them to preach a message of repentance throughout the cities of Galilee

(Mark 6:7–13). Doing so enabled Jesus to multiply the extent of His ministry sixfold, since the apostles were sent out in pairs. As He commissioned them for their task, the Lord instructed them:

> "Go to the lost sheep of the house of Israel. And as you go, preach, saying, 'The kingdom of heaven is at hand.' Heal the sick, raise the dead, cleanse the lepers, cast out demons. Freely you received, freely give. Do not acquire gold, or silver, or copper for your money belts, or a bag for your journey, or even two coats, or sandals, or a staff; for the worker is worthy of his support. And whatever city or village you enter, inquire who is worthy in it, and stay at his house until you leave that city. As you enter the house, give it your greeting. If the house is worthy, give it your blessing of peace. But if it is not worthy, take back your blessing of peace. Whoever does not receive you, nor heed your words, as you go out of that house or that city, shake the dust off your feet. Truly I say to you, it will be more tolerable for the land of Sodom and Gomorrah in the day of judgment than for that city." (Matt. 10:6–15)

All of **the apostles** except for Judas Iscariot were from Galilee, and were therefore familiar with the villages to which they traveled to preach the gospel. Mark does not designate how long the Twelve were gone, but their mission probably lasted weeks, maybe even months. Their ministry efforts created a buzz throughout Galilee, causing even Herod Antipas to take notice (cf. Mark 6:14–16). (For more on the short-term ministry assignment given to the apostles by Jesus, see chapter 20 in this volume.)

When the Twelve returned, they **gathered together with Jesus,** likely in Capernaum, **and they reported to Him all that they had done and taught.** After an extensive ministry tour, the apostles were undoubtedly fatigued from their travels, which included persecution and rejection (cf. Matt. 10:16–23). Adding to their weariness was the news from the disciples of John the Baptist that John, the greatest of all prophets, had recently been executed (cf. Matt. 14:12). When the Lord heard about John's death (cf. Matt. 14:13), and in order to give His disciples a much-needed respite, He instructed them to get into a boat and set sail across the Sea of Galilee. **He said to them, "Come away by yourselves to a secluded place and rest a while." (For there were many people coming and going, and they did not even have time to eat.)** The effort required by the ministry was so intense that they could not even find a few moments for a meal (cf. Mark 3:20).

The Lord recognized their need for rest and responded with tenderness. Following His instruction, the disciples **went away in the boat to a secluded place by themselves.** The boat likely belonged to some of the former fishermen among the Twelve (such as Peter and Andrew or James and John). Even the trip across the lake provided the disciples with an opportunity to enjoy a short reprieve from the pressure of the crowds. According to Luke 9:10, Jesus and the Twelve sailed to an area near the town of Bethsaida. Archaeologists do not know the exact location of Bethsaida. Its name, meaning "house of fish," suggests that "fish town" was one of the many villages that bordered the Sea of Galilee. It may have been located on the northern shore of the lake, to the east of the Jordan River. (Some scholars believe there was another village by the same name on the western shore, near Capernaum [cf. Mark 6:45].) The Gospels indicate that Peter and Andrew were originally from Bethsaida (John 1:44), though they relocated to Capernaum (Luke 4:31, 38). Philip (John 12:21) and possibly Nathanael (John 1:45) were also former residents of the town.

In Luke 10:13–14, Jesus rebuked Bethsaida, along with Chorazin, for its unbelief: "Woe to you, Bethsaida! For if the miracles had been performed in Tyre and Sidon which occurred in you, they would have repented long ago, sitting in sackcloth and ashes. But it will be more tolerable for Tyre and Sidon in the judgment than for you." In Old Testament history, the Phoenician cities of Tyre and Sidon, located on the Mediterranean coast north of Israel, were noted for their rampant idolatry, immorality, violence, pride, and greed. Consequently, God judged both of those cities by totally destroying them (Isa. 23:1–18; Ezek. 26–28; Amos 1:9–10; Zech. 9:3–4). Yet Bethsaida, full of outwardly religious residents, was marked out for even greater judgment than the pagan Phoenicians because they had rejected the Lord and Messiah despite the remarkable miracles and revelation to which they were exposed. (It is likely that some of the apostles had preached there on their recent ministry tour.) As deserving as Tyre and Sidon were of divine wrath, the people in those cities would have repented in sackcloth and ashes if they had witnessed the miracles that Bethsaida experienced (including the miracle recorded in this passage). Because they refused to believe in the face of such overwhelming revelation of the Son of God, the self-righteous Judaistic legalists in Bethsaida would face harsher everlasting consequences than idolatrous pagans (cf. Heb. 10:26–31).

TRUTH FOR THE WANDERING

The people saw them going, and many recognized them and ran there together on foot from all the cities, and got there ahead of them. When Jesus went ashore, He saw a large crowd, and He felt compassion for them because they were like sheep without a shepherd; and He began to teach them many things. (6:33–34)

Given the indefatigable persistence of the crowds that constantly surrounded Jesus and His disciples, it is not surprising that as they pushed out into the lake, **the people saw them going, and many recognized them.** They watched Jesus and His disciples leave in the boat and began traversing the shore on foot in order to follow them. As John writes, the "crowd followed Him, because they saw the signs which He was performing on those who were sick" (John 6:2). Most of those in the crowd were thrill seekers, motivated out of a desire to witness and perhaps personally experience miracles. Those who were sick wished to be healed, and those who were well wanted to be entertained. Some were also fueled by political ambitions, hoping to press Jesus into becoming their political deliverer (cf. John 6:14–15). Noting the direction the boat was headed, the people assessed its general destination **and ran there together on foot from all the cities, and got there ahead of them.**

When Jesus and His disciples reached their destination, the ubiquitous, swarming crowd was already there waiting. **When Jesus went ashore, He saw a large crowd that had already gathered.** Though they violated His privacy, Jesus responded by "welcoming them" (Luke 9:11). The Lord could have ignored them or sent them away; He could have gotten back in the boat and sailed to a different location. Instead, **He felt compassion for them because they were like sheep without a shepherd; and He began to teach them many things.** The verb translated **felt compassion** (from the Greek word *splanchnizomai*) literally means "to be moved in one's bowels," where the feelings of pain are felt, so that the ancients considered them to be the seat of emotions. Jesus was deeply moved by genuine concern for these people because, spiritually speaking, they were wandering as lost **sheep without a shepherd** for their souls.

In an agrarian society, where sheep were a mainstay of agricultural life, the serious dangers faced by **sheep without a shepherd** would have been immediately understood. Without help and guidance, sheep are defenseless, unable to clean themselves, and prone to getting lost. In the Old Testament, the nation of Israel was sometimes pictured as a flock with no shepherd (Num. 27:17; 1 Kings 22:17; 2 Chron. 18:16; Ezek. 34:5). The metaphor depicted the nation as being spiritually vulnerable to deadly enemies and malnourished, threatened by error and sin, and lacking in faithful caretakers and spiritual protectors. As "the good shepherd" (John 10:11), Jesus was willing to feed, cleanse, and protect these lost sheep (cf. Matt. 10:6), and lead them into eternal safety in the fold of salvation. Thus **He began to teach them many things.** According to Luke 9:11, He was "speaking to them about the kingdom of God" (i.e., the realm of salvation), which was the primary theme of His preaching (cf. Mark 1:15; 4:11, 26–32; Luke 4:43; 6:20; 8:1; 11:20; 17:20–21; 18:24–25; John 3:3; Acts 1:3).

As was His usual pattern, Jesus not only taught the people, He also healed them. As Matthew 14:14 explains, "When He went ashore, He saw a large crowd, and felt compassion for them and healed their sick." The Lord's compassion extended beyond the spiritual needs of people to include their physical infirmities as well. Jesus' ability to heal them from temporal ailments was evidence of His ability to offer them spiritual help: salvation not just from the debilitating effects of sin in this life but from the eternal effect of sin itself. The physical healing He provided was limited to this life only, but the eternal life He offered abounds with blessings and benefits both for this life and the next.

FOOD FOR THE WANTING

When it was already quite late, His disciples came to Him and said, "This place is desolate and it is already quite late; send them

away so that they may go into the surrounding countryside and villages and buy themselves something to eat." But He answered them, "You give them something to eat!" And they said to Him, "Shall we go and spend two hundred denarii on bread and give them something to eat?" And He said to them, "How many loaves do you have? Go look!" And when they found out, they said, "Five, and two fish." And He commanded them all to sit down by groups on the green grass. They sat down in groups of hundreds and of fifties. And He took the five loaves and the two fish, and looking up toward heaven, He blessed the food and broke the loaves and He kept giving them to the disciples to set before them; and He divided up the two fish among them all. They all ate and were satisfied, and they picked up twelve full baskets of the broken pieces, and also of the fish. There were five thousand men who ate the loaves. (6:35–44)

After a full day of teaching and healing, Jesus was approached by His disciples, who had collectively decided that the people were hungry and needed to eat. **When it was already quite late** refers to the late afternoon and early evening (sometime between three and six o'clock), just prior to sunset (cf. Matt. 14:15). Due to the lateness of the hour, **His disciples came to Him and said, "This place is desolate and it is already quite late; send them away so that they may go into the surrounding countryside and villages and buy themselves something to eat."** From a human perspective, the disciples' concerns were reasonable. They did not know where to find provisions for such a massive crowd. Aware of the people's hunger, and probably being hungry themselves (cf. Mark 6:31), they encouraged Jesus to dismiss the multitude.

When the disciples noted that the **place** was **desolate,** they were not implying that the location itself was a desert (as some translations make it sound). The Galilean countryside in springtime is beautiful, and the people were sitting on green grass (v. 39). The disciples' observation merely indicates that they were in a remote and unpopulated area, where food was not readily available. So the disciples suggested dismissing the crowds so that the people could head for locations to find dinner for themselves.

Jesus undoubtedly shocked His disciples when **He answered them, "You give them something to eat!"** His words were intended to test the level of their faith, while also forcing them to acknowledge that they had no human solution to the problem. The apostle John records the interaction between Jesus and His disciples regarding this logistical dilemma:

> Therefore Jesus, lifting up His eyes and seeing that a large crowd was coming to Him, said to Philip, "Where are we to buy bread, so that these may eat?" This He was saying to test him, for He Himself knew what He was intending to do. Philip answered Him, "Two hundred denarii worth of bread is not sufficient for them, for everyone to receive a little." (John 6:5–7)

Two hundred denarii equaled about eight months' fair wages for a man. Even that was clearly not enough to feed a crowd of tens of thousands. So **they said to Him, "Shall we go and spend two hundred denarii on bread and give them something to eat?"** The disciples' question evidenced their incredulity and skepticism. Humanly speaking, the problem appeared insurmountable, far beyond the financial resources available to them. The possibility that Jesus might create the necessary food never crossed their minds. They were so focused on the problem, and the need to find a human solution, that they failed to consider the divine power of their Lord.

Jesus **said to them, "How many loaves do you have? Go look!" And when they found out, they said, "Five, and two fish."** Here again John's account fills in the details: "One of His disciples, Andrew, Simon Peter's brother, said to Him, 'There is a lad here who has five barley loaves and two fish, but what are these for so many people?'" (John 6:8–9). The word **loaves** might be literally translated as "bread-cakes," and refers to flatbread wafers or biscuits. The small fish were likely pickled and intended to be eaten with the bread. Together, this constituted a standard lunch for a small boy. That one meal fit for a child could launch a miracle that would feed tens of thousands was never imagined.

But Jesus knew what He was about to do. Speaking of Christ on this occasion, Charles Spurgeon aptly declared:

He it was who thought of the way of feeding them, it was a design invented and originated by himself. His followers had looked at their little store of bread and fish and given up the task as hopeless; but Jesus, altogether unembarrassed, and in no perplexity, had already considered how he would banquet the thousands and make the fainting sing for joy. The Lord of Hosts needed no entreaty to become the host of hosts of hungry men. (Charles Spurgeon, "The Miracle of the Loaves," sermon no. 1218)

Addressing the crowd, Jesus **commanded them all to sit down by groups on the green grass. They sat down in groups of hundreds and of fifties.** The people had been standing as they pressed around Jesus to be healed and instructed by Him. But He ordered them to sit in neatly organized units, to facilitate the distribution of food and so that the people would be comfortable as they ate. Doing so also accentuated the grandeur of this miracle, because it made the vast numbers of people easy to count. With a simple command, Jesus transformed the chaotic crowd into a highly coordinated assembly.

As the people waited to see what He would do next, Jesus **took the five loaves and the two fish, and looking up toward heaven, He blessed the food** by giving thanks to His heavenly Father (John 6:6, 11; cf. 1 Tim. 4:3–5). Then He **broke the loaves and He kept giving them to the disciples to set before them; and He divided up the two fish among them all.** Because there is no human explanation to a divine creative miracle, the Gospels do not attempt to describe the manner in which this miracle took place. It apparently involved continuous creation as Jesus kept producing meals and giving them to the disciples, who were distributing them to the people until everyone was fed.

In the process, thousands of hungry people **all ate and were satisfied.** The word translated "satisfied" (from the Greek *chortazō*) derives its meaning from the world of animal husbandry and describes livestock eating until they are completely full. Thus it speaks of being gratified to the point of not wanting any more. Jesus used this same word in the Beatitudes to promise those who hunger and thirst for righteousness that "they shall be satisfied" (Matt. 5:6). The food Jesus created from nothing was perfect, having never been tainted by the corruption of a fallen world; He made more than enough to satisfy the famished crowds. Per Jesus' instructions, the disciples **picked up** any leftover food (cf.

John 6:12), using small baskets to collect it. That there were exactly **twelve full baskets of the broken pieces, and also of the fish** was obviously no coincidence. As a result of Jesus' perfect providential precision, the apostles each had their own basketful of food. Surely they shared their portions with their Master who created it all.

Mark concludes his account of this remarkable miracle by noting that **there were five thousand men who ate the loaves.** As noted earlier, Matthew 14:21 indicates that there were also many women and children present, meaning that the total number of people in the crowd was far greater than just five thousand. Astonished by the scope of what they had just seen (and the deliciousness of what they had just tasted), the people exclaimed: "This is truly the Prophet [an Old Testament reference to the Messiah] who is to come into the world" (John 6:14). In their euphoria "they were intending to come and take Him by force to make Him king" (v. 15). Obsessed with both His healing and creative power, the crowds longed for Jesus to usher in the ultimate welfare state, in which sickness and hunger would be permanently banished. Here was a Man who could also use His limitless divine power to overthrow Herod and the Romans, as well as gratify their needs.

The people were right to identify Jesus as the Messiah, but as they had all along, they misunderstood the purpose of His coming. Though He will one day return to establish His earthly kingdom with all promised power, provision, and protection as laid out by the Old Testament prophets, at His first coming the Son of God came "to seek and to save the lost" (Luke 19:10) and "to give His life as a ransom for many" (Mark 10:45 ESV). Though the people wanted to make Jesus their political ruler, He was willing only to be spiritual King to those who believed in Him. As generous as He was in the creation of food, Jesus intended the visible display of His power and compassion in the physical world to be a symbol of His might in the spiritual realm. His willingness to give physical rest was a symbol of His offer to give spiritual rest (cf. Matt. 11:28). His desire to teach the truth underscored the fact that He is the truth (cf. John 14:6). And His readiness to make bread and fish was evidence of His ability to provide spiritual food for those who hunger and thirst for righteousness (cf. Matt. 5:6). He is the Bread of Life, such that those who believe in Him will be eternally satisfied (cf. John 6:35).

Jesus refused to be a permanent source of free meals, but He was willing to be an eternal source of spiritual sustenance. Sadly, most of the people were not interested in that. The very next day, most of those who had been miraculously fed rejected Jesus, and many of His disciples stopped following Him altogether (John 6:66). By supernaturally feeding them, He had clearly demonstrated Himself to be the compassionate Creator. By stubbornly rejecting Him, they evidenced the true nature of their hard-hearted unbelief, for which they would be eternally judged in severity. Yet not everyone exhibited such calloused unbelief. Even as many were departing, the apostle Peter articulated the heart cry of every true believer: "Lord, to whom shall we go? You have words of eternal life. We have believed and have come to know that You are the Holy One of God" (vv. 68–69).

Jesus Walks on Water (Mark 6:45–56)

23

Immediately Jesus made His disciples get into the boat and go ahead of Him to the other side to Bethsaida, while He Himself was sending the crowd away. After bidding them farewell, He left for the mountain to pray. When it was evening, the boat was in the middle of the sea, and He was alone on the land. Seeing them straining at the oars, for the wind was against them, at about the fourth watch of the night He came to them, walking on the sea; and He intended to pass by them. But when they saw Him walking on the sea, they supposed that it was a ghost, and cried out; for they all saw Him and were terrified. But immediately He spoke with them and said to them, "Take courage; it is I, do not be afraid." Then He got into the boat with them, and the wind stopped; and they were utterly astonished, for they had not gained any insight from the incident of the loaves, but their heart was hardened. When they had crossed over they came to land at Gennesaret, and moored to the shore. When they got out of the boat, immediately the people recognized Him, and ran about that

whole country and began to carry here and there on their pallets those who were sick, to the place they heard He was. Wherever He entered villages, or cities, or countryside, they were laying the sick in the market places, and imploring Him that they might just touch the fringe of His cloak; and as many as touched it were being cured. (6:45–56)

The remarkable events recorded in this section immediately followed the miraculous creation of a meal for tens of thousands of people on the northeastern side of the Sea of Galilee (cf. Mark 6:33–44). With divine precision, Jesus created just enough food for the massive crowd to be satisfied, and the leftovers filled exactly twelve baskets, one for each of the apostles. The visible magnitude of that supernatural display dramatically demonstrated both the power and compassion of the Son of God— divine attributes that continually characterized the ministry of Jesus.

With the creation of the meal, Jesus reached the peak of His popularity. He had ministered all through Galilee for more than a year, preaching and performing countless miracles. He also extended His ministry by authorizing the twelve apostles to proclaim the gospel message and to exhibit the power He had delegated to them. As a result, the word about Him swept throughout the region, even reaching the ears of Herod Antipas who nervously feared that Jesus might be John the Baptist, whom he beheaded, back from the dead.

Herod had reason to be concerned. When Jesus miraculously created food from nothing and with no apparent effort, the crowd responded with a euphoric attempt to crown Him king (cf. John 6:14–15). They hoped He would overthrow Herod and the Romans, and usher in the millennial kingdom with power and provision like He had displayed. The people's enthusiasm was misguided; their interests were merely material and temporal. Jesus' message, by contrast, focused on truths that were heavenly and eternal. He insisted on a spiritual transformation, not a political revolution (cf. John 18:36). Though He will one day return to establish His kingdom on earth (cf. Rev. 20:1–6) and fulfill all that the prophets predicted about the glories of His reign, such was not the goal of His first coming (cf. Mark 10:45; Luke 19:10).

The Gospels indicate that the apostles generally shared the messianic expectations of the people. They undoubtedly expected Jesus to overthrow Israel's enemies and establish the messianic kingdom head-quartered in Jerusalem, in which they would sit to the right and left of His royal throne (cf. Matt. 19:28; Mark 10:37; Luke 22:30). Yet there was a key distinction between the apostles and the unbelieving crowds. When Jesus' ministry did not fit their preconceptions about the Messiah, the populace rejected Him and later called for His death. Even many of His followers forsook Him (cf. John 6:66). The apostles, by contrast, continued to believe. As He watched the crowds leave and disciples defect, just a day after miraculously feeding them, "Jesus said to the twelve, 'You do not want to go away also, do you?' Simon Peter answered Him, 'Lord, to whom shall we go? You have words of eternal life. We have believed and have come to know that You are the Holy One of God'" (John 6:67–69). Clearly, unlike the crowds, they looked beyond the physical to "eternal life."

Peter's monumental confession raises an important question: What catalyst convinced the Twelve to believe in Jesus when so many others rejected Him? He had created bread and fish to feed thousands the day before. Yet, most of those who experienced that miracle rejected Him. Immediately after the event, even the disciples who remained with Him "had not gained any insight from the incident of the loaves, but their heart was hardened" (Mark 6:52). Their rapid transformation in thinking must have had a powerful cause. The apostles alone experienced the astounding incident recorded in this section (vv. 45–56), which was the catalyst by which they first acknowledged Jesus to be the Son of God (cf. Matt. 14:33). The wondrous event can be divided into three scenes: Jesus' private intercession with the Father, His powerful intervention for the Twelve; and His personal interaction with the crowds. In each scene, the Lord Jesus Christ occupies center stage.

PRIVATE INTERCESSION WITH THE FATHER

Immediately Jesus made His disciples get into the boat and go ahead of Him to the other side to Bethsaida, while He Himself was sending the crowd away. After bidding them farewell, He left for the mountain to pray. (6:45–46)

Hopeful jubilation had swept over the crowd after Jesus miraculously created the meal (cf. Mark 6:33–44). Knowing that even the Twelve were susceptible to the politically charged fervor of the people, **immediately Jesus made His disciples get into the boat. Made** is from the Greek *anagkazō*, meaning "to force" or "to insist." Undoubtedly, they would have wished to stay and bask in the popularity of the moment, but the Lord gave them no choice. He commanded them to depart by boat **and go ahead of Him to the other side to Bethsaida.**

Some scholars have wondered what Mark meant, since John 6:17 explains that their intended destination was Capernaum. Two proposed and reasonable solutions merit consideration. First, some have suggested that there were two different villages named **Bethsaida.** Because the name means "house of fish," it is possible that more than one fishing village near the lake claimed that title. Those who hold this view differentiate between "Bethsaida Julius," located on the northeastern side of the Sea of Galilee, and "Bethsaida of Galilee," which they assert was located on the western side of the lake near Capernaum (cf. John 12:21). According to this view, the meal for the crowd took place near Bethsaida Julius. Upon leaving that area, the disciples sailed toward Bethsaida of Galilee and neighboring Capernaum. A second, perhaps less convincing, solution asserts that there was only one village named Bethsaida (i.e., Bethsaida Julius), based mainly on a lack of archaeological evidence for a second village by that same name. According to this view, the feeding of the five thousand took place in a remote location southeast of Bethsaida (cf. Mark 6:35). When Jesus commanded the disciples to **go ahead of Him to the other side to Bethsaida,** He was actually instructing them to cross the lake by traveling "toward Bethsaida," meaning west. (The Greek preposition *pros* [translated as **to**] can mean "to," "toward," or "with regard to.") As they sailed to the western shore of the Sea of Galilee, they would have initially gone toward Bethsaida, eventually passing it on their way. (It may be that Jesus intended them to follow the shoreline as they traversed the lake, thereby sailing near the village. Bethsaida is part of the larger Plain of Bethsaida that stretches for about three miles along the northern edge of the Sea of Galilee.)

After instructing the disciples to depart, Jesus **Himself was sending the crowd away.** Dispersing tens of thousands of people, held captive by the miraculous, would not have been an easy task, humanly speaking. Yet, in the same way He sovereignly ordered them to sit in groups of fifty and one hundred (cf. vv. 39–40), the Lord exercised divine authority over the crowd and the people complied. Though they enthusiastically wanted to make Him king to suit their own ends, He dismissed them without an argument. As for the people, John 6:22–24 implies they did not travel far. Apparently spending the night in the nearby countryside, they awoke the next morning and returned to the place where Jesus had fed them, only to discover He was no longer there.

The crowd may have been clamoring for a public revolution, but Jesus longed for a time of private intercession with His heavenly Father. Thus, **after bidding them farewell, He left for the mountain to pray.** At the beginning of His ministry, Satan had tempted Jesus with the offer of "all the kingdoms of the world, and their glory" (Matt. 4:8–9). Perhaps, in the wake of the crowd's enthusiasm, Jesus again faced the temptation to bypass the cross and claim an earthly throne immediately. But that was not the Father's will—a point Jesus reiterated the next day when He again addressed the crowds in Capernaum: "For I have come down from heaven, not to do My own will, but the will of Him who sent Me" (John 6:38; cf. Mark 14:36; John 4:34; 5:19). With no interest in the superficial, emotional exuberance expressed by the people, the Lord retreated to a place of private prayer, as He often did (cf. Matt. 14:23; Mark 1:35; Luke 6:12; 22:41–44).

Jesus' prayer that evening undoubtedly included a time of petition for His disciples. Knowing what they were about to experience, He entrusted them into the hands of His Father. Surely, as He did on other occasions (cf. Luke 22:32; John 17:6–26), Jesus asked the Father to grant them true, enduring faith. The Father answered that prayer in a mighty way, granting them faith in response to an unparalleled wonder.

POWERFUL INTERVENTION FOR THE TWELVE

When it was evening, the boat was in the middle of the sea, and He was alone on the land. Seeing them straining at the oars, for

the wind was against them, at about the fourth watch of the night He came to them, walking on the sea; and He intended to pass by them. But when they saw Him walking on the sea, they supposed that it was a ghost, and cried out; for they all saw Him and were terrified. But immediately He spoke with them and said to them, "Take courage; it is I, do not be afraid." Then He got into the boat with them, and the wind stopped; and they were utterly astonished, for they had not gained any insight from the incident of the loaves, but their heart was hardened. (6:47–52)

The phrase **when it was evening** refers to the second evening of the day, between six and nine o'clock at night. Jesus had fed the multitudes earlier, during the first evening (cf. Matt. 14:15), which lasted from three to six. By now, the sun was down and dusk had turned to darkness. With each passing hour, the distance between the disciples and Jesus widened. They were in **the boat,** which **was in the middle of the sea, and He was alone on the land.** Due to the sudden eruption of a terrifying storm, what normally would have been a routine lake crossing had become a treacherous journey. Violent winds (John 6:18) propelled crushing waves that battered the boat (Matt. 14:24). (For more on the fierce storms that sometimes arose on the Sea of Galilee, see chapter 16 in this volume.) Earlier, the disciples had experienced a similar tempest, but Jesus had been with them on that occasion (cf. Mark 4:37–41). This time they were by themselves.

As noted above, Jesus had remained behind to pray, retreating to a nearby mountain to find solitude in order to commune with His Father. Though His disciples were alone by themselves and miles away, they were never outside the reach of His divine protection. In a clear demonstration of divine omniscience, Jesus saw **them straining at the oars, for the wind was against them.** The Lord, aware of their predicament even before it happened, remained in control of the situation at every moment. Both the tempest and the Twelve were in His hands. Though He was too far away to physically see the boat through the stormy darkness, Jesus always knew their precise location. The omniscience of God is unlimited in its scope and universal in its sight. As Proverbs 15:3 declares, "The eyes of the Lord are in every place, watching the evil and the good."

Job reiterated that truth when he asked, "Does He [the Lord] not see my ways and number all my steps?" (Job 31:4; cf. Jer. 16:17). Second Chronicles 16:9 states that "the eyes of the Lord move to and fro throughout the earth" (cf. Zech. 4:10). And the author of Hebrews echoes that reality in these words: "There is no creature hidden from His sight, but all things are open and laid bare to the eyes of Him with whom we have to do" (Heb. 4:13). Even a stormy sea cannot obscure the clarity of God's omniscient gaze. As David famously asked the Lord, "Where can I go from Your Spirit? Or where can I flee from Your presence? If I dwell in the remotest part of the sea, even there Your hand will lead me, and Your right hand will lay hold of me" (Ps. 139:7, 9–10). The omniscient Son of God had not abandoned His disciples to the storm. He knew exactly where they were and how He would deliver them.

That the disciples were **straining at the oars** indicates they were working feverishly to survive. At least four of the disciples (and perhaps as many as seven) were experienced fishermen on that lake, and only an extreme storm would have given them such difficulty. Due to the conditions, a trip that normally would have lasted only an hour or two had become an all-night struggle to keep themselves from drowning. Mark indicates that it was **about the fourth watch of the night** when Jesus finally came to help them (cf. Matt. 14:25). The Romans divided the night into four watches. The first was from six to nine; the second, from nine to midnight; the third, from midnight to three in the morning; and the fourth, from three to six. The disciples, who had left before nine o'clock the previous evening, were still on the lake in the hours just before dawn. In all of that time, probably about nine hours, they had been able to row only a few miles as they were thwarted by the strong squall (cf. John 6:19).

The situation seemed desperate, even hopeless, when Jesus sovereignly intervened. **He came to them, walking on the sea; and He intended to pass by them.** Out of the darkness, in the midst of the howling winds and splashing waves, Jesus moved to the disciples **walking on the sea.** The Creator of the waters and the wind set foot upon the choppy surface as if it were hard as stone and smooth as glass, making His way to them in their hour of despair. The phrase **He intended to pass by them** can be easily misunderstood and would be better translated as "He desired to come alongside them." The Lord knew exactly where they were and He walked on the lake until He arrived alongside their boat.

Understandably, the disciples were shocked when **they saw Him walking on the sea.** No doubt the night of utter exhaustion and constant struggle added to their confusion, and since they could not believe their eyes nor recognize who it was, **they** panicked and **supposed that it was a ghost.** The word **ghost** (in Greek *phantasma*), from which the English words "phantom" and "phantasm" are derived, refers to an apparition or imaginary specter. Popular first-century superstition purported that spirits of the night brought disaster, and the disciples assumed the worst. After hours of yelling at each other in the midst of the storm, they were so startled that in spite of their tired voices, they shrieked in horror. As Mark explains, they **cried out; for they all saw Him and were terrified.** The word **terrified** (a form of the Greek verb *tarassō*) means "to throw into a panic" or "to strike with dread." They had already been afraid of the storm; seeing a figure walk toward them on the water propelled their fear to even higher levels of intensity.

In an attempt to dismiss this miracle, some unbelieving critics have alleged that Jesus was merely walking along the shore, and not on the surface of the lake. That interpretation of the text is untenable for several reasons. First, the boat was miles from the shore, making it impossible for the disciples to have seen Jesus through the stormy darkness. Matthew 14:24 literally says that they were "many stadia" from land; a stadion measured approximately an eighth of a mile. Second, the disciples would not have been gripped with fear if they had merely seen someone walking along the shoreline. No experienced fisherman would be fooled into thinking a bystander on land was actually walking on water. Third, if Jesus were standing on the shore, Peter would not have started sinking when he got out of the boat (cf. Matt. 14:30). After all, Peter stepped out in the same place that Jesus was walking (v. 31), and the water there was deep enough for a grown man to drown. As with all of His miracles, Jesus' walking on the water demonstrated His deity. Because He is the Creator of the universe (cf. John 1:3; Col. 1:16; Heb. 1:2), He not only controls the wind and the waves (cf. Mark 4:41), He walks upon them.

Graciously, the Lord did not allow the disciples' terror to last.

Immediately He spoke with them and said to them, "Take courage; it is I, do not be afraid." The command **take courage** (from the Greek verb *tharseō*) means "to be brave" or "to be of good cheer." It is used by Jesus to call His people to depend on Him as the source of their confidence, even in the midst of impossible circumstances (cf. Matt. 9:2, 22; 14:27; Mark 10:49; John 16:33; Acts 23:11). In the midst of the chaos and confusion, they recognized the voice of the Lord Jesus calling to them.

The phrase **it is I** could literally be translated, "I AM." Not only did that statement identify the speaker as Jesus, it also reflected the self-revelation of God found in the Old Testament (cf. Ex. 3:14). Jesus not only demonstrated His deity through His supernatural power, He also claimed to be God with the words that He spoke (cf. John 5:18; 8:58; 10:30, 33). Realizing it was Jesus, the disciples' fear turned to relief. Matthew records that Peter, in a moment of exuberance, spoke up and said to Jesus:

> "Lord, if it is You, command me to come to You on the water." And He said, "Come!" And Peter got out of the boat, and walked on the water and came toward Jesus. But seeing the wind, he became frightened, and beginning to sink, he cried out, "Lord, save me!" Immediately Jesus stretched out His hand and took hold of him, and said to him, "You of little faith, why did you doubt?" (Matt. 14:28–31)

Peter's faltering faith was representative of all the disciples and exemplified the reason this miracle was necessary, to strengthen their faith. Though Jesus' rebuke was singularly directed at Peter, it fittingly applied to the entire group. That the Lord graciously reached out His hand and rescued Peter, in spite of Peter's doubts, is a wonderful picture of the way in which He graciously helps His own in their hour of need in spite of their weaknesses (cf. Heb. 13:6). (Scholars sometimes wonder why Mark did not include the episode about Peter in his account. It may be that, because Mark wrote his gospel under Peter's influence, and because Peter was a humble man who wanted the focus to be on Christ and not him, Mark intentionally omitted those details. Whatever the explanation, the ultimate answer is that the Holy Spirit only inspired Matthew to include that feature.)

After rescuing Peter, the Lord **got into the boat with them, and the wind stopped; and they were utterly astonished.** The disciples had seen Jesus walking on water and instantaneously calming a fierce storm. They had even watched Peter stand on the surface of the lake. After all that, at the moment Jesus entered the boat, the fierce winds instantly vanished and the storm was gone. Having served its divinely appointed purpose, the tempest disappeared. In that same instant, Jesus miraculously propelled the boat to its destination on the western shore. As John 6:21 reports, "Immediately the boat was at the land to which they were going." One moment, they were battling a raging storm in the middle of the lake; the next, the wind and waves were calm and the boat had arrived at the shore. Understandably, the disciples responded with shock. The word **astonished** comes from the Greek word *existēmi*, meaning "to be beside oneself." The miracle they had just experienced blew their minds.

According to Matthew 14:33, the response of the disciples turned to worship: "Those who were in the boat worshiped Him, saying, 'You are certainly God's Son!'" They recognized that they were in the presence of the Creator (cf. Job 26:14), the One who controls the winds and the waves (cf. Mark 4:41). Perhaps their minds were flooded with Old Testament passages like Psalm 77:19 (NKJV), "Your way is in the sea. Your path is in the great waters and Your footsteps were not known." They may have remembered the words of Habakkuk 3:15, "You walked through the sea with your horses, through the great heap of waters." Or maybe they thought about Job 9:8 (NKJV), "He treads on the waves of the sea."

In their worship, the disciples' astonishment transcended the mere fascination of the crowds. Many people were amazed by Jesus (Matt. 7:28; 12:23; 22:33; Mark 1:22; 9:15; Luke 2:47; 4:32; 11:14; John 7:46), but few truly worshiped Him. The disciples had begun to understand the truth His miracles had pointed to all along: that He was the Messiah, the Son of God (cf. Mark 1:1). That recognition drove them to their knees as they willingly confessed the theological reality expressed throughout the New Testament, namely, "that Jesus Christ is Lord, to the glory of God the Father" (Phil. 2:11).

Worship should have been the disciples' response earlier, when Jesus miraculously fed the crowd of tens of thousands of people. But, instead of falling down in reverence, they apparently allowed themselves to get caught up in the enthusiasm of the crowd. This appearance of Jesus on the water was therefore necessary in order to strengthen their faith, because **they had not gained any insight from the incident of the loaves, but their heart was hardened.** Due to their own spiritual dullness, the disciples had missed the true significance of that earlier display of divine creative power. Safe on the shore in the presence of their almighty Savior, they were convinced of His deity and fell on their knees in adoration and praise.

Personal Interaction with the Crowds

When they had crossed over they came to land at Gennesaret, and moored to the shore. When they got out of the boat, immediately the people recognized Him, and ran about that whole country and began to carry here and there on their pallets those who were sick, to the place they heard He was. Wherever He entered villages, or cities, or countryside, they were laying the sick in the market places, and imploring Him that they might just touch the fringe of His cloak; and as many as touched it were being cured. (6:53–56)

The account of Jesus' walking on the water contains far more than a single miracle. First, it was preceded by the supernatural feeding of the thousands (vv. 33–44). Second, Jesus omnisciently saw the disciples in the midst of the storm (v. 48). Third, He suspended gravity by walking on the surface of the tempestuous lake (v. 48). Fourth, He enabled Peter to walk on water (cf. Matt. 14:29). Fifth, as soon as He entered the boat, the wind stopped and the storm evaporated (Mark 6:51). Sixth, the boat was immediately transported to the shore (John 6:21). And finally, after reaching land, Jesus began to heal the sick who were brought to Him (Mark 6:53–55). Overwhelmed by the wonder of it all, the disciples responded in the worshipful recognition that their Master was the Son of God.

Mark continues his account by noting that **when they had crossed over they came to land at Gennesaret, and moored to the shore.** The plain of Gennesaret lay to the southwest of Capernaum. As noted earlier, John 6:17 indicates that the disciples were crossing the lake toward Capernaum; yet, they landed at Gennesaret. Critics sometimes claim that this represents a discrepancy in the gospel accounts. In reality, it does not. Though the disciples may have originally intended to go directly to Capernaum, the Lord supernaturally and instantaneously placed their boat at Gennesaret. They had undoubtedly drifted off course due to the strong winds, which explains why their boat was no longer headed toward their original destination. Storm or no storm, they landed exactly where Jesus wanted them to be. The close proximity of Capernaum and Gennesaret meant that Jesus and the disciples easily walked to Capernaum after **they got out of the boat.** Capernaum was their ultimate destination, and it was there, in the synagogue, that Jesus preached His sermon on the bread of life (cf. John 6:24, 59).

Once onshore, **immediately the people recognized Him, and ran about that whole country and began to carry here and there on their pallets those who were sick, to the place they heard He was.** As Jesus and the disciples walked from Gennesaret to Capernaum, the Lord continued to show compassion to needy people, both along the way and once He finally arrived in Capernaum. The gospel of John picks up the story at that point, filling in the details of what Jesus preached in Capernaum that day (cf. John 6:26–58). Mark's account, however, zooms out and provides a final summary of Jesus' ministry in Galilee. **Wherever He entered villages, or cities, or countryside, they were laying the sick in the market places, and imploring Him that they might just touch the fringe of His cloak; and as many as touched it were being cured.** Everywhere He went, Jesus mercifully healed all the sick who were brought to Him. His healing power had no limits and His loving-kindness no boundaries. He personally and graciously cared for all who sought Him. Like the woman in Mark 5:28–29, desperate people suffering from all sorts of incurable diseases and disabilities were healed simply by touching the fringe of His cloak. The display, scope, and intent of His matchless power, from the creation of a massive meal to the calming of a violent storm to the healing of countless infirmities, was accompanied by the demonstration of His expansive divine compassion.

Though many who experienced His miracles would never come to embrace Him in genuine saving faith, true believers, like the disciples in the boat, move beyond mere amazement to the place of sincere worship. As did the apostle John on the isle of Patmos, they fall on their faces before the Son of God, paying homage to

> Jesus Christ, the faithful witness, the firstborn of the dead, and the ruler of the kings of the earth. To Him who loves us and released us from our sins by His blood— and He has made us to be a kingdom, priests to His God and Father—to Him be the glory and the dominion forever and ever. Amen. (Rev. 1:5–6; cf. v. 17)

Scripture-Twisting Tradition (Mark 7:1–13)

24

The Pharisees and some of the scribes gathered around Him when they had come from Jerusalem, and had seen that some of His disciples were eating their bread with impure hands, that is, unwashed. (For the Pharisees and all the Jews do not eat unless they carefully wash their hands, thus observing the traditions of the elders; and when they come from the market place, they do not eat unless they cleanse themselves; and there are many other things which they have received in order to observe, such as the washing of cups and pitchers and copper pots.) The Pharisees and the scribes asked Him, "Why do Your disciples not walk according to the tradition of the elders, but eat their bread with impure hands?" And He said to them, "Rightly did Isaiah prophesy of you hypocrites, as it is written: 'This people honors Me with their lips, but their heart is far away from Me. But in vain do they worship Me, teaching as doctrines the precepts of men.' Neglecting the commandment of God, you hold to the tradition of men." He was also saying to them, "You are experts at setting aside the commandment of God in order to

keep your tradition. For Moses said, 'Honor your father and your mother'; and, 'He who speaks evil of father or mother, is to be put to death'; but you say, 'If a man says to his father or his mother, whatever I have that would help you is Corban (that is to say, given to God),' you no longer permit him to do anything for his father or his mother; thus invalidating the word of God by your tradition which you have handed down; and you do many things such as that." (7:1–13)

As the Old Testament repeatedly declares, the only worship that pleases God is that which flows from a heart that sincerely loves Him and seeks to obey His Word (cf. Deut. 10:12; 11:13; 13:13; 26:16; 30:2, 6, 10; Josh. 22:5; 1 Sam. 7:3; 12:20; 12:24). Moses famously articulated that principle to the Israelites as they stood ready to enter the Promised Land: "Hear, O Israel! The Lord is our God, the Lord is one! You shall love the Lord your God with all your heart and with all your soul and with all your might" (Deut. 6:4–5). True worship involves the whole person: heart, soul, and strength. Mere externalism is never acceptable to God (cf. 1 Sam. 15:22). As the Lord told the prophet Samuel regarding David, "God sees not as man sees, for man looks at the outward appearance, but the Lord looks at the heart" (1 Sam. 16:7; cf. 13:14; 1 Kings 8:39). When David passed the kingdom on to Solomon, he gave his son similar instruction, "As for you, my son Solomon, know the God of your father, and serve Him with a whole heart and a willing mind; for the Lord searches all hearts, and understands every intent of the thoughts" (1 Chron. 28:9). At the dedication of the temple, Solomon reiterated those words to the entire nation: "Let your heart therefore be wholly devoted to the Lord our God, to walk in His statutes and to keep His commandments, as at this day" (1 Kings 8:61; cf. 2 Kings 20:3).

In spite of such clear instruction, the nation repeatedly slipped into externalism, hypocrisy, and apostasy. Even Solomon, endowed with supernatural wisdom (1 Kings 3:12), was not immune to allowing his heart to be led astray (cf. 11:4). In response to Israel's calloused unbelief, God raised up prophets who called the people back to wholehearted worship and obedience. As the Lord declared through the prophet Jeremiah (29:13), "You will seek Me and find Me when you search for Me *with all your heart"* (emphasis added). The prophet Joel similarly proclaimed,

> "Yet even now," declares the Lord, "return to Me with all your heart, and with fasting, weeping and mourning; and rend your heart and not your garments." Now return to the Lord your God, for He is gracious and compassionate, slow to anger, abounding in lovingkindness, and relenting of evil. (Joel 2:12–13; cf. Amos 5:21–24)

The Lord was not interested in external symbols of sorrow, like the tearing of clothes, unless they truly represented genuine repentance and heartfelt remorse. The prophet Isaiah similarly rebuked the people of his day for their cold, heartless religion. Although the people offered the correct sacrifices (Isa. 1:11), observed religious festivals (vv. 13–14), and lifted up continual prayers (v. 15), they did so from hearts that were rebellious and unrepentant (vv. 16–17). They were good at observing tradition, yet their hearts were far from God (cf. 29:13). If they refused to repent, they would face divine judgment at the hand of the Babylonians.

Seven centuries later, the Judaism of Jesus' day was characterized by a similar form of empty, lifeless, hypocritical worship. Over the centuries, Jewish tradition had created a legalistic religion of self-righteous externalism, primarily propagated by the Pharisees and scribes. Though their religion was directed at the true God, it was practiced in the wrong way (cf. Rom. 10:2) and was therefore unacceptable to Him.

Jesus confronted the hypocritical worship of His day in the same way the prophets before Him had denounced it in theirs. He came to bring the true religion of the heart (Matt. 5:8, 21–48; 6:19–21). Consequently, He clashed fiercely with the religious leaders of first-century Israel. He called them vipers (Matt. 12:34), condemned them as false shepherds (John 10:8; cf. Ezek. 34:1–10), and cursed them as hypocrites (cf. Matt. 23:13, 15, 23, 25, 27, 29). Though Jesus exhibited meekness, gentleness, and compassion toward the crowds (cf. Mark 6:34), He never hesitated to openly rebuke the purveyors of false religion.

The events described in Mark 6, from the commissioning of the Twelve (vv. 7–13, 30–32) to the feeding of the thousands (vv. 33–44) to Jesus walking on the water (vv. 45–52), represent both the peak of Jesus' popularity and the climax of His Galilean ministry. The people He miraculously fed were so amazed they wanted "to come and take Him by force to make Him king" (John 6:15). But their motivation was merely national and materialistic. The following day, when Jesus articulated spiritual realities regarding the kingdom, the crowd quickly became disenchanted. Many of His followers left Him (cf. v. 66), and His popularity began to decline. From that point forward, Jesus focused more and more of His attention on training the Twelve, preparing them for their ministry to begin after His crucifixion and resurrection.

Contributing to that decline in popularity was the propaganda spread by the Pharisees and scribes, who sought to discredit Jesus by ascribing His power to Satan (cf. Mark 3:22). As noted above, the Lord frequently clashed with the Jewish religious leaders. This section describes one of those episodes, in which the messianic Judge condemned the blatant hypocrisy of apostate Judaism. The passage can be divided into three segments: the interrogation, the indictment, and the illustration.

THE INTERROGATION

The Pharisees and some of the scribes gathered around Him when they had come from Jerusalem, and had seen that some of His disciples were eating their bread with impure hands, that is, unwashed. (For the Pharisees and all the Jews do not eat unless they carefully wash their hands, thus observing the traditions of the elders; and when they come from the market place, they do not eat unless they cleanse themselves; and there are many other things which they have received in order to observe, such as the washing of cups and pitchers and copper pots.) The Pharisees and the scribes asked Him, "Why do Your disciples not walk according to the tradition of the elders, but eat their bread with impure hands?" (7:1–5)

According to John 6:4, the feeding of the thousands took place near the time of the Jewish Passover, one year before Jesus died on the cross. The episode described in this section (Mark 7:1–13), which occurred in Galilee shortly after the miraculous feeding, took place around that same time. (For a harmony of the Gospels, see John MacArthur, *One Perfect*

Life [Nashville: Thomas Nelson, 2012].) A delegation of **Pharisees and some of the scribes gathered around** Jesus. Like an earlier group (cf. Mark 3:22), this commission of clerics **had come** to Galilee **from Jerusalem.** (For more on the Pharisees and scribes, see chapter 7 in the current volume.) Most likely, they came at the request of Galilean members of their sect to help confront Jesus in light of His widespread and threatening popularity. Since Jerusalem was the seat of Jewish religion, the location of both the temple and the Sanhedrin, this delegation represented significant ecclesiastical authority. As the recognized experts in both Old Testament law and rabbinic tradition, the Pharisees were champions of the popular form of legalistic Judaism that dominated first-century Israel. From the outset of Jesus' ministry, the Pharisees and scribes knew His message was a direct assault on their system of self-righteousness. Consequently, they were always seeking ways to discredit His ministry in the eyes of the people, with the ultimate goal of ending His life (cf. Mark 3:6).

A potential opportunity arose for Jesus' enemies when they saw **that some of His disciples were eating their bread with impure hands, that is, unwashed.** Though the Mosaic law prescribed ceremonial washings for priests (Lev. 22:6–7), it did not require others to wash their hands in any particular way before eating. The Pharisees insisted that the Jewish people perform specific ceremonial washings, not because they were biblically commanded but because they were part of rabbinic teaching. They were hardly concerned about sanitation but obsessed with ritual tradition. As Mark explains in his parenthetical note, **the Pharisees and all the Jews do not eat unless they carefully wash their hands, thus observing the traditions of the elders.** The ceremonial washing prescribed by rabbinic praxis involved several steps. First, water was poured from a jar onto both hands with the fingers pointing up, so that the water would run off at the wrists. Then, water was again poured over the hands with the fingers pointing down. Finally, each hand was rubbed with the fist of the other hand. Strict Jews would follow these regulations before every meal and between each course in the meal. (For a fuller discussion of these ceremonial washings, see Alfred Edersheim's *The Life and Times of Jesus the Messiah* [Grand Rapids: Eerdmans, 1972], 2:10–13.)

The washings became more elaborate when people returned home after going out, because they might have been defiled through contact with a Samaritan, a Gentile, or even a fellow Jew who was ceremonially unclean. Thus, as Mark observes, **when they come from the market place, they do not eat unless they cleanse themselves.** Added to this traditional hand-washing was the careful cleansing of cooking instruments and dining utensils. In fact, **there are many other things which they have received in order to observe, such as the washing of cups and pitchers and copper pots.** Together, these ritualistic washings made each mealtime an elaborate and meticulous affair.

The **traditions of the elders** consisted of extrabiblical regulations that had been passed down from the time of the Babylonian captivity (605–535 B.C.). These oral traditions, which pervaded the Judaism of Jesus' day, were eventually written down in the Mishnah around the end of the second century A.D. The Mishnah, along with additional rabbinic commentary called the Gemara, makes up the Talmud (the collection of Jewish tradition that in printed form encompasses thousands of pages of extrabiblical material). According to the Talmud, God gave Moses the oral law, which he passed on to other great men in Israel. These men were charged with personally appropriating the law in their own lives, training others who would teach the law to subsequent generations, and building a wall of protection around the law in order to preserve it. That wall of protection consisted of extrabiblical regulations intended to ensure that the people never came close to breaking the law. In reality, however, those rabbinic rules actually undermined and obscured the law they were intended to protect. Over time, the Jewish people began to measure their spiritual condition in terms of external conformity to traditional requirements and ceremonial rituals, rather than in terms of sincere love for God and humble obedience to His Word (cf. Isa. 66:2).

When the Jewish people returned to their homeland after the Babylonian captivity, scribes (the first of whom was Ezra) began to copy and teach the Scriptures in order to instruct the people in the Word of God (cf. Neh. 8:8). As they explained the Scriptures, they made comments on the text, eventually accumulating a massive body of interpretive material. As the centuries passed, the distinction between Scripture and rabbinic traditions that were based on scribal interpretations of Scripture became blurred. By Jesus' day, **the traditions of the elders** had over-shadowed and supplanted God's Word. Divine truth had been lost, buried under mountains of tradition. Consequently, the rituals of Judaism could be practiced outwardly without regard to the condition of one's heart before God.

The Pharisees and scribes took their traditions very seriously, including hand-washing. Some rabbis suggested that a demon named Shibtah sat on people's hands while they were sleeping. If the demon were not removed by ceremonial washing before eating, he would be transferred to the mouth and could enter the body. Other rabbis turned hand-washing into a salvation issue. As the Jerusalem Talmud asserts, "Whoever is firmly implanted in the land of Israel, who speaks the holy language, *who eats his food in purity* [as required by hand-washing rituals], and recites the *Shema* morning and evening, is assured of life in the world to come" (*Shabbat* 1:3, emphasis added). It is no wonder, then, that the religious leaders accused Jesus' disciples of committing a serious offense. Phrasing their accusation in the form of a question, they incredulously **asked** Jesus, **"Why do Your disciples not walk according to the tradition of the elders, but eat their bread with impure hands?"** Their inquiry was not motivated by curiosity but by outrage. They were incensed that Jesus would allow His disciples to openly disregard a ritual they considered so binding.

THE INDICTMENT

And He said to them, "Rightly did Isaiah prophesy of you hypocrites, as it is written: 'This people honors Me with their lips, but their heart is far away from Me. But in vain do they worship Me, teaching as doctrines the precepts of men.' Neglecting the commandment of God, you hold to the tradition of men." He was also saying to them, "You are experts at setting aside the commandment of God in order to keep your tradition." (7:6–9)

Jesus responded, not by answering the Pharisees' question but by indicting them for their hypocrisy. He would later give an answer to His disciples (vv. 17–23), but to the apostate religious leaders He offered no explanation or excuse. Instead, He confronted the calloused unbelief that characterized the false system that they embraced.

Taking them straight to the Scriptures, Jesus began by pointing to the prophet Isaiah. **He said to them, "Rightly did Isaiah prophesy of you hypocrites."** The Pharisees were **hypocrites** because, although they looked holy on the outside, their hearts were unrepentant and corrupt. As Jesus told them on a later occasion, "Woe to you, scribes and Pharisees, hypocrites! For you are like whitewashed tombs which on the outside appear beautiful, but inside they are full of dead men's bones and all uncleanness. So you, too, outwardly appear righteous to men, but inwardly you are full of hypocrisy and lawlessness" (Matt. 23:27–28). Like the Israelites of Isaiah's day, the Pharisees and scribes emphasized external rituals and extrabiblical regulations while completely neglecting a genuine love for God. Quoting from Isaiah 29:13, Jesus said, **"As it is written, 'This people honors Me with their lips, but their heart is far away from Me. But in vain do they worship Me, teaching as doctrines the precepts of men.'"** Isaiah's words struck at the heart of the Pharisaic system, which pretended to love God, yet worshiped Him in a way that was superficial, contrived, unbiblical, and unacceptable. In case they missed the point, Jesus added, **"Neglecting the commandment of God, you hold to the tradition of men."** The Pharisees and scribes were far more concerned with upholding rabbinic customs than obeying God's law.

First-century Judaism, like all forms of apostate religion, elevated man-made traditions above the teachings of Scripture. The Pharisees prized their rites, rituals, and regulations, allowing that which was merely external to take the place of true worship and heartfelt obedience. Outwardly, they paid homage to God **with their lips,** but inwardly **their** calloused hearts were **far away from** Him. Because they had never been transformed on the inside, their attempts to worship God were inevitably hypocritical. True worship, by contrast, flows from the soul that has been regenerated and eagerly seeks to honor and submit to the will of the Lord. As Jesus explained in John 4:24, the only worship God accepts is that which is "in spirit" (from the heart) and in "truth" (according to sound doctrine). As self-righteous hypocrites who rejected the Messiah, the Pharisees failed on both counts.

These archetypal fakes were outraged that Jesus disregarded their traditions. But the Lord knew that neither He nor His disciples were bound to follow rabbinic customs. Only that which came from Scripture was authoritative; where tradition conflicted with the Word of God, tradition needed to be overturned and its purveyors openly exposed. Consequently, Jesus **was also saying to them, "You are experts at setting aside the commandment of God in order to keep your tradition."** The Pharisees and scribes accused Jesus' disciples of committing a serious offense. In reality, it was they who were guilty of the real crimes against God. They neglected the **commandment of God** and influenced many others to do the same. Their hands may have been washed and cleansed, but their hearts were not. Consequently, they and their followers were headed for eternal judgment (cf. Matt. 23:15).

THE ILLUSTRATION

"For Moses said, 'Honor your father and your mother'; and, 'He who speaks evil of father or mother, is to be put to death'; but you say, 'If a man says to his father or his mother, whatever I have that would help you is Corban (that is to say, given to God),' you no longer permit him to do anything for his father or his mother; thus invalidating the word of God by your tradition which you have handed down; and you do many things such as that." (7:10–13)

After exposing their duplicity from the text of Isaiah 29, Jesus gave the hypocrites an illustration to prove His point. Taking them back to Exodus 20:12 and 21:17, He reminded them that **Moses said, 'Honor your father and your mother'; and, 'He who speaks evil of father or mother, is to be put to death.'** God Himself had instructed His people to honor, respect, and treat their parents with care. Not to do so was both a violation of the fifth commandment and a crime worthy of death.

Inherent in honoring one's father and mother is the responsibility to love and respect them throughout the entirety of their lives, including helping to meet their needs if they become unable to provide for themselves. But rabbinic tradition had grown to undermine that biblical mandate. It brashly suggested that a child could avoid assisting his parents simply by telling them, "Whatever I have that would help you has been given to God" (Matt. 15:5). Though the religious experts knew what God commanded, having committed large portions of the Mosaic law to memory, they used tradition to circumvent it. As Jesus explained, **"But you say, 'If a man says to his father or his mother, whatever I have that would help you is Corban (that is to say, given to God),' you no longer permit him to do anything for his father or his mother."**

The word **Corban** is a Hebrew term that means "devoted to God" and referred to offerings of money or material goods that had been pledged to God. At some point in Israel's history, a tradition arose allowing people to declare their possessions "Corban," thereby promising that they would eventually use their resources for sacred purposes. Even if a man's parents asked him for financial support, he was forbidden from using anything he had declared to be "devoted to God" in order to help them. The rabbinic system thus provided adult children with a loophole by which they did not have to assist their aged or needy parents, and yet could still appear to be loyal worshipers who gave generously to God. Though a person could declare all of his possessions "Corban," he was not required to donate them immediately to the temple or synagogue. For the most part, the pledged possessions remained under his control. In fact, whenever he wanted to use them for his own purposes, he could reverse the vow merely by saying "Corban" over them again. The hypocritical system, promoted by the Pharisees and scribes, allowed people to maintain an external veneer of dedication to God while simultaneously turning their backs on their parents.

Jesus ended His confrontation with the Pharisees and scribes by issuing a blanket, devastating condemnation: "[You are] **thus invalidating the word of God by your tradition which you have handed down; and you do many things such as that."** The Judaism of the Pharisees and scribes was an unbiblical religion that invalidated God's Word. The true faith of the Old Testament had been lost, obscured by layers of rabbinic rules and regulations that the Jewish religious leaders had **handed down**. That they did **many things such as that** indicates that the illustration Jesus used regarding "Corban" was just one of many similar examples of corruption and hypocrisy within the Pharisaical system.

The evil-hearted Pharisees and scribes managed to pervert even the most basic disciplines, from moral behavior to prayer and fasting to giving to the poor (cf. Matt. 5:20; 6:1–6; 23:1–36). In response, the Messiah repudiated their false form of Judaism, teaching that such traditions are meaningless and that what God requires is a heart that loves Him and seeks His glory (cf. Mark 12:29–30).

Though Jesus detested the traditions of the apostate Judaism, it should be noted that tradition itself is not inherently evil. There are many wonderful traditions that believers have celebrated throughout the centuries. Devastating problems arise when those traditions are given an authority equal to or greater than Scripture. Whenever **the word of God** is invalidated by **tradition,** as in the case of the Pharisees and scribes, it is an abomination and an offense. Those who truly love God cherish His Word and eagerly desire to submit to its commands (cf. John 14:15), even if doing so requires breaking with tradition. They look to no higher authority than God's Word.

According to one rabbi who honestly evaluated the Judaism of his day, "There are ten parts of hypocrisy in the world, nine at Jerusalem and one in the whole world" (cited from John A. Broadus, *Commentary on the Gospel of Matthew* [Philadelphia: American Baptist Publication Society, 1886], 335.) Hypocrisy is not limited to ancient Judaism. It is still pervasive in various forms of Christendom today, where it thrives in empty ceremonies, superficial worship, errant doctrines, indifferent prayers, legalistic moralism, and the like. By its very definition, hypocrisy looks good on the outside, but it is corrupt on the inside.

The solution for hypocrisy is the same as for any other sin: repentance. Perhaps no New Testament example better illustrates that truth than the apostle Paul. As a Pharisee, Paul measured his spiritual condition in terms of self-righteous externals and religious accolades. When he became a Christian, he realized those things were worthless. As he explained to the Philippians:

> If anyone else has a mind to put confidence in the flesh, I far more: circumcised the eighth day, of the nation of Israel, of the tribe of Benjamin, a Hebrew of Hebrews; as to the Law, a Pharisee; as to zeal, a persecutor of the church; as to the righteousness which is in the Law, found blameless. But whatever things were gain to me, those things I

have counted as loss for the sake of Christ. More than that, I count all things to be loss in view of the surpassing value of knowing Christ Jesus my Lord, for whom I have suffered the loss of all things, and count them but rubbish so that I may gain Christ, and may be found in Him, not having a righteousness of my own derived from the Law, but that which is through faith in Christ, the righteousness which comes from God on the basis of faith, that I may know Him and the power of His resurrection and the fellowship of His sufferings, being conformed to His death; in order that I may attain to the resurrection from the dead. (Phil. 3:4–11)

By the grace of God, Paul came to understand what every religious hypocrite must recognize, that self-righteous works are like filthy rags before a holy God (Isa. 64:6). But true righteousness is available through Jesus Christ (Rom. 5:19; 2 Cor. 5:21). Those who embrace Him in saving faith will be forgiven and transformed from the inside (cf. Isa. 1:18). They will be made into true worshipers (cf. Phil. 3:3). As Paul declared elsewhere: "Therefore if anyone is in Christ, he is a new creature; the old things passed away; behold, new things have come" (2 Cor. 5:17).

The Inside Story on Defilement
(Mark 7:14–23)

25

After He called the crowd to Him again, He began saying to them, "Listen to Me, all of you, and understand: there is nothing outside the man which can defile him if it goes into him; but the things which proceed out of the man are what defile the man. [If anyone has ears to hear, let him hear.]" When He had left the crowd and entered the house, His disciples questioned Him about the parable. And He said to them, "Are you so lacking in understanding also? Do you not understand that whatever goes into the man from outside cannot defile him, because it does not go into his heart, but into his stomach, and is eliminated?" (Thus He declared all foods clean.) And He was saying, "That which proceeds out of the man, that is what defiles the man. For from within, out of the heart of men, proceed the evil thoughts, fornications, thefts, murders, adulteries, deeds of coveting and wickedness, as well as deceit, sensuality, envy, slander, pride and foolishness. All these evil things proceed from within and defile the man." (7:14–23)

The notion that human beings are basically good persists in the world in spite of constant and ubiquitous evidence to the contrary. Popular psychologists and secular anthropologists insist evil is not inherent in people. Consequently, the blame for destructive behaviors is ultimately placed on external forces and environmental factors. "Other people are bad not me" seems to be the proud excuse easily formed by the deceptive human heart. Unwilling to acknowledge their own guilt, perpetrators often claim to be victims—faulting parents, peers, or circumstances for their criminal behavior.

A biblical understanding of human nature could not be more opposite. Because all people are sinners (cf. Rom. 3:23), they are born with a nature that is already corrupt (cf. Ps. 51:5; Rom. 5:12, 19). The problem is not outside of them but within them. As Jeremiah 17:9 (KJV) explains, "The heart of man is deceitful above all things, and desperately wicked." External factors may provide people with unique opportunities to manifest their sinfulness, but the corruption already exists on the inside. All human beings are sinful, perpetrators of crimes against man and God. They are wicked not because of outside influences but because they are full of pride and lust, and "when lust has conceived, it gives birth to sin" (James 1:15).

The Jewish people of Jesus' day were obviously not affected by the musings of modern psychologists. Yet, they similarly misunderstood the basic truth about where corruption and defilement originates. Thinking that moral contamination came from external sources, they developed an elaborate system of external rituals and ceremonies that they thought would make them pure. They wrongly assumed that if they looked good on the outside by attending the synagogue, honoring the law, and observing the traditions of the elders, God would deem them righteous on the inside (cf. Matt. 23:13–36; Phil. 3:4–6). Consequently, Judaism became a breeding ground for hypocrisy, externalism, and superficial legalism.

In this section (Mark 7:14–23), Jesus confronted that false system by articulating the difference between true and false sources of defilement. Significantly, the word **defile** or **defiles** (from the Greek verb *koinoō*, meaning to pollute or make unclean) appears five times in this passage (vv. 15 [twice], 18, 20, 23). Following His confrontation with the

Pharisees regarding the authority of rabbinic tradition (vv. 1–13), Jesus continued by shattering the notion that moral corruption originates outside a person. In so doing, He also demonstrated that spiritual cleansing cannot be obtained through external rituals and religious ceremonies. The passage can be divided into two parts, each concentrating on the truth about defilement: the truth stated and the truth explained.

THE TRUTH STATED

After He called the crowd to Him again, He began saying to them, "Listen to Me, all of you, and understand: there is nothing outside the man which can defile him if it goes into him; but the things which proceed out of the man are what defile the man. If anyone has ears to hear, let him hear." (7:14–16)

Even as Jesus drew His Galilean ministry to a close, huge crowds of people still accumulated around Him wherever He was (cf. Mark 6:56). His popularity drew the ire of the Jewish religious leaders, whose resentment was so strong that the only thing that would satisfy it was to kill Him (cf. 3:6). At some point shortly after the first miraculous feeding of the thousands (cf. 6:33–44), some Pharisees and scribes traveled from Jerusalem to Galilee to confront Jesus (7:1–13). Their antagonistic interchange with Him undoubtedly attracted a group of curious onlookers, who would have been amazed to hear Jesus openly defy the religious leaders' authority to their faces (cf. 1:22; Luke 11:39–44). **After** the confrontation was over, Jesus **called the crowd to Him again and began saying to them, "Listen to Me, all of you, and understand."** By calling the people to carefully heed His words, Jesus was doing more than just asking for their attention. He was underscoring the eternal significance of what He was about to say.

Speaking of spiritual defilement, Jesus explained that **there is nothing outside the man which can defile him if it goes into him.** The Lord's point was that external things, like meals eaten with ceremonially unwashed hands (cf. 7:2), are not the source of spiritual impurity. Rather, the defilement that offends God is an internal, spiritual reality that has a corresponding internal source. Sinful pollution does not come from outside the sinner but lies within him. In the parallel passage of Matthew 15:11, Jesus explained that it is "what proceeds out of the mouth [that] defiles the man." The Lord's point was that moral contamination is not evidenced by what goes into a person's mouth but what comes out from it (cf. Matt. 12:34; Luke 6:45). The mouth is not the only place where wretchedness manifests itself, but it is the most ready, immediate, and constant exit for the evil inside (cf. James 3:2–12). Proverbs 6:12 characterizes a wicked man as "one who walks with a perverse mouth." Proverbs 15:28 adds: "The mouth of the wicked pours out evil things." When Jesus spoke of the **things which proceed out of the man,** He was referring not only to a person's speech but also the desires, thoughts, and attitudes behind his speech. Because the heart is evil, wicked lusts, words, and actions inevitably gush forth. Those **are what defile the man.**

Jesus' words must have shocked His listeners, all of whom had been raised in a system that prized external morality and ceremonies (cf. Matt. 6:1–6, 16–18). In reality, the Lord was not introducing new ideas but reiterating Old Testament truths that the Jewish people should have known well. They were familiar with passages that taught that "God sees not as man sees, for man looks at the outward appearance, but the Lord looks at the heart" (1 Sam. 16:7; cf. 13:14; 1 Kings 8:39; Prov. 21:2); and that "the Lord searches all hearts, and understands every intent of the thoughts" (1 Chron. 28:9; cf. 1 Kings 8:61; 2 Kings 20:3). Yet, due to their own extrabiblical traditions, they had become preoccupied with a superficial form of purity that was inherently hypocritical because it bypassed the heart.

It is true that some of Israel's rituals and regulations had been prescribed by God in the Mosaic law. Certain foods were forbidden (cf. Lev. 11:1–47), and certain medical issues (such as leprosy [13:11, 44–45], touching a dead body [21:1, 11], and menstruation [15:19]) rendered a person ceremonially unclean. Yet, those things were intended as symbols or illustrations of the true nature of man's sinful heart and his desperate need for divine cleansing. That a person who was ceremonially defiled needed external cleansing to participate in public worship provided a powerful picture of the fact that every sinner requires divine forgiveness and internal cleansing before coming into God's presence.

The fact that Old Testament rituals were only symbols is particularly emphasized throughout the book of Hebrews. Commenting on the Levitical system, the author of Hebrews explained that the priesthood was "a copy and shadow of the heavenly things" (8:5); the sacrifice of bulls and goats foreshadowed the final atoning work of Christ (cf. Heb. 9:13–14); and the Holy Place in the tabernacle was "a symbol for the present time. Accordingly both gifts and sacrifices are offered which cannot make the worshiper perfect in conscience, since they relate only to food and drink and various washings, regulations for the body imposed until ...Christ appeared" (9:9–11). Even the Mosaic law was "only a shadow of the good things to come and not the very form of things," because external conformity to it "can never, by the same sacrifices which they offer continually year by year, make perfect those who draw near" (10:1). Salvation requires internal cleansing, such that God's people can "draw near with a sincere heart in full assurance of faith, having [their] hearts sprinkled clean from an evil conscience and [their] bodies washed with pure water" (10:22).

Like the sacrificial system, circumcision was also a physical act prescribed by God to symbolize a spiritual reality. Even as Israel entered the Promised Land, the Lord reminded the people that His gaze was focused on the circumcision of their hearts:

> "Now, Israel, what does the Lord your God require from you, but to fear the Lord your God, to walk in all His ways and love Him, and to serve the Lord your God with all your heart and with all your soul, and to keep the Lord's commandments and His statutes which I am commanding you today for your good? . . . Circumcise then your heart." (Deut. 10:12–13, 16; cf. Jer. 4:4)

Paul reiterated that truth in Romans 2:28–29,

> For he is not a Jew who is one outwardly, nor is circumcision that which is outward in the flesh. But he is a Jew who is one inwardly; and circumcision is that which is of the heart, by the Spirit, not by the letter; and his praise is not from men, but from God.

After all, Abraham was justified by faith prior to being circumcised (cf. Rom. 4:1–12).

The Old Testament was clear: no attention to commanded ceremony or ritual was pleasing to God unless it came from a heart that sincerely loved Him (cf. (cf. Deut. 10:12; 11:13; 13:13; 26:16; 30:2, 6, 10; Josh. 22:5; 24:23; 1 Sam. 7:3; 12:20, 24; 1 Kings 8:23; 2 Chron. 11:16; Isa. 51:7; 57:15). The notion that external acts—like being circumcised, observing dietary laws, or performing ceremonial cleansing—could provide salvation from sin was utterly alien to God's law. In spite of that fact, the Jewish people, clinging to their sin with corrupt love (cf. John 3:19–20), became preoccupied with external symbols to the exclusion of internal purity. Doing so allowed them to appear religious without being either repentant or righteous (cf. Isa. 1:11–17; 29:13; Amos 5:21–24). By going through the motions while still clinging to their sin, they cultivated a system that thrived on hypocrisy. That is why Jesus said to the Pharisees, "You are like whitewashed tombs which on the outside appear beautiful, but inside they are full of dead men's bones and all uncleanness. So you, too, outwardly appear righteous to men, but inwardly you are full of hypocrisy and lawlessness" (Matt. 23:27–28; cf. Titus 1:15–16). To make matters worse, they added their own man-made rules and regulations to the law—eventually eclipsing the truth of God's Word with the traditions of men (cf. Mark 7:8, 13). Rather than leading them closer to God, their extrabiblical rituals and regulations led them away from Him. In the end, by rejecting and crucifying His Son, they proved that they loved their traditions far more than God Himself.

Jesus protested against their superficial religion by emphasizing the necessity of true internal righteousness (cf. Matt. 5:6, 20–48; Luke 18:9–14). Because the source of their defilement was spiritual and internal, it could not be removed by physical washings and external rituals. It was this very issue that Jesus explained to Nicodemus: "Truly, truly, I say to you, unless one is born of water and the Spirit he cannot enter into the kingdom of God. That which is born of the flesh is flesh, and that which is born of the Spirit is spirit" (John 3:5–6). Being "born of water and the Spirit" was a reference not to literal washing but to spiritual cleansing (Ezek. 36:24–27; cf. Num. 19:17–19; Ps. 51:9–10; Isa. 32:15; 44:3–5; 55:1–3; Jer. 2:13; Joel 2:28–29), a reality accomplished by the Holy Spirit at the moment of conversion (cf. Titus 3:4–7). Just as physical birth cannot produce spiritual life, so only the Holy Spirit can affect the regenerating transformation necessary to enter God's kingdom. The Pharisees and scribes were attempting to remove spiritual corruption through physical, external, and ceremonial means. The result was a whitewashed façade that thinly veiled a blackened heart. As Jesus explained to them, "Woe to you, scribes and Pharisees, hypocrites! For you clean the outside of the cup and of the dish, but inside they are full of robbery and self-indulgence" (Matt. 23:25; cf. Luke 16:15).

Verse 16 adds the phrase **If anyone has ears to hear, let him hear.** Most modern translations place that sentence in brackets because it does not occur in the earliest, most reliable manuscripts of the gospel. Though Jesus used this phrase on other occasions (Matt. 11:15; 13:9, 43; Mark 4:9, 23; Luke 8:8; 14:35; cf. Rev. 3:6, 13, 22), the evidence indicates that it was not part of the original text.

THE TRUTH EXPLAINED

When He had left the crowd and entered the house, His disciples questioned Him about the parable. And He said to them, "Are you so lacking in understanding also? Do you not understand that whatever goes into the man from outside cannot defile him, because it does not go into his heart, but into his stomach, and is eliminated?" (Thus He declared all foods clean.) And He was saying, "That which proceeds out of the man, that is what defiles the man. For from within, out of the heart of men, proceed the evil thoughts, fornications, thefts, murders, adulteries, deeds of coveting and wickedness, as well as deceit, sensuality, envy, slander, pride and foolishness. All these evil things proceed from within and defile the man." (7:17–23)

Sometime later that day **when He had left the crowd,** Jesus and His disciples **entered the house** where He was presumably staying, possibly the home of Peter and Andrew in Capernaum (cf. 1:29). Away from the crowds, the Lord was able to communicate privately with **His disciples,** who **questioned Him about the parable.** According to Matthew 15:12–14:

The disciples came and said to Him, "Do You know that the Pharisees were offended when they heard this statement?" But He answered and said, "Every plant which My heavenly Father did not plant shall be uprooted. Let them alone; they are blind guides of the blind. And if a blind man guides a blind man, both will fall into a pit."

That the Pharisees and scribes were offended by Jesus' words was no surprise. He intentionally struck devastating blows at the heart of their hypocritical form of self-righteous externalism. Though they considered themselves spiritual authorities who represented God, in reality they were blind guides leading people on the road to hell (cf. Matt. 23:15). As false shepherds, they could not aid people in escaping judgment, because they would one day face divine wrath themselves (cf. Ezek. 34:2–10), being uprooted like weeds and cast into the fire (cf. Matt. 13:40–42). Israel's apostate leaders were so far from salvation that Jesus told His disciples to "let them alone." Because they had finally and willfully rejected their Messiah, they had been abandoned to judgment (cf. Mark 3:28–29) and were thus to be ignored.

According to Matthew 15:15, "Peter said to Him, 'Explain the parable to us.'" It is at this point that Mark's narrative picks up the story. Jesus responded and **said to them, "Are you so lacking in understanding also?"** The Lord's question served as a mild rebuke to His disciples. It was less than a year until the cross, and they were still struggling with basic truths like the priority of inner righteousness over external ritual. It is likely that the disciples comprehended some aspects of the truth of what Jesus was disclosing. However, His teaching was so contrary to what they had been taught that they initially found it difficult to accept.

Recognizing their struggle, Jesus patiently explained the truth behind the metaphor: **"Do you not understand that whatever goes into the man from outside cannot defile him, because it does not go into his heart, but into his stomach, and is eliminated?"** As is often the case in Scripture (e.g., Deut. 6:5; Prov. 6:18; 22:15; Jer. 17:10; Rom. 1:21; 1 Cor. 4:5; Eph. 1:18), the **heart** refers not to the physical organ but to the inner person—the seat of one's mental, emotional, and spiritual being. It encompasses one's attitudes, affections, priorities, ambitions, and desires. The Lord's point was that something physical and external, like food eaten with unwashed hands, cannot defile the inner person because it is physical, not spiritual. The condition of one's heart before God is not determined by what one eats.

Mark's parenthetical note explains that in making this statement Jesus in a moment obliterated the dietary laws of Judaism and **declared all foods clean.** The issue is not a person's culinary choices but the spiritual condition of his inner person. Given Mark's close association with the apostle Peter (see Introduction: Authorship), Mark's comment was likely influenced by Peter's own experience in Joppa (Acts 10:15; cf. 1 Tim. 4:3).

In verses 17–23, Jesus transitioned from the physical analogy to clearly express the spiritual reality. **And He was saying, "That which proceeds out of the man, that is what defiles the man."** Spiritual defilement does not come from the outside but from the evil that resides in every human. The source of all wickedness is **from within,** so that **out of the heart proceed evil thoughts.** The word **thoughts** (from the Greek term *dialogismos*) is a general term referring to a person's inward reasoning or perception. Because the heart is evil, man's intentions, designs, ideas, motives, and musings are also depraved (cf. Gen. 6:5; Eph. 2:1–3). Out of the cesspool of the corrupt heart flow evil words, evil actions, and evil attitudes; the Lord enumerated six of each. The Pharisees and scribes loved to produce legalistic lists of external things either to do or to avoid. In response, Jesus articulated His own list defining the true nature of spiritual defilement by delineating the kinds of wickedness that live in and proceed from corrupt hearts.

Jesus' list of six representative evil actions began with **fornications** (a form of the Greek word *porneia*, from which the English word "pornography" is derived), a general reference to sexual sin. Next, He identified **thefts** (a form of *klopē*; the related verb, *kleptō*, provides the basis for the English word "kleptomaniac"); **murders** (a form of *phonos*), denoting the illicit taking of another person's life; **adulteries** (a form of *moicheia*), meaning sexual sin that violates the marriage covenant; and **deeds of coveting** (a form of *pleonexia*), a reference to desires and behaviors motivated by greed and avarice. All four of those actions are included in the second half of the Ten Commandments (cf. Ex. 20:13–17; cf. Rom. 13:9), and the disciples would have immediately recognized them as flagrant transgressions. (According to Matt. 15:19,

Jesus also mentioned bearing false witness in this context.) Completing this category of evil, Jesus added **wickedness** (a form of *ponēria*), a general reference to iniquity that encompassed everything else that violates God's law and holy will.

The Lord continued by denouncing six representative evil attitudes that lie behind those wicked actions (cf. Matt. 5:21–37). These include **deceit** (from the Greek word *dolos*), meaning craftiness, lying, and deception; and **sensuality** (a form of *aselgeia*), a reference to the unbridled lust of a dirty mind. The word **envy** translates two Greek words (forms of *ophthalmos*, meaning "eye," and *ponēros*, meaning "evil") and could be literally rendered as "evil eye." Jesus used it here to describe eyes full of jealousy and hatred. **Slander** (a form of *blasphēmia*) refers to abusive and injurious speech toward others; **pride** (from the Greek word *huperēphania*) describes feelings of superiority, arrogance, and self-promotion. In the same way that the word "wickedness" summarized the evil actions in Jesus' list, **foolishness** (a form of *aphrosunē*) encompassed the previous attitudes that He had articulated. It is a general term for moral folly and senselessness (cf. Prov. 13:16; 18:2; Eccl. 10:1–3). Ensuring that the disciples did not miss the point, Jesus reiterated the truth that **all these things proceed from within and defile the man.** It is not unwashed hands that defile a person but an unwashed soul.

No physical act of ceremonial cleansing or external ritual can purify a depraved heart, out of which flows all wicked actions and evil attitudes. Sinners need to be given a new nature, a new heart. Only the Spirit of God can create that (cf. Jer. 31:33; John 3:3–8). Speaking of the new covenant, the Lord God promised the Israelites:

> "Then I will sprinkle clean water on you, and you will be clean; I will cleanse you from all your filthiness and from all your idols. Moreover, I will give you a new heart and put a new spirit within you; and I will remove the heart of stone from your flesh and give you a heart of flesh. I will put My Spirit within you and cause you to walk in My statutes, and you will be careful to observe My ordinances." (Ezek. 36:25–27)

As Ezekiel's prophecy indicates, salvation requires inner transformation, a new heart. The New Testament identifies that reality as the miracle of regeneration and the new birth (cf. John 1:12–13; 3:3; Eph. 2:4–5; 5:26–27;

Col. 2:13; James 1:18; 1 Peter 1:3, 23–25; 1 John 2:29; 3:9; 4:7). The apostle Paul described regeneration in these words:

> He saved us, not on the basis of deeds which we have done in righteousness, but according to His mercy, by the washing of regeneration and renewing by the Holy Spirit, whom He poured out upon us richly through Jesus Christ our Savior, so that being justified by His grace we would be made heirs according to the hope of eternal life. (Titus 3:5–7)

Salvation is not predicated "on the basis of deeds," including moral works, religious ceremonies, and external rituals. Rather it requires an internal miracle by the Holy Spirit who, according to His sovereign will and power, creates and cleanses the souls of all who embrace Jesus Christ in faith (Acts 15:8–9; cf. Rom. 8:2).

The Pharisees and scribes failed to understand that their corruption was on the inside. Though they appeared fastidiously religious, their superficial self-righteousness was infinitely inadequate (cf. Isa. 64:6; Luke 18:9–14; Phil. 3:4–9). Like all sinners, they needed new hearts that were regenerated by the Spirit of God. Yet, when Jesus confronted their hypocrisy, they spurned Him in angry unbelief, plotted His murder (cf. Matt. 12:24; 26:4; John 11:47–53), and committed spiritual suicide, not unlike Judas Iscariot.

Those who harden their hearts to the good news of the gospel, like the Pharisees and scribes did, will face eternal judgment (cf. Rom. 1:21; 2:5; Heb. 3:15). But those whose hearts have been made new by the power of God (2 Cor. 4:6; cf. Acts 16:14) have become new creatures in Christ (2 Cor. 5:17; cf. Col. 3:10). As those who "hunger and thirst for righteousness" (Matt. 5:6), they delight in hiding God's Word in their hearts (Ps. 119:11; cf. Deut. 6:6; Prov. 3:3; 22:17–18; Jer. 17:1) so that they might serve the Lord in loving obedience (John 14:15; cf. Rom. 6:17; Eph. 6:6; 1 John 5:3) and "fervently love one another from the heart" (1 Peter 1:22; cf. John 13:34; Rom 12:10; Heb. 13:1; 1 Peter 2:17; 3:8). Though their hearts were once characterized by all sorts of wicked actions and attitudes (cf. 1 Cor. 6:9–11), they are now divinely empowered to live in a way that pleases God (cf. Rom. 6:17–18, 22; 13:11–14), as they "flee from youthful lusts and pursue righteousness, faith, love and peace, with those who call on the Lord from a pure heart" (2 Tim. 2:22).

Food from the Master's Table
(Mark 7:24–30)

26

Jesus got up and went away from there to the region of Tyre. And when He had entered a house, He wanted no one to know of it; yet He could not escape notice. But after hearing of Him, a woman whose little daughter had an unclean spirit immediately came and fell at His feet. Now the woman was a Gentile, of the Syrophoenician race. And she kept asking Him to cast the demon out of her daughter. And He was saying to her, "Let the children be satisfied first, for it is not good to take the children's bread and throw it to the dogs." But she answered and said to Him, "Yes, Lord, but even the dogs under the table feed on the children's crumbs." And He said to her, "Because of this answer go; the demon has gone out of your daughter." And going back to her home, she found the child lying on the bed, the demon having left. (7:24–30)

Because Mark wrote his gospel for a Gentile audience, he was careful to highlight the fact that the message of salvation was not limited to Israel but extended to the entire world (cf. Mark 13:10; 14:9; 16:15). For first-century Jews, that notion was radical and revolutionary. Even in the early church, many Jewish believers initially struggled to accept the idea that Gentiles could be saved without first converting to Judaism (cf. Acts 11:1–18; 15:1–11).

The Israelites viewed non-Jews as outcasts who were separated from the kingdom and purposes of God (cf. Eph. 2:11–12). Accordingly, Gentiles were considered unclean, cursed, and consigned to divine judgment. The Jews assumed that they alone (along with proselytes) could receive the blessings of salvation because they were part of God's chosen nation. That myopic perspective reflected a misunderstanding of the Old Testament, which declared Israel to be a kingdom of priests (Ex. 19:6) who would reflect the blessings of salvation to all the families of the earth (cf. Gen. 12:3; 22:18; 26:4; 28:14). God intended the Jews to be His faithful witnesses to the world, so that souls from every nation would join them in glorifying Him. As the book of Psalms exclaims:

> God be gracious to us and bless us,
> And cause His face to shine upon us—Selah.
> That Your way may be known on the earth,
> Your salvation among all nations.
> Let the peoples praise You, O God;
> Let all the peoples praise You.
> Let the nations be glad and sing for joy;
> For You will judge the peoples with uprightness
> And guide the nations on the earth. Selah.
> Let the peoples praise You, O God;
> Let all the peoples praise You.
> The earth has yielded its produce;
> God, our God, blesses us.
> God blesses us,
> That all the ends of the earth may fear Him. (Ps. 67:1–7; cf. 100:1–3)

Thus, the people of Israel were called to be a light to the nations, so that through them the inhabitants of the whole earth would sing God's praise and give Him glory. Engulfed in idolatry and immorality, the nations of the world needed to know about the one true God (cf. Isa. 45:5), without whom they could not be saved (Isa. 43:11; cf. John 14:6; Acts 4:12).

The Lord God always intended the message of salvation to reach the whole world, originally using Israel as the means to that end (cf. Gal.

3:8). Thus, the gospel was given to the Jews first that through them it might extend to the Gentiles (cf. Rom. 1:16). Tragically, Old Testament Israel failed to embrace their missionary role. Perhaps no biblical figure illustrates that failure more vividly than the prophet Jonah, who preferred running away from God to preaching a message of repentance to the Ninevites (cf. Jonah 4:1–3). Rather than viewing the surrounding nations with compassion, the Israelites grew to despise foreigners—treating them as enemies instead of a mission field.

All of that changed with the Messiah's coming. As Isaiah 49:6 predicted regarding the extent of the Messiah's ministry: "It is too small a thing that You should be My Servant to raise up the tribes of Jacob and to restore the preserved ones of Israel; I will also make You a light of the nations so that My salvation may reach to the end of the earth." A few chapters earlier, the Lord God expanded on the Messiah's global impact:

> I will appoint You as a covenant to the people,
> As a light to the nations,
> To open blind eyes,
> To bring out prisoners from the dungeon
> And those who dwell in darkness from the prison....
> Sing to the Lord a new song,
> Sing His praise from the end of the earth!
> You who go down to the sea, and all that is in it.
> You islands, and those who dwell on them.
> Let the wilderness and its cities lift up their voices,
> The settlements where Kedar inhabits.
> Let the inhabitants of Sela sing aloud,
> Let them shout for joy from the tops of the mountains.
> Let them give glory to the Lord
> And declare His praise in the coastlands. (Isa. 42:6–12)

Where the nation failed in its global witness, the Messiah would triumph. He would be the unfailing light to the nations, so that the message of God's salvation would spread throughout the entire world.

The prophecies of Isaiah were clearly fulfilled in the life and ministry of Jesus Christ. Though the focus of His earthly ministry centered on the nation of Israel, His offer of salvation extended to every person—whether Jew or Gentile. For example, He revealed Himself as Messiah to an outcast Samaritan woman in John 4:26. After His death and resurrection, He commissioned His followers to be His witnesses "both in

Jerusalem, and in all Judea and Samaria, and even to the remotest part of the earth" (Acts 1:8; cf. Matt. 28:19–20). Through the power of the Holy Spirit, the early Christians turned their world upside down (cf. Acts 17:6), so that the light of salvation spread to engulf the world (cf. Matt. 5:14–16). The gospel's global reach is perhaps most richly expressed in Revelation 5, a passage that depicts the glorified church in heaven. There, the four living creatures declare to the Lamb: "You were slain, and purchased for God with Your blood men from every tribe and tongue and people and nation" (v. 9). For all of eternity, redeemed people from all ages and all nations will glorify and worship their Savior.

The Messiah's salvation ministry to the entire world is previewed in this text (Mark 7:24–30), as a Gentile woman from Tyre demonstrates saving faith in the Lord Jesus. The passage can be organized under five headings: Jesus' foreign retreat, the woman's fervent request, Jesus' focused reply, the woman's faith-filled response, and Jesus' favorable reaction.

JESUS' FOREIGN RETREAT

Jesus got up and went away from there to the region of Tyre. And when He had entered a house, He wanted no one to know of it; yet He could not escape notice. (7:24)

After more than a year in Galilee, Jesus' extended ministry there had come to an end. Though some believed, the majority of people rejected Him (John 6:66; cf. Matt. 11:20–24), including the residents of His hometown of Nazareth (cf. Mark 6:1–6). The Jewish religious leaders had grown increasingly antagonistic (3:20–30) and sought to kill Him (3:6; cf. Matt. 12:14). King Herod, fearful that Jesus posed a threat to his political power, also wanted to execute Him (cf. Luke 13:31). Aware of the mounting opposition against Him, and knowing the cross was still months away, Jesus left Galilee for a concentrated time of training with His apostles. He did not withdraw out of fear (cf. Luke 9:51; cf. 19:28) but out of a deliberate desire to prepare the Twelve for their coming apostolic challenges. Rather than traveling south into Judea, where it would be nearly impossible to find the privacy He sought, the Lord journeyed north. As Mark explains, **Jesus got up and went away from there to the region of Tyre.**

The **region of Tyre,** situated to the northwest of Galilee, refers to the Gentile territory of ancient Phoenicia, which today is located in southern Lebanon. In his parallel account, Matthew identifies it as "the district of Tyre and Sidon" (Matt. 15:21; cf. Gen. 10:19; 49:13; Josh. 11:8; 1 Kings 17:9). Tyre and Sidon were coastal cities, located about twenty miles apart along the eastern shore of the Mediterranean Sea. According to Mark 7:31, after spending an unspecified period of time in this region, Jesus journeyed through Sidon before traveling east and then south along the eastern side of the Sea of Galilee. In the face of His own people's rejection, Jesus sought rest and seclusion in a Gentile place. Roughly nine hundred years earlier, the prophet Elijah journeyed to this same area during Israel's drought, when wicked King Ahab sought to find him (cf. 1 Kings 17:9; 18:10; Luke 4:25–26).

Arriving in the vicinity of Tyre, Jesus, along with the Twelve, **had entered a house.** That this was a private tour is indicated by the fact that **He wanted no one to know of it; yet He could not escape notice.** Inevitably, as happened wherever Jesus went, news about His arrival quickly spread. Even deep in Gentile territory, roughly thirty-five miles northwest of Capernaum, the people had heard about Him. According to Mark 3:8, people from "the vicinity of Tyre and Sidon" had been among the crowds that followed Jesus during His Galilean ministry (cf. Luke 6:17). They undoubtedly returned home with firsthand reports of the amazing miracles they had witnessed. As a result, word about Him spread far beyond the borders of Israel.

Though the Lord intended this trip for rest and private instruction for His disciples, He also knew of the divine appointment that awaited Him. In fact, that planned encounter was a critical part of the apostles' training to be His witnesses. His meeting with the Gentile woman provided the Twelve with a vivid example of true faith and a preview of what was to come, when they would begin to take the gospel to the ends of the earth.

THE WOMAN'S FERVENT REQUEST

But after hearing of Him, a woman whose little daughter had an unclean spirit immediately came and fell at His feet. Now the woman was a Gentile, of the Syrophoenician race. And she kept asking Him to cast the demon out of her daughter. (7:25–26)

After hearing that He was staying nearby, **a woman whose little daughter had an unclean spirit immediately came and fell at His feet.** Apparently she had previously heard about Jesus. Perhaps she had even traveled to Galilee and seen Jesus' miracles herself. If so, she had already witnessed His power to heal diseases and cast out demons. Like many others who desperately sought help from Jesus, this woman approached Him in humble reverence, falling down before Him (cf. Matt. 17:14; Mark 1:40; 5:22; Luke 17:16; John 11:32). Jesus regularly healed Jews. But as Mark explains, **the woman was a Gentile, of the Syrophoenician race.** From the perspective of first-century Judaism, she had everything going against her. First, she was a **woman,** which even among the Jews meant she was viewed as inferior to a man. Second, she **was a Gentile.** The adjective **Syrophoenician** described people from this area at that time; Phoenicia had been annexed to Syria under a Roman general named Pompey (about 65 B.C.). According to Matthew 15:22, she was a descendant of the Canaanites, the ancient enemies of Israel (cf. Ex. 23:23; Num. 33:52–53; Deut. 7:2; 20:16–17). Third, she came from an area that was engulfed in pagan idolatry and was undoubtedly an idol worshiper herself. Tyre and Sidon were major centers of worship for the fertility goddess Astarte, known as Ashtaroth in the Old Testament (cf. Judg. 2:13; 10:6; 1 Sam. 7:3–4; 12:10; 31:10). In the minds of the Jews, no self-respecting rabbi would ever allow a Gentile, especially an idolatrous woman, to remain in his presence. The Lord wanted to show His disciples that the message of salvation was for the nations, those whom they had been taught were outside Gods' grace and blessing.

The woman had an urgent problem, which is why **she kept asking** Jesus **to cast the demon out of her daughter.** Demons are fallen angels who operate in the kingdom of darkness. In this horrific instance, a demon was cruelly possessing a little girl (cf. Matt. 15:22). (For more on demon possession, see chapter 17 in this volume.) As a mother, this woman's heart was aching for her daughter. With her life and home in satanic turmoil, she had likely performed whatever ceremonies she thought would appease her false gods, but to no avail. When it became obvious that idols of stone could not deliver her child (cf. Ps. 115:4–8; Isa. 44:9–20), she abandoned her pagan practices. Turning away from her impotent idols (cf. 1 Thess. 1:9), she came to Jesus, hoping Israel's Messiah could rescue her daughter.

The fact that she **kept asking** for His help indicates that she was unwilling to give up. Her love for her daughter, the horror of demonic power in her home, combined with her confidence in Jesus' power, fueled her unwavering resolve. That heartfelt persistence was matched by an attitude of humble penitence. As the parallel account in Matthew 15:22 explains, she "began to cry out, saying, 'Have mercy on me, Lord, Son of David; my daughter is cruelly demon-possessed.'" Recognizing her own unworthiness, like the publican in Luke 18:13, she begged for mercy on the basis of His inherent goodness, not her own. Her address to Jesus was also characterized by reverence and a recognition of His messianic role. Even though she was a Gentile, she acknowledged Him as Lord and identified Him by the messianic title "Son of David" (cf. Matt. 21:9). Her words suggest more than a superficial familiarity with the religious beliefs of neighboring Israel. She rightly understood who Jesus was.

Matthew 15:23 indicates that, although she kept asking persistently, initially Jesus "did not answer her a word." At first glance, the Lord's silence may seem a bit startling. He was not being rude or indifferent. Rather, He was illustrating a vital spiritual point—both for her and for His disciples. The reason Jesus did not answer her immediately was to allow the robust character of her faith to be put on display. After experiencing the superficial faith of many in Israel (cf. John 2:24; 6:64, 66), the Lord found true faith in a Gentile woman from the region of Tyre. The barriers He erected were not designed to push her away but to showcase the authenticity of her faith. Unlike the rich young ruler, whose faith crumbled when tested (cf. Matt. 19:16–22), this woman's faith was unbreakable. That the Lord had compassion on her is borne out by the rest of this account (cf. John 6:37).

JESUS' FOCUSED REPLY

And He was saying to her, "Let the children be satisfied first, for it is not good to take the children's bread and throw it to the dogs." (7:27)

The disciples misinterpreted Jesus' silence, assuming His refusal to answer indicated that He wanted the woman to leave. As she continued to plead, their frustration and impatience toward her increased. Not only was she a Gentile and a nuisance, her loud appeals were attracting attention at a time when they sought privacy and seclusion from the crowds. Thus, according to Matthew 15:23, "His disciples came and implored Him, saying, 'Send her away, because she keeps shouting at us.'" They found the woman bothersome and simply wanted her to be silenced and sent away. The Lord, however, intended to teach them a valuable lesson about the character of genuine faith.

In response to the disciples' request, but within earshot of the woman, Jesus "answered and said, 'I was sent only to the lost sheep of the house of Israel'" (Matt. 15:24). The Lord's words reminded the disciples that His initial mission was to the Jewish people (cf. John 4:22; Rom. 1:16; 15:8), and that the time for them to be witnesses throughout the whole earth had not yet arrived. His statement also tested the woman's faith, since it sounded as if He might not help her because she was a Gentile. Those with lesser faith might have erupted in anger or walked away in dejection. Instead, "she came and began to bow down before Him, saying, 'Lord, help me!'" (Matt. 15:25). The phrase "to bow down" (from the Greek word *proskuneō*) is often rendered as **to worship,** and underscores her reverential attitude toward Jesus. Knowing He was her only hope, she humbly refused to be dissuaded from coming to Him (cf. Luke 18:1–8).

Jesus continued to test her faith by again delaying His response. Essentially restating what He had just told the disciples, **He was saying to her, "Let the children be satisfied first, for it is not good to take the children's bread and throw it to the dogs."** With a simple analogy, the Lord reiterated that His ministry priority was first to Israel. A meal prepared for the children should not be given to the dogs. Similarly, the

Messiah's priority was to preach the news of the kingdom to the children of Israel (cf. Matt. 10:5–6; 15:24; Mark 1:14–15; John 1:11; Acts 10:36). Though the gospel would soon be preached to all the nations, that global expansion was waiting for Christ's ascension and the arrival of the Holy Spirit (Matt. 28:18–20; Acts 1:8; cf. John 10:16; 11:51–52). The New Testament uses two different Greek words for **dogs.** One refers to the feral mongrels that roamed the streets in packs and scavenged for garbage (cf. Matt. 7:6; Luke 16:21; Phil. 3:2; 2 Peter 2:22; Rev. 22:15). The **dogs** referred to here (from the Greek word *kunarion*, sometimes translated as "little dogs") were diminutive household pets that were cared for by the family. Thus, Jesus used a term for dogs that was far less harsh than most first-century Jews would have applied to the Gentiles. Even so, the woman understood the Lord's point. His primary focus was on feeding the children of Israel (cf. John 6:35), and she was not included.

The Woman's Faith-Filled Response

But she answered and said to Him, "Yes, Lord, but even the dogs under the table feed on the children's crumbs." (7:28)

The Lord knew the woman's divinely bestowed faith (cf. Eph. 2:8–9) was genuine, and that it would not be discouraged or dissuaded (cf. Luke 13:24; 16:16). Rather than being offended, she responded with undaunted trust. Extending Jesus' analogy, **she answered and said to Him, "Yes, Lord, but even the dogs under the table feed on the children's crumbs."** She recognized her unworthiness and acknowledged her place as a Gentile. Unlike many of the Jews, who responded to Jesus with self-righteous pride, her attitude was very meek and poor in spirit (cf. Matt. 5:3). For her, just the **crumbs** were sufficient. A tiny fragment of Jesus' power could heal her daughter and that was all she sought. Though the priority of Jesus' earthly mission was to the children of Israel, the crumbs of the gospel did fall from their table to satisfy humble Gentiles who hungered for true righteousness (cf. Matt. 5:6). The covenants, Scriptures, and the Messiah may all have been given to Israel (cf. Rom. 9:4–5), but God intended for Gentiles to receive the overflow (cf. Rom. 11:12). The message of salvation that came first to the Jews is the same gospel message that was and would be given to the Gentiles. The several Gentile conversions in the Gospels are previews of the future salvation of souls from all nations.

The woman's response, elicited by the Lord Jesus, expressed a quality of faith that He called "great faith" (cf. Matt. 15:28). On an earlier occasion, the Lord made a similar remark about a Roman centurion who asked Jesus to heal his servant: "I have not found such great faith with anyone in Israel" (cf. Matt. 8:10; Luke 7:9). In both cases, it was a Gentile who demonstrated such remarkable faith. With the woman in Tyre, the context suggests that her faith was more than just a nominal belief in Jesus' healing power. Her humble, reverent, and persistent appeal to Christ implies that God was at work in her heart, drawing her to salvation (cf. John 6:44). Had her faith remained in the pagan deities of her Canaanite culture, it would have been empty and worthless. True faith sets its hope in the one true God (cf. Heb. 11:1, 6) and fixes its "eyes on Jesus, the author and perfecter of faith" (12:2).

The greatness of this woman's faith is magnified when compared to the little that she knew. Born and raised in a pagan culture, she did not share in the privileged heritage of the Jewish people. She was removed from the temple, the sacrificial system, and even the Scriptures. Yet, even though she had received only a little revelation, she believed. The magnitude of her faith was evidenced by her willingness to turn from the pagan deities of her upbringing and embrace Jesus Christ in faith. That response stood in stark contrast to the Jewish religious leaders, who arrogantly condemned their own Messiah as a blasphemer (cf. John 10:33), a friend of sinners (cf. Luke 7:34), and an ally of Satan (cf. Mark 3:22). In Matthew 11:21, Jesus offered this severe warning to the Israelites who rejected Him: "Woe to you, Chorazin! Woe to you, Bethsaida! For if the miracles had occurred in Tyre and Sidon which occurred in you, they would have repented long ago in sackcloth and ashes." Here was a pagan woman from the region of Tyre who proved the truthfulness of Jesus' words. What a rebuke she was to apostate Israel, a Gentile who embraced the Messiah when so many self-righteous Jews rejected Him (cf. Rom. 11:11).

JESUS' FAVORABLE REACTION

And He said to her, "Because of this answer go; the demon has gone out of your daughter." And going back to her home, she found the child lying on the bed, the demon having left. (7:29–30)

Though Jesus prolonged His interaction with this woman, in order to put the nature of genuine faith on display, He knew all along what He was going to do. The Lord never refused anyone, Jew or Gentile, who approached Him in sincere faith (John 6:37; cf. Luke 7:9; John 4:39). After hearing her reply, **He said to her, "Because of this answer go; the demon has gone out of your daughter."** Because she possessed true belief in Him, the process of being tested only strengthened it (cf. Rom. 4:20; 1 Peter 1:7). Her resolve did not waver but intensified. And Jesus was highly pleased with her response.

The Lord granted her request by casting the demon out of her daughter. He had such control over the spiritual realm that He did not need to be with her. His power was omnipresent, and the evil spirit was immediately compelled to evacuate. Having embraced the Lord Jesus in faith, the woman returned home confident in His power. **And going back to her home, she found the child lying on the bed, the demon having left.** That her daughter was lying down in bed suggests both that the child was exhausted due to the struggle with the demon (cf. Mark 1:26; 9:20) and that she was finally able to rest peacefully, now that the evil spirit was gone. Undoubtedly, like Jairus and his wife upon the resurrection of their daughter (cf. Mark 5:42) or the countless others whom Jesus healed, this woman responded in joy-filled astonishment that her daughter had been delivered.

The daughter's healing, though wonderful, is not the primary point of this account. Rather, the focus centers on both the substance of this woman's faith—being characterized by humility, penitence, reverence, and persistence—and the object of her faith—namely, the Lord Jesus Christ. This woman's story is a magnificent illustration of the fact that genuine saving faith forsakes idols, abandons pride, and reverently yet persistently begs for divine mercy and grace (cf. Matt. 7:7). In some ways she is like Job, whom God tested to demonstrate the genuineness of his faith. True faith persists and endures until it receives the grace it seeks.

To Speak or Not to Speak (Mark 7:31–37)

27

Again He went out from the region of Tyre, and came through Sidon to the Sea of Galilee, within the region of Decapolis. They brought to Him one who was deaf and spoke with difficulty, and they implored Him to lay His hand on him. Jesus took him aside from the crowd, by himself, and put His fingers into his ears, and after spitting, He touched his tongue with the saliva; and looking up to heaven with a deep sigh, He said to him, "Ephphatha!" that is, "Be opened!" And his ears were opened, and the impediment of his tongue was removed, and he began speaking plainly. And He gave them orders not to tell anyone; but the more He ordered them, the more widely they continued to proclaim it. They were utterly astonished, saying, "He has done all things well; He makes even the deaf to hear and the mute to speak." (7:31–37)

These verses might be introduced with a riddle: Who is permitted to speak but not able, and able to speak but not permitted? That enigmatic question finds its answer in this dramatic account.

After more than a year of public ministry in Galilee, Jesus took His disciples away for a time of isolated instruction. The Twelve had recently affirmed that He was the Son of God (Matt. 14:33) who alone spoke words of eternal life (John 6:68). The time had come for the Lord Jesus to focus His efforts more intently on preparing them for their ministry after His death and resurrection. They would be commissioned as the first generation of gospel preachers, charged with launching the truth toward the ends of the earth (cf. Matt. 28:19; Acts 1:8).

Jesus and His disciples journeyed first to the northwest, traveling outside of Israel into the region of Tyre (modern Lebanon). There they encountered a Gentile woman who desperately sought Jesus' help and, in the process, exhibited genuine faith in Him (cf. 7:24–30). Her humble persistence provided the apostles with a vivid illustration of their future missionary work. It would not be long before they would see many Gentiles similarly displaying faith in Christ as the gospel spread beyond the borders of Israel (cf. Acts 10:11–48; 11:1–18, 20–25).

After their stay near Tyre ended, Jesus and the Twelve **went out from the region of Tyre, and came through Sidon to the Sea of Galilee, within the region of Decapolis.** Traveling in a circuitous route, in order to extend the time with His disciples, the Lord continued going north through the city of Sidon (situated on the Mediterranean coast about twenty miles from Tyre) before journeying east and then south to His destination on the southeastern shores of the Sea of Galilee.

The **region of Decapolis,** located on the southeast side of the lake, was home to Gentiles and outside the territory of Herod Antipas. The region encompassed ten city-states (the name **Decapolis,** from the Greek *deka* ["ten"] and *polis* ["city"], literally means "ten cities"). Archaeological discoveries indicate that these towns were centers of Greek paganism, littered with idols honoring pagan deities like Zeus, Aphrodite, Artemis, and Dionysus. Though the nation of Israel was still Jesus' priority, His willingness to minister in this Gentile area, much like His interaction with the woman from Tyre, previewed the fact that the gospel was always intended to be preached throughout the whole world. (For more on this point, see chapter 26 in the current volume.) By traveling to Decapolis, Jesus returned to the vicinity of Gerasa where He had earlier healed a man possessed by a legion of demons (cf. Mark 5:1–20). Through the witness of that man (v. 20), along with others from Decapolis who had traveled to Galilee to see Jesus (cf. Matt. 4:25), the news about Jesus had already spread to this area.

The Lord's time of instruction with the Twelve was ended as massive crowds gathered around Him once again. Matthew 15:29–31 sets the scene:

> Jesus went along by the Sea of Galilee, and having gone up on the mountain, He was sitting there. And large crowds came to Him, bringing with them those who were lame, crippled, blind, mute, and many others, and they laid them down at His feet; and He healed them. So the crowd marveled as they saw the mute speaking, the crippled restored, and the lame walking, and the blind seeing; and they glorified the God of Israel.

Though the residents of Decapolis were idol worshipers, they had heard about Jesus' power and knew He could do what their pagan deities had never done. Consequently, they rushed those who were physically disabled to Him, and He healed them, immediately and completely. Predictably, they "marveled" (from the Greek *thaumazō*, meaning to be struck with awe) and began to glorify the true God. Ironically, the Jewish leaders of Israel who saw the same miracles rejected Jesus, accusing Him of operating by Satan's power (Mark 3:22); the Gentile pagans of Decapolis recognized that His power came from God. For the moment, turning from their idols, they offered praise to the God of Israel.

It is in that context that the account described in this passage (Mark 7:31–37) took place. Whereas the parallel passage in Matthew 15:29–31 provides an overview of Jesus' healings, Mark is the only gospel writer who includes this encounter. Initially, the deaf man described here was unable to speak. By Christ's will and power, he was enabled to speak. Finally, when the Lord commanded him to keep quiet, he was unable not to speak.

UNABLE TO SPEAK

They brought to Him one who was deaf and spoke with difficulty, and they implored Him to lay His hand on him. (7:32)

Friends or family members **brought** a man **who was deaf and spoke with difficulty** to see Jesus. His deafness was likely congenital or long-term; without being able to hear as a child, he was unable to learn how to speak, thereby resulting in a severe speech impediment. In that world, no remedies existed for such a condition. Those suffering from such physical impairments were ostracized by society. Even in Israel, deaf people, because of their hearing loss and speech defects, were generally regarded as mentally handicapped. Adding insult to injury, the Jews alleged that disabilities like deafness or blindness were the direct result of God's judgment for sin (cf. John 9:1–2). That this man lived in a pagan society likely meant that the ill treatment and disdain he endured was even worse.

Nonetheless, some cared enough about this man to bring him to Jesus, **and they implored Him to lay His hand on him.** In this context, the verb **implored** (from the Greek verb *parakaleō*) means "to beg" or "to entreat" with a sense of urgency. In desperation they pled on behalf of their friend, who could not speak for himself, that Jesus would enable him to hear. Jesus often laid His hands on people to visually and tangibly demonstrate His power to the sufferers (cf. Mark 1:31, 41; 5:41; 6:5; 8:22, 25). Unlike the Pharisees and scribes, who considered themselves to be above the common people, Jesus gladly mingled with the crowds and willingly extended His touch toward those in need. Doing so displayed His and heaven's tender compassion and personal care. It also demonstrated that He was not afraid of ceremonial defilement. Jesus was never defiled by those whom He touched—whether it was a leper (1:40–41), a woman with a hemorrhage of blood (5:25–34), a dead body (5:41–42), or a Gentile man who suffered from deafness. Rather than being corrupted by them, they were cleansed and restored by Him.

ENABLED TO SPEAK

Jesus took him aside from the crowd, by himself, and put His fingers into his ears, and after spitting, He touched his tongue with the saliva; and looking up to heaven with a deep sigh, He said to him, "Ephphatha!" that is, "Be opened!" And his ears were opened,

and the impediment of his tongue was removed, and he began speaking plainly. (7:33–35)

Responding with compassion as He always did (cf. Matt. 9:36; 14:14; Mark 1:41; 8:2, etc.), **Jesus took** the man **aside from the crowd, by himself.** In the midst of the pressing throng, with many others waiting to be healed, the Lord Jesus gave His attention to one desperate man who had surely been ignored and neglected throughout his life. For as long as the man could remember, he had been scorned, ostracized, and despised. But in that moment, he received the undivided attention and compassion of the Creator Himself.

In an act of profound kindness, the Lord began to communicate in sign language, using gestures and nonverbal signals. Jesus used four specific signs to make His point. First, He **put His fingers into** both of **his ears** to indicate that He recognized the man's physical problem. Jesus understood that he was not stunted mentally or possessed by demons, as some may have thought; he simply could not hear. The Lord used a symbolic gesture to demonstrate that He had rightly diagnosed the medical issue. Second, **after spitting, He touched his tongue with the saliva.** Jesus again employed a physical gesture to identify the man's speech disability. Though Jesus used **saliva** in His healings on two other occasions (cf. Mark 8:23; John 9:6), it obviously had no power. However, ancient people generally believed that saliva had healing properties. The deaf man would have understood that Jesus' use of saliva meant He intended to heal him. Third, **looking up to heaven,** Jesus demonstrated that the creative power He exercised came from God. Even as a pagan, the man would have understood what Jesus meant by gazing toward heaven. Fourth, by giving **a deep sigh,** the Lord communicated a sincere sympathy for the long agonies of this man's disability. An honest groaning visibly projected pain and heartache on the man's behalf. So, using nonverbal communication, the Lord Jesus taught this man about both God's power and His compassion. The Son of God would heal him, with power that came from above, because He cared deeply about him.

Those two wonderful truths must have filled the man's heart and mind as the miraculous happened. **Jesus said to him, "Ephphatha!" that is, "Be opened!"** By using the Aramaic term **Ephphatha,** Mark provided an exact quote of Jesus' words, since the colloquial language He spoke was Aramaic. However, Mark immediately translated it for his Greek-speaking readers: **"Be opened!"** With a command from the incarnate Creator, the man was immediately given new hearing organs and his tongue was miraculously loosed to speak. As Mark explains, **his ears were opened, and the impediment of his tongue was removed, and he began speaking plainly.** The word **impediment,** from the Greek word *desmon*, means "bond" or "chains." It was as if his speech had been imprisoned in the dungeon of deafness. Immediately, he was set free and able to hear perfectly and speak plainly.

The extent of the miracle went beyond merely repairing the man's physical faculties. He was also given the ability of miraculous language acquisition. Not only could he hear sounds, he was able to understand and articulate words without needing any linguistic training or speech therapy. The word **plainly** comes from the Greek word *orthōs*, meaning "straight" or "right." The English medical terms "orthopedics" and "orthodontics" are derived from that Greek term. In an instant, the One who created the world (John 1:1–3), and upholds it with "the word of His power" (Heb. 1:3), supernaturally enabled this man to hear and speak fluently. Like every miracle Jesus performed, this healing was an act of divine creative energy through His word, the same way He made the universe in the beginning (cf. Gen. 1:3,6,9,14,20,24,26).

<h2 style="text-align:center">U<small>NABLE</small> N<small>OT</small> <small>TO</small> S<small>PEAK</small></h2>

And He gave them orders not to tell anyone; but the more He ordered them, the more widely they continued to proclaim it. They were utterly astonished, saying, "He has done all things well; He makes even the deaf to hear and the mute to speak." (7:36–37)

No doubt, the man's reaction was one of exuberant joy. Naturally, his instant impulse was to tell everyone what happened. But Jesus instructed him and his friends to keep quiet—an immense restraint in light of such an experience. Yet, **He gave them orders not to tell anyone.**

Orders (from the Greek *diastellomai*) refers to a command. That Jesus commanded this man to remain quiet may seem strange, not only because He had just given him the ability to speak but also because the Lord had earlier told the Garasene demoniac to do the exact opposite:

> He said to him, "Go home to your people and report to them what great things the Lord has done for you, and how He had mercy on you." And he went away and began to proclaim in Decapolis what great things Jesus had done for him; and everyone was amazed. (Mark 5:19–20)

One might wonder why Jesus instructed the former demoniac to spread the news about Him throughout the region of Decapolis and later told the former deaf man to keep quiet. There was an important difference. The former demoniac was the first missionary to that Gentile area. But now, largely through his witness, the news about Jesus' miracle-working power was well-known throughout the region, resulting in widespread euphoria. The situation had reached epic proportions due to the unbridled enthusiasm of the unwieldy crowds. As in Galilee, the Lord had no desire to add fuel to the fire of their inherently materialistic and political expectations about Him (cf. John 6:15).

Jesus issued similar commands at other times as well (cf. Matt. 8:4; 9:30; 12:16; 17:9; Mark 1:25, 34, 44; 3:12; 5:43; 7:36; 8:26, 30; 9:9; Luke 4:41; 9:21). On certain occasions, the Lord insisted on silence because He knew the report would amplify the enthusiastic fervor of the crowds, which would only hinder His ministry (cf. Mark 1:40–45; John 6:14–15). As noted above, that was likely part of Jesus' concern on this occasion since large crowds were already flocking to Him in the Decapolis (cf. Mark 8:1–10). At other times, the gag order served as an act of judgment on unbelievers by obscuring the truth from those who had permanently rejected Him (cf. Luke 9:21).

However, the primary reason Jesus repeatedly insisted on this kind of silence is found in Mark 8:30–31. After His disciples identified Him as the Messiah and the Son of God (v. 29; cf. Matt. 16:18), "He warned them to tell no one about Him. And He began to teach them that the Son of Man must suffer many things and be rejected by the elders and the chief priests and the scribes, and be killed, and after three days rise again." Knowing that His earthly mission would not be accomplished until after His death and resurrection, Jesus instructed even His own disciples to remain quiet until after the story was complete. Many whom He healed knew Him merely as a miracle worker, but Jesus had come for a far more glorious purpose (cf. Luke 19:10). A message that highlighted only His miraculous healings would be inadequate. The full message about Him must include the truth that "Christ died for our sins according to the Scriptures, and that He was buried, and that He was raised on the third day according to the Scriptures" (1 Cor. 15:3–4).

Aware of their uncontainable elation, the Lord repeated His instruction, **but the more He ordered them, the more widely they continued to proclaim it.** In spite of His repeated commands, the man and his friends, unable to contain their joy, proved disobedient. Ironically, though Jesus had healed his ears, the man refused to listen to the Lord's instruction. It is likely that Jesus' admonition was also aimed at bystanders in the crowd who had witnessed this stunning miracle. The disciples must have wondered also why Jesus would issue such a command. Even they would only later come to understand the full story of Jesus' work—including His death and resurrection (cf. Mark 9:32; Luke 9:45; 18:34; John 12:16).

Upon seeing the miraculous wonders He did, including the transformation of this deaf man, the people in the crowd **were utterly astonished.** The word **utterly** comes from the Greek term *huperperissōs*, meaning "exceedingly," "above all measure," or "superabundantly." **Astonished** translates a form of the word *ekplessō*, which means "to be struck with amazement" or, colloquially, "to be blown out of one's mind." The people were completely awestruck and unable to contain themselves. So, in spite of Jesus' instruction to the contrary, they too spread the word everywhere.

In their excitement, the people exclaimed, **He has done all things well. He makes even the deaf to hear and the mute to speak.** The adverb **well** translates the Greek word *kalōs*, meaning "rightly," "correctly," or "appropriately." The people were commenting on the perfection of His miracles. He made the blind to see, the lame to walk, **the deaf to hear and the mute to speak.** Their recovery was immediate, and their restoration complete. Jesus' healings never failed; they were perfect every time.

The word **mute** comes from the Greek word *alalos*, meaning "without speech." That term is used only three times in the Gospels, all in Mark (cf. 7:37; 9:17, 25). Earlier, in verse 32, Mark used an even less common word to describe this man's condition. The phrase "spoke with difficulty" translates a form of the Greek word *mogilalos*, occurring only here in the New Testament. Significantly, that same word occurs only once in the Septuagint (the ancient Greek translation of the Old Testament) in Isaiah 35. That prophetic passage describes the wonders of the future millennial kingdom when Christ returns to reign on the earth: the desert will blossom with beautiful flowers (vv. 1–2), Israel and the surrounding nations will see the glory of the Lord God (v. 2), the weak and feeble will be encouraged (v. 3), and God's enemies will be judged and the righteous saved (v. 4). In that context, Isaiah writes, "Then the eyes of the blind will be opened and the ears of the deaf will be unstopped. Then the lame will leap like a deer, and the tongue of the mute will shout for joy" (vv. 5–6). The word "mute" (from the Hebrew word *'illem*) is translated by a form of the Greek word *mogilalos* in the Septuagint. By using that same rare term, Mark connected his account with the prophecy of Isaiah 35. The healings Jesus performed, like the curing of a deaf man with a severe speech impediment, were previews of the glories of His future messianic kingdom, when death and disease will be greatly diminished (cf. Isa. 29:18; 30:23; 32:14–15; 65:20).

Isaiah 35:8–10 continues its description of the millennial kingdom with a beautiful picture of the redeemed who will dwell there:

> A highway will be there, a roadway,
> And it will be called the Highway of Holiness.
> The unclean will not travel on it,
> But it will be for him who walks that way,
> And fools will not wander on it.
> No lion will be there,
> Nor will any vicious beast go up on it;
> These will not be found there.
> But the redeemed will walk there,
> And the ransomed of the Lord will return
> And come with joyful shouting to Zion,
> With everlasting joy upon their heads.
> They will find gladness and joy,
> And sorrow and sighing will flee away.

While the people Jesus healed physically during His ministry were right to rejoice, their momentary exuberance cannot compare to the eternal joys that await those whom He has saved spiritually and to whom He has promised eternal glorified bodies (cf. John 11:25–26; 1 Cor. 15:20–28, 35–56). During the millennial kingdom (cf. Rev. 20:1–6) and then forever on the new earth (cf. Rev. 21:1–22:5), the redeemed will exult in the wonder of their completed salvation.

By healing temporal maladies, the Lord Jesus pointed people to something greater: the hope of eternal life (cf. John 5:40; 6:35; 10:10; 17:2–3). Through Him, forgiveness from sin and reconciliation with God are readily available to everyone who believes the gospel, whether Jew or Gentile (cf. Rom. 1:16; 2 Cor. 5:20–21; Gal. 3:28). Jesus is infinitely more than a miracle worker and the greatest teacher. He is the only Savior (John 14:6; Acts 4:12) who died to pay the penalty for sin (cf. Isa. 53:4–5; Rom. 4:25; Col. 2:13–14; 1 Peter 3:18) and rose victoriously to demonstrate His power over death (cf. Acts 2:24; 17:31; Rom. 8:11; 1 Cor. 15:20–22, 54–56). Those who repent and believe in Him savingly will experience His life-giving power for all of eternity (cf. John 4:14; 7:38; Rev. 7:17; 21:6). Spiritually, their sinful hearts are cleansed at the moment of conversion (cf. Acts 10:43; 15:9; Rom. 8:1; 2 Cor. 5:17; Titus 3:4–7). Physically, their bodies will one day be resurrected, never to experience disease or decay again (cf. John 5:28–29; 1 Cor. 15:42–56; 2 Cor. 5:1–4; Rev. 21:4). In that state of glorified perfection, free from both sin and sickness, they will forever worship their Redeemer and King (cf. Rev. 5:13; 19:1–6; 22:3–4).

The Compassionate Provider
(Mark 8:1–10)

28

In those days, when there was again a large crowd and they had nothing to eat, Jesus called His disciples and said to them, "I feel compassion for the people because they have remained with Me now three days and have nothing to eat. If I send them away hungry to their homes, they will faint on the way; and some of them have come from a great distance." And His disciples answered Him, "Where will anyone be able to find enough bread here in this desolate place to satisfy these people?" And He was asking them, "How many loaves do you have?" And they said, "Seven." And He directed the people to sit down on the ground; and taking the seven loaves, He gave thanks and broke them, and started giving them to His disciples to serve to them, and they served them to the people. They also had a few small fish; and after He had blessed them, He ordered these to be served as well. And they ate and were satisfied; and they picked up seven large baskets full of what was left over of the broken pieces. About four thousand were there; and He sent them away. And immediately

He entered the boat with His disciples and came to the district of Dalmanutha. (8:1–10)

Shortly after the feeding of the five thousand (Mark 6:35–44) and the sermon on the bread of life (cf. John 6:35, 51), the Lord left Galilee for an extended time of private training with the Twelve. He and His disciples went first to the region of Tyre, where Jesus ministered to a Syrophoenician woman who exhibited great faith in Him (7:24–30). Next, they traveled north through Sidon, and then east and south to the region of Decapolis on the southeastern side of the Sea of Galilee (v. 31). In all, their circuitous journey through Gentile territory likely lasted for two or three months, providing the Twelve with focused personal instruction from their Lord.

During that time, the disciples would have been acutely aware that they were not in the land of Israel, a reality that fit the teaching purposes of Jesus as He began to prepare them for the Great Commission: to go into all the world and preach the gospel to people of every nation (Matt. 28:19–20; Acts 1:8). Like the reluctant prophet Jonah, the Israelites of Jesus' day despised the Gentiles and had no desire for their salvation. The disciples undoubtedly were affected by the racial bias of their culture (cf. Luke 9:54). That deeply rooted prejudice was opposite the heart of God, who from eternity's original decree intended the message of salvation to spread from His chosen people to all nations (cf. Gen. 12:3). It was critically important for the Twelve to understand that the gospel was a message for the whole world.

Their foray into Gentile territory ended in the region of Decapolis (Mark 7:31), which bordered the southeastern shores of the Sea of Galilee. The people there had heard about Jesus (cf. Mark 5:20), so that when He arrived, massive crowds came out to meet Him on a mountainside near the lake (cf. Matt. 15:29). There, He healed the sick who were brought to Him, including the lame, crippled, blind, deaf, mute, and many others (v. 30; cf. Mark 7:31–37). As a result, the Gentile multitude "marveled as they saw the mute speaking, the crippled restored, and the lame walking, and the blind seeing; and they glorified the God of Israel" (Matt. 15:31).

The event recorded in Mark 8:1–10 culminates Jesus' journey through those Gentile areas. This passage can be divided into four segments: the merciful compassion of the Lord, the myopic consternation of the disciples, the miraculous creation of a meal, and the ministry cultivation of the Twelve.

THE MERCIFUL COMPASSION OF THE LORD

In those days, when there was again a large crowd and they had nothing to eat, Jesus called His disciples and said to them, "I feel compassion for the people because they have remained with Me now three days and have nothing to eat. If I send them away hungry to their homes, they will faint on the way; and some of them have come from a great distance." (8:1–3)

The first feeding of thousands (Mark 6:35–44) took place on the northeast side of the Sea of Galilee, near the time of the feast of Passover (John 6:4), when the hills around the lake were lush with grass (cf. Matt. 14:19; John 6:10). Several months had likely passed since that miraculous event, a point suggested by the description of the hillsides as mere "ground" on this occasion (Matt. 15:35; Mark 8:6). Under the intense heat of summer, the green grass of spring would begin to wither away and die.

It was **in those days** that **there was again a large crowd and they had nothing to eat.** The massive multitude had been drawn to Jesus by His miracles (cf. Matt. 15:29–31; Mark 7:31–37). Though they were Gentiles from a pagan region, their response was one of praise to the God of Israel. Mark uses the word **again** to indicate that this **large crowd** with **nothing to eat** should not be confused with the earlier Jewish multitude whom Jesus fed near Bethsaida. (For more on the distinction between those two events, see the discussion below.)

Jesus called His disciples and said to them, "I feel compassion for the people." Though the gospel writers repeatedly state that Jesus felt compassion toward people (cf. Matt. 9:36; 14:14; 15:32; 20:34; Mark 1:41; 6:34; Luke 7:13), only here and in the parallel passage (Matt. 15:32) did Jesus, speaking in the first person, declare this about Himself. The verb translated **feel compassion** (from the Greek word *splanchnizomai*) literally means "to be moved in one's bowels," the visceral organs where the feelings of pain are felt, so that the ancients considered them to be the seat of emotions. The idea was similar to modern expressions like a "gut-wrenching" emotion or a feeling "in the pit of one's stomach." The English word **compassion** comes from a Latin word meaning, "to suffer with," and conveys feelings of deep sympathy, pity, and kindness toward those who are hurting.

Throughout the Old Testament, God repeatedly revealed Himself as the God of compassion. In Exodus 34:6, the Lord God declared Himself to be "compassionate and gracious, slow to anger, and abounding in lovingkindness and truth." Moses reiterated that divine attribute to the Israelites in Deuteronomy 4:31, "For the Lord your God is a compassionate God; He will not fail you nor destroy you nor forget the covenant with your fathers which He swore to them." The book of Psalms echoes that truth: "The Lord is compassionate and gracious, slow to anger and abounding in lovingkindness" (Ps. 103:8; cf. 111:4). Even when the nation of Israel proved unfaithful, "the Lord was gracious to them and had compassion on them and turned to them because of His covenant with Abraham, Isaac, and Jacob, and would not destroy them or cast them from His presence until now" (2 Kings 13:23; cf. 2 Chron. 36:14; Neh. 9:17; Joel 2:13). As the prophet Jeremiah declared, even after the fall of Jerusalem, "The Lord's lovingkindnesses indeed never cease, for His compassions never fail" (Lam. 3:22; cf. Mic. 7:19).

Because He is God, divine compassion marked the life of Christ. Jesus expressed merciful care both for people's spiritual needs (cf. Matt. 9:36; Mark 6:34) and for their physical afflictions (Matt. 14:14); He extended that care to both Jews and Gentiles (cf. Matt. 8:5–13; 15:22–31; Mark 7:31–37). On this occasion, the Lord felt compassion for this crowd specifically **because they** had **remained with** Him for **three days** with **nothing to eat.** In their eagerness to hear Jesus' teaching and witness His miracles, the people refused to go home—even if it meant sleeping outside and missing a few meals. Overwhelmed with the Lord Jesus, they put hunger aside. He recognized what perhaps they themselves did not even realize. Speaking to His disciples, the Lord said, **If I send them away hungry to their homes, they will faint on the way; and some of them have come from a great distance.** The word **faint** (from the Greek verb *ekluō*) means "to weaken" or "to collapse," like a bowstring that goes limp when unstrung. Knowing that the people had not eaten for three days, and that some of them would be traveling long distances to return home, Jesus responded with compassion.

THE MYOPIC CONSTERNATION OF THE DISCIPLES

And His disciples answered Him, "Where will anyone be able to find enough bread here in this desolate place to satisfy these people?" And He was asking them, "How many loaves do you have?" And they said, "Seven." (8:4–5)

The disciples answered Jesus by asking, **"Where will anyone be able to find enough bread here in this desolate place to satisfy these people?"** At first glance, the Twelve seem to react in almost the same way as before, during the feeding of the thousands near Bethsaida (6:35–37). Certainly, they had not forgotten what Jesus had done a few months earlier. So why did they ask almost the same question as before? Did they not know the Lord Jesus could provide as He had done earlier? The answer is that they did. Their question is best understood as a kind of tongue-in-cheek acknowledgment of the earlier miracle, and their own admission that they had again no adequacy or resources for such a vast need. It was not intended to cast doubt on Jesus' miraculous power, but rather to emphasize the fact that, if a crowd this large was going to be fed in that remote location, it would require another creation of food. The word translated **to satisfy,** from the Greek verb *chortazō*, derives its meaning from the world of animal husbandry where it described livestock eating until they were completely full. It is the same word used to describe the satisfied multitude in Mark 6:42.

If the disciples had any doubts about what was about to happen, it was not Jesus' power they questioned but His purpose. This crowd consisted of Gentiles, people outside of the Abrahamic covenant whom the Jews considered to be unclean. It was one thing for Jesus to heal them, but the creation of a meal went one step further. For Jewish people to eat with Gentiles was forbidden by rabbinic regulations (cf. Acts 10:28; 11:3; Gal. 2:18). Understandably, that idea would likely have caused consternation among the disciples. Yet, Jesus was teaching them an important lesson about how far the gospel would extend. Thus, this miracle served as a fitting climax to the time He and the Twelve spent traveling through Gentile territory.

In order to highlight the miraculous nature of what He was about to do and perhaps to remind the disciples of what He had done before, Jesus **was asking them, "How many loaves do you have?" And they said, "Seven."** In verse 7, Mark explains that "they also had a few small fish." Before the previous creation of food for thousands, the disciples found five loaves and two fish (Mark 6:41). On this occasion, they managed to collect seven loaves and several fish. Bread and fish comprised the typical meal for those who lived around the lake. Obviously, such meager supplies were useless in feeding such a massive crowd. The apostles knew that, but they also knew the power of their Creator Lord.

THE MIRACULOUS CREATION OF A MEAL

And He directed the people to sit down on the ground; and taking the seven loaves, He gave thanks and broke them, and started giving them to His disciples to serve to them, and they served them to the people. They also had a few small fish; and after He had blessed them, He ordered these to be served as well. And they ate and were satisfied; and they picked up seven large baskets full of what was left over of the broken pieces. About four thousand were there; and He sent them away. (8:6–9)

As Jesus had done before, **He directed the people to sit on the ground,** perhaps in groups of hundreds and fifties (cf. Mark 6:40) in order to separate them for the distribution of the meal. **Taking the seven loaves,** a form of flatbread, **He gave thanks and broke them.** By giving thanks to the Father, Jesus not only modeled what it means to depend on God for daily provisions (cf. Matt. 6:11), He also signified to the crowd of onlookers that the power behind the miracle was divine.

Without any apparent exertion or strain, Jesus **started giving** pieces of bread **to His disciples to serve to them, and they served**

them to the people. They also had a few small fish; and after He had blessed them, He ordered these to be served as well. As with the previous miraculous provision, no natural explanation is possible. This was the spontaneous and continuous creation of bread and fish by the Creator of all things Himself (cf. John 1:3; Col. 1:16; Heb. 1:3). The Lord kept bringing meals into existence out of nothing as the disciples distributed them to those in the crowd until everyone was fed. Of course, in addition to miraculously creating the food, Jesus could have supernaturally distributed it to the people. The Lord involved His disciples in order to allow them to participate in the expression of heavenly compassion. Their involvement also symbolized their future role as soul-feeding messengers of the life-giving gospel. Soon, they would distribute the message of the bread of life to the whole world.

With the food created and disseminated, the people **ate and were satisfied.** The word **satisfied** comes from the same Greek word found in verse 4 and indicates that the hungry crowds, after three days without eating, feasted until they were totally satisfied. When the meal was over, the Twelve **picked up seven large baskets full of what was left over of the broken pieces.** As they had done previously at the meal near Bethsaida, when they collected twelve baskets of food (6:43), the disciples gathered what was left. None of the food was wasted. **Large baskets** translates a form of the Greek word *spuris*, the same word used to describe the basket that lowered Paul over the side of a Damascus wall (Acts 9:25). These baskets were different than the small baskets (from the Greek *kophinos*) that the disciples used on the previous occasion. Jesus later distinguished between the two miraculous meals by reminding the disciples of the different baskets they had used. In Mark 8:18–20, Jesus asked them,

> "Do you not remember, when I broke the five loaves for the five thousand, how many baskets [from *kophinos*] full of broken pieces you picked up?" They said to Him, "Twelve." "When I broke the seven for the four thousand, how many large baskets [from *spuris*] full of broken pieces did you pick up?" And they said to Him, "Seven."

The different types of baskets are not the only distinction between this miraculous feeding and the one that occurred earlier (in Mark 6:35–44).

The locations (Bethsaida vs. Decapolis); the audience (Jews vs. Gentiles); the number of men present (5,000 vs. 4,000); the length of time the crowd lingered beforehand (one day vs. three days); and the number of loaves (five vs. seven) were all different. Moreover, Jesus Himself distinguished between the two events (Mark 8:18–20); Matthew and Mark recorded both occasions as being two separate miracles. Though some modern skeptics suggest these two events should be conflated, that notion is clearly unsupported by the biblical text.

Mark's comment that **about four thousand were there** refers only to the total number of men. The parallel passage in Matthew 15:38 makes that point explicit, "Those who ate were four thousand men, besides women and children." With four thousand households represented, the crowd could have easily numbered between fifteen and twenty thousand. Neither Matthew nor Mark record the response of the people, though they were undoubtedly elated. Perhaps some of them wanted to make Jesus king, just as the multitude had tried to do near Bethsaida (cf. John 6:15). As on that occasion, after the meal, **He** ended the astounding event and **sent them away.**

The Ministry Cultivation of the Twelve

And immediately He entered the boat with His disciples and came to the district of Dalmanutha. (8:10)

After the three days of intense ministry, filled with miraculous healings and culminating in a supernatural meal, Jesus left the region of Decapolis to return to Galilee for a short time. **Immediately He entered the boat with His disciples and came to the district of Dalmanutha.** The parallel passage, Matthew 15:39, identifies their destination as "the region of Magadan." The two accounts are not contradictory but use two different names to refer to the same area between the towns of Magdala and Capernaum. Jesus' return to Galilee brought His excursion into Gentile territory full circle—from Tyre to Sidon to Decapolis and back to Galilee. The cross was now less than a year away, and it would not be long before Jesus transitioned His ministry focus to Judea and Jerusalem.

As noted above, Jesus' journey into Gentile lands provided the Twelve with an extended time of personal training and critical instruction. In the process, they received invaluable preparation in at least four areas. First, they were exposed to Jesus' divine person. They witnessed His authority over demons (Mark 7:29–30), His power over disease (7:31–37), and His ability to create food spontaneously (8:1–9). They watched as people with incurable diseases and physical disabilities—from blindness to paralysis to deafness—were brought to Jesus and healed immediately and completely by Him. The disciples understood that only God could be the source of such power, which is why they confessed Jesus to be God's Son (cf. Matt. 14:33; 16:16).

Second, they learned that the ultimate priority in life is worship. As Jesus had earlier explained to a woman in Samaria, "An hour is coming, and now is, when the true worshipers will worship the Father in spirit and truth; for such people the Father seeks to be His worshipers. God is spirit, and those who worship Him must worship in spirit and truth" (John 4:23–24). During their journey outside of Galilee, the disciples saw that principle fleshed out in a Gentile context. It was a Syrophoenician whom Jesus commended for her great faith (Matt. 15:28). And it was the Gentile crowds in the region of Decapolis who witnessed Jesus' miracles and "glorified the God of Israel" (v. 31). By contrast, the religious leaders of Israel had substituted coldhearted religion full of rabbinic rules and restrictions for true worship (Mark 7:1–13). It is essential to recognize that difference.

Third, having been there for both of the meals Jesus miraculously created, the disciples began to understand the divine resources available to them. Though their faith was still weak in this regard (cf. 8:16–21), it was necessary for them to embrace the promise of Matthew 6:31–33,

> Do not worry then, saying, "What will we eat?" or "What will we drink?" or "What will we wear for clothing?" For the Gentiles eagerly seek all these things; for your heavenly Father knows that you need all these things. But seek first His kingdom and His righteousness, and all these things will be added to you.

The disciples had no ability in themselves to feed hungry crowds or give spiritual life to wasted souls. But Jesus did. His resources were infinite,

His power limitless, and His providential precision perfect. They simply needed to depend on Him (cf. Heb. 13:5–6). By involving them in the distribution of food to the multitudes, the Lord provided them with a vivid illustration of God's inexhaustible care that was especially designed not for the body but the soul.

Fourth, the disciples witnessed the Lord's compassion dramatically displayed toward people whom first-century Jews generally treated with scorn and disdain. It made sense to them that the Messiah would perform miracles for the people of Israel. But to think that He would also cast out demons, heal diseases, and create meals for Gentiles represented a major paradigm shift. Yet, it was a lesson the disciples desperately needed to learn, as Jesus prepared them to take the message of salvation to the ends of the world. As one commentator explains:

> From the church fathers onward the church has rightly perceived that in the feeding of the four thousand Jesus brings saving bread to the Gentiles, as he brought it earlier to the Jews in the feeding of the five thousand. The journey to the Gentiles in 7:24–8:9 has evinced that they are neither beyond the reach of salvation nor inured to it. Like the book of Jonah, the three vignettes in Mark 7:24–8:9 reveal that supposed Gentile outsiders are in fact surprisingly receptive to the word of God in Jesus. The journey of Jesus to Tyre, Sidon, and the Decapolis proves that although the Gentiles are ostracized by the Jews, they are not ostracized by God. Jewish invective against the Gentiles does not reflect a divine invective. There is a lesson here for the people of God in every age, that its enemies are neither forsaken by God nor beyond the compassion of Jesus. (James R. Edwards, *The Gospel according to Mark* [Grand Rapids: Eerdmans, 2002], 232)

A short time earlier, Jesus' Galilean ministry had culminated with thousands of Jews being miraculously fed. His foray into Gentile territory similarly ended with the creation of a supernatural meal. Both occasions were previews of the coming glories of the messianic kingdom, in which all of the redeemed, both Jew and Gentile, will participate in the celebratory banquet of the Lamb (cf. Rev. 19:9).

As demonstrated by all of Jesus' miracles, it is the nature of God to care for those in need. Whenever Jesus healed an infirmity, cast out a demon, raised a dead person to life, or fed a hungry multitude, He put God's compassion on display. That compassion reached its highest point at the cross. As the Lord Himself said on the night before His death, "Greater love has no one than this, that one lay down his life for his friends" (John 15:13; cf. Heb. 2:17; 1 John 3:16). To satisfy the crowd's physical hunger after three days required compassion and supernatural power, but to save their souls for eternity required something far more— supernatural sacrifice. Jesus willingly went to the cross to bear the full weight of divine punishment for the sins of all who would ever believe in Him (cf. 2 Cor. 5:21).

Spiritual Blindness (Mark 8:11–26)

29

The Pharisees came out and began to argue with Him, seeking from Him a sign from heaven, to test Him. Sighing deeply in His spirit, He said, "Why does this generation seek for a sign? Truly I say to you, no sign will be given to this generation." Leaving them, He again embarked and went away to the other side. And they had forgotten to take bread, and did not have more than one loaf in the boat with them. And He was giving orders to them, saying, "Watch out! Beware of the leaven of the Pharisees and the leaven of Herod." They began to discuss with one another the fact that they had no bread. And Jesus, aware of this, said to them, "Why do you discuss the fact that you have no bread? Do you not yet see or understand? Do you have a hardened heart? Having eyes, do you not see? And having ears, do you not hear? And do you not remember, when I broke the five loaves for the five thousand, how many baskets full of broken pieces you picked up?" They said to Him, "Twelve." "When I broke the seven for the four thousand, how many large baskets full of broken pieces did you

pick up?" And they said to Him, "Seven." And He was saying to them, "Do you not yet understand?" And they came to Bethsaida. And they brought a blind man to Jesus and implored Him to touch him. Taking the blind man by the hand, He brought him out of the village; and after spitting on his eyes and laying His hands on him, He asked him, "Do you see anything?" And he looked up and said, "I see men, for I see them like trees, walking around." Then again He laid His hands on his eyes; and he looked intently and was restored, and began to see everything clearly. And He sent him to his home, saying, "Do not even enter the village." (8:11–26)

Since the fall of Adam and Eve into sin (Gen. 3:6–19), every human being has been born spiritually blind (cf. Rom. 1:21; 3:23). The eyes of their hearts are clouded by sin (cf. Eph. 4:17–18) and darkened by Satan (cf. 2 Cor. 4:3–4), so that they naturally love the darkness and hate the light (John 3:19–20). Unable to comprehend truth (1 Cor. 2:14), they stumble through life groping for answers (cf. Acts 17:27) as they wander in moral and spiritual confusion (Ps. 82:5; Prov. 4:19).

For some, this blindness is temporary. By God's grace, their minds are illuminated by the Holy Spirit to see the light of the gospel and embrace the Lord Jesus Christ in saving faith (cf. Acts 26:18; 1 John 2:8). As Jesus Himself explained, "I have come as Light into the world, so that everyone who believes in Me will not remain in darkness" (John 12:46; cf. John 1:9; 8:12; 9:5). The reception of such spiritual sight requires a supernatural work of God (cf. Col. 1:13). The apostle Paul compared it to the miracle of creation: "For God, who said, 'Light shall shine out of darkness,' is the One who has shone in our hearts to give the Light of the knowledge of the glory of God in the face of Christ" (2 Cor. 4:6). As new creatures in Christ (2 Cor. 5:17), believers are given the mind of Christ by which they can understand and appropriate spiritual truth (1 Cor. 2:10–16; Eph. 5:8; 1 Thess. 5:5). Such understanding is only possible because the eyes of their hearts have been enlightened (cf. Eph. 1:18).

For many others, their blindness is permanent and eternal. Refusing to embrace the Lord Jesus in saving faith, they remain in the total darkness of sinful rebellion and unbelief (cf. John 1:4–5; 1 John 2:9).

Though they may be externally religious, in reality they are spiritually ignorant and self-deceived (cf. John 12:35). The Jewish religious leaders of Jesus' day, for example, considered themselves to be the most enlightened of all people (cf. John 9:41). Yet, the Lord condemned them as "blind leaders of the blind" (Matt. 15:14 KJV). Though they had been given the Old Testament Scriptures and the biblical covenants, their spiritual blindness was so acute that they refused to receive their own Messiah (John 1:11).

When sinners persist in rejecting the truth, there comes a point when God gives them over to the consequences of their unbelief (Rom. 1:24, 28–32). They are thus confirmed in their blindness as an act of divine judgment, and the truth is hidden from them (cf. Mark 4:12). Jesus referred to this form of blindness when He wept over Jerusalem, "saying, 'If you had known in this day, even you, the things which make for peace! But now they have been hidden from your eyes" (Luke 19:41–42). Because the religious leaders would not repent but continually hardened their hearts instead, they crossed a line past which they could not repent (cf. Mark 3:28–30). Thus, judgment became inevitable (cf. Luke 19:43–44; John 3:18).

This section (Mark 8:11–26) illustrates the difference between those who are permanently blind and those whose blindness is only temporary. On the one hand, the Pharisees' unwillingness to receive the truth signified a terminal condition with everlastingly devastating consequences. On the other hand, Jesus' disciples eagerly desired to embrace the truth. Though they sometimes struggled to comprehend spiritual realities, their lack of clarity was only temporary. Finally, by healing a blind man, Jesus provided a vivid illustration of temporary blindness and spiritual sight.

THE PERMANENT BLINDNESS OF THE PHARISEES

The Pharisees came out and began to argue with Him, seeking from Him a sign from heaven, to test Him. Sighing deeply in His spirit, He said, "Why does this generation seek for a sign? Truly I say to you, no sign will be given to this generation." (8:11–12)

After spending an extended time with His disciples in Gentile territory, traveling from Tyre (7:24–30) to Sidon (7:31) to the Decapolis (7:31–8:9), Jesus returned to the Jewish region of Galilee (8:10). Having arrived in Dalmanutha in the region of Magadan (Matt. 15:39), located somewhere along the western shore of the lake not far from Capernaum, the Lord was soon confronted by a hostile group of Pharisees. Motivated by spite and malice, their only interest in Jesus was to discredit Him and plot His murder. Their menacing attitude stood in stark contrast to that of the Gentiles, who had welcomed Jesus and praised God because of Him (Matt. 15:31; Mark 7:37).

In their confrontation with Jesus, the Pharisees exhibited three characteristics of those with permanent spiritual blindness. First, they found common ground in their hatred for the Light. According to the parallel passage in Matthew 16:1, **the Pharisees** who **came out** to meet Jesus were accompanied by a group of Sadducees. Under normal circumstances, the Pharisees and Sadducees were bitter rivals (cf. Acts 23:6–10). The Pharisees were fastidious legalists who sought to separate themselves from any form of moral or cultural defilement. Zealous to protect institutional Judaism from Greek influence, they elevated rabbinic traditions to a place of equal authority with Scripture (cf. Mark 7:8, 13). (For more on the Pharisees, see chapter 7 in this volume.) The Sadducees, by contrast, had no regard for the oral traditions of the Pharisees. Though they paid lip service to the Torah, they denied key doctrines like the existence of angels, the resurrection of the body, and the immortality of the soul (cf. Mark 12:18; Acts 4:1–2; 23:8). Generally aristocratic, the Sadducees (many of whom were priests—cf. Acts 4:1; 5:17) were the guardians of temple policies and operations, including lucrative (and corrupt) practices like money changing and the sale of sacrificial animals (cf. Mark 11:15–19; John 2:14–17). Despite their significant animosity toward each other, the Pharisees and Sadducees were united by their common rejection of the Savior.

Fueled by a mutual hatred for Jesus, representatives from both parties **began to argue with Him, seeking from Him a sign from heaven.** A popular Jewish superstition alleged that demons could mimic earthly miracles (like the signs performed by the magicians in Pharaoh's court; Ex. 7:11–12, 22), but only God could work wonders in the sky. The religious leaders could not deny that Jesus performed miracles on earth, but they insisted that He did so through the power of Satan (cf. Mark 3:22). Thus, if Jesus were unable to perform a miraculous sign in the heavens, it would bolster their claim to the people that He was not empowered by God.

Clearly, making the demand for **a sign from heaven** was nothing more than setting a trap, intended **to test** Jesus in the hopes that He would fail and be discredited. As it was, Jesus had already provided ample evidence to demonstrate His divine power (including heavenly signs—cf. Mark 1:9–11; 4:39–41), but they stubbornly refused to believe in Him. The religious leaders clearly did not need to receive more proof by seeing another miracle; even if Jesus accommodated their request, their unbelief would have remained unchanged (cf. John 12:37–40). Among the Pharisees who interacted with Jesus, Nicodemus is the only recorded example of one whose salvation faith began to come to life when he recognized the self-evident truth that Jesus' power was divine. As he said to Christ, "Rabbi, we know that You have come from God as a teacher; for no one can do these signs that You do unless God is with him" (John 3:2). Yet, most of the religious leaders rejected Jesus anyway. They did not recognize that Jesus, the incarnate Son of God standing in their midst, was Himself the ultimate sign from heaven (cf. John 8:23).

On this and other occasions, the religious leaders exhibited a second characteristic of permanent spiritual blindness: they responded to additional light with more intense rejection. The Pharisees and Sadducees were no different than Pharaoh who, with each sign that Moses performed, hardened his heart even more (Ex. 8:32; 9:12, etc.). Rather than responding in faith to the light of the Savior, they retreated even farther into the darkness. Jesus responded emotionally to their resolute faithlessness by **sighing deeply in His spirit.** A simple form of this same verb is found in Mark 7:34, where Jesus sighed in response to the suffering of a deaf man. Here, the compound form expresses even stronger emotion. The willful blindness of the religious leaders broke the Lord's heart, later causing Him to weep over the people of Jerusalem (Luke 19:41).

Jesus rebuked their inexcusable unbelief with a condemning question. **He said, "Why does this generation seek for a sign?"**

Looking beyond just the Pharisees and Sadducees who stood before Him, the Lord indicted the entire generation of Israelites who followed their apostate teaching (cf. Matt. 16:4). Like their ancestors who fell into apostasy (cf. Deut. 32:20; Judg. 2:10–11) and persecuted the prophets (cf. Matt. 23:29–36), the Jews of Jesus' day proved similarly faithless. Their willful rejection was such that no sign would convince them to believe. When confronted by the light, they ran deeper into the shrouded gloom of their self-righteous traditions. There was therefore no reason for Jesus to perform another miracle, since it would have only compounded their guilt. The permanence of their blindness was such that Jesus issued an unalterable verdict: **Truly I say to you, no sign will be given to this generation.** The Lord would not oblige the wicked demands of hard-hearted unbelievers.

The parallel passage in Matthew 16:1–5 expands on Mark's account:

> The Pharisees and Sadducees came up, and testing Jesus, they asked Him to show them a sign from heaven. But He replied to them, "When it is evening, you say, 'It will be fair weather, for the sky is red.' And in the morning, 'There will be a storm today, for the sky is red and threatening.' Do you know how to discern the appearance of the sky, but cannot discern the signs of the times? An evil and adulterous generation seeks after a sign; and a sign will not be given it, except the sign of Jonah." And He left them and went away.

Because the Pharisees and Sadducees insisted on seeing a sign in the sky, Jesus used an illustration involving the heavens to expose their folly. Their method of predicting the weather by looking to the color of the sky was primitive and crude. Yet, ironically, they were better meteorologists than theologians. They could recognize a coming storm from something as subtle as a ruddy morning hue, but they failed to recognize the coming of the Messiah in spite of the abundant evidence that was right in front of them. If the countless miracles Jesus had already performed could not convince them, nothing else would (cf. John 5:36; 10:37–38). Jesus' reference to the sign of Jonah referred to His death and resurrection (cf. Matt. 12:39–40), the ultimate testimony to His power and His victory over sin, death, and Satan. Sadly, even that would be knowingly rejected by the religious leaders, who bribed the Roman soldiers, instructing them to spread lies about what actually took place at the tomb (cf. Matt. 28:11–15).

In their hard-hearted stubbornness, the religious leaders illustrated a third characteristic of permanent spiritual blindness: persistent rejection of the light inevitably brings eternal darkness. The beginning of verse 13 spells out the terminal consequences of their willful unbelief: Jesus left them (cf. Matt. 16:4). Knowing the Pharisees and Sadducees would not believe, He abandoned them to their own self-righteous delusions (cf. Rom. 1:24, 26, 28). They were blind men (Matt. 23:17, 19) and blind guides (v. 24) leading their followers to hell by knowingly refusing to believe (cf. Matt. 23:15). The consequences of their terminal blindness were forever irreversible. They had long since rejected the Messiah (cf. Mark 3:6, 22), and He had consequently rejected them. The Bible appropriately describes hell as "outer darkness" (Matt. 8:12; 22:13; 25:30) because it is a place of everlasting spiritual blindness. The tragic reality is that the whole world is filled with people who, like these apostate religious leaders, have rejected the light. Because they love the darkness of their sin (John 3:19), they will one day be cast into the darkness of everlasting punishment.

That Jesus left the Pharisees and Sadducees signified more than a temporary separation. This exchange constituted Jesus' final conflict with the religious leaders in Galilee. Once again, they tried to put Him to a test He would fail (cf. Deut. 6:16). And once again, they failed and He rebuked them for their hard-hearted unbelief. From this point forward, the Lord's miracles, like His parables, would primarily be intended for His disciples, and not for the religious leaders or even the crowds. Moreover, His public ministry in Galilee had come to its end. When He later made a trip through the region, He did so secretly (cf. Mark 9:30). The populace of Galilee had been given ample opportunity to repent and believe, but they did not (cf. Matt. 11:20–24). Having been finally rejected by them, Jesus shifted His focus to Judea and Jerusalem, and ultimately the cross.

THE TEMPORARY BLINDNESS OF THE DISCIPLES

Leaving them, He again embarked and went away to the other side. And they had forgotten to take bread, and did not have

more than one loaf in the boat with them. And He was giving orders to them, saying, "Watch out! Beware of the leaven of the Pharisees and the leaven of Herod." They began to discuss with one another the fact that they had no bread. And Jesus, aware of this, said to them, "Why do you discuss the fact that you have no bread? Do you not yet see or understand? Do you have a hardened heart? Having eyes, do you not see? And having ears, do you not hear? And do you not remember, when I broke the five loaves for the five thousand, how many baskets full of broken pieces you picked up?" They said to Him, "Twelve." "When I broke the seven for the four thousand, how many large baskets full of broken pieces did you pick up?" And they said to Him, "Seven." And He was saying to them, "Do you not yet understand?" (8:13–21)

In contrast to the Jewish religious leaders and the apostate generation they represented, a small remnant of true believers saw the light and followed it (cf. John 1:12). That group, known as the disciples (from the Greek word *mathētēs*, meaning "learners"), included the twelve apostles and other loyal followers of Jesus. Unlike the Pharisees, who loved the darkness, the disciples loved the light and sought the truth. They willingly rejected the blind religious leaders in order to follow Jesus (cf. Mark 10:28), because they knew Him to be the Light of the World (cf. Mark 8:29; John 6:69).

Leaving the incorrigible Pharisees and Sadducees behind, Jesus and His disciples again **embarked and went away to the other side** of the Sea of Galilee, crossing the lake to its northeastern shore. Jesus' departure symbolized a tragic reality: the religious leaders of Galilee had rejected the light, and darkness settled in because the light was gone. But the Lord was accompanied by His disciples, those who had embraced Him in saving faith. Though they had once been spiritually blind like the Pharisees, the veil over their hearts had been lifted by divine regeneration so that they could believe (cf. 2 Cor. 3:15–18). Even so, there were still times when the disciples failed to understand the things Jesus taught them (cf. Mark 9:32; Luke 2:50; 9:45; John 12:16; 14:9; 20:9). Unlike the religious leaders, their lack of clarity about spiritual matters was only temporary.

On this occasion, the disciples demonstrated their obtuseness when, in spite of the significant interchange that had just occurred, they became preoccupied with the mundane. As they traveled across the lake, growing increasingly hungry, they realized **they had forgotten to take bread, and did not have more than one loaf in the boat with them.** The northeastern shores near Bethsaida were less populated and fairly remote (cf. Mark 6:35), and the disciples wondered where they would eat their next meal. Though they had been so long with Jesus, their thinking still operated primarily on a natural level.

Jesus, however, was focused on matters of eternal significance. In light of His confrontation with the religious leaders, there were important lessons the disciples needed to learn. **And** so, ignoring their hunger, **He was giving orders to them.** The imperfect tense of the verb **giving orders** (from the Greek word *diastellomai*, meaning "to charge" or "to command") indicates that this emphatic instruction from Christ was repeated and ongoing. The Lord's insistent warning to the disciples was, **Watch out! Beware of the leaven of the Pharisees and the leaven of Herod.** The parallel account in Matthew 16:6 notes that Jesus' admonition also included the leaven of the Sadducees. **Leaven,** or yeast, is used in Scripture to illustrate influence. Because a small amount of yeast is able to permeate a relatively large amount of dough and cause it to rise, leaven served as a fitting illustration of spiritual influences that produce dramatic effects—whether positive (cf. Matt. 13:33; Luke 13:21) or negative, as in this passage.

The Pharisees, Sadducees, and Herodians comprised three influential parties in first-century Israel. They were very divergent from each other, yet all three hated Jesus (cf. Matt. 16:1; Mark 3:6; John 11:47–53), and each posed a serious spiritual threat to the disciples. The **leaven of the Pharisees** included both their doctrinal errors and personal hypocrisy (cf. Luke 12:1). Their system of works-righteousness and superficial externalism produced spiritual frauds who looked good on the outside but inwardly were full of death and uncleanness (cf. Matt. 23:27). The leaven of the Sadducees consisted of pragmatism, rationalism, and materialism. Their denial of key doctrinal truths, like the resurrection of the body and the immortality of the soul, and their willingness to use the temple to exploit people financially, made their teachings as dangerous as those of the Pharisees (cf. Matt. 16:12). **The leaven of Herod** referred to the depraved, immoral behavior that characterized Herod Antipas and all who emulated him (cf. Mark 6:21–28). The Herodians were secularists who openly welcomed the immoral influences of Roman culture. But that kind of worldliness had no place among the followers of Christ (cf. 1 John 2:15–17). Thus, Jesus' admonition provided a somber warning against the ever-present temptations of legalism, hypocrisy, rationalism, materialism, immorality, and worldliness.

Incredibly, the disciples responded to Jesus' instruction by thinking only about physical food. The Lord had been using figurative language to warn them about destructive spiritual influences, but they thought He was talking about literal yeast (cf. Matt. 16:12). With dinner on their minds, **they began to discuss with one another the fact that they had no bread.** Though the cross was less than a year away, Jesus' followers were still more concerned about physical realities than spiritual truths. Consequently, they completely missed the significance of the Lord's instruction. As on other occasions, their response demonstrated the weakness of their faith (cf. Matt. 6:30; 8:26; 14:31). Though their eyes had been opened to embrace the truth of the gospel, some elements of spiritual dullness clearly remained. **Aware of this,** the Lord exhibited patience in His response to the disciples, although He was undoubtedly grieved by their thickheadedness. Jesus **said to them, "Why do you discuss the fact that you have no bread?"** The nature of their conversation evidenced a level of immaturity, lack of understanding, and weak faith.

Earlier, when Jesus explained that He would teach the multitudes in parables, He told His disciples, "To you has been given the mystery of the kingdom of God, but those who are outside get everything in parables, so that while seeing, they may see and not perceive, and while hearing, they may hear and not understand, otherwise they might return and be forgiven" (Mark 4:11–12). On this occasion, Jesus turned those statements into rhetorical questions that formed a mild rebuke for the disciples: **Do you not yet see or understand? Do you have a hardened heart? Having eyes, do you not see? And having ears, do you not hear?** The disciples were not in the same category as the unbelieving crowds. They had been given spiritual understanding and their hearts were not hard. Thus there was no excuse for their utter lack of perception.

The last thing the disciples needed to worry about was where to find food. On two recent occasions, they had witnessed Jesus miraculously create meals for thousands of people (Mark 6:33–44; 8:1–10). In light of His power, they had no reason to be anxious about what they would eat. Jesus reminded them of this truth by further asking them, **"And do you not remember, when I broke the five loaves for the five thousand, how many baskets full of broken pieces you picked up?" They said to Him, "Twelve." "When I broke the seven for the four thousand, how many large baskets full of broken pieces did you pick up?" And they said to Him, "Seven."** Because they were in the presence of the Creator, there was obviously no need to be distracted by a lack of food. Their focus needed to be on the vital spiritual lessons Jesus was teaching. Graciously yet firmly, the Lord moved His disciples toward divine truth. After making it clear that He was not talking about literal leaven, **He was saying to them, "Do you not yet understand?"** Matthew 16:12 indicates that they finally did.

Though the disciples exhibited confusion on this occasion, their lack of spiritual understanding was not permanent like that of the Pharisees and Sadducees. A clear contrast can be seen between the two. The religious leaders found common ground in their hatred for Jesus; the disciples were united in their love for Him. The Pharisees and Sadducees reacted to additional light with greater rejection; the disciples responded with a deeper desire to learn more. The leaders' darkness deepened, the disciples' darkness dissipated. By persisting in their unbelief, the religious leaders were abandoned by Him and ultimately cast into everlasting hell. By embracing the Lord Jesus in saving faith, the disciples were embraced by Him and ultimately welcomed into eternal heaven.

Thus, in spite of the disciples' weaknesses and shortcomings, the Lord was glad to teach them. Whereas the religious leaders were shut off from divine revelation due to their unbelief, Jesus' followers (especially the Twelve) were the privileged recipients of His constant instruction. Even after His death and resurrection, the Lord continued to teach for forty days until He ascended into heaven (Acts 1:3). Though no longer physically present with them, He had already promised the apostles that He would continue to reveal truth to them through the Holy Spirit. On the night before His death, He told them, "The Helper, the Holy Spirit, whom the Father will send in My name, He will teach you all things, and bring to your remembrance all that I said to you" (John 14:26). He later added,

> "I have many more things to say to you, but you cannot bear them now. But when He, the Spirit of truth, comes, He will guide you into all the truth; for He will not speak on His own initiative, but whatever He hears, He will speak; and He will disclose to you what is to come. He will glorify Me; for He will take of Mine, and will disclose it to you. All things that the Father has are Mine; therefore I said, that He takes of Mine, and will disclose it to you." (John 16:12–15)

That revelation, given by Christ to the apostles through the Holy Spirit (e.g., "the apostles' teaching" in Acts 2:42), is preserved for every generation of believers in the writings of the New Testament.

Though the Lord has not given new revelation since the close of the New Testament canon and the passing of the apostolic age, believers have been given the complete Scripture, the Word of Christ (Col. 3:16), empowered and illuminated by the Holy Spirit (1 Cor. 2:14–16; cf. Ps. 119:18). Divine revelation in the Scripture is all that they need for life and godliness (cf. 2 Tim. 3:16–17; 2 Peter 1:2–3). As believers immerse themselves in the truth of Scripture, they inevitably grow in sanctification (1 Peter 2:1–3) and Christlikeness (2 Cor. 3:18). It was the Spirit who initially opened their eyes to the truth, and it is the Spirit who continues to elucidate that same truth of God's Word in their hearts (1 John 2:27). For those who know the Lord Jesus, any confusion they might have in this life is only temporary. One day they will enter the eternal light of heaven (cf. Rev. 21:23–25). As Paul expressed to the Corinthians, "For now we see in a mirror dimly, but then face to face; now I know in part, but then I will know fully just as I also have been fully known" (1 Cor. 13:12).

AN ILLUSTRATION OF TEMPORARY BLINDNESS

And they came to Bethsaida. And they brought a blind man to Jesus and implored Him to touch him. Taking the blind man by the hand, He brought him out of the village; and after spitting on his eyes and laying His hands on him, He asked him, "Do you see anything?" And he looked up and said, "I see men, for I see them

like trees, walking around." Then again He laid His hands on his eyes; and he looked intently and was restored, and began to see everything clearly. And He sent him to his home, saying, "Do not even enter the village." (8:22–26)

After sailing across the lake, Jesus and the disciples arrived at their destination on the northeastern shore. **They came to Bethsaida,** the hometown of Peter, Andrew, Philip, and possibly Nathanael (cf. John 1:44–45). The town of Bethsaida was near the place where Jesus fed the five thousand men plus women and children (Mark 6:41–44), and it is likely that many of the local residents were fed in that meal. (For more on Bethsaida, see chapter 22 in the current volume.)

Word undoubtedly spread quickly when Jesus arrived, and people began coming to be healed by Him. Among them were the friends or relatives who **brought a blind man to Jesus.** According to Jewish sources, blindness was widespread in the ancient world (cf. Lev. 19:14; 21:18; Deut. 27:18; 28:29; 2 Sam. 5:6, 8; Job 29:15), and Jesus healed a number of blind men throughout His ministry (Matt. 9:27–31; 11:5; 12:22; 15:30–31; 20:30–34; 21:14; Mark 10:46–52; Luke 4:18; 18:35–42; John 9:1–12; cf. Isa. 42:7). Those who suffered from blindness were helpless and reduced to begging (cf. Mark 10:46). Additionally, like others with disabilities or debilitating diseases, they were considered cursed by God (cf. John 9:1–2). That kind of stigma made living with blindness doubly painful.

The friends or relatives who brought this man to Jesus **implored Him to touch him.** The Lord often healed people, even those whom the Jewish religious establishment considered untouchable, by touching them. When Peter's mother-in-law was sick with a fever, Jesus took her by the hand and raised her up (Mark 1:31). When a leper fell before Him, the Lord "stretched out His hand and touched him" in order to heal him (v. 40). According to Mark 3:10, "He had healed many, with the result that all those who had afflictions pressed around Him in order to touch Him." In Mark 5:23, Jairus pleaded for his dying daughter, asking Jesus to come lay His hands on her. Along the way, a woman with an incurable hemorrhage was healed simply by touching the hem of Jesus' robe (vv. 27–29). Even in unbelieving Nazareth, Jesus "laid His hands on a few sick people and healed them" (6:5). Mark later reports that "wherever He entered villages, or cities, or countryside, they were laying the sick in the market places, and imploring Him that they might just touch the fringe of His cloak; and as many as touched it were being cured" (6:56). The Lord's willingness to touch the sick and suffering demonstrates His infinite loving-kindness. Unlike the aloof religious leaders of Israel, who avoided anything or anyone that might cause ceremonial defilement, Jesus did not keep His distance from hurting people. He reflected the compassion of God and demonstrated that merciful tenderheartedness through personal touch.

Jesus responded with divine mercy to this man's predicament. **Taking the blind man by the hand, He brought him out of the village.** Graciously and tenderly, the Lord escorted him to a place where they could have more privacy. This is one of two miracles (along with the healing of the deaf man in 7:32–37) that are recorded only by Mark. Much like He had done earlier for the deaf man (7:33; cf. John 9:6), Jesus used saliva to symbolize the transfer of healing power from Him to the man. Obviously, the saliva was not some sort of magic potion. The Lord did not need any props to accomplish His miracles, but it symbolized His healing power for a blind man who could feel the spittle on his eyes.

After spitting on his eyes and laying His hands on him, He asked him, "Do you see anything?" And he looked up and said, "I see men, for I see them like trees, walking around." The verb translated **looked up** (from the Greek *anablepō*) is the same verb used elsewhere to describe those whom Jesus healed of blindness (cf. Mark 10:51–52; John 9:11, 15). The fact that the man saw **men** looking **like trees, walking around** implies that the things he saw were badly out of focus. He understood that he could see other people, but they were so fuzzy that they were indistinguishable from the trees. (The **men** whom he saw were probably the disciples, who had accompanied Jesus and the blind man out of Bethsaida.) **Then again He laid His hands on his eyes; and he looked intently and was restored, and began to see everything clearly.** For a second time, Jesus touched the man's eyes. This time, the man **looked intently** (from the Greek verb *diaplebō*, meaning "to see through" or "to see with a penetrating gaze"). The fog was gone. His vision was in perfect focus, so that he was able to see everything with sharp clarity.

Modern faith healers sometimes allege that this verse supports the notion of incomplete healings, but it clearly does not. None of the Lord's healings ever resulted in partial, imperfect, or gradual restoration, nor was there ever a period of rehabilitation necessary. This miracle was no exception. In a matter of moments, the blind man went from debilitating blindness to perfect vision. Such is obviously a far cry from the fraudulence and failure that characterizes self-proclaimed healers today. (For a full critique of modern faith healing, see chapter 8 in John MacArthur, *Strange Fire* [Nashville: Thomas Nelson, 2013].)

Jesus often instructed those He healed not to tell anyone about their experience. (For more on why the Lord did that, see chapter 18 in the current volume.) He did the same here. After restoring the man's sight, Jesus **sent him to his home, saying, "Do not even enter the village."** In this case, the Lord's prohibition served as a confirmation of divine judgment. Like the apostate religious leaders, the residents of Bethsaida had no excuse for their unbelief. They had witnessed many miracles, yet they refused to repent (Matt. 11:20–24). Consequently, the Lord would issue a stinging rebuke against them:

> "Woe to you, Bethsaida! For if the miracles had been performed in Tyre and Sidon which occurred in you, they would have repented long ago, sitting in sackcloth and ashes. But it will be more tolerable for Tyre and Sidon in the judgment than for you." (Luke 10:13–14)

By escorting the man outside of the town, and by denying him the opportunity to go back and proclaim what happened, Jesus confirmed the permanence of Bethsaida's unbelief and His own judgment. Like the Pharisees whom Jesus confronted earlier (Mark 8:11–13), the residents of Bethsaida were sentenced to eternal spiritual blindness.

The account of this miracle is simple enough for a child to comprehend. Yet, the setting in which it is placed gives it significant meaning. It is no coincidence that the healing of a physically blind man immediately followed the demonstration of permanent spiritual blindness by the religious leaders (8:11–13) and temporary spiritual blindness by the disciples (8:14–21).

This was a private miracle performed by Jesus for His disciples, and it underscored a number of important truths for them. First, it served as a confirmation of Jesus' deity, since only divine power could open the eyes of the blind (cf. Ps. 146:8). In the very next section of Mark, perhaps thinking back on this miracle, Peter rightly confessed, "You are the Christ, the Son of the Living God" (Matt. 16:16; cf. Mark 8:29). Second, it provided the disciples with a glimpse of the future messianic kingdom, when Christ will reign from Jerusalem for a thousand years (cf. Rev. 20:1–6). During that time, death and disease will be greatly reduced, including maladies like blindness (cf. Isa. 29:18; 35:5). Third, it marked a turning point in Jesus' ministry. The Lord's public ministry in Galilee was over, and His focus was on training His disciples. From this point forward, with the cross only months away, Jesus began to speak plainly to the Twelve about His coming death (cf. Mark 8:31; 9:31; 10:32).

Finally, this miracle served as an illustration for the disciples of temporary spiritual blindness. Spiritually speaking, they had once been like that blind man. Having been raised in traditional Judaism, they had been taught to follow the guidance of the blind Pharisees and scribes (Matt. 23:16). Even with the light of Old Testament Scripture (cf. Ps. 119:105), and the advantages inherent in being part of God's chosen nation (cf. Rom. 3:2; 9:4–5), their understanding of spiritual truth had been hopelessly blurred by centuries of rabbinic tradition and religious hypocrisy. All of that changed when they met the Savior. His saving touch removed the veil of darkness that once shrouded their unbelieving hearts (cf. 2 Cor. 3:14–15). In an act of infinite compassion, the Lord Jesus miraculously gave them eyes of faith, as He does for every sinner whom He saves, so that they could clearly apprehend truth for the first time. He is, as the apostle John describes Him, "the true Light which, coming into the world, enlightens every man" (John 1:9).

The Ultimate Good News and Bad News (Mark 8:27–33)

30

Jesus went out, along with His disciples, to the villages of Caesarea Philippi; and on the way He questioned His disciples, saying to them, "Who do people say that I am?" They told Him, saying, "John the Baptist; and others say Elijah; but others, one of the prophets." And He continued by questioning them, "But who do you say that I am?" Peter answered and said to Him, "You are the Christ." And He warned them to tell no one about Him. And He began to teach them that the Son of Man must suffer many things and be rejected by the elders and the chief priests and the scribes, and be killed, and after three days rise again. And He was stating the matter plainly. And Peter took Him aside and began to rebuke Him. But turning around and seeing His disciples, He rebuked Peter and said, "Get behind Me, Satan; for you are not setting your mind on God's interests, but man's." (8:27–33)

No question is more important than,"Who is Jesus Christ?" It is of ultimate significance because how people respond to the Lord Jesus determines their eternal destiny (John 3:36; cf. John 14:6; Acts 4:12). Those who wrongly answer that question will face divine judgment (cf. John 3:18; 1 Cor. 16:22). They may view Jesus as a good teacher, a moral example, or even a human prophet. As this passage demonstrates, those designations are woefully inadequate and incomplete.

The Bible reveals that Jesus was far more than a benevolent teacher or inspirational leader. As Mark states at the outset of his gospel, He is the "Christ, the Son of God" (Mark 1:1). The Lord Jesus is the divine Messiah, God incarnate, of whom the apostle John declared:

> In the beginning was the Word, and the Word was with God, and the Word was God. He was in the beginning with God. All things came into being through Him, and apart from Him nothing came into being that has come into being. . . . And the Word became flesh, and dwelt among us, and we saw His glory, glory as of the only begotten from the Father, full of grace and truth. (John 1:1–3, 14)

Repeatedly and clearly, the four Gospels reiterate the theme that Jesus is both the Messiah (e.g., Matt. 1:18; 16:16; 23:10; 26:63–64; Mark 1:1; 14:61–62; Luke 2:11, 26; 4:41; 24:46; John 1:17, 41; 4:25–26; 11:27; 17:3) and the Son of God (e.g., Matt. 8:29; 27:43, 54; Mark 3:11; 15:39; Luke 1:35; 3:21–22; 4:41; 9:35; 22:70; John 1:34, 49; 5:18; 10:30, 36; 11:4; 14:9–10; 19:7). The very reason the gospel accounts were written was to demonstrate those dual truths. As John explained, speaking for himself and the other gospel writers, "These have been written so that you may believe that Jesus is the Christ, the Son of God; and that believing you may have life in His name" (John 20:31; cf. 1 John 5:20).

The fundamental question of who Jesus is forms the crux of this passage (Mark 8:27–33). At this point in the Lord's ministry, the Twelve had been with Him for more than two years. Their hopeful expectation from the beginning was that He was the Messiah and the Son of God. As Andrew told Peter, after first meeting Jesus, "We have found the Messiah" (John 1:41); Nathanael similarly exclaimed, "Rabbi, You are the Son of God; You are the King of Israel" (John 1:49). The disciples were likewise familiar with the testimony of John the Baptist, who declared Jesus to be the Son of God (John 1:34) and the Lamb of God who would take away the sin of the world (John 1:29). Over the course of Jesus' ministry, the apostles had been amazed by His authoritative teaching (cf. Mark 1:22, 27; John 6:68), awestruck by His divine power (cf. Mark 2:12; 4:41), and aware of their own sinfulness in contrast to His divine perfection (Luke 5:8; cf. Mark 2:5–7). Only a few months earlier, after Jesus miraculously walked on water and instantly calmed a violent storm (Mark 6:45–52), they had responded by worshiping Him and saying, "You are certainly God's Son!" (Matt. 14:33). The following day when many of Jesus' followers deserted Him (cf. John 6:66), Peter said on behalf of his fellow apostles, "We have believed and have come to know that You are the Holy One of God" (John 6:69).

As those examples demonstrate, the incident recounted in these verses was not the first time the Twelve had recognized the deity and messiahship of the Lord Jesus (though it is the first such confession recorded in Mark's gospel). However, it was on this occasion (Mark 8:29; cf. Matt. 16:16; Luke 9:20) that the apostles, through their spokesman Peter, stated that truth with greater conviction and confidence than ever before, doing so against the backdrop of widespread confusion among the crowds and increasing hostility from Israel's religious leaders. That which began as a hope-filled expectation had become a heart-fixed certainty. Appropriately, this passage marks the climax of Mark's gospel and the culmination of Jesus' training of the Twelve. Their discipleship had been intensified over the previous few months, as the Lord increasingly withdrew from the Galilean multitudes to focus on mentoring His apostles. After weeks of concentrated instruction, this essentially constituted their final exam.

From the perspective of Peter and the other disciples, this passage also represents the ultimate emotional trauma: the highest high followed by the lowest low. Peter's confession about Jesus marks the christological apex of Mark's gospel, while his subsequent confrontation of Jesus was met by the most stinging reprimand any believer could ever receive.

THE GOOD NEWS: PETER'S CONFESSION

Jesus went out, along with His disciples, to the villages of Caesarea Philippi; and on the way He questioned His disciples, saying to

them, "Who do people say that I am?" They told Him, saying, "John the Baptist; and others say Elijah; but others, one of the prophets." And He continued by questioning them, "But who do you say that I am?" Peter answered and said to Him, "You are the Christ." And He warned them to tell no one about Him. (8:27–30)

After His final miracle in Bethsaida, the healing of the blind man (8:22–26), **Jesus went out, along with His disciples.** They traveled north of the Sea of Galilee, walking some twenty-five miles **to the villages of Caesarea Philippi,** located near the ancient Israelite town of Dan (cf. Judg. 20:1; 1 Chron. 21:2), about forty to fifty miles southwest of Damascus. Situated at the foot of Mount Hermon, near a large spring that fed the Jordan River, Caesarea Philippi was originally named Paneas (or Panias), after the Greek deity Pan (a mythological half goat, half man famed for his flute-playing). When Philip the Tetrarch inherited the territory from his father, Herod the Great, he greatly enlarged the city. In A. D. 14, he renamed it Caesarea in honor of Caesar Augustus. To distinguish it from Caesarea Maritima, located west of Jerusalem on the Mediterranean coast, the city became known as Caesarea Paneas or Caesarea Philippi (so called in honor of Philip the Tetrarch). The city itself was largely populated by Gentiles and thus filled with pagan idols. By again journeying outside of Galilee (cf. Mark 7:24–8:10), Jesus and the apostles enjoyed a reprieve from the oppressive crowds, the antagonistic religious leaders, and the threat posed by Herod Antipas (cf. Luke 13:31). Mark explains that it was while they were still **on the way** to the region surrounding Caesarea Philippi that the conversation recorded in these verses took place.

According to Luke 9:18, Jesus had been praying, as was His custom (cf. Matt. 14:23; 19:13; 26:36, 39, 42, 44; Mark 1:35; 6:46; 14:32, 35, 39; Luke 3:21; 5:16; 6:12; 9:28–29; 11:1; 22:32, 41–45). After returning to the disciples, He presented them with a "final exam" consisting of only two questions. The first surveyed human opinion about Jesus' identity; the second zeroed in on the divine truth about who He truly is.

First, **He questioned His disciples, saying to them, "Who do people say that I am?"** By **people** (a plural form of the Greek word *anthrōpos*, a general term for "man" or "person"), Jesus was referring not to the religious leaders but to the uncommitted throngs of people who flocked to hear Him teach and especially to witness His miracles (cf. John 6:2). The parallel passage in Luke 9:18 uses the word *ochlos*, meaning "crowds" or "multitudes." Of course, the Lord already knew what the masses thought about Him (cf. John 2:24–25). But He wanted the apostles to fully appreciate the contrast between perception and the truth.

Responding to His question, the disciples recounted the varied popular opinions. **They told Him** that some, like Herod Antipas, considered Jesus to be **John the Baptist** raised from the dead (Mark 6:14–16). **Others** assumed Jesus was **Elijah,** whom God promised to send "before the coming of the great and terrible day of the Lord" (Mal. 4:5). **But others** thought He might be **one of the prophets,** like Jeremiah, whom Jewish tradition held would return with the ark of the covenant at the establishment of Messiah's kingdom. In spite of the countless and universally acknowledged miracles Jesus had performed, all of which testified to Him (cf. John 5:36; John 10:37–38), the people still did not believe in Him. They knew He had divine power and thus considered Him to be a prophet like Elijah, Jeremiah, or John. However, because they expected the Messiah's agenda to include being a military deliverer who would overthrow the pagan occupiers from Rome and establish a temporal and autonomous kingdom in Israel (cf. John 6:14–15), they were unwilling to embrace Him as the Messiah.

After hearing them answer, Jesus followed with a second, all-important query. **He continued by questioning them, "But who do you say that I am?"** In all three gospel accounts of this event, the word **you** is emphatic (cf. Matt. 16:15; Luke 9:20). Surveying the opinion of the crowds may have been an educational exercise for the disciples, but Jesus' follow-up question got to the crux of the matter. Nothing was more important than how they answered.

Like all first-century Jews, the disciples had been raised expecting the Messiah to vanquish Israel's enemies and establish His kingdom in Jerusalem. When it became clear that the religious leaders had rejected Jesus (e.g., Mark 3:6, 22), and that He would not use His miraculous power to overthrow Rome (cf. John 6:15), the disciples must have wondered if He truly was the Messiah. Those same considerations caused John the Baptist to express similar reservations. As Matthew reports, "When John, while imprisoned, heard of the works of Christ, he sent word by his disciples, and said to Him, 'Are you the Expected One, or shall we look for someone else?'" (Matt. 11:2–3). The Lord responded to John by pointing to His miracles, which clearly established His messianic credentials (cf. vv. 4–6). But, as John's example demonstrates, even the most faithful Israelites struggled to overcome their preconceived notions of what the Messiah would be and do.

Nonetheless, in stark contrast to the popular opinion of their countrymen, the disciples expressed what every believer knows to be true (cf. John 20:31a), and what Mark's gospel was written to demonstrate (cf. Mark 1:1), that Jesus is the Messiah and the Son of God. Speaking for the rest of the Twelve as he often did (e.g., Matt. 15:15; 19:27; John 6:68), **Peter answered and said to Him, "You are the Christ."** Peter's full statement is recorded in Matthew 16:16, "You are the Christ, the Son of the living God." Significantly, this is only the second time in Mark's gospel that the title **Christ** (*Christos,* the Greek word for "Messiah") has been used; the first being in the opening verse (1:1). The term "Messiah," from the Hebrew word *mashiach,* means "anointed one" (cf. Luke 4:18; Acts 10:38; Heb. 1:9). A royal title, it was used in the Old Testament to refer to the divinely appointed kings of Israel (cf. 1 Sam. 2:10; 2 Sam. 22:51) and later came to refer specifically to the great eschatological deliverer and ruler whose coming was eagerly anticipated by the Jews (cf. Dan. 9:25–26; cf. Isa. 9:1–7; 11:1–5; 61:1). With clarity and conviction, and without a shade of doubt or equivocation, Peter proclaimed Jesus to be God's supreme "Anointed One," the Savior of the world. After more than two years of following the Lord, the apostles' doubts about who Jesus was had vanished. Both His deity and His messiahship were firmly anchored in their minds. To be sure, they would still exhibit times of failure and weakness (cf. Mark 14:66–72). But they had come to know that Jesus was indeed the Messiah, the Son of God.

The resolute conviction that filled their hearts was not of their own doing. As Jesus told Peter in response, "Blessed are you, Simon Bar-jona, because flesh and blood did not reveal this to you, but My Father who is in heaven" (Matt. 16:17). The disciples could take no credit for this theological breakthrough of faith. They believed only because the Father had drawn them (John 6:44), the Son had revealed Himself to them

(Matt. 11:27), and the Spirit had opened their eyes to the truth (1 Cor. 2:10–14; 2 Cor. 3:15–18).

With minds full of faith and certainty, the apostles were undoubtedly eager to spread the news about Jesus that Peter had just articulated. But the Lord **warned them to tell no one about Him.** The word **warned** (from the Greek verb *epitimaō*) refers to a strong admonition or stern rebuke (cf. Mark 1:25; 3:12; 4:39; 9:25; 10:13, 48). In this case, Jesus' insistence on their silence was motivated by more than a desire to quell the unbridled enthusiasm of the multitudes (cf. John 6:14–15). The Lord knew His work was not yet finished, and thus the gospel message was still incomplete (cf. 1 Cor. 15:1–4). It would be premature for the apostles to go into the world and preach the good news until after His death and resurrection (Matt. 28:19–20; Acts 1:8). To demonstrate that this was the primary motivation behind His warning, the Lord immediately began to discuss the events of His passion (Mark 8:31; cf. Matt. 16:20–23; Luke 9:21–22). (For further discussion regarding the reason Jesus issued these types of warnings, see chapter 18 in this volume.)

THE BAD NEWS: PETER'S CONFRONTATION

And He began to teach them that the Son of Man must suffer many things and be rejected by the elders and the chief priests and the scribes, and be killed, and after three days rise again. And He was stating the matter plainly. And Peter took Him aside and began to rebuke Him. But turning around and seeing His disciples, He rebuked Peter and said, "Get behind Me, Satan; for you are not setting your mind on God's interests, but man's." (8:31–33)

The last thing the disciples expected to hear on the heels of this grand moment of revelation and clarity was a death announcement from Jesus. Understandably, the declaration devastated them. They knew Jesus was the Messiah, but they could not fathom the thought that He would suffer and be killed.

Mark notes that Jesus **began to teach them** about His death, indicating that from this point forward His death would be a repeated theme of His instruction to them (cf. Matt. 17:9, 12, 22–23; Mark 9:31; 10:33, 45; John 12:7). The title **the Son of Man,** a name Jesus applied to Himself more than eighty times in the Gospels, designated both His divine messiahship (Dan. 7:13; Acts 7:56) and His humanity (cf. Phil. 2:6–8; Heb. 2:17).

As the Lord foretold what would take place, He explained that He **must suffer many things.** By using the word **must,** Jesus indicated that the torments He would endure were an unchangeable part of the Father's purpose for Him. Though Peter failed to grasp that truth on this occasion (cf. v. 32), he would later come to clearly understand and proclaim that Jesus was "delivered over [to be crucified] by the predetermined plan and foreknowledge of God" (Acts 2:23; cf. Luke 22:22, 37; Acts 3:18; 4:27–28; 13:27–29). The cross was no accident; it was part of the divine plan of salvation from eternity past. As Jesus Himself explained regarding the purpose of His earthly mission: "For even the Son of Man did not come to be served, but to serve, and to give His life a ransom for many" (Mark 10:45).

The suffering Jesus would face meant that He would **be rejected by the elders and the chief priests and the scribes, and be killed, and after three days rise again.** The religious leaders of Israel would reject their own Messiah, putting Him through a mock trial, delivering Him to the Romans, and unjustly and hatefully orchestrating His execution. Though Jesus had previously spoken about His death, He had done so in veiled ways. In Matthew 12:40, He told the Pharisees, "For just as Jonah was three days and three nights in the belly of the sea monster, so will the Son of Man be three days and three nights in the heart of the earth." He similarly declared to the temple authorities, "Destroy this temple, and in three days I will raise it up" (John 2:19). Now **He was stating the matter plainly** to His disciples, with a level of clarity that not even they could misunderstand (cf. Mark 8:14–21).

The news sent the apostles reeling. They were convinced of His divine person, but now they struggled with the divine plan. In their bewilderment, they either completely missed or badly misunderstood the part about the resurrection (cf. John 20:9), perhaps thinking Jesus was referring to the final resurrection on the last day (cf. John 11:24). The disciples had no paradigm in which the Messiah, the Anointed One of God who would bring salvation and blessing to Israel and the world, would be rejected and killed by the very people He came to save (John 1:11). Like most of their fellow Jews, they had inherited misinterpretations of familiar Old Testament passages that predicted that the Messiah must suffer (cf. Pss. 16:10; 22:1, 7–8, 16–18; 69:21; Isa. 50:6; Zech. 11:12–13; 12:10). As Isaiah prophesied seven centuries earlier regarding Christ:

> He was despised and forsaken of men,
> A man of sorrows and acquainted with grief;
> And like one from whom men hide their face
> He was despised, and we did not esteem Him.
> Surely our griefs He Himself bore,
> And our sorrows He carried;
> Yet we ourselves esteemed Him stricken,
> Smitten of God, and afflicted.
> But He was pierced through for our transgressions,
> He was crushed for our iniquities;
> The chastening for our well-being fell upon Him,
> And by His scourging we are healed.
> All of us like sheep have gone astray,
> Each of us has turned to his own way;
> But the Lord has caused the iniquity of us all
> To fall on Him.
> He was oppressed and He was afflicted,
> Yet He did not open His mouth;
> Like a lamb that is led to slaughter,
> And like a sheep that is silent before its shearers,
> So He did not open His mouth.
> By oppression and judgment He was taken away;
> And as for His generation, who considered
> That He was cut off out of the land of the living
> For the transgression of my people, to whom the stroke was due?
> His grave was assigned with wicked men,
> Yet He was with a rich man in His death,
> Because He had done no violence,
> Nor was there any deceit in His mouth.
> But the Lord was pleased
> To crush Him, putting Him to grief;
> If He would render Himself as a guilt offering,
> He will see His offspring,
> He will prolong His days,
> And the good pleasure of the Lord will prosper in His hand.
> As a result of the anguish of His soul,
> He will see it and be satisfied;
> By His knowledge the Righteous One,
> My Servant, will justify the many,

As He will bear their iniquities.
Therefore, I will allot Him a portion with the great,
And He will divide the booty with the strong;
Because He poured out Himself to death,
And was numbered with the transgressors;
Yet He Himself bore the sin of many,
And interceded for the transgressors. (Isa. 53:3–12)

In spite of that passage, they were shocked by Jesus' announcement. In his resistance to his Lord's words, Peter went from being a spokesman for God (Matt. 16:17) to being the mouthpiece of Satan. As Mark recounts, **Peter took** Jesus **aside and began to rebuke Him.** Incredibly, a former fisherman had the audacity to contradict the Creator Himself, the one he had just identified as the Messiah and the Son of God. Rather than submitting to his sovereign Lord, Peter confronted Jesus with an abrasive retort, "God forbid it, Lord! This shall never happen to You" (Matt. 16:22). **Rebuke** translates the same word Mark used earlier to speak of Jesus' stern admonition to the disciples (v. 30). The word implies a level of authoritative judgment from a superior to someone under his command or oversight. Not only had Peter presumptuously elevated his own authority above Jesus, he directly contradicted the redemptive purposes of God. What Jesus said must take place, Peter brashly insisted would "never happen."

If Peter had been shocked by Jesus' earlier words about Himself regarding His coming death, he must have been utterly shaken by what the Lord said about him. **Turning around and seeing His disciples, He rebuked Peter and said, "Get behind Me, Satan; for you are not setting your mind on God's interests, but man's."** Matthew 16:23 notes that Jesus also added, "You are a stumbling block to Me." The fact that Jesus turned around for all the Twelve to hear suggests that Peter was articulating what all of them were thinking. They recoiled at the thought that their Lord would suffer and die, though only Peter had the rash boldness to actually confront Jesus about it. Thus, they all needed to hear Jesus' rebuke. The word **rebuked** translates the same word that Mark used of Peter's confrontation of Christ in verse 32.

Peter's intentions may appear noble on the surface. He naturally reacted to the thought that the Lord and Messiah whom he loved would be rejected and murdered. Furthermore, he and the other apostles had sacrificed a great deal to follow Jesus (cf. Matt. 19:27). In addition to their hopes for kingdom glory in the future, they had come to depend on Him completely in the present. It seemed impossible that He could be taken from them. But by rebuking Jesus, Peter, beyond forgetting his place, put his own selfish desires above the plans and purposes of God. The short-sighted apostle needed to be reminded that God's plans transcend human reasoning (cf. 1 Cor. 1:18–31). As God Himself explains, "'My thoughts are not your thoughts, neither are your ways My ways,' declares the Lord. 'For as the heavens are higher than the earth, so are My ways higher than your ways, and My thoughts than your thoughts'" (Isa. 55:8–9; cf. Ps. 92:5–6; Rom. 11:33–36). The disciples did not yet understand God's plan, but Jesus was operating in perfect accordance with the Father's will (cf. Mark 14:36; John 4:34; 5:30; 6:38).

In response, Jesus leveled a devastating rebuke that must have hit Peter like a deathblow, **"Get behind Me, Satan."** By opposing the purposes of God and demanding Jesus avoid the cross, Peter had actually become a spokesman for the devil. The Lord understood that the plan of redemption and the path to glory required suffering and death (Phil. 2:8–11; Heb. 12:2). Therefore, He would not yield to any temptation that promised a kingdom without the cross (cf. Matt. 4:8–9). He refused to put a desire for personal comfort above His submission to His heavenly Father (cf. Luke 22:42–44). Though the devil tempted Jesus intensively in the wilderness (Mark 1:13), Satan's attacks did not end there. According to Luke 4:13 (NKJV), after the forty days ended, Satan "departed from Him until an opportune time," meaning that he was continually looking for ways to tempt Jesus (cf. Heb. 2:18; 4:15). Peter's severe transgression provided that opportunity on this occasion. Knowing that the cross would spell his downfall and defeat (cf. Gen. 3:15; John 12:31; Col. 2:14–15; Heb. 2:14), Satan tried vigorously to derail God's plan of redemption. Jesus never succumbed to those temptations (cf. Heb. 2:18; 4:15).

Peter erred greatly on that day near Caesarea Philippi, but he would soon come to understand and cherish the cross deeply. Less than a year later, on the day of Pentecost, he would boldly stand in Jerusalem with the other apostles and proclaim the gospel of a crucified and resurrected Messiah (Acts 2:22–24). Near the end of his life, writing to believers in Asia Minor, Peter explained the glorious significance of the crucifixion: "For Christ also died for sins once for all, the just for the unjust, so that He might bring us to God, having been put to death in the flesh, but made alive in the spirit" (1 Peter 3:18; cf. 2:24). What the disciples considered to be the ultimate bad news on that day near Caesarea Philippi was, in reality, the best news the world has ever received. It was the very heart of the gospel. By dying and rising again, Jesus Christ, the Son of God, paid the penalty for sin and conquered death, so that all who believe in Him might have eternal life (c.f. John 3:16; 6:40; Rom. 10:9–10; 2 Cor. 5:20–21; 1 Tim. 1:15).

Losing Your Life to Save It (Mark 8:34–38)

31

And He summoned the crowd with His disciples, and said to them, "If anyone wishes to come after Me, he must deny himself, and take up his cross and follow Me. For whoever wishes to save his life will lose it, but whoever loses his life for My sake and the gospel's will save it. For what does it profit a man to gain the whole world, and forfeit his soul? For what will a man give in exchange for his soul? For whoever is ashamed of Me and My words in this adulterous and sinful generation, the Son of Man will also be ashamed of him when He comes in the glory of His Father with the holy angels." (8:34–38)

Following Peter's great confession of Jesus as the Messiah and Son of God (8:29; cf. Matt. 16:16), this passage gleams like a crown jewel for which the rest of Mark provides the gilded setting. It is at this point that Jesus Himself, the divine evangelist, invites all sinners to embrace Him in saving faith and become His disciples.

In contrast to the man-centered, feel-good platitudes that pervade contemporary Christendom, the gospel preached by Jesus was a sobering call to self-denial, suffering, and absolute surrender. False gospels entice their hearers with promises of material prosperity, physical healing, earthly success, self-esteem, and an easy life. The true gospel deals a deathblow to such counterfeits. The Lord Jesus calls His followers to humble brokenness, a life of self-sacrifice, and a willingness to endure hardship for His sake.

This brief but fundamental sermon from Jesus is recorded in all three of the Synoptic Gospels (cf. Matt. 16:24–28; Luke 9:23–27), and reflects the Lord's consistent teaching on the character of saving faith and the cost of discipleship (cf. Matt. 10:32–33; Mark 10:17–27, 39; Luke 9:57–62; 12:51–53; 13:23–24; 17:33; John 8:31; 12:24–25). As Jesus had earlier told the Twelve when He sent them throughout Galilee (cf. Mark 6:7–13),

> "He who loves father or mother more than Me is not worthy of Me; and he who loves son or daughter more than Me is not worthy of Me. And he who does not take his cross and follow after Me is not worthy of Me. He who has found his life will lose it, and he who has lost his life for My sake will find it." (Matt. 10:37–39)

On a later occasion, the Lord similarly challenged a large crowd to consider the cost of following Him, "Whoever does not carry his own cross and come after Me cannot be My disciple. For which one of you, when he wants to build a tower, does not first sit down and calculate the cost to see if he has enough to complete it?" (Luke 14:27–28). The gospel Jesus preached was neither an appeal to people's felt needs nor a message of easy believism. He called for total submission and unreserved commitment to Him.

This concise, powerful portion of Scripture may be sorted into three headings: the principle of true discipleship, the paradox of true discipleship, and the punishment for false discipleship.

THE PRINCIPLE

And He summoned the crowd with His disciples, and said to them, "If anyone wishes to come after Me, he must deny himself, and take up his cross and follow Me." (8:34)

The recognition that Jesus was the divine Messiah, as articulated by Peter's confession (8:29), represented a euphoric moment of realization and clarity for the apostles. Their joy was quickly eclipsed by the news that Jesus must suffer and die (v. 31). The Twelve had difficulty accepting the notion of a suffering Messiah, as evidenced by Peter's impetuous reaction (v. 32). In reality, they were setting their minds on man's interests (v. 33), thinking only of glory and blessings for themselves in the messianic kingdom. What they failed to understand was that God's plan of redemption required a sacrifice for sin (cf. Isa. 53:10–12; John 1:29).

Having explained to the apostles that He was going to die, Jesus **summoned the crowd with His disciples** and began to disclose that suffering and persecution would be the lot for **anyone** who **wishes** to follow Him. The sobering nature of Jesus' words affirmed the reality of the apostles' faith. They had already experienced the cost of leaving families, homes, and occupations behind to follow Jesus (Mark 10:28–30). His teaching in this passage reinforced their absolute commitment to Him. For the unbelievers in the crowd, Jesus' words **come after Me** comprised an open invitation to place their faith in Him and join His disciples. To do so would cost them everything. As the Lord made transparent, true saving faith is characterized by self-denial, cross bearing, and submissive obedience.

Self-denial. The person who desires to follow Christ first **must deny himself.** The verb **deny** (from the Greek *aparneomai*) is a strong term, meaning "to have no association with" or "to disown completely." The same word is used to describe Peter's denial of Jesus (Mark 14:30–31, 72) and Christ's denial in heaven of those who deny Him before men (Luke 12:9). The Lord's point was that those who wished to follow Him must be willing to disown themselves and give up everything for His sake (cf. Matt. 13:44–46). They must abandon both their self-righteousness and their sin, submitting all their ambitions and agendas to Him.

Inherent in the reality of self-denial is the affirmation that the sinner cannot gain entrance into heaven through his own self-righteous or religious efforts. For those in the crowd still trapped in the legalism of the Pharisees and scribes, the call to self-denial was a command to abandon their apostate system of externalism, works-righteousness, and hypocrisy (cf. Matt. 5:20–48). That was the very message Jesus preached in the Sermon on the Mount, when He insisted that salvation is given to those who are poor in spirit (Matt. 5:3), meaning those who recognize their spiritual bankruptcy before a holy God (cf. Isa. 64:6). Grace is not extended to those who think they are well but to those who know they are sick (Mark 2:17). It was not the self-assured Pharisee whom Jesus declared to be righteous but the undeserving and self-confessed unworthy sinner who cried out for mercy (Luke 18:14).

Jesus' hearers needed to recognize that they could not merit God's favor through outward conformity to the rituals and traditions of Judaism. Unable to keep the law perfectly (James 2:10), they fell woefully short of God's standard of holy perfection (Rom. 3:23), and thus deserved divine condemnation and eternal death (Rom. 6:23). Only by rejecting their self-righteous efforts as worthless and clinging to God's gracious gift of righteousness through faith in Christ could they be saved (cf. Rom. 3:24–28). When the apostle Paul was regenerated by God, he denounced his former good works as a Pharisee, calling them worthless (Phil. 3:3–8). As he explained, true righteousness is not a "righteousness of [one's] own derived from the Law, but that which is through faith in Christ, the righteousness which comes from God on the basis of faith" (v. 9). The sinner denies himself when he abandons self-reliance and self-confidence, instead depending on Christ's power and mercy alone for salvation.

The gospel call to self-denial also necessitates repentance from sin and selfish ambition (Luke 5:32; 14:26; 24:47). Those who follow Christ must do so on His terms, not theirs. They must be willing to break completely with their former way of life (cf. Isa. 55:6–7), turning to God from falsehood (1 Thess. 1:9) and abandoning the old habits of their sinful flesh (Rom. 6:6; 7:18; Eph. 4:22; Col. 3:5). All that they used to love must be rejected (1 John 2:15–17; cf. Rom. 13:14), having been replaced with undivided love for their Master (Matt. 10:37; John 8:42; 14:15, 23).

Thus, to pursue Christ not only requires embracing Him as Savior

but also wholeheartedly submitting to Him as Lord. At the moment of salvation, those who formerly were slaves of sin are transformed into slaves
of righteousness (Rom. 6:17–18) and slaves of Christ (1 Cor. 7:22; 1 Peter
2:16), so that His desires, purposes, and will become dominant in their
lives. His Word becomes their mandate and His glory their highest ambition (2 Cor. 5:9). Thus, the redeemed can declare with Paul "For to me, to
live is Christ" (Phil. 1:21); and elsewhere, "I have been crucified with
Christ; and it is no longer I who live, but Christ lives in me; and the life
which I now live in the flesh I live by faith in the Son of God, who loved
me and gave Himself up for me" (Gal. 2:20; cf. 6:14).

Cross bearing. The person who wishes to come after Christ must,
secondly, **take up his cross.** The cross in Jesus' day was not the iconic,
sentimental symbol that it has become over two millennia of history. For
those living in the first century, a cross was universally understood as an
instrument of execution, similar to the way an electric chair might be
viewed in modern times. Unlike contemporary forms of execution, crosses
were designed to prolong the agony of death for as long as possible. As
instruments of torture, shame, and execution, they were reserved for the
worst criminal offenders and enemies of the state. The Romans crucified
their victims in public, along highways, as a gruesome reminder of what
happened to those who defied Caesar's imperial authority. Estimates suggest that as many as thirty thousand Jews were crucified during Jesus'
lifetime. Thus, when the Lord used a cross to explain the cost of discipleship, His audience knew precisely what He meant.

Jesus' point was that those who desired to be His disciples, rather
than seeking prosperity and ease, must be willing to endure persecution,
rejection, hardship, and even martyrdom for His sake. To follow Christ was
to embark on a path of adversity and maltreatment. As the Lord later
explained to His disciples,

> If the world hates you, you know that it has hated Me before it hated
> you. If you were of the world, the world would love its own; but because
> you are not of the world, but I chose you out of the world, because of
> this the world hates you. Remember the word that I said to you, "A slave
> is not greater than his master." If they persecuted Me, they will also per-
> secute you; if they kept My word, they will keep yours also. But all these
> things they will do to you for My name's sake, because they do not
> know the One who sent Me. (John 15:18–21; cf. Matt. 10:24–25)

Not every believer will die as a martyr, but every faithful follower of Jesus will love Christ so fully that even death is not too high a price for eternal joy. All believers inevitably suffer to some degree because the world hates those who belong to Him (2 Tim. 3:12). Thus, to take up the cross is a metaphor for being willing to pay any price for the glorious gift of life He gives (cf. 1 Peter 4:12–14). True conversion causes a person to view the Lord Jesus and the hope of heaven as so precious that no personal sacrifice is too much. As the apostle Paul explained to the believers in Corinth, "For momentary, light affliction is producing for us an eternal weight of glory far beyond all comparison, while we look not at the things which are seen, but at the things which are not seen; for the things which are seen are temporal, but the things which are not seen are eternal" (2 Cor. 4:17–18).

Those who initially profess Christ, but are unwilling to suffer for His sake, expose the fact that they are not truly His disciples. As the Lord Himself explained in the parable of the soils, "These are the ones on whom seed was sown on the rocky places, who, when they hear the word, immediately receive it with joy; and they have no firm root in themselves, but are only temporary; then, when affliction or persecution arises because of the word, immediately they fall away" (Mark 4:16–17). Conversely, those who endure trials and hardship for the honor of Christ prove the genuineness of their faith (1 Peter 1:6–7).

Loyal obedience. Third, as Jesus' words **follow Me** indicate, discipleship requires loyal and continual obedience to Him. The verb **follow** (a form of the Greek word *akoloutheō*) is the same verb found in John 10:27, where Jesus described believers as His flock, "My sheep hear My voice, and I know them, and they follow Me." Like sheep submitting to the voice of their shepherd, genuine followers of Christ are characterized by loving obedience to Him and His Word. As the Lord explained to a group of "Jews who had believed Him, 'If you continue in My word, then you are truly disciples of Mine'" (John 8:31)

At the end of His ministry, Jesus reiterated the truth that faith in Him necessitates submission to Him. Using imagery similar to this passage (Mark 8:34–38), the Lord declared, "He who loves his life loses it, and he who hates his life in this world will keep it to life eternal. If anyone serves Me, he must follow Me; and where I am, there My servant will be also; if anyone serves Me, the Father will honor him" (John 12:25–26). On the night before His death, in the upper room with His disciples, the Lord reminded them, "If you love Me, you will keep My commandments" (John 14:15), and "If anyone loves Me, he will keep My word" (v. 23), and again, "You are My friends if you do what I command you" (John 15:14; cf. 14:21, 24; 15:10). Clearly, Jesus considered a life of obedience to be a nonnegotiable reality of genuine discipleship.

The rest of the New Testament echoes that same reality. Though believers are not saved on the basis of their good works (Eph. 2:8–9; Titus 3:5–7), those who have been saved will inevitably demonstrate the fruit of a righteous life (cf. Matt. 3:8; Gal. 5:22–23). Thus, obedience becomes a litmus test for regeneration (cf. Luke 6:43–45). As the apostle John explained,

> By this we know that we have come to know Him, if we keep His commandments. The one who says, "I have come to know Him," and does not keep His commandments, is a liar, and the truth is not in him; but whoever keeps His word, in him the love of God has truly been perfected. By this we know that we are in Him: the one who says he abides in Him ought himself to walk in the same manner as He walked. (1 John 2:3–6; cf. 3:24; 5:3; 2 John 6).

Those who live in obedience to Christ demonstrate that they are truly His disciples. Conversely, those who persist in unrepentant sin give evidence that they do not belong to Him (cf. 1 John 3:4–10).

It is important to note that self-denial, cross bearing, and obedience are not meritorious works that somehow earn salvation. Nor do they comprise a list of sequential steps that must be followed to be saved from sin. Rather, they are the inherent characteristics of repentant faith and the new birth, which is the gift of God (Eph. 2:8; 2 Tim. 2:25) imparted by His Spirit at the moment of salvation. Those whom God saves He transforms, giving them a new heart (cf. Ezek. 36:25–27), so that out of love for the Savior, they eagerly deny themselves, endure suffering, and submit obediently to His Word.

THE PARADOX

For whoever wishes to save his life will lose it, but whoever loses his life for My sake and the gospel's will save it. For what does it profit a man to gain the whole world, and forfeit his soul? For what will a man give in exchange for his soul? (8:35–37)

The Lord expounded on the nature of true discipleship by using a paradox. As Jesus explained, **For whoever wishes to save his life will lose it, but whoever loses his life for My sake and the gospel's will save it.** Those unwilling to surrender their lives to Christ, choosing instead to cling to sin, selfish ambition, and acceptance by the world, will one day lose their souls to everlasting death. But those willing to abandon everything for the sake of Christ will receive eternal life. Jesus, of course, was not suggesting that every form of self-sacrifice has spiritual or eternal value but only that which is done **for** His **sake and the gospel's.**

In Matthew 13, the Lord illustrated this paradoxical principle with two parables about the kingdom of salvation:

> The kingdom of heaven is like a treasure hidden in the field, which a man found and hid again; and from joy over it he goes and sells all that he has and buys that field. Again, the kingdom of heaven is like a merchant seeking fine pearls, and upon finding one pearl of great value, he went and sold all that he had and bought it. (Matt. 13:44–46)

In the same way that one might sell all he owns to gain something of far greater value, so believers are eager to give up everything to gain Christ and the salvation He alone provides. As the apostle Paul explained, speaking of the self-righteous works he abandoned for Christ's sake, "I count all things to be loss in view of the surpassing value of knowing Christ Jesus my Lord, for whom I have suffered the loss of all things, and count them but rubbish so that I may gain Christ" (Phil. 3:8).

The Lord continued by posing two rhetorical questions: **For what does it profit a man to gain the whole world, and forfeit his soul? For what will a man give in exchange for his soul?** To obtain all of the riches, respect, and religious accolades this life could offer and yet die apart from Christ is to be eternally destitute. The world and all it contains is passing away (1 John 2:17), soon to be consumed with fire (2 Peter 3:10–12). But each person's soul will live forever. For those who joyfully embrace that reality, it is incredible to think that anyone would forfeit eternity in heaven for a few fleeting decades of self-indulgence in this life. Yet that is what most people do (Matt. 7:13). Such is the power of human sinfulness (cf. John 8:42–47).

On a different occasion, the Lord Jesus illustrated this truth with a parable about a wealthy fool who thought only of the present and failed to plan for eternity. As Luke reports,

> And He told them a parable, saying, "The land of a rich man was very productive. And he began reasoning to himself, saying, 'What shall I do, since I have no place to store my crops?' Then he said, 'This is what I will do: I will tear down my barns and build larger ones, and there I will store all my grain and my goods. And I will say to my soul, "Soul, you have many goods laid up for many years to come; take your ease, eat, drink and be merry."' But God said to him, 'You fool! This very night your soul is required of you; and now who will own what you have prepared?' So is the man who stores up treasure for himself, and is not rich toward God." (Luke 12:16–21)

To gain the whole world but reject Christ is to lose one's soul to hell. But to give up everything this world offers for the sake of following Him is to gain eternal riches (cf. Matt. 6:19 – 21).

THE PUNISHMENT

For whoever is ashamed of Me and My words in this adulterous and sinful generation, the Son of Man will also be ashamed of him when He comes in the glory of His Father with the holy angels. (8:38)

The purpose of Jesus' first coming was to suffer and die as the only sacrifice for sin acceptable to God (Mark 10:45). But, as He reminded His audience, a future day is coming when He will return as sole sovereign in triumph and judgment (cf. Rev. 19:11–16). As the divine Judge (John 5:22), Jesus Christ is the determiner of every person's eternal destiny.

Whoever rejects Christ in this life, being **ashamed of** Him **and** His **words,** will be rejected by Him at the judgment (cf. Matt. 10:32–33). In this context, **ashamed** (from the Greek verb *epaischunomai*) means to despise, reject, or refuse to accept. The only people who will be saved are those who are ashamed of themselves but not ashamed of Him.

Every sinner ought to be utterly ashamed over his own wicked thoughts, words, and actions, even over self-righteous pride and hypocrisy. As noted earlier, the gospel calls sinners to deny themselves by abandoning both sin and self-righteousness. True believers are characterized by brokenness, humility, and a sorrow that leads to repentance. By contrast, unbelievers are ashamed, not of themselves but of Christ. They love their sin, so that their "glory is in their shame" (Phil. 3:19; cf. Jer. 6:15); they prize the approval of this world (John 12:43), and are therefore unwilling to embrace the suffering inherent in following Christ. Moreover, they see no need for the gospel, thinking they can gain heaven through a righteousness of their own making (cf. Rom. 10:3). Consequently, they find the message of the cross to be offensive and foolish (1 Cor. 1:18,23).

Although the Lord Jesus deserved honor, glory, and worship, He was rejected by His own people (John 1:11). The nation of Israel had eagerly awaited His arrival for centuries. But when He came, the religious leaders and the people were ashamed of their own Messiah. The Lord referred to them (and all people like them) as **this adulterous and sinful generation.** In using that description, Jesus was not referring to literal adultery but to spiritual harlotry (cf. Isa. 57:3–10; Ezek. 16:35–36; Hos. 2:13). First-century Judaism had replaced true religion with dead traditions and superficial legalism. Though the nation no longer worshiped physical idols, Pharisaical religion had created one great idol out of the rabbinic system of ceremonies, traditions, and external rituals (Mark 7:6–13; cf. Matt. 23:13–36).

If anyone is ashamed of Christ in this life, like the apostate leaders of Israel were, **the Son of Man will also be ashamed of him when He comes in the glory of His Father with the holy angels.** Using Old Testament imagery that was readily familiar to His listeners, Jesus declared the terrifying end that awaits all who reject Him (cf. Matt. 25:31–46). In Daniel 7:9–14, the prophet recounted a powerful vision of that future judgment:

I kept looking
Until thrones were set up,
And the Ancient of Days took His seat;
His vesture was like white snow
And the hair of His head like pure wool.
His throne was ablaze with flames,
Its wheels were a burning fire.
A river of fire was flowing
And coming out from before Him;
Thousands upon thousands were attending Him,
And myriads upon myriads were standing before Him;
The court sat,
And the books were opened....
I kept looking in the night visions,
And behold, with the clouds of heaven
One like a Son of Man was coming,
And He came up to the Ancient of Days
And was presented before Him.
And to Him was given dominion,
Glory and a kingdom,
That all the peoples, nations and men of every language
Might serve Him.
His dominion is an everlasting dominion
Which will not pass away;
And His kingdom is one
Which will not be destroyed.

By using the title **Son of Man** (a designation He applied to Himself more than any other in the Gospels), Jesus directly connected Himself to Daniel's vision. One day, in fulfillment of that prophecy, the Lord Jesus will return as King and Judge (Mark 14:62). He will return to earth in glory to establish His reign over the whole world. The rugged cross will be replaced by a royal throne. When that day of reckoning comes, the Lord will destroy His enemies (2 Thess. 1:7–10), and they will be cast into eternal hell (cf. Rev. 14:10–11).

For believers, the return of Christ is their blessed hope, a comforting promise that they eagerly wait to see fulfilled (Titus 2:11–14; Rev. 22:20). In the meantime, they are not ashamed of Christ or His Word (Rom. 1:16; Phil. 1:20; 2 Tim. 1:12; 1 Peter 4:16). Having abandoned their sin and self-effort, and wholly embraced the Lord Jesus in faith, they rest confident in the knowledge that they are forgiven and redeemed. The wondrous reality is that their Savior is not ashamed of them either. As the book of Hebrews reveals, Jesus "is not ashamed to call them brethren" (Heb. 2:11), and "God is not ashamed to be called their God" (Heb. 11:16).

For unbelievers, the certainty of final judgment is a terrifying reality (Heb. 10:29–31). As the Scriptures declare, "It is appointed for men to die once and after this comes judgment" (Heb. 9:27). On that day, those who refused to abandon their sin or who trusted in their self-righteous efforts will be irrevocably and eternally condemned to hell (cf. Matt. 7:21–23; cf. Rev. 20:11–15). But those who obeyed the invitation of the gospel—embracing the Lord Jesus Christ in humble, repentant faith—will not be put to shame (Rom. 9:33). Having abandoned this world for the sake of Christ, they will live with Him forever in the world to come. As the Lord Himself promised, speaking of the glories of the new earth, "He who overcomes will inherit these things, and I will be his God and he will be My son" (Rev. 21:7).

Bibliography

Brooks, James A. *Mark*. New American Commentary. Nashville: Broadman Press, 1991.

Cole, R. Alan. *The Gospel According to St. Mark*. Tyndale New Testament. Grand Rapids: Eerdmans, 1961.

Cranfield, C. E. B. *The Gospel According to Saint Mark*. Cambridge Greek Testament Commentary. New York: Cambridge University Press, 1972.

Edwards, James R., *The Gospel According to Mark*. Pillar New Testament Commentary. Grand Rapids: Eerdmans, 2001.

France, R. T. *The Gospel of Mark*. New International Greek Testament Commentary. Grand Rapids: Eerdmans, 2002.

Garland, David E. *Mark*. NIV Application Commentary. Grand Rapids: Zondervan, 1996.

Grassmick, John D. "Mark" in John F. Walvoord and Roy B. Zuck, eds., *Bible Knowledge Commentary*. Vol. 2. Wheaton: Victor Books, 1985.

Hendricksen, William. *The Gospel of Mark*. Grand Rapids: Baker, 1975.

Hiebert, D. Edmond. *Mark: A Portrait of the Servant*. Chicago: Moody Press, 1974.

Horne, Mark. *The Victory According to Mark*. Moscow, ID: Canon Press, 2003.

Hughes, R. Kent. *Mark: Jesus, Servant and Savior*. Preaching the Word Commentary. Westchester, IL: Crossway, 1989.

Lane, William L. *The Gospel According to Mark*. New International Commentary on the New Testament. Grand Rapids: Eerdmans, 1974.

Paisley, Harold. *Mark: What the Bible Teaches*. Kilmarnock, Scotland: John Ritchie, 1984.

Stein, Robert H. *Mark*. Baker Exegetical Commentary. Grand Rapids: Baker Academic, 2008.

Swete, Henry B. *Commentary on Mark*. Reprint; Grand Rapids: Kregel, 1977.

Taylor, Vincent. *The Gospel According to St. Mark*. New York: St. Martin's Press, 1966.

Wuest, Kenneth S. *Mark in the Greek New Testament*. Grand Rapids: Eerdmans, 1957.

Indexes

Index of Hebrew/Aramaic Words

Index of Greek Words

Index of Scripture

12:7–12	240	20:1–3	70	21:2	130
14:10–11	433	20:1–6	324	21:7	434
14:11	244	20:2	240	21:14	172, 285
19:1–6	382	20:7–10	240, 244	21:23–25	406
19:7	130	20:10	65	22:1–5	49
19:9	392	20:10–15	58	22:12	216
19:11–16	431	20:11–15	434	22:17	130
19:11–20:6	191	21:1–22:5	70		

Index of Subjects

dogs, 369
dove, 34

eating and drinking, 118
ecumenism, 124
eczema, 87
Edomites, 190
Egypt, 86
Ekron, 181
Elijah, 23, 298, 302, 416
Elisha, 298, 302
Elizabeth, 30
envy, 358
Ephphatha, 377–78
"eruvs," 140
Esau, 190
eternal kingdom, 48, 49
eternal life, 382, 431
Eusebius of Caesarea, 3
evangelism, 5, 65, 206, 212, 215, 250
Eve, 70, 270
evil, 357, 358
evil spirits, 62, 65
    See also demons
exclusivity, 124
exorcism, 65, 239
extrabiblical regulations, 354, 355
    See also traditions
Ezra, 61, 342

faith
    and Christ's healing miracles, 280
    and falling away, 203
    genuine, 103, 228, 327, 367–72
    and obedience, 91
    and salvation, 261
    saving, 68, 180, 198, 210, 348, 424
    test of, 91, 233, 331
faith healers, 74, 76, 409
fall away, 203
fallen angels, 58, 63, 65, 245, 246
    See also demons
false disciples, 216
false religion, 62, 125, 133, 134, 339
false teachers, 136, 216, 288, 291
family of God, 186–88
fasting, 44, 127–28

fear
    of God's presence, 106–7, 234–35, 248
    of Herod Antipas, 303–5, 309–10
    of man, 192
feeding of the five thousand
    and feeding of the four thousand, 390
    location, 318
    organization of, 319–20
    scale of, 312–13, 321
feeding of the four thousand, 388–90
fever, 73
fishermen, 51, 230
fishers of men, 51, 54
fishing industry, 50, 51, 60, 72
the flood, 270
flute-players, 263, 264
following, 51, 52
forgiveness
    of Matthew, 116
    of the paralytic, 102, 103, 105, 107
    and repentance, 22
    and sin, 96, 97, 107, 125
fruit-bearing, 205–6, 207, 212
fulfilling all righteousness, 31–33
fulness of time, 48
Fulvia, 308
funerals, 263–64

Gadara, 241
Galilee
    Herod Antipas's rule of, 300
    as Jesus' home, 29
    Jesus' ministry in, 47, 271, 284, 286, 312
    Jewish disdain for, 28
    unbelief of, 401
Gemara, 342
Gennesaret, 333, 334
Gentiles
    baptism of, 29
    of Galilee, 28
    gospel extension to, 362–63, 364, 391–92
    Jewish people eating with, 387–88
    receptiveness of, 392

of healing, 163
public nature of, 162
See also specific miracles by name
Mishnah, 115, 342
money, love of, 204
money changing, 398
moral folly, 358
Mosaic law
　on contagious skin diseases, 90, 91
　on fasting, 128
　Pharisees' adherence to, 149, 346
　symbolic nature of, 352, 353
Moses, 298
Most High God, 244
Mount Hermon, 414
mourners, 263, 264
Mozambique, 229
Mt. Hermon, 228
multitude. *See* crowds
murder, 357
musicians, 263, 264
mustard seeds, 219, 220
mystery, 197, 198, 214

Nahum, 60
nakedness, 242–43
Nathaniel, 15, 161, 169, 171, 315
Nazareth, 28, 65, 178, 179, 270–81
Nazirites, 24
Nero, 3
New Covenant, 168
Nicodemus, 256, 354, 399

oaths, 307–8
obedience
　of Christ, 32, 33
　in discipleship, 428–29
　and faith, 91
　and fruit-bearing, 206, 213
　in proclaiming the gospel, 294–95
Old Covenant, 139
old garments, 132
Old Testament
　law/requirements, 90, 120–21, 155,
　　156
　Pharisaic ignorance of, 143
　promises of, 18, 231–32
　Sabbath, 141

omniscience, 327–29
ordinary men, 172, 284–85
Origen, 3
Our Great Savior (hymn), 236

pain warning system, 88
Pan (Greek deity), 414
Paneas, 414
Papias of Hieropolis, 2–3
parables
　as divine judgment for unbelief,
　　182, 214
　purpose of, 193, 194, 197–99
paralysis, 101
pardon. *See* forgiveness
parents, 345–46
Paul, 1, 2, 2
penitence, 367
　See also repentance
Pentecost, 26, 168
people, 414–15
Perea, 300
perpetual virginity doctrine, 277
persecution, 278, 279, 298, 300
persistence, 367, 374
Peter
　calling of, 40, 50, 161
　in Christ's inner circle, 263
　faith of, 325, 331, 411–13
　fishing operation of, 60
　friendship with Mark, 2, 4
　healing of mother-in-law, 73–74
　leadership of, 169
　residence of, 72–73, 315
　as the rock, 170
　as Satan's instrument, 420–21
　sermons of, 2, 168
Pharaoh, 398, 399
Pharisees
　hard-heartedness, 85
　and the Herodians, 157–58
　hostility toward Jesus, 202, 271, 279
　John the Baptist's response to, 31
　lifestyle, 24
　philosophy, 99–100
Pharisees and Sadducees, 398, 400
Pharisees and scribes
　as false teachers, 136, 166

hostility toward Jesus, 153, 165
legalistic Judaism of, 153, 341
Philip, 161, 169, 171, 315
Philip the Tetrarch, 300, 304, 414
Phoenicia, 365
physical torment, 243
Pilate. *See* Pontius Pilate
Plain of Bethsaida, 326
political revolution, 324, 325
poll taxes, 114
Pompey (Roman general), 366
Pontius Pilate, 300, 309
power of Jesus
over disease and death, 254, 260, 334, 377
over Satan and demons, 65–67, 239, 240, 246
over storms, 334
prayer
Jesus and, 78–79, 327, 328
in Judaism, 128
preaching
Christ's emphasis on, 54, 80–81, 84, 227
by the disciples, 167, 286
of John the Baptist, 22, 25
purpose of, 47, 48
on repentance, 287
pride, 358
priests, 91, 145
The Problem of Pain (Lewis), 174
prophets
call to obedience by, 338–39
Elijah and John the Baptist as, 17, 18, 23–24
mistreatment of, 298, 299
psoriasis, 87
publicans. *See* tax collectors

Q document, 6
Quelle (source), 6

rabbinic rules/restrictions
on caring for parents, 345–46
on caring for the sick, 153
on hand washing, 343
hypocrisy of, 344, 347

on the Sabbath, 139–40, 143, 150–51
rabbis, 61
reaping, 142, 144
rebuke, 420–21
Red Sea, 229
redemption, 77–78
regeneration, 25–26, 116, 218
relativism, 124, 134
repentance
evidence of, 21, 22
John the Baptist's call for, 20, 287, 303–4
and the kingdom of God, 48
through gospel preaching, 80–81, 287
riddles, 221
See also parables
righteousness
as gift of grace, 32, 33, 112, 122
of the scribes and Pharisees, 119
true, 150, 348, 354
roads, 180, 195
rocky/stony ground, 195, 202, 303
Roman centurion, 270
Roman crucifixion, 427
Rome, 3
roof, removing, 101–2
royal messengers/heralds, 16–19
Rufus, 4

Sabbath
for church age believers, 140–41
God's purpose for, 145–46
observance of, 137
rabbinic rules/regulations for, 139–40, 143, 150–51, 153
synagogue attendance, 60
work prohibitions, 75
sacrifices, 37
Sadducees
agents of Satan, 202
John the Baptist's response to, 31
lifestyle, 24
and Pharisees, 271, 279
rejection of Jesus, 165
saliva, 377, 408

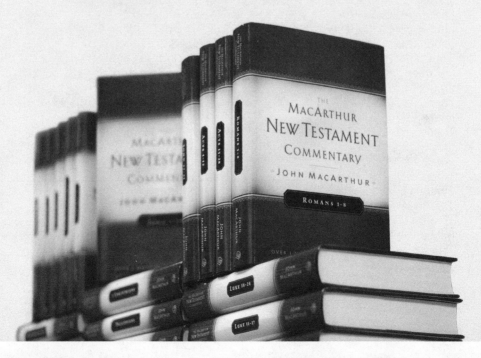

The MacArthur New Testament
Commentary series includes: